# Risk and the War on Terror

This book offers the first comprehensive and critical investigation of the specific modes of risk calculation that are emerging in the so-called war on terror.

*Risk and the War on Terror* offers an interdisciplinary set of contributions which debate and analyse both the empirical manifestations of risk in the war on terror and their theoretical implications. From border controls and biometrics to financial targeting and policing practice, the imperative to deploy public and private data in order to 'connect the dots' of terrorism risk raises important questions for social scientists and practitioners alike.

- How are risk technologies redeployed from commercial, environmental and policing domains to the domain of the war on terror?
- How can the invocation of risk in the war on terror be understood conceptually?
- Do these moves embody transformations from sovereignty to governmentality; from discipline to risk; from geopolitics to biopolitics?
- What are the implications of such moves for the populations that come to be designated as 'risky' or 'at risk'?
- Where are the gaps, ambiguities and potential resistances to these practices?

In contrast to previous historical moments of risk measurement, governing by risk in the war on terror has taken on a distinctive orientation to an uncertain future. This book will be of great interest to students and researchers of international studies, political science, geography, legal studies, criminology and sociology.

**Louise Amoore** is Lecturer in Political Geography in the Department of Geography at Durham University, UK.

**Marieke de Goede** is Senior Lecturer in the Department of European Studies at the University of Amsterdam, The Netherlands.

# Risk and the War on Terror

Edited by Louise Amoore and
Marieke de Goede

Routledge
Taylor & Francis Group

LONDON AND NEW YORK

First published 2008
by Routledge
2 Park Square, Milton Park, Abingdon, Oxon OX14 4RN

Simultaneously published in the USA and Canada
by Routledge
270 Madison Avenue, New York, NY 10016

*Routledge is an imprint of the Taylor & Francis Group, an informa business*

Transferred to Digital Printing 2009

Typeset in Garamond by
Taylor & Francis Books

*British Library Cataloguing in Publication Data*
A catalogue record for this book is available from the British Library

*Library of Congress Cataloging in Publication Data*
Risk and the war on terror / edited by Louise Amoore and Marieke de Goede.
p. cm.
Includes bibliographical references and index.
ISBN 978-0-415-44323-4 (hardback : alk. paper) – ISBN 978-0-415-44324-1
(pbk. : alk. paper) – ISBN 978-0-203-92770-0 (e-book : alk. paper) 1.
Terrorism–United States–Prevention. 2. Terrorism risk assessment–United States.
3. Privacy, Right of–United States. 4. Ports of entry–Security measures–United
States. 5. Terrorism–Prevention. 6. Privacy, Right of. I. Amoore, Louise. II.
Goede, Marieke de, 1971-
HV6432.R567 2008
363.325'12–dc22
2007047895

ISBN10: 0-415-44323-7 (hbk)
ISBN10: 0-415-44324-5 (pbk)
ISBN10: 0-203-92770-2 (ebk)
ISBN13: 978-0-415-44323-4 (hbk)
ISBN13: 978-0-415-44324-1 (pbk)
ISBN13: 978-0-203-92770-0 (ebk)

In memory of Richard V. Ericson (1948–2007)

# Contents

# Figures

# Contributors

**Louise Amoore** is Lecturer in Political Geography in the Department of Geography, Durham University (UK). Her current research focuses on the politics of risk expertise and decision, the public contestation of border technologies, and artistic interventions ·in apparently securitized spaces. She has published her work in journals such as *Political Geography, Economy & Society, Security Dialogue* and *Antipode*. She is currently completing a book, *Economies of Exception*, on the conditions of the contemporary security decision.

**Claudia Aradau** is Lecturer in International Studies in the Department of Politics and International Studies, The Open University (UK). Her research interrogates the effects of politics deployed at the horizon of security and of catastrophe. She has worked on the securitization of human trafficking and migration, governing terrorism and exceptionalism. Her current research focus lies in the exploration of the political and historical relations between security, freedom and equality. She is the author of *Rethinking Trafficking in Women: Politics out of Security* (Palgrave, 2008). She is also co-writing a book on *The Politics of Catastrophe* together with Rens van Munster.

**Susan Bibler Coutin** is Associate Professor in the Department of Criminology, Law and Society at the University of California, Irvine (USA) and Director of the UCI Center in Law, Society and Culture. She is the author of *The Culture of Protest: Religious Activism and the US Sanctuary Movement* (1993), *Legalizing Moves: Salvadoran Immigrants' Struggle for US Residency* (2000) and *Nations of Emigrants: Shifting Boundaries of Citizenship in El Salvador and the United States* (2007). Her current research examines the relationships that 1.5 generation Salvadorans (individuals who were born in El Salvador but who immigrated to the United States at young ages) are forging with their countries of origin and residence.

**Marieke de Goede** is Senior Lecturer in the Department of European Studies at the University of Amsterdam, The Netherlands. She writes on the cultural history of modern finance and the politics of fighting terrorist finance. She is the author of *Virtue, Fortune and Faith: A Genealogy of Finance* (2005) and editor of *International Political Economy and Poststructural Politics* (2006). She is a member of the editorial board of *Environmental and Planning D: Society and Space*.

**Charlotte Epstein** lectures in International Relations at the University of Sydney, Australia. She was previously a George Lurcy Visiting Scholar at the University of California, Berkeley (USA). With a background in Philosophy and Literature (Université de Paris-Sorbonne), on the one hand, and International Relations (Cambridge University), on the other, she is interested in forms of 'productive' power and how they transform the state and the international system. Her forthcoming book, *The Power of Words in International Relations: Birth of an Anti-Whaling Discourse*, seeks to develop a discursive approach to the study of International Relations. Other publications have appeared in *International Political Sociology*, *The Encyclopaedia of Governance*, *Global Environmental Politics*, *International Journal of Peace Studies* and *Cambridge Review of International Affairs*.

The late **Richard V. Ericson** was Professor and Director, Centre of Criminology, University of Toronto, Canada. His books include *Crime in an Insecure World* (Polity Press, 2007), *The New Politics of Surveillance and Visibility* (edited with Kevin Haggerty, 2006) and *Uncertain Business: Risk, Insurance and the Limits of Knowledge* (with Aaron Doyle, 2004). His research focused on the new politics of security and its implications for law and surveillance practices; the role of coroners in death investigation and public safety; and reputation, security and trust in financial institutions.

**Wendy Larner** is Professor of Human Geography and Sociology, School of Geographical Sciences, University of Bristol (UK). Recent publications span the fields of political economy, governmentality, economic geography and social policy, including 'Expatriate Experts and Globalising Governmentalities' (*Transactions of the Institute of British Geographers*, 2007) and 'Globalisation, Cultural Economy and Not-so-Global Cities' (*Environment and Planning D: Society and Space*, 2007).

**Bill Maurer** is Professor and Chair of the Department of Anthropology at the University of California, Irvine (USA). He has written widely on the anthropology of money, finance and property. He is the editor of several collections, as well as the author of *Recharting the Caribbean: Land, Law and Citizenship in the British Virgin Islands* (1997), *Pious Property: Islamic Mortgages in the United States* (2006) and *Mutual Life, Limited: Islamic Banking, Alternative Currencies, Lateral Reason* (2005). The last title received the Victor Turner Prize in 2005.

**Rita Raley** is Associate Professor at the University of California, Santa Barbara (USA), where she researches and teaches in the areas of new media and global studies. Her book, *Tactical Media*, a study of new media art in relation to neoliberal globalization, is forthcoming from the University of Minnesota Press.

**Mark B. Salter** is Associate Professor at the School of Political Studies, University of Ottawa, Canada. He received a Master's degree from the London School of Economics and a doctorate from the University of British Columbia. He is currently researching the use of risk management in Canadian border policing and editing *Politics of/at the Airport*. He is the author of *Rights of Passage: the Passport in International Relations*, and editor with Elia Zureik of *Global Policing and Surveillance: Borders, Security, Identity*. Salter has also published in *International Political Sociology*, *Alternatives*, *Security Dialogue* and the *Journal of Air Transport Management*. He also acted as a consultant for the Canadian Air Transport Security Authority and Transport Canada and has presented papers at numerous conferences, including AVSEC World and the Canadian Aviation Security Conference.

**Jonathan Simon** is Associate Dean for Jurisprudence and Social Policy at UC Berkeley (USA). His work explores the roles of risk and crime in the governance of late modern societies. His most recent book is *Governing through Crime: How the War on Crime Transformed American Democracy and Created a Culture of Fear* (2007).

**Matthew Sparke** is Professor of Geography and International Studies at the University of Washington (USA). Funded by a National Science Foundation CAREER grant, his recent research and teaching have been about globalization, neoliberal governance and, in particular, the impact of free market regimes on the geography of politics. He is the author of *In the Space of Theory: Postfoundational Geographies of the Nation-State* (2005), and is currently writing a textbook on globalization and a dictionary of globalization that are both to be published by Blackwell. More information about his other recent articles on border regions, cosmopolitanism, structural violence, global health and the global South can be found at http://faculty.washington.edu/sparke/.

**Rens van Munster** is Assistant Professor in International Politics at the Department of Political Science, University of Southern Denmark, Odense. His research explores the political implications of securitizing immigration in the EU as well as the links between risk and security within liberal orders of governance. He has (co-)published various articles in international journals such as the *International Journal for the Semiotics of Law*, the *European Journal of International Relations* and *International Relations*. He is also the author of *Immigration, Security and the Politics of Risk in the EU* (forthcoming 2008). Together with Claudia Aradau, he is co-writing a book on *The Politics of Catastrophe*.

**William Walters** teaches in the Department of Political Science at Carleton University, Canada. His research explores the geopolitical sociology of state borders and migration in Europe and North America. His publications include *Global Governmentality* (co-edited with Wendy Larner, 2004), *Governing Europe* (co-authored with Jens Henrik Haahr, 2005) and *Unemployment and Government: Genealogies of the Social* (2000).

# Acknowledgements

This book is the product of an ongoing series of conversations and collaborations between scholars with backgrounds in various disciplines. The question of the specific modalities of risk deployed in what has come to be known as the 'war on terror' resonates across the arts, humanities and social sciences. Fortunately for us, the compelling and timely nature of the question was also recognized by funding bodies. For scholars to talk across disciplines and, of course, across the distance of continents requires some resource commitment to make it possible. We are grateful for the support of the International Studies Association, the British Council, Nederlandse Organisatie voor Wetenschappelijk Onderzoek (NWO) and the Institute for Culture and History of the University of Amsterdam.

The initial drafts for most of the chapters in the book were presented and discussed at a workshop 'Governing by Risk in the War on Terror', held prior to the annual conference of the International Studies Association in San Diego, March 2006. Since that time, the group has continued its conversations, drawing in new people and raising new themes and questions. We are profoundly grateful to all the workshop participants, as well as to those who have contributed at a later stage, for their faith in the project. We have been demanding editors and very much appreciate the judicious and thoughtful responses to our queries.

It is, as ever, not possible to acknowledge the many people whose comments and interventions have shaped the course of the project. Suffice to say that we are grateful to the many audiences and seminar participants whose intellectual input has helped to push the boundaries of what we thought possible with the work. The comments of anonymous reviewers, and particularly the ever insightful Michael J. Shapiro, have been inspiring. Our special guest, Bill Maurer, has supported the project from its inception and delivered what we consider to be a quite remarkable preface on rusing with risk. Media and visual artist Rozalinda Borcila is, it seems fair to say, used to unusual requests and quirky collaborations. Her responses to our peculiar requests have been unwavering. We have found her work on reversing the gaze of risk and security to be extraordinarily powerful. We are honoured that she has produced original visual work for our cover. Heidi Bagtazo and her team at Routledge/Taylor and Francis have been their usual supportive, efficient and good humoured selves. Tatjana Das and Sara Dondorp of the Department of European Studies, University of Amsterdam, have done marvellous formatting work on the final manuscript. Thank you to Polity and Elsevier for granting permissions to reprint sections from published work.

Gunther, Paul, Caspar and Grace have supported the obsession with risk and the ever increasing KLM airmiles with love and generosity. Thank you.

# Foreword

## Rusing risk[1]

*Bill Maurer*

A ruse, says the *Oxford English Dictionary*, is a "detour; a doubling or turning of a hunted animal to elude the dogs." The term derives from the French "ruser," from which English also acquired the word "rush," as in a frontal impact that drives an opposing force away, leading it in turn to ruse, to flee and scatter in all directions. This quality of turning about and scattering in all directions, like game in the hunt, also lends the word its more common and more modern English meaning of trickery. Hunted animals, it would seem, deceive in order to escape their pursuers. In doing so, they take unexpected tacks and twists in direction, thwarting the hunters' forward rush.

The chapters assembled in this fascinating collection lend new significance to the techniques of misdirection and meandering of the ruse. For, in documenting efforts to govern through risk in the recent history of the "war on terror," the authors demonstrate that new forms of governance are attempting to meet the doubling and turning of an apparently elusive prey with increasingly complicated probabilistic models, the complexity of which may itself be a ruse masking older forms of power. What is being evaded, too, by those who would "protect" by governing through risk, is the relationship between truth and justice, the latter held in abeyance by the drive to secure the former through more and more complex probabilistic models.

I am reminded of the ruse in reading these chapters by the iconic image of the man, woman and child running across the border on signs lining the freeway between Irvine and San Diego, California, reproduced in Rita Raley's chapter here and targeted for mockery by a performance art group she discusses. In the artists' resignification, the figures (let us for the sake of argument call them a family) are both rusing from pursuers and rushing toward jobs in the name of the free market. The art group thus draws attention to shifting modalities of governance tracked in the volume as a whole, from the territory-based governance of sovereignty to the market-based governance of risk and uncertainty.

The difficulty in trying to account for these emerging modalities of governance, however, is that, in attempting to track the present and recent past, we frequently lose sight of the past in the present and the contorted temporalities that infuse past, present and future with one another, sometimes out of phase and sometimes in sync. Our grammar does not help us here. In the construction "from … to … " in written and spoken English, the position of the prepositions in the sentence mimics their meaning: an unfolding over time. Like the fleeing family, the sign that resembles what it signifies, this grammatical construction demonstrates the linguistic property of iconicity (Haiman 1980). Like the family in the sign, however, the prepositional construction, as it is colloquially used, may also suggest an array of unrelated objects and objectives, a meandering or scattering through space or time. "She conducts research on everything from statistics to kinship terminology." Grammar books frown upon this usage. But I think that this "ungrammatical" sense of the phrase can be useful in coming to terms with governance through risk. For what we discover in the chapters that follow is a diversity of aims and targets and, in fact, a series of competing and often contradictory notions of risk, calculation, governance and sovereignty, sometimes coming into phase in the same instant, other times oscillating from one to the next and back again, and still other times overlaying one another like the patina on an African fetish object on which offerings have been poured since unrecorded time.

Take risk itself. Paired with uncertainty, as in Frank Knight's classic early twentieth-century discourse on economic profit, risk signifies a calculable probability, as opposed to the unmeasurable uncertainty of the incalculable future. It was in the latter that Knight saw the potential for profit:

> Profit arises out of the inherent, absolute unpredictability of things, out of the sheer, brute fact that the results of human activity cannot be anticipated and then only in so far as even a probability calculation in regard to them is impossible and meaningless.
>
> Knight (1921: 311)

Risk and uncertainty have a much older lineage, as well, harking back to Aristotle's distinction in the *Nichomachean Ethics* between science and practical wisdom: the former rooted in certainties, however difficult to arrive at, and the latter in a sense of what is to be done without any clear guide. Prudence, here, involves a *judgment* of what is to be done (Book VI, section 5). Arriving at that judgment is a practice of virtue in the face of the unknown and incalculable. This notion of virtuous judgment in Aristotle recalls the medieval and Renaissance European understanding of the probable not as a quality of calculability but as a quality of the weight of an argument.

One could easily chart an historical shift in conceptions of the probable in the West, then. This historical shift would move from (A) ideas about the virtuous attempt to weigh evidence in favor of taking one course of action over another without more stable a warrant for one's choice than one's own history of judgment and one's location in a community of interpretants and their collective norms; to (B) ideas about calculating the probability of one outcome over another based on one's choices today, a risk–benefit analysis undergirded by statistical norms. The problem with such a chart, however, is that both modes of assaying the probable are available in the present. The latter may seem dominant, but it makes no sense without the former, which is also continuously being reasserted. Judgment is always contingent, but not necessarily always calculative. Prudence is a kind of "older" probability, but it too resides in the present and there is no reason to think it will not accompany calculative rationalities in the future.

For Renaissance thinkers in Europe, the prudential course summoned a further problem. As Richard Regosin puts it in an essay on Montaigne, "how to respond to the moral imperative to 'be just' without knowing what it means to be just" (Regosin 2006: 56)? This is a familiar conundrum to early twenty-first-century inheritors of the European tradition, as well, who have by now absorbed some of the lessons of relativism and post-foundationalism in philosophy, politics and law. It is often decried in discussions around the "war on terror," too, for the position that there must be moral certitudes and universal values in this "war" and in its everyday battles provides the ideological cover for those many, everyday instances when those certitudes and values are abrogated in their own name, as the chapters here attest. Rather than continuing to move back and forth between universalism and relativism, however, Regosin suggests that Montaigne had an answer to this conundrum, one that post-structuralist thinkers echo: "one must ruse with the law" (Regosin 2006: 56). One must adopt an "oblique and crippled knowledge," say Detienne and Vernant in their commentary on the *Nichomachean Ethics* (quoted by Regosin 2006: 57; my translation). Regosin continues that, in the few places where Montaigne mentions the ruse:

> In each case rusing takes place in situations whose conditions are not authored by its players – be it war, the social position of women, or his own old age – situations marked by instability, uncertainty, and the absence of clear or obvious directives, where suppleness of mind and the ability to foresee consequences serve to bring about a desired end.
>
> Regosin (2006: 57)

The conditions described in this volume are also not authored by their players, and let us not fool ourselves here: those who would attempt to calculate and thereby govern by risk are not in control of that which they author, and neither are they the authors of a seamless or hegemonic totality. The very logic they are carried along with allows, indeed compels, acts such as those of the performance artists described by Raley or the immigrants discussed by Coutin. For risk, in seeking to quantify and control uncertainty, also reveals the "nonlinear temporalities" – Coutin's term – and the "looking sideways" and "looking forward" of the UK Treasury's effort against "terrorist financing" discussed by de Goede, that inevitably evade that control.

How, though, to respond – politically, analytically, morally – to the politics of preemption, precaution or preparedness and vigilance that seemingly pervade the present and recent past? Simply asserting opposition, calling forth "truths" or by raising consciousness? Counterposing qualitative judgment and justice against quantitative calculation and management? Valorizing the subject against the sovereign or the person against the market?

No. One must also ruse with risk.

## Notes

1  I would like to thank the editors of this volume for inviting me to contribute this Foreword, and Tom Boellstorff and Susan Coutin for their helpful comments and suggestions.

# Introduction

## Governing by risk in the war on terror

*Louise Amoore and Marieke de Goede*

They were turning her from a woman into cartoons, headlines, opinions, fears, fate. They were morphing her into what she was not – the unknown terrorist.

Flanagan (2006: 261)

How do we thwart a terrorist who has not yet been identified?

Michael Chertoff (2006)

## Automated targeting

In December 2006, a new computer-based screening program called Automated Targeting System (ATS), deployed by the US to screen international travelers at all air, land and sea borders, became the subject of public discussion. ATS was developed for the specific purpose of screening cargo and container shipments into US ports, assigning a risk score to all imports in advance of their arrival at the border. As the Department of Homeland Security's Privacy Impact Assessment for ATS states, the risk assessments enable the "identification of previously unknown areas of note, concern or pattern" (2006: 9). The system for identifying "unknown" threats in mobile goods and objects has now been exported in full to the risk management of mobile people at US borders. ATS analyzes a variety of passenger data – including address, financial records, "no show" history, how tickets were purchased, motor vehicle records, past one-way travel and seating preference – in order to assign a risk score to individual travelers. The score is used to determine whether passengers or border crossers are placed on a "selectee list" for further attention, stopped and questioned at the border or, indeed, denied entry. The risk assessment calculation in ATS is classified, and the results can be kept on file for up to forty years (Sniffen 2006).

Civil liberties groups voiced objection to the program. According to Barry Steinhardt of the American Civil Liberties Union (ACLU), ATS casts suspicion on millions of innocent travelers, while seriously threatening privacy and constitutional liberties. While the system explicitly seeks to make visible an unknown person who would not otherwise be seen, assigning a risk value to every recoverable life transaction, the risk calculation itself is never made visible. Because the system screens the entire population of travelers in the search for the "unknown terrorist," people can never meaningfully access, challenge or correct their risk category. One of Steinhardt's concerns is the absence of limits to the data authorities may want to access for security screening. "Does the government get to scrutinize every address at which you've ever lived?" wonders Steinhardt (2007), "Quiz you about the fact that you once went for 12 months without a job? About your web surfing, your online book purchases, your school transcripts ... your associations?"

However, Stewart Baker (2006) of the Department of Homeland Security asserts that ATS has been successful in turning back individuals who pose a high security risk while offering "faster service for most travelers." Baker reveals that the most important feature of ATS is its ability to do "a quick link analysis" that checks travelers against terrorism watch lists, so being able to identify, for example, "travelers who gave the airline a phone number that's also used by a known terrorist." Baker concludes by emphasizing the need to connect the dots of available data, suggesting that data analysis may have prevented 9/11:

> This is a lesson we learned from September 11. After-the-fact reviews of the hijackers' travel reservations showed that we might have been able to uncover the plot if we'd had better computer systems and better access to travel data ... *We didn't connect those dots before 9/11, but we should have.* We learned that lesson, and now ATS allows us to look for these links.
>
> Baker (2006, emphasis added)

Risk-based calculative models and practices are emerging as a key means of identifying vulnerable spaces and suspicious populations in the war on terror. The imperative to "connect the dots" means that all kinds of new data analysis programs are being developed and implemented across the public and private sectors, such as automated screening programs, financial risk assessments and telecommunications link analyses (Levi and Wall 2004; Amoore and de Goede 2005; Amoore 2006; Ericson 2007). Although ATS has been the subject of dispute between the US and the European Union (EU), as Europe does not want its passenger data to become part of the program, we cannot assume that the turn to risk in the war on terror is a specifically American phenomenon. European welfare states such as The Netherlands and Germany are at the forefront of fusing public and private databases in the name of security, without, in fact, provoking much public debate at all. Shortly after 9/11, for example, the German government screened the data of more than five million males (*Rasterfahndung*), in order to identify potential Al Qaeda "sleeper cells." Data were collected from universities, private companies, municipal authorities and immigration authorities by a set of criteria that included sex and country of origin. The objective of the process was to find connections between otherwise insignificant pieces of data that in combination were thought to be cause for suspicion. As one analysis notes, "There is no 'insignificant' data left in times of automatic data processing" (Achelpöhler and Niehaus 2004: 497; also Zehfuss 2003). The German search did not yield any terrorist suspect or prosecution.[1] More generally, the EU has demonstrated itself to be a proponent of the deployment of data in the fight against terror, regarding it as a preferred non-militaristic solution to the threats of terrorism (de Goede 2008).

This book engages with the turn to risk management and measurement as practices of governing in the contemporary war on terror. The imperative to deploy public and private data in order to "connect the dots" of terrorism risk raises important questions for social scientists and practitioners alike. Although we are profoundly interested in the changing practices of surveillance after 9/11 (cf. Lyon 2003; Amoore and de Goede 2005; Lyon and Bennett 2008), it is not surveillance *per se*, but rather the specific questions surrounding risk as a technology of preemptive targeting that concern the contributions to this volume. How are risk technologies redeployed from commercial, environmental and policing domains to the domain of the war on terror? How can the invocation of risk in the war on terror be understood conceptually? Do these moves embody transformations from sovereignty to governmentality; from discipline to risk; from geopolitics to biopolitics? What are the implications of such moves for the populations that come to be designated as "risky" or "at risk?" Where are the gaps, ambiguities and resistances to these practices? This volume offers an interdisciplinary set of contributions which debate and analyze both the empirical manifestations of risk in the war on terror and their theoretical implications, from the standpoints of human geography, law, criminology, cultural studies, international relations and political science.

Expanding on Steinhardt's questions about ATS, three specific issues can be raised that are at the heart of this volume's concerns. First, Steinhardt's main concern is with government access to personal data, which substantially increases under ATS. However, the turn to risk in the war on terror is not only, and perhaps not even primarily, about the newly expanded authority and access for public bodies to private data. Indeed, the citizens of European welfare states have long been accustomed to such government access to personal data. Instead, the application of risk techniques in the war on terror fosters complex new spaces of governing in which public and private authorities, knowledges and datasets cooperate closely, and sometimes become practically indistinguishable. ATS itself relies primarily on commercial data collected by airlines, but also on public data collected at ports, immigration and through communications monitoring (Sniffen 2006). Other programs, such as the risk analysis of financial transactions, entail decision-making concerning what is and is not suspicion *inside* private spaces such as banks (see de Goede, this volume). It is the public/private hybrid spaces of governing and their implications for our understanding of risk that are at the heart of the concerns of this volume.

Second, while Steinhardt is concerned, understandably, with the millions of innocent (American) citizens whose records are scrutinized and registered under the program, it is probably correct to say, as Baker does, that under ATS many travelers will be confronted with *less* scrutiny, not more. In other words, risk-based screening is offered to civil liberties groups as being more objective, neutral and expert led than the potentially discriminatory and prejudicial decisions taken by airport security personnel and border guards. It is also thought to ensure, as Baker (2006) puts it, that "grandmothers and infants" don't have to go through security searches. In the process, however, decisions concerning *which* passengers need "a closer look" and *which* qualify for "faster service" (Baker 2006) are displaced inside bureaucratic and technological spaces that are difficult to understand, and even more difficult to challenge. Thus, for example, the US Secretary for Homeland Security targets British citizens "of Pakistani origin" for a stark choice between withdrawal of the visa waiver and the submission of data that "focuses on behaviour not race or ethnicity" (Chertoff 2007). Of course, inside these data, designations of exception and exemption are always already made on grounds that are absolutely racialized and prejudicial. It is the work done inside such "spaces of exception" that is a core concern of this volume (Edkins, Pin-Fat and Shapiro 2004; Agamben 2005).

Third, it is important to enquire whether ATS's desire to connect the dots "*before* a hijacker boards a plane" gives rise to novel political concerns that cannot find some form of resolution in a recourse to the rights of privacy or, indeed, to civil liberties (Chertoff 2006, emphasis added). For Homeland Security Secretary Michael Chertoff (2006), the challenge of ATS and other risk technologies in the war on terror is how to "thwart a terrorist who has not yet been identified." Indeed, we could say that ATS is trying to identify terrorists who are not (yet) terrorists. This desire for preemptive identification and disruption is at the heart of the deployment of risk in the war on terror. As will be explored throughout this volume, such politics of preemption draw on but go beyond established languages and techniques of risk. This has political implications that cannot be adequately addressed by established political categories of rights and freedoms. The contributions in the fourth part of this volume, by Salter, Raley and Coutin, explore the gaps, ambiguities and resistances in risk technologies, in order to make them subject to political questioning in new ways.

## From the risk society to the war on terror

The central question for risk society, as Ulrich Beck sees it, is "how to feign control over the uncontrollable" (2002: 4). Although this book departs substantially from Beck's thesis, for us it is precisely this feigning of control that has dominated the rise in risk discourses in the war on terror. Risk in this sense is categorically not about reducing risk, achieving control, or even about ensuring safety or security – what matters instead is that the *appearance* of securability and manageability is sustained. We do not see the significance of the idea of risk within the war on terror, then, residing in life "in a world risk society," in which potentially catastrophic and uninsurable risks proliferate (Beck 1999: 4; see also Beck 1992, 2000). Instead, following a growing critical body of scholarship on the discourses and practices of risk, risk is a construction, a "way in which we govern and are governed" (Adam and van Loon 2000: 2; O'Malley 2000: 458). As these critical risk studies remind us, risk cannot be isolated as a tangible entity or event, for it is performative – it produces the effects that it names (Butler 1990, 1993). It is not strictly the case that observable new risks have come into being, but that society has come to understand itself and its problems in terms of risk management (Ewald 1991). To consider risk as the dominant technology of the war on terror, then, is to engage with the practices that are enacted *in the name of* managing risk and uncertainty (Amoore 2004; O'Malley 2004; de Goede 2005).

The proliferation of risk techniques in the war on terror, then, is essentially about a particular mode of governing – a means of making an uncertain and unknowable future amenable to intervention and management. Despite a growing focus on new articulations of risk governance across the academy, however, there has largely been silence on the specifics of risk as a practice of governing in the war on terror (but see Rasmussen 2004; Spence 2005; Ericson 2007). Yet, what we see happening here has fundamental implications for how we think about risk and how we theorize security. The practices that are discussed in this book differentiate ever more finite categories of risk across diverse spheres, defining new and mobile exceptions, exclusions and special zones. As Mariana Valverde and Michael Mopas argue, practices of "targeted governance" shift the arts of government from discipline to risk, where "discipline governs individuals individually, risk management, by contrast, breaks the individual up into a set of measurable risk factors." These means of governing by risk, then, permit the mobile drawing of lines within and between individuals, with knowledge data giving the impression of a "smart, specific, side-effects-free, information-driven utopia of governance" (Valverde and Mopas 2004: 239).

Perhaps the most significant aspect of the techno-expert deployment of risk in the war on terror is what Michael Levi and David Wall call dataveillance or "the proactive surveillance of what effectively become suspect populations, using new technologies to identify risky groups" (2004: 200). The war on terror involves the classification, compilation and analysis of data – on airline passenger manifests, financial transactions or social security information, for example – on an unprecedented scale (Salter 2004; Amoore and de Goede 2005; Sparke 2006). These techniques rely heavily on sophisticated computer technology and mathematical modeling to mine data and map "normal" patterns of behavior so that deviations can be singled out and targeted. For contemporary geopolitics, such techniques have important implications: in what ways are practices of knowledge and intelligence changing post 9/11? How are particular patterns of behavior designated as the "norm?" In what ways do commercial applications such as frequent flier schemes and financial instruments become useful to the construction of the "risky" or "at risk" body? What are the political implications of using privately collected data for the purposes of public governance and law enforcement? What counts as evidence in extra-legal judgments made in advance of the event?

## A risk beyond risk

According to Richard Ericson and Aaron Doyle (2004a: 141), "terrorism strikes at the foundation of risk society." The risk society is characterized by a tendency to understand an increasing number of society's ills and insecurities through the lens of risk, in order to tame and eradicate them through calculative technologies. In this context, it is the sheer unpredictability and incalculability of terrorist attack that, according to Ericson and Doyle, presents "a stark reminder of the limits to risk assessment and management" (see also Ericson, this volume). Put simply, an event such as a terrorist attack serves to puncture the illusion of a fully managed risk and reminds us of the essential unknowability of the future. As Wendy Larner discusses in this volume, a "global imaginary" of a new, dispersed and particularly unpredictable terrorism underpins the war on terror's ambiguous relationship with the risk society (see also Mythen and Walklate 2006).

Paradoxically, however, this recognition of incalculability does not lead to an abandonment of calculative techniques in favor of, for example, a political–philosophical recognition of the fragility of modern life. Indeed, the very advent of the idea of risk as a means of governing coincides with a security apparatus that no longer seeks to prevent, to order or to withhold, but instead to preempt, to allow to play out, to make probabilistic judgments. Foucault's question, posed some thirty years ago, remains the important one: "Can we say that the general economy of power in our societies is becoming a domain of security?" In his histories of the technologies of security, delivered at the Collège de France, Foucault elucidates how the specific space of security refers to a "series of possible events; it refers to the temporal and the uncertain" (2007: 20). Such an orientation to the uncertain future inhabits the very idea of risk. In his delineation of practices of security from those of discipline, Foucault locates "the absolutely crucial notion of risk" (2007: 61). Working through a painstaking genealogy of smallpox, Foucault identifies new "fields of application and techniques" of risk. No longer did the management of disease "follow the previous practice of seeking purely and simply to nullify the disease [ ... ] or to prevent contact between the sick and the healthy." Instead, he notes "the emergence of a completely different problem" that is concerned with "allowing circulations to take place, of controlling them, sifting the good and the bad, ensuring things are always in movement" (2007: 65; see also Walters 2006; Elden 2007; Lobo-Guerrero 2007). With the idea of risk is always already the possibility to govern on the very basis of uncertainty and mobility – via "differential risks," "risk zones," "different curves of normality" (Foucault 2007: 63).

In a system such as ATS, then, we find precisely the modes of risk management that foster new and imaginative ways of dealing with uncertainty, amounting to an intensification of the search for anticipatory decision-making across all domains of social life. As Aradau and van Munster discuss in this volume, and following Foucault's insights, the deployment of risk in the war on terror is to be understood through the *dispositif of Precaution*: in which a desire for zero risk joins a vision of worst case scenarios in order to enable preemptive action against perceived terrorist threats. Terrorism, in other words, is understood to be "*a risk beyond risk*, of which we do not have, nor cannot have, the knowledge or the measure" (Ewald 2002: 294, emphasis added). If no longer based on the appearance of science and calculation, what then provides the basis for security decisions in a politics of preemption? Precautionary risk practices exceed the logic of (statistical) calculability and involve, instead, imaginative or "visionary" techniques such as stress testing, scenario planning and disaster rehearsal (O'Malley 2004: 5). Such imaginative new ways of dealing with uncertainty continue to deploy the language of risk, while outstripping, in practice, established technologies of risk calculation. Certainly, there is historical precedent of the incorporation of various uncertainties into risk governing practices. Bougen's (2003) analysis of the new governability and profitability of catastrophe risk (including earthquakes, hurricanes, strikes and terrorism) is one relevant example. Bougen (2003: 258) notes that rendering catastrophe insurable involves the deployment of techniques with "a particularly fragile connection to statistical technologies" that are perhaps better understood as "a special kind of alchemy" (cf. O'Malley 2002).

Indeed, ATS itself has to be understood as one form of just such an alchemy: while both its proponents and its opponents have couched the program in terms of a risk assessment exercise, its most important methodology entails data mining and "link analysis," whereby passenger data are compared with data on terrorist suspects. First deployed in Las Vegas casinos in order to ban card-counting gamblers, link analysis as a security technology entails imaginative and associative methodologies that accord dangerousness to particular individuals and that depart significantly from statistical risk calculation. Similarly, it is precisely the algorithmic alchemists of 1990s consumer data mining and profiling who now lead the "mathematical sciences role in homeland security" (BMSA 2004). Commercial techniques that were previously used to imagine and visualize an as-yet-unknown consumer are now actively in use to preempt the as-yet-unknown terrorist.

While not without historical precedent, then, the invocation of imagination in dealing with terrorism risk, as analyzed in this volume by Mark Salter among others, entails novel practices of approaching and deploying risk. One of the central themes of this volume is the ways in which "risk of terrorism" both appropriates and exceeds established risk practice and deploys new calculative techniques as well as cultural imaginations in order to govern society. Drawing on, for example, the historical lineages of risk literature (see Aradau and van Munster, this volume) and border control (see Walters, this volume), this volume is able to explore both the novel norms of post 9/11 risk management and the ways in which it is already historically present. Through its empirical examples and theoretical reflections, the book seeks to unsettle the current limits of the risk literature, thinking differently about the politics of what is done in the name of risk.

## Sovereignty/governmentality

The paradigm of governing enabled in the risk society depends upon what a number of authors have called neoliberal governmentality (Dean 1999; Larner and Walters 2004; O'Malley 2004; Simon 2007a). As summarized by Deborah Lupton (2006: 14), this paradigm holds that "more and more risk avoiding practices are required of the 'good citizen.' Risk avoidance has become a moral enterprise relating to issues of self-control, self-knowledge and self-improvement." Understanding risk as a practice of governmentality, clearly, is indebted to Foucault's conceptualizations of modern power as operating through the self-governing and self-assessing capacities of citizen/ subjects (Burchell, Gordon and Miller 1991; Foucault 1991). "Marked by a diffuse set of strategies and tactics", Butler explains (2004: 52), "governmentality gains its meaning and purpose from no single source, no unified sovereign subject. Rather, the tactics characteristic of governmentality operate diffusely, to dispose and order populations, and to produce and reproduce subjects, and their beliefs." In the war on terror, such individual responsibility for risk avoidance has manifested itself in national programs that encourage citizens to be ready for disaster, by, for example, keeping emergency kits, being aware of catastrophe risks and taking everyday precautions like not opening post that has no return address. As Ericson (2007: 63) writes of such programs: "the citizen must be ready for the malicious demon of terrorism in all places at all times" (see also Hay and Andrejevic 2006). Such "readiness" may also entail monitoring for "suspicion" throughout routine, everyday activity, such as shopping, traveling and driving. Citizens are encouraged to engage "vigilant visualities" in their daily lives, looking out for the "out of the ordinary" and reporting unusual sightings to "anti-terror hotlines" (Amoore 2006, 2007a).

At the same time, however, the deployment of risk in the war on terror does not fit seamlessly into a paradigm of neoliberal governmentality. The politics of preemption diffuses and defers responsibility for catastrophe, and at least partly legitimates a return of collective "risk management" or indeed preemptive intervention by state institutions. For James Hay and Mark Andrejevic (2006: 335), homeland security is the new "social security," whereby sovereignty rules through "strategies of security," while simultaneously rendering citizens individually accountable. We have seen that Steinhardt worries about unlimited new government access to personal data in the name of terrorism risk monitoring. Others point to the preemptive strike in Iraq and signal the strengthening of borders against transnational flows of goods, money and people (Andreas and Snyder 2000). A burgeoning literature on the return of imperialism discusses and analyzes such interventions as a manifestation of the return of (state) sovereignty in the post-9/11 era (Andreas and Biersteker 2003; Harvey 2003). This literature, however, fails to take into account adequately the ways in which risk technologies, private expertise and commercial datasets play an unprecedented role in contemporary security interventions.

Neither a continuing paradigm of neoliberal governmentality, nor an unequivocal return of the sovereign state, then, the deployment of risk in the war on terror invites us to think about the complex new interplays of public and private, governmentality and sovereignty, biopolitics and geopolitics (cf. Campbell 2005). As explored in this volume by Matthew Sparke among others, much of the new sovereignty is located in technologies of risk management in which state power is revitalized via alliances with expertise. The authority of private risk assessment firms, biometrics companies, homeland security consulting, financial data mining firms and so on suggests a significant realigning of public and private power in the war on terror. Judith Butler coins the term "petty sovereigns" in order to denote the immigration officials, mid-level bureaucrats and private actors who render unilateral and unaccountable preemptive security decisions. "Petty sovereigns abound" writes Butler (2004: 56), "reigning in the midst of bureaucratic ... institutions mobilized by aims and tactics of power they do not inaugurate or fully control." We may argue that the deployment of risk technologies in the war on terror precisely enables petty sovereigns to do their work and accords them a semblance of objectivity and scientific certainty.

In effect, two worlds of globalization are represented through risk practice in the war on terror: one populated by legitimate and civilized groups whose normalized patterns of financial, leisure or business behavior are to be secured; and another populated by illegitimate and uncivilized persons whose suspicious patterns of behavior are to be targeted and apprehended (Coutin 2000; Coutin, Maurer and Yngvesson 2002). In order that the licit and legitimate world of profitable movements of money, goods and people may remain an alluring and enduring prospect, then, control over the illicit world of terrorism, trafficking or illegal immigration must be made credible. Software sorting through risk paradigms plays a crucial role in the constitution of the two worlds of post-9/11 globalization (Graham 2005).

As Sparke's chapter suggests, the very promise of smart border risk technologies is to deliver "economic liberty and homeland security with a high-tech fix."

The work of risk technologies in the war on terror, we have argued, can be understood to be the banal face of the preemptive strike (Amoore and de Goede 2008). The preemptive decisions of the battlefield have their echoes in really quite prosaic and everyday domains where action is taken on the basis of anticipation (Massumi 2007). The violence of the banal preemptive strike is located in the continuous "drawing of lines" around particular groups of people, sorting the suspicious from the "normal," the "risky" from the "at risk" (Edkins and Pin-Fat 2004). The arrest and detention of travelers at the border, the freezing of financial transactions, the preemptive disruption of plots and indictment of suspects, the stopping and searching of young Muslim men in the city subway, the entry of a name onto a selectee list – all advance an invisible political violence, taking unaccountable and often unchallengeable decisions. In this sense, the risk-based governing of people flows and money flows is properly understood as a *continuation* of risk-based military practices more directly visible in other domains of the war on terror (Graham 2004; Gregory 2004; Rasmussen 2006). In comparison with the visible devastating violence on the battlefields in Iraq and Afghanistan, the invisible violences inside the software models that sort travelers and financial transactions, or within new classifications of migrant illegality, garner far less critical attention. It is precisely this conjuncture of software sorting, risk assessment and political violence that this volume will illuminate.

## Chapter outlines

The cover of this book shows video stills from media artist Rozalinda Borcila's project *Geography Lessons*. Borcila produces what she calls "counter surveillance" videos of airport security and urban transport systems. Turning the camera back on what have become normalized and prosaic security practices, Borcila attends to the risk calculations that we thought we could never see. Intervening in "apparently controlled spaces" that are "policed through technologies of visualization and information management" (Borcila 2006), the artist inverts the risk logics that pervade so much of contemporary security practice. In contrast to a security apparatus that deploys risk logics in order to preempt or anticipate, Borcila's installations suggest to us the fragilities and uncertainties within security screening, displaying for our perusal that which is already screened out. Our decision to use Borcila's work as the opening to the book is very much bound up with her unsettling of the appearance of securability that we encounter at the airport and in the city subway. Yet, for us it also reflects something of the ethos of the conversations and engagements that brought this project into being. Scholars from across the arts, humanities and social sciences came together to discuss that which is conducted in the name of risk, and in a sense to make visible precisely the modes of calculation and governing that would otherwise be concealed inside techno-science. Rather as Borcila's multiple screen films render extraordinary what have become ordinary practices – searching, removing shoes and belts, interrogating, detaining – so the contributions to this book seek to "make facile gestures difficult" (Foucault quoted by Campbell 1998: 215).

The structure of the book is organized around four key thematic sections:

# I
## Risk, precaution, governance

The first section opens some of the conceptual themes of the book, providing a theoretical and philosophical orientation to the specific modes of risk that are emerging in the security practices of the war on terror. The chapters in this section draw on the leading edge analysis of scholars in security studies, geography and criminology. Claudia Aradau and Rens van Munster provide a powerful counter reading of the notion of a risk society that reaches its limits with catastrophic terrorism. Drawing on Foucault's sense of a *dispositif* of risk – a heterogeneous assemblage for governing social problems – Aradau and van Munster carefully probe the idea of risk as precisely a technology of limits, always capable of exceeding the limits. In contrast to a world of prudential insurance (characterized by data collection, statistical analysis, scientific and expert knowledges), they observe the precautionary principle (characterized by screening of whole populations, probabilistic judgments and decisions beyond science and expertise) to be at work in the war on terror. The implications for the rule of law, as they suggest, are considerable: "rendering the future as catastrophic turns law into a policy instrument to prevent such disastrous occurrences."

Wendy Larner's chapter argues that the specific imaginaries deployed in the war on terror are fully reconcilable with the visualizations of economic globalization. This is an important contribution for it begins to outline precisely how a world of "openness" and "flows" is extended and not inhibited by the novel security practices of the war on terror. Put simply, could it be new modes of risk management that suture together the imaginary we see affixed to the walls of every US airport: "keeping America's doors open, our nation secure?" Larner outlines the governmental techniques and calculative practices that "reconstitute terrorism risk as a global business practice." Focusing on *Risk Management Solutions'* "catastrophe maps", the chapter echoes empirically some of what Aradau and van Munster argue conceptually: that the insurability of terrorist risk is extended beyond limits by cartographical imaginations that draw together unknown threats – landslide, earthquake, tornado and terrorism (cf. Shapiro 2007).

Richard Ericson's chapter offers the reader a deep engagement with the idea of preemptive security and, importantly, its implications for law and juridical judgment. Throughout the book, Agamben's state of exception and, particularly, the suspension of the rule of law in favor of the force of law is a central theoretical strand. Here, Ericson casts the incisive eye of a critical criminologist on the question of what kinds of counter laws flourish when preemptive security becomes the norm. "Preemptive security," he writes, "is based on a precautionary logic that normalises suspicion." Taking up the themes of precaution raised by Aradau and van Munster, Ericson elaborates a mode of risk that sanctions a society where "the legal order must be broken to secure the social order." Exploring rich examples of the direct effects of his "laws against law," such as the USA Patriot Act, Ericson depicts a world where counter laws take decisions based on suspicion and supposition. In so doing, he elaborates a key theme of the book: that specific forms of risk management exceed past forms of risk calculation precisely because they incorporate imagination, visualization and uncertainty.

## II
### Crime, deviance, exception

The chapters in this section provide in-depth analysis of the deployment of risk techniques in the specific context of crime and deviance. Increasingly, the "external" security of army and warfare and the "internal" security of police/crime and welfare are irrevocably intertwined (cf. Andreas and Price 2001; Bigo 2002). In this section, leading critical legal scholar Jonathan Simon contextualizes the war on terror within the specific conditions of the war on crime. Tracing a careful genealogy of the "war on" metaphor that resonates across "war on crime," "war on cancer," "war on terror," Simon opens up the operation of risk to a broader sense of the security apparatus. The very making of normalcy and deviance in the war on terror, as he powerfully suggests, has a broader relation to ideas about crime and crim-inality (also Simon 2007a). "The war on terror that has unfolded since September 11 2001," he writes, "has been profoundly shaped by the field of crime, politics and governance in ways that may ratify the skew toward security." At stake in situating contemporary risk practices in a genealogy of wars by other means, of course, is a deliberate and insistent demand that we do not seek out only the novelty of the novel.

Marieke de Goede's chapter offers an analysis of how changing financial border practices both appropriate and exceed discourses of risk, deploying increasingly "imaginative" approaches such as social network analysis (see also de Goede 2003; Maurer 2005). Exemplifying many of the themes raised by Aradau and van Munster and Ericson, in particular, de Goede powerfully exposes the violent dividing practices that are at work inside the war on terrorist finance. This is a compelling example of the risk *dispositif*, and also of the deployment of counter laws. Because the monitoring, tracing and freezing of financial assets can operate in place of law – with a lower threshold for intervention and evidence – the tracking and tracing of financial transactions becomes an important war by other means. Situating her analysis in a world where the UK Prime Minister Gordon Brown wants to see financial data as the "modern day Bletchley Park" for cracking the "code of the terrorist," de Goede demands that we see the targeting of *Hawala* networks and Islamic charities as more than mere "collateral damage," indeed as inherent to the risk technology itself.

Finally, Louise Amoore's chapter discusses the growing phenomenon of homeland security citizenship. She argues that the risk practices of the war on terror are becoming prosaic and ordinary, to the point that the call for private expertise also calls up inexpert and everyday calculations of risk. From Citizenscorps and USAonwatch to the calling up of London commuter's mobile phone images following the July 2005 bombings, the settling out of a normalized way of life becomes a means of identifying multiple anomalies. Thus, the decision of the exception – to take outside *"ex capere"* in order to include within – is both deferred into expert algorithmic calculations and diffused into ordinary everyday suspicions. Amoore suggests that a decision that simply invokes a risk calculation – this person to be on a selectee list, that person to have their assets frozen, that call to the anti-terror hotline to be prioritized – can never meaningfully be an ethical decision that confronts the unknowability of the future.

## III
### Biopolitics, biometrics, borders

The chapters in this section address the deployment of risk in the domain of border controls and border management. Measures such as the USA Patriot Act, Homeland Security Act, US VISIT and trusted traveler schemes such as Nexus are given analytical attention here. Matthew Sparke's chapter offers his cutting edge findings on the co-presence of securitized nationalism and free market transnationalism. "What new forms of sub-citizenship and sub-ordination," asks Sparke, "are emerging as the underside of expedited border-crossing privilege?" Tracing the proximity of global "kinetic elites" to other exceptional offshore spaces of rendition and removal, Sparke suggests vividly the practices of risk displacement and deferral that accompany contemporary risk management (see also Baker and Simon 2002).

William Walters' work on the border has received interdisciplinary attention, particularly for the way that it historically situates the "biopolitical border" (Walters 2002) and its governmental practices of security and immigration. In this chapter, Walters' key concern is to unsettle the sense of a clear "post 9/11" securitization of the border. Opening with Foucault's insight that "it is a time like any other, or rather a time which is never quite like any other," Walters analyses the US–Mexico "Wetback crisis" of the 1950s. As a specific historical moment when risk becomes attached to the figure of the migrant, his story powerfully unsettles certainties about contemporary security and migration. "What we today call 'risk' and 'security,'" argues Walters, "are in fact not at all constant, but the correlates of specific kinds of political genealogies and governmental techniques."

Finally, Charlotte Epstein considers the role of biometric practices in the post-9/11 management of the border. Focusing on the deployment of biometric systems as a system of risk management, Epstein situates the body at the heart of the technologies of biometric power. Following in a sense from Walters' discussion of Deleuze's "dividual" – the fragmentary subject, divided both within and without – Epstein explores how the body is (re)configured in and through biometric technologies. Situating her discussion in the US VISIT program, she shows how "the logic that regulates the functioning of biometric systems has spilled over into the practices by which we are governed today."

## IV
### *Risks, tactics, resistances*

At the same time as exploring how transformations of governance are taking place within the war on terror, the editors and the contributors to this book consider it important to explore the ambiguities and resistances that are emerging. The chapters in the final section suggest the ways in which the ambivalent, antagonistic and undecidable moments of risk technologies might be revealed (cf. Raley 2004). In Rita Raley's chapter, the militarized practices at the US–Mexico border are revealed and resisted through the tactics of radical artists and tactical media groups. "As securitisation procedures and policies intensify," writes Raley, "so too does the art-activist response." In the artistic interventions of groups such as Critical Art Ensemble and the Electronic Disturbance Theater, Raley locates a critical capacity to disrupt the practices of normalization (and anomaly production) that are inherent to risk technologies. The meaning of risk in a post-9/11 world is itself unsettled by the images and interventions of artist-activists.

Susan Bibler Coutin's chapter argues that, "when risk is rendered catastrophic yet incalculable, oppositional discourses and tactics, like security discourses themselves, *must enter the unknown.*" In a powerful essay on the possibilities for subversion of risk practices, Coutin argues that, because approaches to risk in the war on terror attempt to read the future into the present, it is precisely a disruption of this grid of intelligibility that makes classification and categorization more difficult. Understood in this way – and following the arguments in other chapters that contemporary risk is preemptive and not preventative, precautionary and not prudential – the practices of resistance must themselves embark on novel temporal interventions. Articulating models of "consciousness raising" used by 1980s social movements to challenge cold war security discourses, Coutin identifies a move to scientific uncertainty that "disables such knowledge-based critiques." Exploring a novel and path-breaking mode of "engaging unknown unknowns," the chapter proposes a philosophy of indistinct lines suspicious/ normal agent/terrorist.

Finally, Mark Salter explores the ways in which a specific mode of risk, highly dependent on forms of imagination, is emerging as a key paradigm in the war on terror. Thus, in this final concluding chapter, we are taken into the realm where risk management meaningfully loses its attachment to disciplinary or preventative governance and enters a world of imagined scenarios. Like Richard Ericson, Salter cites the findings of the 9/11 Commission Report: the chief failure was one of imagination. Illustrating his analysis with discussion of Condoleeza Rice's public defense, and with filmic and literary imagining, Salter persuasively argues that contemporary risk management represents the imagination as the very site of policy and decision. Echoing the calls of Raley and Coutin for a means of unsettling and making strange that which has identifying the "norm" at its very core, Salter turns to laughter and humor: "the use of humour tells us something about the way risk and imagination are at work."

## Note

1 The search did not cause much public debate but, in 2006, the German High Court ruled it unconstitutional after a prolonged court battle commenced by a Moroccan student who objected to his data being screened (Achelpöhler and Niehaus 2004).

# Part I

# Risk, precaution, governance

# 1 Taming the future

## The *dispositif* of risk in the war on terror

*Claudia Aradau and Rens van Munster*

The message is that there are no knowns. There are things that we know that we know. There are known unknowns. That is to say there are things we now know we don't know. But there are also unknown unknowns – things we don't know we don't know.

Donald Rumsfeld (2002)

Responsible science and responsible policymaking operate on the precautionary principle.

Tony Blair (2002)

## Introduction

After 9/11, catastrophe has become once more the dominant political imaginary of the future. Even if the catastrophic extent of 9/11 has been subject to debate, the projected future is one of expected and undeniable catastrophe. As the deputy Secretary of Defense pointed out at the fifth anniversary of 9/11: "[T]he reason (terrorists) killed 3,000 people that day is because they didn't know how to kill 30,000 or 300,000 or 3 million. But if they had known how to ... they would have" (Miles 2006). Comparing the terrorist attacks of 9/11 with the Chernobyl disaster of the 1980s, Ulrich Beck (2002) has claimed that September 11 drove home the lesson that we now live in a risk society, a society in which there are uncontrollable and unpredictable dangers against which insurance is impossible and where questions of compensation, liability and harm minimization have lost all their social and political significance.

In the post-September 11 conditions of extreme uncertainty, decision-makers are simply no longer able to guarantee predictability, security and control (Rasmussen 2004). Rather, "the hidden central issue in world risk society is how to *feign* control over the uncontrollable – in politics, law, science, technology, economy and everyday life" (Beck 2002: 41, emphasis added; see also the Introduction to this volume). According to theorists of risk society, control is ideological, doomed to fall short of the measure of reality.

As insurance companies sustained unprecedented losses as a result of the 9/11 attacks, Beck's observations on the uninsurability and uncontrollability of risk appeared to carry considerable empirical value. Yet, a closer look at the developments in the governance of risk illuminates that his sweeping statements about uncontrollable risks in an age of extreme uncertainty are inattentive to the institutional measures and actions that have accompanied the tragic events of 9/11. Against the backdrop of radical contingency and incalculability, organizations – public as well as private – have attempted to devise means to minimize or avoid the catastrophic promise of the future, seeking for alternative ways to predict and master the risk of terrorism (for an overview, see Ericson and Doyle 2004a).

Our analysis of the risk practices deployed in the "war on terror" breaks with Beck's risk society thesis and explores the deployment of a governmental *dispositif* of risk (Aradau and van Munster 2007). Formulated in the context of environmental struggles in Germany in the 1970s, Beck's narrative of risks as produced by modernity does not travel well to the current practices and technologies of risk deployed in the war on terror.[1] Drawing upon Foucault's work on governmentality and recent social analyses of risk, this chapter will therefore explore how a *dispositif* of risk is deployed in the "war on terror" at the horizon of catastrophic future and radical uncertainty. This approach takes as its starting point the conceptualization of risk as a *dispositif*, i.e. a heterogeneous assemblage of discursive and material elements for governing social problems.[2]

Unlike Beck's uninsurable risks, a Foucauldian approach focuses on how presumably incalculable catastrophic risks such as terrorism are governed. Rather than ideological attempts to "feign control", as intimated by Beck, it will be argued that different policies such as war, surveillance, injunctions to integration and drastic policies against antisocial behaviour in fact function within a *dispositif* of precautionary risk. What is new is not so much the advent of an uncontrollable risk society as the emergence of a "precautionary" element that has given birth to new rationalities of government that require that the catastrophic prospects of the future be tamed and managed. In conjunction with a neoliberal rationality of risk, the *dispositif* of precautionary risk creates convergent effects of depoliticization and de-democratization.[3]

Beyond the empirical connections between Beck's earlier analysis and 9/11, his uninsurable risk society also carries profound political consequences. Indeed, for Beck, the advent of risk society harbours the possibility for reinventing the international along more democratic and cosmopolitan lines as expert rule gives way to deliberation in global public forums (Beck 1992, 1999). Against this optimistic view, however, others have pointed out that the representation of catastrophic risks, especially in the wake of 9/11, has brought about exceptional practices beyond and outside the law, imperial reinventions of liberty and democracy and securitization of boundaries of difference.[4] But framing the alternatives to the international as either "imperial" or "exceptional" (Walker 2006) on a general level does not shed light on their relationship to the heterogeneous practices deployed in the war on terror. We argue, therefore, that exceptionality and imperialism in the wake of 9/11 need to be understood against the background of how governing terrorism is problematized at the horizon of a catastrophic future to be avoided at all costs.

At the same time, Beck (2003) maintained that the advent of risk society signalled the end of neoliberalism, as no companies or other private actors would be willing to embrace the risk of terrorism and other catastrophic events. However, this chapter will argue that the new meanings of the exceptional and imperial that define the securitizing practices post-9/11 reify the status quo through a specific rendering of politics as the social and economic continuity of neoliberalism. The *dispositif* of risk in the war on terror is profoundly depoliticizing, inasmuch as it suspends the contestation of political decisions on the exception and displaces social antagonisms. In conjunction with a neoliberal rationality of governance, it is de-democratizing inasmuch as it undermines political agency that challenges the inegalitarian neoliberal global world order. The argument will proceed in three stages: first, we outline a genealogy of the *dispositif* of risk. Second, we explore the specific configuration of risk practices deployed in the "war on terror". Third, we analyse the political implications of the precautionary *dispositif* for the philosophy of the exception, imperial and securitizing practices, and its intersections with the rationality of neoliberalism.

## Taming the future: insurance, neoliberalism and precaution

Contrary to Beck's emphasis on the univocal logic of modernity that leads to incalculable risks, scholars using an analytic of government inspired by the work of Michel Foucault have been attentive to the diversity of risk practices. In this approach, risk can be understood as a *dispositif* to govern social problems. A *dispositif* consists of "discourses, institutions, architectural forms, regulatory decisions, laws, administrative measures, scientific statements, philosophical, moral and philanthropic propositions" (Foucault 1980a: 194). The heterogeneous elements that make up a *dispositif* of risk can be understood more systematically as a combination of rationalities and technologies, a "family of ways of thinking and acting, involving calculations about probable futures in the present followed by interventions into the present in order to control that potential future" (Rose 2001: 7). A *dispositif* of risk is the product of contingency and invention, not the result of the logic of modernity (O'Malley 2004: 7). Hence, a *dispositif* of risk creates a specific relation to the future, which requires the monitoring of the future, the attempt to calculate what the future can offer and the necessity to control and minimize its potentially harmful effects.

Importantly, the identification of risk is not the same as recognizing the uncertainty of future events. On the contrary, the identification and management of risk is a way of organizing reality, taming the future, disciplining chance and rationalizing individual conduct (Hacking 1990). Identifying the future as bearing catastrophic risks is therefore linked with visions of order and ways to constitute and reproduce it.[5]

A *dispositif* of risk is subject to transformation and modification, depending on the knowledgeable representations of the problems and objects to be governed and on the available technologies to produce particular effects in the governed. Risk inscribes reality as harbouring "potential dangerous irruptions" (Castel 1991: 288) and deploys technologies to avert these events in the future. The heterogeneity of risk practices can be unravelled both synchronically and diachronically. Thus, although risk was thought for a long time to be co-extensive with the insurable, a genealogy of risk reveals different *dispositifs* developed in particular historical contexts and in response to specific social problems (Donzelot 1984; Ewald 1986).

The first *dispositif* of risk is that of nineteenth-century liberalism, which imposed not only legal duties and restrictions upon individual freedom, but equally moral ones. The *dispositif* of responsibility functions under the moral motto "do no harm to others". Responsibility was the responsibility of prudent individuals who negotiated the vicissitudes of fortune on their own and avoided becoming a burden on the others. The second *dispositif* of risk, insurance, emerged at a time when politics and economics proved incapable of managing social problems. Insurance provided an answer to the "scandal of the poor" in the post-revolutionary French *République*, when neither political equality nor capitalism could (Donzelot 1984). Despite equality before the law and equal sovereignty, the poor had no property and were therefore forced to sell their labour. Yet, free access to work did not mean the end of their indigence. The resolution of the social question – impossible through either political claims or economic measures – was given in the form of mandatory insurance. Risk could convert conflicting demands within the *République* and mitigate the "shameful opposition between the owners of capital and those who, living only by their labour, remain enslaved to them at the same time as they are proclaimed politically sovereign" (Donzelot 1988: 396). The wage system was the first form of collective risk insurance, guaranteeing rights, giving access to benefits outside work and protecting workers from the peril of indigence.

In this context, a growing number of social problems of industrial modernity became governed by technologies of insurance. The *dispositif* of insurance emerged out of a contestation over means to deal with a social problem and, given its non-revolutionary claims in dealing with society, became a dominant way of framing social events such as, for example, the work accident.[6] Solidarity through insurance could thus make up for the shortcomings of society, compensate for the effects of poverty and reduce the negative effects of oppression. With insurance, state actions targeted only the forms of social relations and not the structures of society. The injured, sick or unemployed worker did not need to demand justice before a court or to take to the streets as the proletarians had done in 1848. Instead, the worker could be indemnified by the state, the greatest social insurer. Through insurance, workers could be protected against unemployment or accidents, in a word against indigence, the great political concern of the century.

The *dispositif* of risk insurance modified the traditional understanding of risk as individual responsibility. With risk insurance, individuals are no longer directly and solely responsible for their fate. The state creates a general principle of responsibility in which individuals cannot be disentangled from one another.[7] Currently, however, insurance itself is undergoing further transformations linked with the historical context in which its technologies are deployed. On the one hand, insurance is under attack from neoliberalism; on the other, it is challenged by scientific discoveries.

First, with the rise of neoliberalism, the practice of collective risk management tends to be supplanted by "prudentialism", in which subjects are required to prudently calculate, and thereby minimize, the risk that could befall them. This does not however reactivate the nineteenth-century understanding of risk, but redirects the *dispositif* of insurance towards the individual – hence the reference to the notion of "new prudentialism" (O'Malley 1992: 261). Society is once more disintegrated; solidarity trickles down to categories of the population defined by the redeployment of private insurance. Insurance becomes a matter of individual responsibility rather than societal solidarity; it functions as a market which individuals enter for the provision of their own security. Neoliberalism thus entails a shift towards private security arrangements and a rediscovery of individual responsibility. Baker and Simon have aptly described this shift as a move from "spreading risk", concerned with the socialization of risks by spreading them out over the whole population, to "embracing risk" leading to a de-pooling of collective risks towards individual responsibility (Baker and Simon 2002).

Second, insurance has undergone another modification which, until recently, has been given relatively little attention in the literature on governmentality. This second modification concerns not the rationality of neoliberalism but, rather, the rationality of scientific knowledge that has underpinned the insurance *dispositif*. If insurance has been modified as a result of neoliberalism, traditional strategies of risk insurance have also come under attack from the scientific discoveries that undermine the very logic of calculability and the possibility of providing calculations for the future. As Ewald has succinctly formulated this latter challenge, risk "tends to exceed the limits of the insurable in two directions: toward the infinitely small-scale (biological, natural, or food-related risk), and toward the infinitely large-scale ('major technological risks' or technological catastrophes)" (Ewald 1993: 222).[8]

Therefore, the *dispositif* of insurance undergoes a double modification. On the one hand, the rationality of neoliberalism steers it towards market-based organization of the social, the subject and the state. According to Wendy Brown, neoliberalism casts the political and social sphere as dominated by market concerns and organized by market rationality (Brown 2006: 694). On the other hand, the rationality of scientific knowledge steers it towards radical uncertainty. As Tom Baker has astutely noted, both rationalities are reactions to the limits of insurance: precautionary risk is a reaction to the limits of insurance to prevent dangerous occurrences, while embracing risk is a reaction to the inability of the insurance state to effectively spread loss (Baker 2002: 351).

The precautionary rationality challenges insurance to tame the infinities of risk and integrate it within a *dispositif* of governance.[9] While these two "infinities" of risk appear reminiscent of Beck's incalculable risks of modernity, infinity is not synonymous with incalculability. After all, the limit of knowledge has always confronted insurance technologies. Insurance *is* the art of making the seemingly incalculable subject to calculation (Ericson, Doyle and Barry 2003: 284). The first element of infinity that undermines a politics of insurance is the *catastrophic element*, the grave and irreversible damage that an event can cause. The second element of infinity is that of *uncertainty*. Ewald's infinitely small or infinitely large-scale risks are both related to scientific knowledge. When knowledge is unable to define the prospect of the future, to compute its own effects upon the future, the logic of insurance is surpassed (Ewald 2002). Traditionally, insurance requires the identification of risk and the statistical estimation of an event happening.

At its core, the precautionary element is derived from environmental politics. The environment was the first area in which catastrophic events were possible, yet not scientifically provable. Formulated initially within the legal realm, the precautionary principle has its roots in the German *Vorsorgeprinzip*, or foresight principle, which emerged in the early 1970s and developed into a principle of German environmental law.[10] Since then, it has informed international policy statements and agreements – initially recognized in the World Charter for Nature, which was adopted by the UN General Assembly in 1982; and subsequently adopted in the First International Conference on Protection of the North Sea in 1984. The European Commission, which recognized it for the first time in relation to the environment in the 1992 Maastricht Treaty, later extended it to other situations (European Commission 2000). The definition of the precautionary principle is however most often traced back to the 1992 Rio Declaration (United Nations 1992), which states that action should not be dependent upon "full scientific certainty". Similarly, the European Environment Agency has urged us to take actions on the basis of what we do not know: "Forestalling disasters usually requires acting before there is strong proof of harm" (European Environment Agency, quoted in Stern and Wiener 2006: 394).

Notwithstanding its familiar ring, precaution can be reduced neither to traditional responsibility in the face of dangers nor to neoliberal prudentialism. It is not a reminder of precautions that must be taken individually by entering the insurance market. Precautionary risk introduces within the computation of the future its very limit, the infinity of uncertainty and potential damage. It is therefore exactly the opposite of prudence: if the latter recommended what "precautions" to take under conditions of knowledge, the former demands that we act under scientific and causal uncertainty. The weight of the future is not simply that of contingency, but that of catastrophic contingency. This double infinity of risk makes infinite risks difficult to govern by the technologies of insurance. Yet, this does not mean, as Beck wrongly hypothesized, that these technologies dwindle out of existence or that governmentality is suspended. Social problems are always subjected to the imperative of governmentality. The representation of the double infinity of terrorism has rather led to the deployment of a precautionary *dispositif*, which has been grafted upon the "old" insurantial technologies of risk management.

Precautionary risk has not, however, spelled the death of insurantial risk or of prudentialism. It has reconfigured insurance in a new *dispositif* that deploys already available rationalities and technologies of risk. The precautionary element is grafted upon the existing technologies of insurance, other forms of calculation and relationality to the future. The rationality of neoliberalism and the rationality of precaution are not mutually exclusive, but converge in the emphasis on market agents as risk embracing and the simultaneous (if contradictory) need to control the conditions of markets as well as the conditions of the future.[11] Precautionary risk relies on the neoliberal idea that the future is radically uncertain. Radical uncertainty is, after all, the motor of market and competitive behaviour. If, in the neoliberal rationality, uncertainty is seen to foster more innovation and economic profit, the precautionary rationality emphasizes the other side of neoliberalism, namely that of the need to govern markets and create the conditions of their functioning. As will be shown in the following sections, precautionary risk and its focus upon risk avoidance do not involve the end of insurance, but also open up novel and profitable ways of embracing risk in and by the insurance business.

## Precautionary risk in the war on terror

While it originated in the environmental sphere, we argue that precautionary risk has also emerged in the *dispositif* of risk to govern terrorism, where other, traditional technologies are considered fallible or insufficient.[12] Here, Rumsfeld's tautological quote that opened this chapter can be read as an overview of risk management. The "known knowns" activate technologies of responsibility, while the "known unknowns" are the risks that can still be integrated by insurance technologies. They refer to the unknown future that can be governed through statistical probabilities and other forms of computation. Finally, the "unknown unknowns" can be said to represent the catastrophic events that disturb the existing modalities of taming uncertainty and the future. According to Ewald, "the precautionary principle does not target all risk situations but only those marked by two principal features: a context of scientific uncertainty on the one hand and the possibility of serious and irreversible damage on the other" (Ewald 2002: 282).[13] Or, as Blair put it in the other opening quote, when faced with uncertainty, responsible decision-making is based upon the precautionary principle.

As we have seen, a *dispositif* of risk generally consists of rationalities and technologies to monitor and predict dangerous occurrences in the future. Precautionary risk, more specifically, is based on four interlinked rationalities that allow for the deployment of specific technologies to manage the "unknown unknowns" of terrorism. These rationalities are: zero risk, worst case scenario, shifting the burden of proof and serious and irreversible damage (Ewald 2002). They are derived from the catastrophic and radically contingent elements of the future, and they modify the three rationalities typical of insurance: risk identification, risk reduction and risk spreading. These four rationalities, triggered by the double infinity of catastrophe and uncertainty, can be clearly discerned in President Bush's outline of the Iraqi threat:

> Many people have asked how close Saddam Hussein is to developing a nuclear weapon. Well, we don't know exactly, and that's the problem ... Facing clear evidence of peril [the attacks of September 11], we cannot wait for the final proof – the smoking gun – that could come in the form of a mushroom cloud ... Understanding the threats of our time, knowing the designs and deceptions of the Iraqi regime, we have every reason to assume the worst, and we have an urgent duty to prevent the worst from occurring.
>
> Bush (2002a)

As this passage shows, the worst case scenario and its irreversible damages logically lead to a politics of extreme risk avoidance. At the same time, however, practices of risk management such as "contingency planning" increasingly derive from the realization that the catastrophe will happen. Hence, the worst case scenario is simultaneously to be avoided at all costs and essentially unavoidable. Thus, as Andrew Lakoff has rightly noticed, precaution is increasingly joined to "preparedness" as a technique for managing catastrophic futures through "operational criteria of response" rather than total avoidance (Lakoff 2006: 9).

The concern with taming an uncertain, catastrophic future has also modified the logic of profiling present in insurantial technologies. The insurance paradigm of risk was based on scientific calculus and group profiling. Profiling as a technology of "social sorting" (Lyon 2002) depends on the categorization of social groups, their profiling and statistical computation of risk. Once terrorist suspects cannot be clearly identified through technologies of profiling, we have a renewed panopticism, forms of surveillance that target everybody, as the potential terrorist could be any of us (see also de Goede, this volume; Coutin, this volume). Gordon Woo, one of the best known risk analysts of the London-based firm Risk Management Solutions, has formulated this dilemma of the undetectable terrorist:

> What would be especially puzzling to security forces is the apparently haphazard variation in the commitment of a specific individual to the terrorist cause. Such individuals would not be classified as hard-liners, and would soon disappear from the terrorist radar screen ... These individuals may not themselves have any prolonged history of links with radical groups, so they would be hard to identify in advance as potential suspects ... .
>
> Woo (2002)

Traditional technologies of risk management become more extensive as profiling and surveillance attempt to encompass the whole population (van Munster 2004). As the underestimation of intelligence and knowledge is considered irresponsible from the viewpoint of precautionary risk, the scope and field of intelligence need to be enlarged accordingly. Yet, at the limit of knowledge, intelligence itself becomes insufficient. The Home Office official report on the 7/7 London bombings points out this conundrum: nothing marked out the four men involved in the attacks, they were all "unexceptional" (Home Office 2006). 9/11 has therefore given way to more proactive forms of surveillance of suspect populations, leading to a surplus supply of data and an overprediction of threats (Lyon 2003; Levi and Wall 2004; Amoore and de Goede 2005). Precautionary technologies therefore change the relation to social groups, to the population as created by the traditional *dispositif* of insurance. Statistical computation and risk management relied upon the scientific representation of social groups that were to be governed; profiling was an important technology for selecting these groups and targeting them.

Moreover, whereas insurance operates with a view that (financial) losses can be distributed evenly within a population, a scenario of immeasurable and irreparable damage dictates that the "burden of proof" is no longer on the state to show guilt but on the suspects to prove that they are and will remain harmless. Their responsibility is uncertain and prior to the event and therefore impossible to accommodate by the juridical notions of guilt and innocence. The inclusion of "indefinite detention", "house arrest" in the UK and the creation of "legal limbos" such as Guantánamo all capture the inadequacy of law to deal with situations of the double infinity of extreme uncertainty and a catastrophic future. As the rationality of zero risk makes those considered potentially dangerous a priori responsible, judgements of responsibility are transferred to the sphere of administrative decisions against juridical procedures. What counts is a coherent scenario of catastrophic risk and imaginary description of the future. The other's actions are no longer relevant. It is against this background, perhaps, that George Bush's "infinite justice" gains its full meaning. The sanctioning of those deemed responsible becomes itself immeasurable, therefore infinite.

The four rationalities of precautionary risk, then, bring to light that the contingent relation to knowledge combined with a catastrophic imaginary of the future instigates a politics of decision that has severed its relation with science, expertise and management. At the limit of knowledge, the relation to representation becomes an arbitrary connection. Political decisions can no longer sustain the imaginary of being grounded in the certainties of science, as the precautionary principle severs or rather exposes in its contingency the very relation between knowledge and representation. When faced with the limits of surveillance, biographical profiles, biometric identifiers, decisions must be taken beyond the horizon of certainty. As a consequence, the rationality of catastrophic risk translates into policies that *actively* seek to prevent situations from becoming catastrophic at some indefinite point in the future. War and preparedness are mobilized alongside other technologies of precaution in a governmental *dispositif* to avoid terrorist irruptions in the future.

The "war on terror" – as fought in Afghanistan and Iraq for example – can therefore not be criticized as simple (imperial) warmongering, but should be made sense of within the context of a *dispositif* that activates all the technologies imaginable in the face of uncertainty and looming catastrophe.[14] Consider Tony Blair's response to criticism against his position on the war in Iraq:

> Sit in my seat. Here is the intelligence. Here is the advice. Do you ignore it? But, of course, intelligence is precisely that: intelligence. It is not hard fact. It has its limitations. On each occasion, the most careful judgement has to be made taking account of everything we know and advice available. But in making that judgement, would you prefer us to act, even if it turns out to be wrong? Or not to act and hope it's OK? And suppose we don't act and the intelligence turns out to be right, how forgiving will people be?
>
> Blair (2004)

Expert knowledge is exposed as an insufficient and unreliable resource for political decisions. If the contingency of political decisions could be "hidden" under the weight of knowledge and the necessity of expertise, they now reappear as ungrounded, arbitrary attempts to subdue the contingency of the future. When the limits of technical or scientific knowledge are exposed, politics discloses its own necessary decisionism, its immanent limit. Yet, this does not imply that knowledge no longer plays any role in risk management, that the imaginary of knowledge grounding politics has been undone. On the contrary, Blair's approach to the war in Iraq has wavered between an initial reliance on intelligence and a later invocation of the "uncertainty" of this knowledge. Rather, it demonstrates that the computation of the future has become decisional.[15]

## The "unknown knowns" of neoliberalism: the politics of risk in the war on terror

At the beginning of this chapter, we suggested that an analysis of the *dispositif* of risk allows us to gauge the political consequences of the exceptional and imperial practices deployed in the "war on terror". Precautionary risk will also expose the de-democratizing effects of the neoliberal rationality of governance. In the post-9/11 academic world, Carl Schmitt's theory of the exception has experienced a fast revival. Torture, indefinite detention, Guantánamo, extraordinary rendition, to name a few examples, are all assigned as exceptional practices deemed to be simultaneously inside and outside the law (see also Ericson, this volume). While scholars have been grappling with the paradoxical relation between exceptional measures and the institutional and legal consequences of the war on terror, the revival of Schmitt's theory of the exception has brought home the aporias of the rule of law. As Judith Butler, in a passage reminiscent of Hannah Arendt's work, has made clear, law itself contains its own exceptions:

> ... there is also a problem with the law, since it leaves open the possibility of its own retraction, and, in the case of the Geneva Convention, extends 'universal' rights only to those imprisoned combatants who belong to 'recognizable' nation-states, but not to all people. Recognizable nation-states are those that are already signatories to the convention itself. This means that stateless people or those who belong to states that are emergent or 'rogue' or generally unrecognized lack all protections.
>
> Butler (2004: 86)

Yet, most analysts drawing on Agamben seem to agree that what distinguishes the current exception is its permanent nature, the shift from a temporally confined decision to a "normal" form of governance (Neal 2004). Agamben himself hints at a similar reading when he argues that the state of exception is not so much an exceptional measure, but a technique of government that relies on security (Agamben 2005).[16] The exceptionality of these practices, in turn, has been described as a crossing of the threshold from the international to the imperial, where "all rules of international order are pushed back so as to reveal the always potential possibility of empire as the regulative negation of modern political life" (Walker 2006: 72; see also Hardt and Negri 2000). In these accounts, the exceptional figures as a claim to decisionism that suspends the normal rules of the game where law is either transcended or transformed into an instrument for political objectives (Huysmans 2006a).

An analysis of the precautionary *dispositif* of risk offers a new perspective on the much debated status of exceptional practices and their relation to the role of law and imperialism. To begin with, the former, the *dispositif* of risk, points to important continuities in the role of law, but also to discontinuities in its functioning in the war on terror. Whereas exceptional practices in the wake of 9/11 are generally said to have changed the character of law, turning it into a mere instrument for politics, such changes in the character of law can already be traced back to the invention of insurance, which transformed law into a technique for governing social problems (Huysmans 2004). As John McCormick has argued, a significant temporal connection exists between Schmitt's theory of the exception and the birth of the welfare state insofar as the forms of intervention of the welfare state in the economy have brought about the "materialization" of the law, which the theoretical formalism of liberalism only serves to conceal (McCormick 2000: 1693). Rather than a formal guideline, law is part of the material reality of society. As Ewald has argued:

> The norm is a means of producing social law, a law constituted with reference to the particular society it claims to regulate and not with respect to a set of universal principles. More precisely, when the normative order comes to constitute the modernity of societies, law can be nothing but social.
>
> Ewald (1990: 154–5)

Thus, the very essence of law – its predictability, universality, absolutism and non-retroactivity – can no longer perform its functions when it is made subordinate to the specific concerns of a particular society.[17] With insurance, the statistical, probabilistically established norm appears as a common and objective basis for governing populations, whereas formal expressions of the law lose their significance (see also Ewald 1991: 201).

In the war on terror, law has a singular function inasmuch as it is adjusted to the representation of the future as catastrophic. Rendering the future as catastrophic turns law into a policy instrument to prevent such disastrous occurrences. Rather than a completely novel state of exception, the transformation in the role of law is best understood as dependent upon the representation and governmentality of the future. Law is deployed at the horizon of a future whose representation has already been fixed. However, where the exceptionalism of insurance had the objective to expand substantial justice and social rights not (yet) guaranteed by the law, the precautionary paradigm lacks such progressive potential.[18] In contrast to insurance, the precautionary approach portrays the status quo as worth preserving as a value in itself: "It is concerned with ensuring the continuity of the future with the past. The precautionary principle is counter-revolutionary. It aims to restrict innovation to a framework of unbroken progress" (Ewald 2002: 284).

The precautionary *dispositif* also draws attention to the paradoxical role of the sovereign decision. Although Schmittian analyses have seen the United States as the global sovereign *par excellence*, precautionary risk shows that the sovereign decisions are often withdrawn, suspended rather than asserted. Precautionary risk turns any decision into a radically contingent one. Decisions are simultaneously based in the knowledge that a catastrophe will happen and distanced from it: we cannot know the future any more. Precautionary risk subverts the critical potential that the linkage between the exception and political decisions had. The sovereignty of "decisions" is withdrawn in the impossibility both to deny and to know the catastrophic risks of the future.[19] This double bind of "knowing/not knowing" has been most visible in the run-up to the Iraq war. At the horizon of the worst case scenario, decisions were presented as both rooted in knowledge and rendered unaccountable to the radical contingency of the catastrophe. By promoting an imaginary of catastrophe as worst case scenario and by shifting the burden of proof, the *dispositif* of precautionary risk simultaneously grounds decisions in concrete representations of catastrophe and deprives them of accountability by pointing to the radical contingency and unknowability of these catastrophic visions.[20]

If the *dispositif* of risk against the uncertain and catastrophic future helps in rethinking Schmittian exceptionalism, it also exposes another facet of imperial practices. The United States and their allies have been mainly castigated for their imperial incursions into Afghanistan and Iraq, which have been conducted in the name of our values. As Blair argued:

> Tyrannical regimes with WMD and extreme terrorist groups who profess a perverted and false view of Islam ... have different motives and different origins but they share one basic common view: they detest the freedom, democracy and tolerance that are the hallmarks of our way of life.
>
> Blair (2003)

Yet, critical commentators have argued that this democratic rhetoric harbours a neoliberal rationality of governance. For instance, Wendy Brown has commented that "our way of life" is designated less in democratic than in neoliberal terms, i.e. as:

> the ability of the entrepreneurial subject and state to rationally plot means and ends and the ability of the state to secure the conditions, at home and abroad, for a market rationality and subjectivity by removing impediments to them (whether Islamic fundamentalism or excessive and arbitrary state sovereignty in the figure of Saddam Hussein).
>
> Brown (2003)

Along similar lines, Slavoj Žižek has intriguingly pointed out that what is missing from Rumsfeld's pairings of the known/unknown are the so-called "unknown knowns" – the things we do not know that we know, the so-called disavowed beliefs and suppositions, the obscene practices we pretend not to know about (Žižek 2004). According to him, the "obscenity" of the war on terror exists in ignoring the fact that the "war on terror" also precludes politics and social struggle. As he asks rhetorically: "What if the war on terror is not so much an answer to the terrorist attacks themselves as an answer to the rise of the anti-globalization movement, a way to contain it and distract attention from it" (Žižek 2004: 61). Žižek's analysis is not far removed from Brown's: the unknown known of the war is that of sustaining neoliberal practices and therefore targeting forms of dissent against its practices.

What, then, does the precautionary *dispositif* of risk add to these analyses that emphasize the role of neoliberalism and dissent? In addition to these approaches, the analysis of risk reveals not only imperialism as neoliberal imperialism; it also shows that, historically, preserving the capitalist way of life has figured predominantly in the *dispositif* of risk. To explore this in more detail, it is useful to briefly revisit Donzelot's account of the birth of insurance as a means of displacing the conflict between workers and the owners of capital. Via insurance, workers' demands for restructuring society could be replaced by attempts to modify social relations within the capitalist structure. This account of insurance is less optimistic than that of Ewald, who sees in social insurance "a technology of justice" that transcends class divisions and reconstitutes both working class and capitalists as citizens in relation to the state.

According to Donzelot, however, insurance did not contribute to transgressing class struggle. For him, insurance never called for the reorganization of society but merely for compensation of damages caused by the social division of labour – and this is not done in the name of a fundamental injustice (Donzelot 1988). Actually, insurance as a technology of governance "normalized" social struggles and avoided the partisan appropriation of the state by the workers. Workers' compensation schemes, in this view, are an instrument of government serving the political and economic objectives of minimizing a cause of industrial conflict and maximizing capital accumulation, while simultaneously managing the conduct of the injured worker. Thus, "[s]ocial security is also an insurance against revolution" (Ewald 1991: 209).

Similarly, two risk management experts recently argued in an article on terrorism that the insurance industry contributes to the social and economic continuity of the country (Kunreuther and Michel-Kerjan 2005: 51), while George W. Bush claimed that "[t]oday, with terrorism insurance, we're defending America by making our economy more secure" (Bush 2002b). Insurance, here, is directly related to the protection of the American homeland, understood as the indefinite survival of its economic structures. Moreover, Gordon Lafer has pointed out that the "war on terror" aims at "undoing workers' power in the workplace; pushing back against labor's growing political clout; and breaking apart the labor–community coalitions that threatened to exercise too much democratic control over capital" (Lafer 2004: 334). From forbidding the right of unionization to security personnel at airports to branding as unpatriotic those workers who refused to accept wage and benefit cuts, Lafer shows how the "war on terror" has served to constantly undermine the power of the labour force and any attempts at rolling back corporate capital. The technologies of risk deployed in the war on terror seek to foster subjects who are consistent with the neoliberal logic of capitalism and entrench a vision of the social where antagonisms have been displaced or are suspended by an overwhelming concern with the continuity of social and economic processes.

In practice, therefore, terrorism risk has become increasingly equated with the risk that the capitalist structure is interrupted by exceptional events. One example is AON Corporation, a global leader in risk management, insurance and reinsurance broking, which publishes a "Global Terrorism Risk Map" that ranks the risk of terrorism in relation to foreign investment potential. The risks included under the heading of global terrorism range from extreme right violence, religious extremism to separatism, single-interest groups and Marxist-inspired violence (AON 2005). Bundled under the label "terrorism", these risks have little in common other than that these are all social disorders that can lead to a destabilization of the economic structure of society. Similarly, ACE USA provides insurance against acts that do not follow the federal definition of insurance as provided in the Terrorism Risk Insurance Act. With the purpose to "protect businesses from the devastating financial impact of terrorism" (ACE 2004), it insures companies against a wide variety of politically and criminally motivated acts – many of which can hardly be called catastrophic in scope.

In sum, precautionary risk draws attention to the continuity of economic practices beyond the liberal/neoliberal discontinuity that Michel Foucault (Foucault 2004), governmentality studies (e.g. Rose 1996a; Dean 1999) and analysts of risk (Baker and Simon 2002; Ericson, Doyle and Barry 2003) have located. Under the neoliberal imperative, what is changing, rather, are the ways in which companies embrace and capitalize on the risk of terrorism. Depending on their financial credentials and degree of risk aversion, companies are still willing to take on the risk of terrorism even in cases of extreme uncertainty. Hence, the precautionary rationality in no way displaces the rationality of embracing risk. One needs only to think of the transferral of precautionary risks to the capital market, where they are subjected not to calculations of frequency and severity but to capital market speculations as one of the ways in which the forces of catastrophes are transformed into business opportunities (Ericson and Doyle 2004a).

History does not simply pass from an imaginary of classical liberal democracy to that of a neoliberal subject, as is sometimes suggested in analyses of exceptionality and imperialism. Rather, liberal and neoliberal democracies are sustained by an imaginary of a capitalist subject whose life and property need to be protected against dangerous occurrences in the future. The *dispositif* of risk in the war on terror thus sustains an ideal imaginary of the social that is – and should be – devoid of political conflict. It wants to safeguard the indefinite continuity of an unmodified present, guaranteeing the non-interruption of social and economic processes and normality.

In doing so, insurance companies create a "security continuum" on which terrorism is connected to (other) risks to the global liberal economy such as re-nationalization, the re-imposition of taxes and tariffs, government inter-ference in international investment and the re-regulation of financial mar-kets. For instance, the US Governor responsible for Iraq's reconstruction, Paul Bremer, in his former capacity as chairman of the company Crisis Consulting, identified terrorism as an international business risk without drawing distinctions between terrorism, the anti-globalization movement or nationalist sentiments (Cooper 2004: 15). Consequently, the *dispositif* of risk in the war on terror – combining a precautionary rationality with a neo-liberal one – risks blurring the categories between terrorism, crime and political resistance in an attempt to maintain the neoliberal status quo. Thus, exceptional and imperial practices are harnessed to the securitization of any form of destabilization to the neoliberal global order. The con-vergence of neoliberal and precautionary rationalities of governance has not only suspended the democratic desire of a more egalitarian society, it is also undermining reforms that might challenge neoliberal governance across society.

## Conclusion

Departing from Beck's risk society thesis of the uncontrollability of risks, this chapter has taken up a conceptualization of risk as a *dispositif* to explore the political implications of governing terrorism. For a governmental approach, what counts is not whether terrorism can be controlled or not, but the *dispositif* that is being deployed to make action upon the contingent occurrence of terrorism thinkable and practicable. The historical modifica-tions and reconfigurations of this *dispositif* have, in turn, allowed us to understand the multiple and heterogeneous practices that are currently grouped under the label "war on terror". We argued that the "war on terror" is best made sense of through the prism of precautionary risk, which has given birth to complex technologies and political rationalities that were grafted upon and modified the earlier *dispositif* of insurance.

The *dispositif* of risk deployed to prevent terrorist events is made possible by the representation of terrorism as doubly infinite in its catastrophic effects and the uncertainty of its occurrence. The infinity of risk does not, as Beck hypothesized, lead to a democratic politics that debates what is to be done, but to intensified efforts and technological inventions on the part of the risk managers to adjust existing risk technologies or to supplement them. Technologies of intervening upon the future are always failing; their failure, however, is part of governmentality, the very motor of the continuous requirement for new technologies and more knowledge. Governing terrorism through risk entails drastic prevention at the catastrophic horizon of the future as well as generalized and arbitrary surveillance at the limit of knowledge. New technologies such as biometrics are supposed to enlist everybody under the category of suspicion (see Epstein, this volume). The possibility of irreparable damage severs suspicion from knowledge. Thus, suspected terrorists can be indefinitely detained independent of any evidence that exists against them.

The limit of knowledge and catastrophe mobilized in the precautionary *dispositif* introduces a decisionist form of politics as a form of governmentality of the future. Examining in more detail what it means to govern terrorism through risk can bring more nuanced analyses of exceptional practices and their relation to law, on the one hand, and exceptional practices and their relation to the capitalist structure, on the other. Alluded to by Žižek's notion of "unknown knowns", we argued that, while insurance always has depoliticized conflict, the depoliticizing effects have been more radically pronounced within the precautionary paradigm. The convergence between the precautionary and neoliberal *dispositif* of governance has intensified these depoliticizing and de-democratizing effects. Underwriting terrorism fosters the imaginary of the present as the indefinite continuity of current economic structures. Terrorism risk advances a form of continuity between actions deemed destabilizing to social and economic processes and aspires to a society stabilized and tranquillized in the present, whatever its inequalities and injustices.

## Notes

1 Elsewhere we have provided a more extensive critique of Beck's understanding of risk and its problematic appropriation in IR theory and security studies (Aradau and van Munster 2007).
2 Despite the peril of exoticism, Foucault's coinage *"dispositif"* has been preserved as such in English contexts due to the perceived inadequacy of translations such as mechanism and apparatus. Neither equivalent could account for the heterogeneity that *dispositifs* imply.
3 The term de-democratization is used by Wendy Brown to refer to the effects of the accidental symbiosis of neoliberalism and neoconservatism in American politics (Brown 2006).
4 Huysmans (2006a), Gregory (2004), Harvey (2003), van Munster (2004) and Walker (2006).
5 It is important to note that a *dispositif* is also a reservoir of resistance. It consists of a set of heterogeneous practices and is therefore not structurally closed (see also Coutin, this volume). In this chapter, however, we focus mainly on the rationalities and technologies deployed as part of the *dispositif* on risk in the "war on terror".
6 The discovery of the work accident could have had disrupting effects upon the social fabric, given its disputable claims to responsibility and the exacerbation of questions of exploitation. However, as the rationality of risk shifted from responsibility to insurance, accidents could be reformulated as something inherent to work, against which workers could nonetheless be protected through insurance.

7 Yet, with the expansion of insurance beyond the wage system, solidarity is simultaneously undermined insofar as insurance depends upon the division and classification of
  populations into high risk/low risk groups. As risks of muggings, crime, AIDS, cancers,
  illegal migration all rely on the classification of groups, the *dispositif* of insurance is based
  upon technologies of categorization. Risk profiling and statistical computation entered
  the *dispositif* of insurance by using probabilistic and epidemiological knowledge to identify factors associated with the risks of certain pathologies (Rose 2001: 8).

8 Of course, it depends on cultural and social dispositions which risks are qualified as catastrophic. See Douglas and Wildavsky (1982).

9 We borrow the term "taming" from Ian Hacking's (1990) formulation, "the taming of
  chance" in relation to probabilities and statistical laws.

10 Whereas the German word "*Vorsorge*" (foresight) refers to the precautionary principle, the
  insurantial model of solidarity is best described in German as "*Umsorge*" (taking care,
  caring).

11 See also Baker's (2002) discussion of the precautionary principle and embracing risk.

12 Obviously, the *dispositif* of precautionary risk produces different effects depending on the
  sphere in which it is articulated.

13 Ewald sees the possibility of the precautionary principle being exported outside its original
  territory (2002). Baker (2002) and Sunstein (2005) claim that the precautionary principle
  increasingly permeates other forms of risk as well.

14 Christopher Coker, too, has pointed out that war is one option for avoiding the bleak
  promise of the future, for "when we do turn to the military option we do so to reduce the
  opportunities for bad behaviour, to prevent them from posing an even greater risk in the
  future" (Coker 2002).

15 In an earlier article, we have pointed out that the *dispositif* of precautionary risk is particularly useful for security studies, because it reconciles decisionist discourses on the
  exception (the Copenhagen School) with the more routine-like technologies of risk
  management stressed by Didier Bigo and his colleagues (Aradau and van Munster 2007).

16 Others see it as the atemporal characteristic of law, a law that can only be understood
  through its inherent relation to violence. In post-structuralist and Marxist analyses, law *is*
  (institutionalized) violence (Derrida 1992; Neocleous 2000).

17 Schmitt's argument is stronger, inasmuch as this liberal definition of law is seen as
  hypocritical. Law is always defined by moments of exceptionalisms; it always needs
  "power outside the law" to constitute it.

18 This is also recognized by Ewald who, while seeing insurance as a technology of justice, is less
  optimistic about the transformative potential of the precautionary approach (see below).

19 For a more in-depth discussion of the changing role of law in the "war on terror", see
  Aradau (2007).

20 The conundrum of knowing/not knowing and the sovereign decision deprived of
  accountability is also visible in Bush's outline of the Iraqi threat: "Some have argued we
  should wait – and that's an option. In my view, it's the riskiest of all options, because the
  longer we wait, the stronger and bolder Saddam Hussein will become. We could wait and
  hope that Saddam does not give weapons to terrorists, or develop a nuclear weapon to
  blackmail the world. But I'm convinced that is a hope against all evidence. As Americans, we want peace – we work and sacrifice for peace. But there can be no peace if our
  security depends on the will and whims of a ruthless and aggressive dictator ... Failure to
  act would embolden other tyrants, allow terrorists access to new weapons and new resources,
  and make blackmail a permanent feature of world events" (Bush 2002a).

# 2 Spatial imaginaries

## Economic globalization and the war on terror[1]

*Wendy Larner*

## Introduction

Does the new focus on security and risk-based technologies associated with the so-called "war on terror" mark the end of economic globalization? Whereas in the 1990s, both political and scholarly attention focused on identifying and explaining transnational flows of capital, goods, services and people, more recently, attention has focused on efforts to categorise and contain the movement of particular commodities, forms of information and population groups deemed as "risky" by virtue of their ethnic, national, religious or political origins and/or affiliations. This reorientation has been particularly notable in the increased visibility of technologies aimed at population management, including those associated with biosocial profiling, screening, modelling and mapping explored in this book. This chapter argues that, rather than being a paradox, the increased security at borders, monitoring of the financial and everyday lives of citizens and restrictions on civil liberties associated with the war on terror are premised on the same political–economic imaginary as the fostering of open borders, free markets and active citizenship associated with economic globalization.

There can be no doubt that the recent emphasis on identifying, monitoring and profiling "risky populations" and the rapid introduction of new forms of surveillance and security is a notable phenomenon. This new emphasis is also explicitly linked to a shift in overall political rationalities characterized by a return to more exclusionary, state-centric approaches to global movements and relationships. Should we, however, support the claim that 9/11 and subsequent events have fundamentally challenged the conventional view of economic globalization as "an irresistible historical trend" (Gray 2001: 1). Have these new surveillance and security technologies indeed "brought back the walls" (Friedman 2002) and drastically curbed the flows of money, goods and people across national boundaries? Will the first decade of the twenty-first century be seen as "the period in which the seemingly inevitable process of economic globalization faltered" (OECD Observer 2002)? More conceptually, is globalization indeed "over theorised in terms of social openness and under theorised in terms of social closure" (Shamir 2005)?

Most immediately, answering these questions requires us to reconsider wider claims about the inevitability of economic globalization.[2] It is not the first time that the still all-too-common portrayal of economic globalization as a monolithic process that will result in a borderless world has been challenged. The anti-globalization movement and a wide range of critical scholars have long countered the claim that "there is no alternative" (TINA) to the further liberalization of national economies and societies. For these critics, economic globalization is a political project that emerged out of neoliberal experiments in the 1980s and structural adjustment programmes in the 1990s, and is driven largely by international institutions, hegemonic economic actors and their domestic supporters. They argue the problem is that the "more-market" programmes advocated by the International Monetary Fund (IMF), the World Bank and their allies are exclusionary projects that create further economic and social polarization. But it was the events of 9/11 that gave these longstanding claims about the political specificity of economic globalization additional traction. In the months that followed the inexorable political push towards a borderless free market, the world seemed to grind to a halt as new discourses of homeland security, protection of citizens, policing and risk emerged as the focus of attention among politicians, policymakers and academic commentators.

It is already clear, however, that the confident predictions about the demise of economic globalization that immediately followed 9/11 were premature. After a brief hiatus, global flows of goods, services and people have continued unabated since 2001. But this is not the issue that is at the heart of this chapter. As commentaries about the relationships between economic globalization and the war on terror began to proliferate, it became apparent that there was something else at stake, something that was associated with the ways in which new political configurations are portrayed. Take, for example, the following observation: "The protagonists are not the agents of states, but organisations whose relationships with governments are oblique, ambiguous and some times indecipherable" (Gray 2001: n.p.). The reference here is to those responsible for the attacks on the World Trade Center, but could equally apply to management consultants, transnational social movements, diasporic political alliances or non-government organizations (NGOs). Similarly, former World Bank economist Joseph Stiglitz (2002: n.p.) argued that "(T)he borderless world through which goods and services flow is also a borderless world through which other things can flow that are less positive". Is it simply a discursive coincidence that both economic globalization and terrorism are now being described and analysed in terms of supranational flows, networks and mobilities? And what about the political mechanisms through which these flows, networks and mobilities are governed? Are there family resemblances between the techniques used to govern globalizing production processes and those being developed to combat terrorism?

Various versions of the argument that there is indeed a link between economic globalization and terrorism can be found in existing literatures. There are claims, either that economic globalization has gone too far to be turned back, or that the war on terror is a means of advancing the "neo-liberal agenda of global economic transformation" (Lafer 2004: 324) It has also been argued that economic globalization is *in* terrorism, as in analyses that emphasize the role of telecommunications, the internet and data sharing in the mobilizing and financing of terrorist activities across national boundaries (Hughes 2002). In these discussions, the relationship between economic globalization and terrorism is seen as part of an overall increase in interdependence on a world scale. Others reverse this claim by arguing that terrorism is the *mirror image* of economic globalization: that terrorists are "NGOs of violence" (Beck 2003) in competition with states, economies and societies; that terrorism is a "negative globalisation" (Bauman and Galecki 2005; Smith 2005) or "a dark form of globalisation in which terrorist tactics are imported from Baghdad to Birmingham" (Stevenson 2007: n.p.). Finally, there are those who argue that economic globalization *is* terrorism. Vandana Shiva (2006), for example, explicitly names a form of "economic terrorism" in which the "World Terrorism Organisation" advocates coercive rules of trade and trade liberalization. Ours, she argues, is a world divided between the "free market terrorism" of bin Laden/al Qaeda and the "state sponsored formal terrorism" though which the US and the UK are attempting to reassert geo-economic control.

This chapter contributes to debates about the relationships between economic globalization and terrorism by drawing on accounts of "global governmentality" (Larner and Walters 2003, 2004). The immediate aim is to shift attention beyond the actions of particular governments and politicians, or the political orientations of particular programmes, by exploring the claim that apparent relationships between economic globalization and terrorism are associated with a broader shift in political–economic imaginaries and governmental forms. Because I enter these debates as a scholar of globalization rather than security studies, the chapter focuses on wider questions about the political rationalities and technologies through which the global is being governed, and the spaces and subjects that these rationalities and technologies constitute. It is the content of this political–economic imaginary, the way in which it is shaping understandings of both economic globalization and terrorism, and what this reveals about the spaces and subjects of governance assumed and constituted through the so-called war on terror, that will be examined under the chapter's remit of global governmentality.

## Rethinking economic globalization

Whereas economic globalization is still most often seen as a socio-structural process associated with capitalist expansion, this chapter draws on accounts that emphasize the "imaginaries" of economic globalization. What is meant by this term? It is not simply a reference to the disciplinary formations captured by the term "geographical imaginations", which emphasize the role of place, space and landscape in the constitution of social life. Nor is it simply a reflection of broader humanist usages in which "imaginaries" describe the complex ways in which people come to understand the world and situate themselves in it. Rather, it is a term that captures the growing trend in social science literatures – including economic history, human geography, anthropology and sociology – to pay greater attention to the discursive framing of economic, political and social spaces. In political–economic literatures, a variety of cognate terms can be found including "spatial imaginaries" (Larner 1998), "economic imaginaries" (Jessop 2004) and "imagined economies" (Cameron and Palan 2004). Also relevant are the "relational" or "topological" ways of conceptualizing space associated with the work of geographers such as Massey (2005), Latham (2002) and Amin (2002).

In these literatures, the use of the term "imaginary" marks not only a rise in interest in political–economic representations, but also a way of grappling with changing conceptions of the world. It is now widely accepted that the nation-state is no longer the sole container for political–economic processes, if indeed it ever was. For those who are more socio-structurally inclined, the intellectual response to the problem of methodological nationalism has been to analyse the "rescaling" of political–economic processes, showing how new "state spaces" premised on supranational, regional, urban and local economies have taken on greater visibility and political importance (see, for example, Brenner *et al.* 2003; Keil and Mahon 2008). In these analyses, new state spaces are institutional realignments that follow in path-dependent ways from broader changes in the reorganization of capitalism. This is not to argue that they are deterministic accounts – the recent rediscovery of Polanyi is particularly significant in this context – but they do represent an intellectual commitment to approaches in which the explanation for new spatialities ultimately lies in an analysis of capitalist processes.

This intellectual position can be contrasted with the post-Marxist, post-structuralist and relational accounts that have also come to prominence in recent years under a variety of labels, including governmentality (Dean 1999; Rose 1999), post-structuralist political economy (Larner and Le Heron 2002), cultural economy (Amin and Thrift 2004), cultural political economy (Jessop 2004), feminist political economy (Gibson-Graham 1996, 2006) and cultural anthropologies of the state (Sharma and Gupta 2006). While there are important disciplinary and theoretical differences between these literatures, seen together, they unsettle the taken-for-grantedness of our analytical categories and encourage us to consider more carefully how concepts we use to understand the world have come to take the forms they have. This intellectual approach is not simply a linguistic turn in political economy, nor is it just the conception of "social construction" found in fields such as international relations and international political economy. Rather, the focus is on the constitutive aspects of social scientific concepts and categories. The intellectual project is to identify the specificity of these concepts and categories, to understand how they have become hegemonic and to reveal the work that they do in framing our understandings of the world we live in.

A great deal of attention has been paid to the changing nature of the social in these literatures. The influential governmentality literature, for example, has highlighted the shift from the singular conceptions of society that characterized the postwar formations of Keynesian welfarism and developmentalism to the multiple and heterogeneous conceptions of community associated with advanced liberalism. More relevant to the discussion herein, however, is the increasing attention being paid to how the economy has been imagined and constituted in particular forms. To date, these analyses have largely focused on the national economy, showing that "the economy" is a territorially defined form of economic relations made statistically measurable and nationally regulated during the 1930s and 1940s (Mitchell 2002). This image and knowledge of the national economy was subsequently transported to developing countries in embodied forms, in turn helping to constitute these as nationally bounded economic spaces and creating a new set of development "problems" (Escobar 1995; Suzuki 2006). There is a parallel, and also useful, discussion in state theory, which underlines how the "state effect" is constituted from an assemblage of discourses, institutional forms and practices (Hansen and Stepputat 2001; Sharma and Gupta 2006). Rather than seeing the state as having an a priori conceptual or empirical form, these accounts show how "the state" comes to be understood as a centralized authority ruling over a territorially defined polity. Such accounts have helped us to recognize that the understandings of economy, state and society that dominated both academic and political life during much of the last century were historically and spatially specific. Economy, state and society were imagined as nationally bounded and territorially co-terminous separate spheres. Tellingly, they also show that this economic, political and social imaginary underpinned governmental projects of both the "left" and the "right".

If the now voluminous literature on economic globalization reveals anything, it is that economy, state and society are no longer imagined as either nationally bounded or territorially co-terminous. Globalization is a political–economic imaginary premised on openness and mobility rather than on boundedness and territoriality. It is one in which global flows, networks and mobilities are seen as ubiquitous and increasingly the norm, despite the fact that the vast majority of the world remains immobile (Shamir 2005). For example, the economy is now talked about in terms of financial flows, commodity chains and production networks. In the political arena, the shift from government to governance and the rise of the so-called "disaggregated state" (Slaughter 2004) have underpinned a new focus on supranational institutions, epistemic communities, NGOs and transnational policy networks. Cosmopolitans, immigrant workers, refugees and asylum seekers, internet communities and diasporas are the focus of heightened attention among social commentators. Scholars of security studies now focus on flows of drugs, oil and armaments and their implications for the governance of both nations and states.

Nor are analyses of terrorism exempt from this more general trend. Rather than terrorism being seen as an interstate or intrastate threat, as has been the case previously, following 9/11, the emphasis has been on mobility, fluidity and networks. As Krebs (2002: 1) observes, "We were all shocked by the tragic events of September 11, 2001. In the non-stop stream of news and analysis one phrase was continuously repeated – 'terrorist network'". He then sets out to map these network patterns, emphasizing their incomplete nature, their fuzzy boundaries and their dynamic nature. Similarly, Ettlinger and Bosco (2004) claim that terrorism involves transnational networks of resistance, interspersed with nodes such as madrasas, mosques and refugee camps. Bauman and Galecki (2005: 4) also argue:

> (T)oday's terrorism, being a phenomenon of this era of globalisation, is by definition 'extra territorial'. This is a very peculiar military adversary; it has no headquarters, no military base, no barracks to be bombed. This military force appears from nowhere and then disappears into thin air. There is no commander; there are no orders and hierarchies, yet for some reasons so many separate individuals follow the same path, even more in the same way.

It is in this context that globalization and terrorism can be understood as based on the same political–economic imaginary. Of course, it is not the only such political–economic imaginary – new spatialities are diverse and multiple and include regions, sectors, cities and clusters – but it is notable that it is through and against globalization that these other spatial imaginaries are often understood (Amin 2004a; Larner, Le Heron and Lewis 2007). We also need to think carefully about the legacies of earlier imaginaries including colonialism, welfarism and developmentalism, as well as the resurgence of the civilizational ethos made manifest in the neo-conservative politics of Huntington and others, to make sense of the multiple forms of power that characterize the present (Larner and Walters 2002). But neither of these is the task here. If we understand economic globalization and terrorism to be part of the same political–economic imaginary, what more might we say? How is that we have come to understand the nation-state-centred world as being profoundly challenged by global flows, networks and mobilities? How are these flows, networks and mobilities being made visible? And does this political–economic imaginary also underpin a range of political projects that we might initially think of as diametrically opposed?

## Globalization as an imaginary

Let me be clear about what is not being argued! This is not an argument that globalization has somehow displaced the national economy; that we are seeing the rise of a borderless free market world. This is to reject both the depoliticized "end of ideology" debates associated with Fukuyama (1992), the "globality" of Robertson (1992) in which the world is now a single "imagined community", and claims about deterritorialization made manifest in hyperbole about the "death of distance" and the "end of geography" (O'Brien 1992). But nor is to argue the opposite: that there is nothing new about economic globalization (Hirst and Thompson 1996). Rather, it is an effort to move away from readings of economic globalization that position it as a meta-process or a structural backdrop that can be used to explain subsequent changes in economies, states and societies. As Neil Smith (2004) recognizes, despite all the debates about how globalized the world is or otherwise, it is the power of the "idea" of globalization that is critical. If we begin from this point, then the task becomes that of grasping the distinctiveness of this particular political–economic imaginary. In this regard, we need to be attentive not only to the specificity of the understandings made manifest in this imaginary, but also to how things work and the effects they have.

So how has this new imaginary of global flows, networks and mobilities been constituted? It would be easy – and remains quite tempting – to argue that economic globalization is a market-oriented ideology. Sparke (2003: 375), for example, sees globalization as "the smooth, decentered, globalist, masculinist geo-economic view of the world advocated by TNCs and their supporters". Massey (2005: 83) echoes these claims in her wider ranging account of economic globalization:

> The imagination of globalisation in terms of unbounded free space, that powerful rhetoric of neoliberalism around 'free trade', just as was modernity's view of space, is a pivotal element in an overweaning political discourse. It is a discourse which is predominantly produced in the countries of the world's North (though acquiesced in by many a government in the South). It has its institutions and its professionals. It is normative; and it has effects.

If we took this approach, then both economic globalization and the war on terror would be seen as part of a broader ideological strategy promoted by hegemonic actors. Particular emphasis would be placed on how relationships between major American companies, the military and the US government are furthering the privatization of both the American and the Iraqi economies. Supporters of this argument might also identify how the imperatives of global capital are being supported by educational, financial and legal practices (Sparke 2003).

Another approach, following James Scott's (1998) book *Seeing like a State*, would be to argue that this new political–economic imaginary is an example of states simplifying and making legible the spaces they have to intervene in. Whereas Scott's concern was to identify how state power enforces physical placement, his analytical approach could also be used to explore the schematic categories that describe, aggregate and compare global processes. But, if there is one thing that all the recent talk about economic globalization, disaggregated states and the rise of networks should alert us to, and as Scott (2005) himself has recently stressed, it is that it is not simply firms or the state with which we are concerned here. There is a new role for what are still being called "intermediaries" – this naming, of course, marking the legacies of our earlier conceptual categories in which we understood the economy, state and society as discrete categories. Whether they be economic intermediaries (management consultants, export promotions agencies, immigration consultants), cultural intermediaries (advertising, public relations, media), political intermediaries (NGOs, think tanks, civil society organizations) or social intermediaries (case workers, community and voluntary sectors), these actors also imagine the world as made up of global flows, networks and mobilities.

The various intermediaries might work with or against hegemonic actors. In the literatures that concern many of the contributors to this book, there has been a great deal of discussion about the commodification of security: the use of private security firms and insurance companies to govern risk and the ways in which these new "intermediaries" are contributing to the new understandings of insiders and outsiders through population profiling and risk management techniques (see, for example, Amoore 2006; see also Amoore this volume; Epstein, this volume). Of particular interest are the new actors who have emerged to offer "risk management solutions" that involve modelling and predicting the likelihood of macro-terrorist attacks in various parts of the world. But there is a whole raft of other intermediaries positioned in quite different ways. Nancy Fraser (2005), for example, has recently written about the politics of redistribution and recognition being reframed in a globalizing world and explores the ways in which the politics of class, race and gender are being reconfigured in global social justice movements. The key point is that security guards working in the newly commodified fields of security, the architects of the US terrorism risk model and NGO workers in the global social justice movements take for granted the "fact" of the globalizing world.

These comments also alert us to the fact that social scientists are significant contributors to these new political–economic imaginaries. Substantively, social scientists are increasingly preoccupied by efforts to explain the increased importance of trade, the emergence of new supranational governance regimes manifest in bilateral and multilateral agreements on trade, production and security, globalizing production processes, the nature of new global institutions, new forms of migration, the changing nature of borders and so on. Through their efforts to explain and measure the effects of globalization, they also contribute to its centring as *the* way to think about the world. These substantive concerns segue with high profile conceptual debates. As Holton (2005: 210) recently observed, networks are the metaphor of the current global moment. Similarly, Amin, Massey and Thrift (2003: 6) argue that "We live in an era of increasingly geographically extended spatial flows". More generally, Castellian "spaces of flows", Appadurian notions of "scapes", neo-Foucauldian "assemblages", the "always becoming" subjects of Deleuze and the networks of ANT are also contributing to this new political–economic imaginary. Indeed, arguably, social scientists and political theorists began to talk about the world as fluid, networked and mobile well before politicians and policymakers began to act on understandings of an interconnected world and make efforts to measure global processes.

It should be quite clear by now that globalization is not simply a placeless, spaceless, meta-concept. But nor can this new political–economic imaginary be reduced to geo-economic views of the world or new state spatialities. While economic globalization may take its hegemonic form in what we now call neoliberal globalization, it is well recognized that there are multiple, heterogeneous and diverse globalizations. Discussions of struggles between "the globalisers" (Woods 2006) and anti-globalization movements and between empire and multitude (Hardt and Negri 2000) have underlined the point that the flows and networks of globalization are directional, disjunctive and uneven. More conceptually, Urry (2005) recently distinguished between global networks and global fluids. But the broader point is that all these debates take place in the name of the global. It is in this context that it can be argued that globalization has become a "governmentality", an increasingly normalized and taken for granted context in which economic, political and social activities are understood to take place. Massey's (2005: 84) observation that globalization is a powerful imaginative geography that legitimizes its own production is also pertinent here. Understood in these terms, it is also useful to think of global flows, networks and mobilities as "irreal spaces" (Rose 1999) that are both imagined and partially constituted by this new political rationality.

## Governing globalization

This new political–economic imaginary is not only made manifest in academic, policy and practitioner discourses. We are also seeing new strategies, technologies and techniques that are helping to reconstitute the world as global. This analytical terrain is less developed than that discussed in the section above. To date, there has been a great deal of attention paid to the discourses of globalization, but much less attention has been paid to the techniques of globalization even though these too are critical to the constitution of these new flow-based, political–economic imaginaries (for exceptions, see

Barry 1993; Larner and Walters 2004). This section will not simply rehearse longstanding claims about the shift from government to governance, made manifest in processes such as deregulation, devolution and privatization, and marked by the rise of non-state actors. Rather, it shifts the emphasis on to the actual techniques through which the global is being governed.

Again, there has been quite a lot of discussion about the relationships between governmental techniques and new political formations in the context of national economies, states and societies, but much less in the context of the new global configurations. If censuses (Hannah 2000) and passports (Torpey 2000) were an important way in which we came to understand territorially bounded, nationally based, singular conceptions of society, and Keynesian economics was an important part of the way in which we came to understand economic activity as nationally bounded (Suzuki 2006), what can we say about the governmental techniques that underpin global imaginaries? It is well understood that economics now presents us with a world of free markets, rational decision-makers and choice. But is this disembedded, disembodied, individualized view of the world the only governmental understanding being constituted through new political technologies?

Contributors to the governmentality literature have emphasized how expert knowledges play a key role in the formation of modern governmental practices (Rose-Redwood 2006). Of particular interest have been the ways in which the systematization of knowledge involves measurement and inscription in systems of reporting and monitoring. This not only makes objects and subjects visible in particular forms, these knowledges also embody particular conceptions of how these objects and subjects should be governed. These discussions can be usefully extended to explore new modes of global governance. We are seeing the rise of a range of practices that allow us to understand the world as global and act accordingly. These new "calculative regimes" (Miller 1992) bring together techniques such as benchmarking, standards, best practice, ranking, risk practices and expert knowledge into an assemblage that makes it possible to put objects and subjects in to the same space even though they may be geographically dispersed. These governmental objects and subjects include not only nation-states, but also firms, public and private sector organizations, NGOs, community organizations and individuals.

The proliferation of international standards is one obvious example by which this is happening. Developed initially to govern production processes within firms, International Organization for Standardization (ISO) standards are now being used to compare economic, political, social and environmental processes across countries, institutions and sectors. The audit processes required to realize the various standards render visible these objects and subjects in particular forms, and simultaneously constitute them as global. Another example is the proliferation of global league tables (on topics including the wealth of individuals, size of firms, status of universities, quality of mathematics teaching, levels of child well-being) in recent years. These comparisons put disparate entities, people and places into new spaces through the creation of indices that allow the "global benchmarking" of activities, processes and outcomes. A third example is the new efforts to measure "global" processes. Whereas previously economic and social data were measured within the container of the nation-state, new efforts are being made to measure "cross-border" – again note the legacies of earlier ways of thinking – flows. A high profile example is the A. T. Kearny/Foreign Policy Globalization Index which measures degrees of openness using indicators such as information technology (IT), finance, trade, politics, travel and personal communication. The Organization for Economic Cooperation and Development (OECD) has begun to measure remittances and offshore populations. Also relevant here are discussions about the need for replacement indicators for gross domestic product (GDP), such as "gross national income" (GNI), which would add in net income received from nationals living abroad.

In the context of the war on terror, an interesting example of these new calculative practices is the "catastrophe" maps produced by a firm called Risk Management Solutions (RMS). In their work, long established "risks" (natural hazards such as earthquakes, hurricanes, tornados and hailstorms) are being placed alongside the new "risk" of terrorism in an effort to provide rigorous insurance data that quantify, manage and transfer risks for firms scanning the world for investment opportunities. Importantly, their work involves global representations based on dynamic computational models that work at fine grained levels to establish the geographical likelihood of losses from terrorism from a range of right and left wing groups. Not only do such efforts "visibilize" terrorism as a global problem, they also reconstitute terrorist risk as a global business practice. In this regard, it is notable that the firm is also launching training programmes to "prepare current and future generations of leaders to effectively manage the threat of violence" (RMS 2006). As Aradau and van Munster argue in this collection, such strategies are contributing to a new formulation of risk in which firms and governments all act on the assumption that our future is one of globalized uncertainty and potential catastrophe.

Seen together, these diverse efforts represent a move away from nation-state bounded measurements, calculations and comparisons. The gathering of knowledge about economies, polities and populations is no longer territorially bounded by the nation-state. It is not simply that "government at a distance" severs the direct link between a central authority and the actors and activities being governed. These new techniques and the indicators on which they depend no longer measure component parts of an imagined (national) whole. While these governmental techniques were all initially developed for quite different purposes, they now take as their point of departure the notion of a global world. Comparators, opportunities and risks are understood to exist across national borders rather than being clearly within or without. Moreover, these new "topologies of global regulation" (Amin 2004b) are not simply about the realignment of activities in a new supranational space. Rather, the economic, political and social spaces these practices help to constitute are multiple. Nor is there any clear sovereign authority; as talk among regulatory experts of the shift from political regulation to transactional regulation, and from disciplinary regimes to incentive regimes underlines.

These "advanced liberal" (Rose 1999) techniques are polysemic; they are understood to be equally effective whether governing World Bank programmes or local community organizations. Nor are they politically aligned in particular ways. For example, the ISO is now creating indicators to measure corporate social responsibility, and a small UK-based NGO has just developed a global benchmarking tool to advance gender equity. What holds these globalizing calculative practices together is not simply that they are measurements; rather, it is the aim of these comparisons. The overall ambition is to construct enabling environments in which strategies are being constantly developed to improve performance. For example, the statistical information prepared by the OECD is accompanied by recommendations that set standards for desirable development and the future of socioeconomic change (Alusuutari 2005). Moreover, whereas the imaginaries that underpinned the economic and social policies of the second half of the last century saw the task as that of "catching up", now the overarching ambition is ongoing improvement of processes and future focused outcomes. Finally, it is not simply "objective" categories such as people, goods and services that are being measured in the name of improving performance, but also "subjective" attributes such as innovation, creativity, leadership and skills feature centrally. Both individuals and organizations are to be active, self-responsible and self-actualizing. The aim is to construct enabling environments in which individualized strategies (from microcredit to global risk management) are increasingly the norm.

How then does this emphasis on global "technologies of performance" (Dean 1999) fit with the recent efforts to categorise and contain particular individuals and organizations associated with the war against terror? Put another way; in this globalized, ever changing, aspirational world, what is the "state effect" of these practices? Arguably, governments now see their role as that of channelling these heterogeneous global flows and networks. As Bislev, Salskov-Iversen and Hansen (2001) suggest, the problem of governance has now become that of how to manage economic and social processes in a way that retains competitiveness towards other localities in a global context. This can be seen very clearly in the debates following the clampdown on student visas in the US after 9/11. While framed initially in terms of domestic security, the fear was that international students would go elsewhere, having an impact on the international competitiveness of the US. Similarly, the economic logics that inform the imposition of new security processes at airports focus on the impact that delays might have for business if they were such that they discouraged flying. It is this problematic – how to foster mobility while at the same time monitoring movement – that is giving rise to the integrated risk management strategies that classify individuals and organizations according to perceived threats and risks discussed elsewhere in this collection in detail (see also Sparke, this volume). The aim is to identify and separate out these flows, in order to be able to better oversee mobility. Borders are thus both closed and porous at the same time as new technologies are being used to distinguish between those subjects and objects who can pass freely and those who should not.

## Global subjects

Who are the "irreal" subjects being constituted through these political–economic imaginaries and calculative practices? If we turn our attention back to the literatures on globalization, the broader emphasis on global flows, networks and mobilities can also be seen clearly in diverse and contradictory discussions of global nomads, transnationals, cosmopolitans, asylum seekers, economic refugees, migrants, diasporic citizens and religious fanatics (see, for example, Desforges, Jones and Woods 2005). What brings these discussions together is an increasingly naturalized assumption that subjects are either physically moving or should aspire to move. Nor is it the cosmopolitans of the global North who are mobile and the poor of the South who are not. Rather, the distinction is between those whose movement is facilitated and those whose movement is forced (Bauman 1998). Whether cosmopolitans or asylum seekers, these subjects are active and entrepreneurial (in the broadest sense of the word). They are seeking a better life and looking for new ways to perform familiar tasks. And even those who do not actually move are now understood to have desires and fantasies that are transnational (Grewal 2005).

In this generalized assumption of movement, people are no longer simply either here or there. While these attributes may be most often associated with discussions of transnational elites who have risen to power and visibility by aligning themselves with global markets, in the debates about cosmopolitans, transnational communities and terrorists, we can see the new assumption of subjects with hybrid subjectivities and multiple allegiances who are "thinking and feeling beyond the nation" (Cheah and Robbins 1998). Moreover, it is not simply that citizens themselves are increasingly networked. In the growing number of discussions about political transnationalism and extraterritorial citizenship, we can see that the nation itself is being networked into a global system of social, political and economic interdependency (Mitchell 2003). This is manifest in discussions of how state-sponsored diasporic networks offer new possibilities for economic and social development (Larner 2007), as well as accounts of how social movements (anti-globalization, environmental, feminist and indigenous people's movements) have become globally networked forms of political practice.

This new emphasis on mobile subjects is associated with reconfigured understandings of inequality. Ong (1999) writes about a new form of "graduated sovereignty" in which corporate entities increasingly set the terms of economic and social engagement for certain groups, pointing to the enhanced mobility of financiers, senior managers and consultants as one consequence of these new distinctions between populations. More recently, she argued that these efforts are giving rise to new "states of exception" (Ong 2006) in which mobile bodies are differentially linked across nation-states. She compares the experiences of transnational elites, whose primary allegiance is to global flows and networks, with those of illegal migrants and refugees whose experiences of these global processes are quite different. As she rightly argues, this is how gendered and racialized subjects are now talked about. Those who are unable to move because of poverty, lack of skills or political repression are understood to be somehow lacking in relation to the norm.

How are populations to be managed in this era of mobility, transnational citizenship and hybrid subjectivities? How are global networks to be accessed and movements to be traced? This is where discussions of the rise of so-called "managed migration regimes" (Kofman 2005) and "biometric borders" (Amoore 2006) become relevant. In an era of generalized movement, some subjects have their movements facilitated and others are to be prevented from moving. We could conceptualize this in terms of processes of enclosure, entrapment and containment (see, for example, Shamir 2005); however, efforts to monitor and control global movements are not the same as actually stopping movement. For example, governments want to attract technical and scientific subjects who will contribute to "brain gain" but they don't want these subjects if they are "likely" to apply their knowledge to terrorist activities. Thus, contrary to the assumptions of some commentators (Desforges, Jones and Woods 2005), increasing surveillance and regulation does not necessarily go together with tightened control on international mobility. The aim is to make visible and monitor movements rather than halt them. As Walters (2004a: 252) astutely points out, "It is the challenge of devising systems of security that are compatible with government conducted in the name of the 'mobile world'".

This globalized approach to population management is based on what one author has called "ethnic arithmetic" (Perera 2006). Individuals are now profiled and classified according to perceived threats and risks. Moreover, not only does this involve rational calculation by state agencies but, as Isin (2004) has argued, the securitization of the state, massive border controls and surveillance technologies also produce "neurotic subjects" whose energies are channelled into managing their own anxieties and insecurities. It is clear that these processes are giving rise to new dividing practices between those who are legitimate and those who are illegitimate, those who are understood to constitute potential risk and those who are not. For those from countries who experienced imperialism and colonialism, these practices have a very familiar feel to them; however, the critical point about these new dividing practices is that we are now all subject to them. As a US border guard reassured me shortly after the introduction of biometric profiling for New Zealanders entering the United States: "Don't worry – it's just a matter of time before we are photographing and finger printing our own people". Seen in this light, it is clear we are indeed all now potentially destructive subjects. As Agamben (2004: 41) argues "Humanity itself has become a dangerous class".

## Conclusion

This chapter is deliberately and unapologetically programmatic. It has argued that the political response to terrorism is not a return to the nationally bounded imaginaries of the postwar period. In doing so, the aim has been to sketch out the contours of a political–economic imaginary that shapes our understanding of both economic globalization and the war on terror. This political–economic imaginary makes manifest an understanding of the world as made up of global flows, networks and mobilities. It is not simply the outcome of efforts by transnational corporations (TNCs), supranational institutions or other hegemonic actors to purposefully shape a transnational governance regime. Rather, the chapter has traced broad shifts in meaning that diverse actors, including states, firms, NGOs, social movements, academics and individuals, are all attaching themselves to. The constitutive aspects of this new political–economic imaginary have also been emphasized. In a focus on the techniques by which the global flows are being measured and compared, it was shown that it is not simply that globalization requires global systems of management, but rather that techniques of governing are part of the process through which the global is being constituted.

Having identified this generalized move to flows, networks and mobilities, how might we challenge this particular understanding of the world? How do we avoid an epochal view of change in which there used to be nation-states and now there is globalization? There are at least two broad options, both of which require us to be very careful about the analytical stories we tell about these new global imaginaries. The first possibility is to show that there are multiple globalizations, to continue proliferating accounts of globality (see, for example, Urry 2005). However, the risk is that this strategy would underline the taken-for-grantedness of globalization and re-inscribe the emphasis on flows and mobilities. Perhaps our counter discourses might more usefully take the form of analyses that emphasize other aspects of our contemporary world, revealing that our imaginaries are multiple not singular. For example, how should we think about the religious and civilizational discourses that are also part of the war on terror? How are connections made between the crusades of the twelfth century and the "clash of civilizations" of the present?

The second option is to make very specific claims about how we have come to understand the world as global. It is highly likely that this work will reveal unexpected histories and genealogies. We certainly should not assume that global imaginaries were invented in the "core" and somehow "diffused" to the rest of the world. Just as we know that colonial populations were subject to experiments in public health, forced resettlement, police administration and penal institutions and that those experiments that "succeeded" were re-imported back to the metropole (Scott 2005), and that market-based governance mechanisms were first experimented with under colonialism before being used in the neoliberal experiments of the 1980s and 1990s (Hindess 1998; Larner 2007), we might also examine how the "global" has come together in distinctive forms. These would not be stories of diffusion or hybridity, but rather translation and assemblage. How are particular discourses, techniques and subjects being constituted? What are the vectors of movement, mutating the content and political effects of these discourses, techniques and subjects in particular contexts? Answering these questions will reveal a great deal about the contingency and the specificity of our contemporary spatial imaginaries in general, and those associated with the war on terror in particular.

## Notes

1 Thank you to the editors for their comments and in particular for drawing my attention to the work of Risk Management Solutions, and to the members of the Geographies of Political Economy working group at the University of Bristol for their constructive feedback.
2 Commentators have distinguished between economic, political and cultural globalization (see, for example, Waters 1995). This chapter focuses primarily on economic globalization, namely the generalized claim that technological developments in telecommunications, transportation and materials, together with the rise of flexible production processes, have encouraged the growth of multinational companies, the emergence of new markets and altered the role of the state. That said, the argument made herein is likely to have wider relevance.

# 3 The state of preemption

## Managing terrorism risk through counter law

*Richard V. Ericson*

## Introduction

The American response to the terrorist attacks of 9/11 highlighted a trend toward preemptive security that was already under way across Western societies (Agamben 2005; Dershowitz 2006; Ericson 2007). Preemptive security is based on a precautionary logic that normalizes suspicion (see Aradau and van Munster, this volume). There is perpetual vigilance for signs of danger on the assumption that everyone is guilty of criminal intent. There is also a strong urge to criminalize not only those who actually cause harm, but also those merely suspected of being harmful, as well as authorities who are deemed responsible for security failures.

Preemptive security requires a radical reconfiguration of law. I call this reconfiguration "counter law", which takes two forms (Ericson 2007). Counter law I is law against law. New laws are enacted and new uses of existing law are invented to erode or eliminate traditional principles, standards, and procedures of criminal law that get in the way of preempting imagined sources of harm. Counter law II takes the form of surveillant assemblages (Foucault 1977: 221–3; Haggerty and Ericson 2000, 2006). New surveillance infrastructures are developed and new uses of existing surveillance networks are extended that also erode or eliminate traditional principles, standards, and procedures of criminal law that get in the way of preempting imagined sources of harm.

The legal fine print and surveillance practices of counter law regimes are often hidden. However, counter law as a strategy for preemptive security is highly visible in political culture. Central authorities extol the virtues of counter law measures as the only way to preempt dangers and effect security. Counter law is officially expressed as a "state of exception" (Agamben 2005). Normal legal principles, standards, and procedures must be suspended because of a state of emergency, extreme uncertainty, or threat to security with catastrophic potential. The legal order must be broken to save the social order. However, the state of exception is no longer the exception but has become the normal state. "The declared state of exception has been replaced by an unprecedented generalization of the paradigm of security as the normal technique of government" (Agamben 2005: 87). This is the state of preemption. There is incessant elaboration of laws against law and surveillant assemblages that facilitate preemptive security.

This chapter initially considers Jihadist terrorism and the politics of risk and security surrounding it. It then describes and analyzes the counter law measures that have emerged in the wake of 9/11. The description and analysis show how managing terrorism risk through counter law has further institutionalized the state of preemption, with disturbing consequences for social justice.

## Terrorism and the politics of risk and security

Terrorism is a politics of uncertainty. For example, Jihadist terrorism targets the values, science, technology, and law of Western risk societies, seeking to transform them into uncertain societies. Terrorists are in the business of uncertainty, playing on randomness to keep whole populations in fear, anticipation, and disestablishment. They underscore the potential ungovernability of modern societies, how those with little power can work cheaply and efficiently against powerful institutions to destroy (Stehr and Ericson 2000).

Terrorists stage destructive events that ensure they will live on in the "vast metaphorical spectator spaces" of mass media (Taylor 2004: 170). These events strike at the Western liberal valorization of life at all costs and an orderly death. They do so by making death unpredictable, irrational, and highly symbolic (Bayatrizi 2005). Terrorists transcend life as order, security, prosperity, and freedom by glorifying a different symbolic state: a destiny, a cause, a pride, a sacrifice (Baudrillard 2003: 68).

Suicide bombers construct the Western obsession with uncertainty and fear of death as weakness and even cowardice, juxtaposed with their fearless embracing of death (Reuter 2004: 15). Often supported by family and community, theirs is a spiritual mission in which martyrdom and the afterlife rise above any desire to survive. The spiritual instructional manual for the 9/11 attack on the World Trade Center informed participants, "You will notice that the plane will stop, then will start to fly again. This is the hour in which you will meet God."

The al-Qaeda ideology of destruction, while apparently rooted in the Islamic tradition, ignites followers from different nations and backgrounds. To the extent that an al-Qaeda network exists, it is mainly in the form of dispatching its own loyalists to scenes of local conflict where natives are converted to the view that their struggle is part of a global clash of civilizations. "Thus, injustices perpetuated in Chechnya or on the West Bank can stir up hatred within Morocco and Saudi Arabia, and unintentionally provide aid and comfort to opportunists who stoke the flames of righteous anger everywhere" (Reuter 2004: 18). This disparate nature of al-Qaeda has led Burke (2004) to conclude that it is more an ideology than an organization.

There was an al-Qaeda infrastructure in Afghanistan, but it has been destroyed, and many of bin-Laden's associates are on the run or have been detained or killed. However, the ideology remains strong and is spreading well beyond any link to bin-Laden or his immediate associates. Indeed, bin-Laden has become part of the ideology, in the sense that his role model is used to advance the "Jihadi International" cause.

While rich with myths and symbols that make it seem highly irrational in the context of Western conceptions of life and death, the bin-Laden model is highly rational. Indeed, the myth and symbol are a crucial part of the rationality, mobilizing adherents to strategic action that one Central Intelligence Agency (CIA) analyst views as exhibiting "brilliance, eloquence, sanity, religious sincerity, [and] astute tactical skills" (Scheuer 2004).

The rationality includes methods and targets of attacks that provide poignant reminders of the limits of scientific and technological efforts at risk management. Many attacks, most spectacularly 9/11, involve the use of science and technology against itself. Science and technology simply reward the suicidal will. All attacks expose the limits of risk assessment and management in conventional terms of frequency and severity (Ericson and Doyle 2004a). Frequency is extremely difficult to ascertain for a given target. Terrorism is intentional catastrophe, and the same target can be struck repeatedly or not at all. Severity is also extremely difficult to estimate. Moreover, the consequences of a terrorist attack are assumed to be so severe that terrorism by definition is a risk beyond price.

The rationality also includes methods and targets of attack that provide poignant reminders of the limits of law in risk assessment and management. The new asymmetries of power between nation-states in conflict with non-nation-state actors blur the boundaries between war and peace, and with them the laws of war and domestic law enforcement. There is a new sense of permanent war and absence of peace requiring new laws of both war and domestic peacekeeping. The deterrent capacity of the legal power to punish is destroyed because terrorists express a desire to die. The relationship between law, power, and the state is radically reconfigured as an integral part of terrorism as intentional catastrophe.

> [Terrorists] annihilate the entire logic of power, since no credible threat can be made against someone who has no desire to survive. All of our notions of security and our civilization have been based on this unspoken assumption, which we heretofore have believed to be self-evident. For example, consider that for airport security checks, up until now, the only precaution thought necessary was the matching of every piece of luggage with an on-board passenger, since, as everyone knew, no one would think of blowing themselves up in midair. Or so we thought. The presumption of individual self-interest and fear of death underlies the function of the market economy and the power of the state: suicide bombers cancel these out. Deterrence, punishment, and retaliation all

become meaningless when faced with an aggressor who will impose the utmost penalty for himself at the very moment of his victory.

Reuter (2004: 3)

Terrorism makes precautionary logic obvious. Following 9/11, political speech in the U.S. took a dramatic turn aimed at making precautionary logic part of everyday life. President Bush hit home in various sound-bites the need to preempt the terrorist threat "before it fully materializes." His then National Security Advisor, Condoleeza Rice, declared that extraordinary police and military mobilization against terrorism is necessary before the "smoking gun becomes a mushroom cloud" (Janus 2004: 577–8).

Investigations of the failure to prevent the events of 9/11 focused on the problems of bureaucracy, communication, and tunnel vision in the Federal Bureau of Investigation (FBI), CIA, and other security agencies, and stressed the need to exercise the catastrophic imagination as a crucial ingredient of future security. The 9/11 Commission Report (Kean and Hamilton 2004: 339) said the 9/11 attacks reflected security agencies' failure of "imagination – the lack of organisational capacity to imagine such an attack" (see also Salter, this volume). Ironically, it recommended efforts to bureaucratize imagination: "It is therefore crucial to find a way of routinizing, even bureaucratizing, the exercise of imagination" (ibid: 334). While a bureaucratized imagination seems paradoxical, what is being recommended is the embedding of precautionary logic in the security systems of organizations. In all of their planning, strategies, and practices, security agents are to imagine a kind of sea monster intent on leaving tsunami-like destruction in its wake.

Precautionary logic has become central to the U.S. politics of risk and security, feeding into and fed by other features of its political culture. There is a concerted effort to conflate the need for preemption at home with preemptive strikes against terrorism abroad. This conflation was a key feature of Bush's strategy in the 2004 presidential election, continuing the post-9/11 campaign to simultaneously terrorize the American population into the preemptive policies of homeland security, and populations in Iraq and elsewhere in the Middle East through preemptive attacks.

This conflation of security at home with aggression abroad is effected through the view that the U.S. is at war with terrorists however defined. The U.S. has long used "war on" metaphors to identify suitable enemies and justify extreme security measures against them: "the war on crime," "the war on drugs," even "the war on poverty" when welfarism had a glimmer of hope in the American political culture of the 1960s (see also Simon, this volume). "The war on terrorism" in some respects encapsulates all of these "war on" campaigns because it is not only directed at foreign enemies and global security, but also at enemies within, blurring into preemptive approaches to domestic crime, drugs, welfare fraud, and anything else signifying moral degeneracy (Barak 2005).

Agamben (2005) links the pervasiveness of "war on" metaphors in American culture to the fact that the sovereign power of the president is based in declared emergency linked to a state of war.

> [O]ver the course of the twentieth century the metaphor of war becomes an integral part of the presidential political vocabulary whenever decisions considered to be of vital importance are being imposed. Thus, in 1933, Franklin D. Roosevelt was able to assume extraordinary powers to cope with the Great Depression by presenting his actions as those of a commander during a military campaign ... President Bush's decision to refer to himself constantly as the "Commander in Chief of the Army" after September 11, 2001, must be considered in the context of this presidential claim to sovereign powers in everyday emergency situations. If, as we have seen, the assumption of this title entails a direct reference to the state of exception, then Bush is attempting to produce a situation in which emergency becomes the rule, and the very distinction between peace and war (and between foreign and civil war) becomes impossible.
>
> Agamben (2005: 21–2)

Richard Clarke, a former member of the U.S. Security Council, even argues that al-Qaeda is a "phantom enemy" manufactured through the precautionary logic of instrumental politicians: "those with the darkest imaginations become the most powerful" (Clarke 2004). Raban (2005: 22) observes there is now "a world of chronic blur, full of slippery words that mean something different from what they meant before September 2001." It is the blur of a war on everything, envisaged by U.S. military officials long before 9/11:

> In broad terms, fourth generation warfare [involving a nation-state in conflict with a non-state actor] seems to be widely dispersed and largely undefined; the distinction will be blurred to the vanishing point. It will be nonlinear, possibly to the point of having no defineable battlefields or fronts. The distinction between "civilian" and "military" may disappear. Actions will occur concurrently throughout all participants' depth, including their society as a cultural, not just a physical, entity. Major military facilities, such as airfields, fixed communications sites, and large headquarters will become rarities because of their vulnerability; the same may be true of civilian equivalents, such as seats of government, power plants, and industrial sites (including knowledge as well as manufacturing industries.). Success will depend heavily on effectiveness in joint operations as lines between responsibility and mission become very blurred.
>
> Lind, Nightengale and Schmitt (1989: 22–6)

Fundamentalist religiosity is also integral to precautionary logic in American political culture and the war on everything that flows from it. Radical political conservatism is entwined with a religious ethos powered by disgust with all manner of moral degeneracy believed to characterize Western societies. In this respect at least, there is an affinity with militant Islamism. As Moyers (2005) observes, the religious right has become a powerful force in U.S. electoral politics. Before the 2004 elections, 186 members of Congress were backed by the religious right, a number that has increased since the election. In the Senate, forty-five members were similarly backed following the election.

The religious right also has an enormous mass media infrastructure to ensure a strong presence in public culture, including approximately 1,600 Christian radio stations and 250 Christian television stations. There are also thousands of assembly halls in which church as theater is performed to live audiences. The *Toronto Star* church theater critic, Tom Harper, attended a one-day conference at a Baptist church in Florida on the theme, "Left Behind: A Conference on Biblical Prophecy about End Times" (ibid). He described conference speeches as full of "venom and dangerous ignorance" about a range of suitable enemies, including Islam as "a Satanic religion" and Muslims who intend "to impose their religion on all of us." A "final" war was said to be inevitable, but believers in the church's "Rapture" do not have to worry because sometime in the next four decades they will be swept to heaven. In this rapturous mindset, there is no need to worry about myriad sources of catastrophic loss or even where oil supplies will come from beyond the next four decades. The apocalypse was foretold in the Bible, and believers will rise above it all just as the terrorists of 9/11 imagined they would take a second flight that day to meet their God.

## Counter law I: laws against law

Counter law flourishes in this political culture of precautionary logic and war on everything. As Robert Chesney (2005) wrote in *The Sleeper Scenario: Terrorism Support Laws and the Demands of Prevention*, there is a need to develop enabling legal regimes to aid in the search for malicious demons everywhere. "[T]he overriding priority of the Department [of Justice] since 9/11 is to prevent attacks before they occur using all available tools ... [these tools will produce] significant internal incentive [for security officials] to expand their capacity for prevention" (ibid: 578).

Following 9/11, the U.S. government moved swiftly to enact counter law. The primary move was the enactment of the USA Patriot Act – The Uniting and Strengthening of America by Providing Appropriate Tools Required to Intercept and Obstruct Terrorism Act 2001 (Pub. L. No 107–56, 115 Stat 272) – codified in various sections of the United States Code.

The USA Patriot Act erases established principles, standards, and procedures of criminal law in the name of national security. It places no limit on Presidential authority to criminalize those deemed "unlawful enemy combatants," including U.S. citizens. "Unlawful enemy combatants" is a dangerous offender-like status that criminalizes suspects for imagined future harm they might cause, rather than past crime. People can be assigned this status on the basis of categorical suspicion: the wrong face in the wrong place at the wrong time. There is also suspicion by association: someone is suspected because they know someone who is suspected. Otherwise legitimate acts of non-violent political dissent may also be constituted as dangerous.

Unlawful enemy combatants can be held without specific charges and for an indefinite period. At the beginning of 2005, only four out of 549 prisoners held for two to three years at the Guantánamo Bay detention camp had been charged with a specific offence. The designation of enemy combatant is made at hearings held by military Combatant Status Review Tribunals (CSRT). The suspect is not allowed a lawyer, only a Personal Military Representative who is a military officer without legal training and obliged to serve his superiors who run the CSRT. Witnesses may be called, but only as screened by the military and said to be available. Stafford Smith (2005: 44) observes that the CSRT process "is just another form of interrogation . . . They've been interrogating these guys for two to three years, and now they send someone in who they say is your Personal Rep, and he gets to ask you more questions, and then he goes back and reports to the other side." At the beginning of 2005, there had been CSRT hearings for 440 suspects, and 439 were deemed unlawful enemy combatants subject to indefinite detention.

Unlawful enemy combatants are subject to extreme interrogation tactics including torture. While initial revelations of torture in the mass media suggested that it occurred in isolated cases involving aberrant security operatives – more dangerous offenders – it is now clear that torture was carefully planned as an integral component of the counter law infrastructure. Greenberg and Dratel (2005) have published over 1,000 pages of legal memoranda documenting how the U.S. government argued away laws and conventions against torture. In spite of its enormous expenditure on sophisticated surveillance technology and networks, the U.S. government did not have adequate intelligence on Jihadist terrorism. Information extracted through torture of captured terrorist suspects was to be the answer to the information deficit. The best legal minds in the Justice Department and Defense Department were mobilized in a manner akin to how corporate lawyers help their clients overcome legal obstacles to the interests they wish to pursue. Dratel (2005: xxii) refers to this as

> the "corporatization" of government lawyering: a wholly result-oriented system in which policy makers start with an objective and work backward, in the process enlisting the aid of intelligent and well-credentialed lawyers who, for whatever reason – the attractions of power, careerism, ideology, or just plain bad judgment – all too willingly failed to act as a constitutional or moral compass that could brake their client's descent into unconscionable behavior constituting torture by any definition, legal or colloquial.

The legal memoranda show how the U.S. government internalized the view that the Third Geneva Convention rules on who is a soldier, spy, terrorist, or innocent, and how the issue is to be decided by a competent tribunal, were not applicable to what they planned. Against the advice of Secretary of State Powell and the long history of U.S. policy and practice in this area, the White House proceeded to legitimate torture. In a memorandum to President Bush, White House Counsel Alberto Gonzales argued:

> "[T]he nature of the new war [on terrorism] places a high premium on ... the ability to quickly obtain information from captured terrorists and their sponsors in order to avoid further atrocities" ... He said this "new paradigm renders obsolete Geneva's strict limitations on questioning of enemy prisoners" and made other Geneva provisions "quaint" ... Seven months later Assistant Attorney General Jay S. Bybee hardened the "constitutionally dubious" argument into a flat assertion of presidential immunity from legal restraints on torture. In a memorandum to White House Counsel Gonzales, Bybee said that in a war like the one against terror, "the information gained from interrogations may prevent future attacks by foreign enemies. Any effort to apply [the criminal law against torture] in a manner that interferes with the President's direction of such core war matters as the detention and interrogation of enemy combatants thus would be unconstitutional." The argument got further elaboration in a memorandum of March 6, 2003 ... from an ad hoc group of government lawyers to Secretary of Defense Donald Rumsfeld ... "Congress may no more regulate the President's ability to detain and interrogate enemy combatants," it argued, "than it may regulate his ability to direct troop movements on the battlefield." So presidential power overrode the International Convention Against Torture, to which the United States is a party, and the Congressional statute enforcing the convention.
>
> Lewis (2005: xv)

Donald Gregg, a former national security advisor to the U.S. government, subsequently wrote an article in the *New York Times* in which he made it clear that torture of illegal enemy combatants is a product of this counter law rather than of a few bad apples in the military. In his view, the legal memoranda "cleared the way for the horrors that have been revealed in Iraq, Afghanistan and Guantánamo and make a mockery of the administration's assertions that a few misguided enlisted personnel perpetuated the vile abuse of prisoners" (cited by Lewis 2005: xvi).

The legal memoranda document not only the desire to abrogate the Geneva Convention, but also document strategies to place detainees beyond the reach of any court of law, and to absolve security operatives implementing the policies of liability for war crimes (Dratel 2005). The Guantánamo Bay detention camp location was chosen not only as a secure site, but also because it could be purported to be outside the jurisdiction of U.S. courts and perhaps any other courts. Various legal analyses were undertaken "to give the policy architects and those who implemented it the benefit of the doubt on issues of intent and criminal responsibility while at the same time eagerly denying such accommodations to those at whom the policies were directed. Such piecemeal application of rights and the law is directly contrary to our principles: equal application of the law, equal justice for all, and a refusal to discriminate based on status, including nationality or religion" (ibid: xxi).

Some aspects of this law against law have considerable support in prominent legal and academic circles (e.g., Dershowitz 2002; Ignatieff 2004; Posner 2004). For example, Posner (2004) invokes law and economics language to argue that the "marginal costs" of civil liberties have increased significantly since 9/11, and that there is a need to formulate a new threshold in cost–benefit tradeoffs that preempts "Johnny-one-note civil libertarians uttering fallacious slogans" with their "bromides about free speech" and obsession over "coercive interrogation." Posner prefers the "war on" metaphors of American political culture as a way to instill precautionary logic and justify laws against law.

> It has been a commonplace since Thomas Hobbes wrote Leviathan that trading independence for security can be a profitable swap … In wartime we tolerate all sorts of curtailments of our normal liberties … conscription, censorship, disinformation, intrusive surveillance, or suspension of habeas corpus. A lawyer must say that this is because war is a legal status that authorizes such curtailments. But to a realist it is not war as such, but danger to the unusual degree associated with war, that justifies the curtailments. The headlong rush of science and technology has brought us to the point at which a handful of terrorists may be more dangerous than an enemy nation because the terrorists (unlike an enemy nation) may be undeterrable, may have both the desire and the ability to cause a global catastrophe, and may be able to conceal not only their plans and their whereabouts but their very existence from the world's intelligence services.
>
> Posner (2004: 216, 230)

Posner's will includes legalized surveillance and restriction on a wide range of people in everyday life. For example, he feels scientists should be legally subjected to surveillance and enforceable standards of preventive security in order to preempt the threat that they will become the accomplices of bioterrorists, unwittingly or otherwise. University students from suspect countries need to be subject to enhanced security screening. One-half of all foreign students return home, and "it is doubtful that all those who [do so have] … by virtue of their sojurn in the United States, become inoculated against rabid anti-Americanism" (ibid: 232).

The USA Patriot Act includes unprecedented powers of surveillance. Based on the premise that malicious demons might be sleeping anywhere, law enforcers are given sweeping access to private spaces, places, and communication networks. In this legislation, the old model of resourceful police intelligence is replaced by one of universal suspicion that spells the end of innocence: everyone is suspect and treated as such to a degree, everyone is on a continuum of risk.

There is a legalization of access to communication and database infrastructures that might yield signs of suspicious activity, for example those of telephone companies, Internet Service Providers (ISPs), libraries, retailers (e. g., book stores, travel agencies, car dealers), and schools (e.g., under a "foreign student monitoring program"). Restrictions are eased regarding court orders and warrants to search for information. For example, court orders pertaining to telephone communications are extended to cover email and internet communications, and to cover the entire country rather than only the judicial district in which the order is issued, which was the previous practice. ISPs are given incentives to provide access to information about their customers even without a court order. Incentives include holding them immune from legal liability if they provide such access in "good faith" with government, and offering them compensation for costs associated with their assistance.

The USA Patriot Act also provides for the widening of surveillance powers under the Foreign Intelligence Surveillance Act. For example, there is a widening of the duration of court orders, the scope of access to private sector business records, access to email, and "roving surveillance" schemes. The much laxer legal standards of the Foreign Intelligence Surveillance Act regarding physical searches, wiretaps, and access to private sector databases are extended to criminal investigations as long as domestic law enforcers can argue that there is an element of foreign intelligence gathering in their investigations.

While using the USA Patriot Act and related legislation to legalize its access to the spaces, places, and communications of other entities, the U.S. government has simultaneously tried to draw the veil of administrative decency over its own operations. For example, in signing a November 2002 bill related to federal law enforcement activities, President Bush attached a statement regarding reporting obligations laid down by Congress in which he asserted his Presidential authority "to withhold information 'the disclosure of which could impair foreign relations, the national security, the deliberative processes of the Executive, or the performance of the Executive's constitutional duties', as defined in each case by the President" (Whitaker 2006: 153–4). There is growing recognition that this asymmetry of knowledge and power violates U.S. First Amendment constitutional rights of free speech and access to information (Janus 2004: 579). Total information awareness is for some and not others.

This national security regime of law against law is designed to cast the net as widely as possible, identify suitable enemies, not worry about false positive identifications, drop any pretense of due process of law, and effect summary justice through incapacitation, torture, and elimination. It ignores *mens rea*, the legal principle that criminalization must be based on a specified criminal act. Indeed, there is not even a pretense of what might be termed *probabilis reus*: criminalization on the basis of actuarial knowledge of risk. There is only the law against law principle of *finus reus*: when criminalization appears necessary for national security, no other justification is needed and established legal principles are preempted, finished (Brodeur 1981; Brodeur and Leman-Langlois 2006).

In the aftermath of 9/11, the U.S. government used a variety of other legislative maneuvers to circumvent normal legal process. While most laws against law were designed to ferret out and criminalize terrorists, there was also swift counter law action to protect selective aspects of the economy. For example, extraordinary steps were taken to protect the airline industry, which was already in difficulty before 9/11. In addition to liabilities for the four airplanes destroyed and lives lost in 9/11, the industry suffered an immediate decrease in passenger traffic. *The Air Transportation Safety and System Stabilization Act* (ATSSSA), passed by Congress within twelve days of 9/11, provided a number of temporary financial measures to bail out and stabilize the industry: US$5 billion direct compensation; US$10 billion loan guarantees for both 9/11 costs and any subsequent terrorist attack; a US$100 million liability cap on future terrorist attack claims; discretionary reimbursement of airline insurance premium increases; discretionary reinsurance protection; and an interim insurance program (Campbell 2002; Standard and Poor's 2002: 4).

The most extraordinary provision of the ATSSSA was the Victims Compensation Fund (VCF). This provision was designed to compensate victims of 9/11 in a direct and timely manner, as an alternative to the tort liability system. Anyone who suffered personal injury in the terrorist attacks of 9/11, or beneficiaries of those who experienced wrongful death, could apply to the VCF. As the claim was payable by the U.S. Treasury, the VCF was not really a "fund" or insurance but simply a contribution to disaster relief. The VCF payment was reduced by collateral sources available to the claimant, such as life and health insurance, pension benefits, and specified charitable donations the victim received from the Liberty Fund or similar sources.

If the victim or beneficiary opted for the VCF, they were required to relinquish any right to sue through the tort liability system. As such, the VCF arrangement was consistent with the many other laws against law following 9/11 that short circuited legal process or avoided it altogether. The events of 9/11 precipitated *the* mass tort of all time, and the VCF provided an alternative that would preempt the extraordinary legal, time, and psychic costs of litigation. The fact that, if litigated, all cases would be assigned to one court, the Southern District of New York, ensured a crippling backlog of cases. Indeed, cases from the 1993 terrorist attack on the World Trade Center were still pending in this court when the 2001 attack occurred!

The VCF was the "purest" no-fault statute ever adopted in the U.S.. The statute was drafted by leading representatives of the plaintiffs' bar, a group that would benefit enormously from litigation. The plaintiffs' bar cooperated in the VCF process because it felt it had no choice but to do so. Indeed, it not only helped to develop the VCF alternative to the tort system, but also offered free legal services to victims and their families as a gesture of solidarity.

On one view the VCF was "an unprecedented social welfare relief program" (Campbell 2002: 211). It was the first direct obligation federal bill since Medicare thirty-six years earlier, social security being the only other direct obligation provision in U.S. history. The official in charge of the program called it an "Unprecedented expression of compassion on the part of the American people to the victims and their families ... designed to bring some measure of financial relief to those most devastated by the events of September 11 ... [and] an example of how Americans rally around the less fortunate" (ibid: 15–16).

The VCF was also an example of how Americans rally around their less fortunate industries, providing a form of socialism for business enterprise. The VCF was a crucial ingredient in efforts to bail out the airline industry, as signified by the fact that it was included in the ATSSSA. The ATSSSA capped airline liability for 9/11 to their insurance coverage at the time. In effect, the VCF provided a federal immunity to commercial entities (airlines) for state-based tort claims, dispossessing the states of legal jurisdiction. In the legal opinion of some, the fact that taking the VCF option preempted the victim's right to sue also made it unconstitutional.

Many other strategic uses of law have developed in the ongoing "war on terror" campaign. For example, Welch (2002, 2005) reveals how the U.S. Justice Department initially charges some terrorist suspects with immigration infractions under civil law in order to circumvent the due process standards of criminal law that might be invoked by defense attorneys if there were criminal proceedings. Indeed, under U.S. immigration law, unlike criminal law, those arrested are not entitled to legal aid attorneys and many are thereby immediately rendered defenseless.

## Counter law II: surveillant assemblages

As we have already documented, laws against law help to support the surveillant assemblages of national security. However, these assemblages are based on additional foundations. Existing technologies are reconfigured and new technologies are invented to facilitate surveillance. Similarly, existing organizational arrangements are reconfigured, and new organizations are created to enhance surveillance and visibility. These technological and organizational transformations in turn mobilize various private sector entities as an integral part of the national security surveillant assemblages.

The technological infrastructures for surveillance have greatly expanded in the name of national security (Levi and Wall 2004; Amoore and de Goede 2005; C. Bennett 2005). Caught up in the marketing of preemptive security following 9/11, organizations bought into an array of surveillance technologies aimed at monitoring people and lethal weapons. According to the publisher of the new *Homeland Defence Journal*, "The Sept. 11 attacks will be the biggest catalyst for U.S. technological innovation since the Soviets launched their Sputnik Satellite in 1957, spurring the competing U.S. space program" (Krane 2002: D16). In the year following 9/11, technology companies opened sales offices in Washington and staffed them with retired military and security officials. The big players included Microsoft, IBM, Dell Computers, and Oracle Corporation, which proposed a national identity card and database. Smaller firms also saw the opportunity for expansion. For example, "Visage Technology Inc., a small Massachusetts company that makes drivers' licenses, used a post-Sept. 11 investment of $25 million to purchase a biometrics firm, open an office with a view of the U.S. Capitol and recruit John Gannon, a former deputy director for intelligence at the CIA, as a board member. The company hopes to sell face recognition kiosks to government" (ibid).

There is of course a long history of developing the latest technologies of surveillance and identification in the name of national security. For example, J. Edgar Hoover gained control of the fingerprinting system as part of establishing the FBI as a domestic surveillance agency in the 1920s (Cole 2001: 246–7). Hoover's dream of total information awareness "saw universal fingerprinting as the key to a national web of individualized surveillance, under his personal control" (ibid). While his dream was never fully realized, Hoover did manage to develop the largest fingerprint file in the world through the requirement of the *Alien Registration Act* (1940) that all immigrants and other "aliens" be fingerprinted. "Hoover returned fingerprinting to its origins, as a mechanism for state monitoring and surveillance of citizens, especially those deemed foreign, politically radical, or otherwise dangerous" (ibid).

The key difference in the contemporary era is the capacity to combine different surveillance technologies into a surveillant assemblage, yielding new forms of knowledge and control. A single surveillance technology such as a closed circuit television (CCTV) camera is usually a mile wide but only an inch deep because it does not in itself provide detailed knowledge about the person whose behavior is being momentarily captured and made visible. However, when combined with other technologies – for example, combining digitized CCTV systems with computer databases – depth and intensity of surveillance are achieved. In particular, new computer-based systems of data matching and data mining create new patterns of human traces – a person's "data double" (Haggerty and Ericson 2000) – that can identify them as a particular type of person, suspicious or otherwise. Many surveillant assemblages that were originally developed in commercial contexts to market segment consumers are also models and sources for population data potentially useful in national security contexts (Amoore and de Goede 2005; Turow 2006; Gandy 2006). For example, insurers use data matching and data mining systems to identify "prospects as suspects" (Ericson, Doyle and Barry 2003: chap. 7) – insurance applicants they should not insure – as well as those who are suspected of making fraudulent insurance claims (ibid: chap. 9). The technological infrastructures and algorithmic models used in this commercial context of identifying suspects have applications to any effort to identify suspicious behavior.

The new surveillant assemblages of national security post-9/11 seek both breadth and depth. Breadth is to be achieved through CCTV systems that aim to protect key urban venues in ways similar to the systems that proliferated in the U.K. in the wake of IRA terrorism. For example, "[a]ided by a federal grant of $5.1 million, the city of Chicago is spending $8.6 million on a system of smart video cameras, equipped with software that will raise the alarm when the cameras spot people loitering, wandering in circles, hanging around outside public buildings, or stopping their cars on the shoulders of highways" (Raban 2005: 25). The aim is to ensure that "Anyone walking in public [is] to be almost constantly watched" (*New York Times*, September 21, 2004). Depth is signified by the very name of the FBI's CARNIVORE "super search engine which, when installed on Internet service providers, is capable of trolling through email traffic and flagging communications of interest to the agency based on the identities of senders and receivers, keyword recognition, etc." (Whitaker 2006: 143). Breadth and depth are achieved through surveillant assemblages that cast nets for all manner of possible threats to homeland security, hoping to land big fish as well as the small fry.

> The Department of Homeland Security is the co-sponsor, with the FBI and the Justice Department, of Operation Predator, intended to track down pedophiles via their use of the Internet – presumably because pedophiles, whose civil liberties are held in high esteem by almost nobody, are indeed guinea pigs for a more sweeping exercise in cyber-spying that might net terrorists ... our e-mails, shared files, and visits to suspect Internet sites are obviously more likely to identify us as al-Qaedist than any tendency we may exhibit to wander in circles in front of tall buildings. When FBI director Robert Mueller announced that Operation Predator "sends a clear message that the digital environment will not offer sanctuary to those pedophiles who lurk in peer-to-peer networks. We will identify you. We will bring you to justice," it seems improbable, given the DHS's involvement in the scheme, that he had pedophiles only, or mainly, in mind.
>
> Raban (2005: 25); see also Janus (2004)

While electronic surveillance technologies have the breadth to traverse organizational boundaries and the depth to make visible previously unknown spaces and population profiles, they do not do so on their own. Organizational change occurs in conjunction with technological change, and the transition is not straightforward.

The U.S. government created the Department of Homeland Security as an umbrella organization for bringing closer together a number of different security-related organizations, including the FBI and CIA. This organizational change is a means of trying to break down divisions between different government agencies that have worked semi-autonomously and at times in competition and conflict with each other. It also serves to advance the conflation of war abroad and the war on threats to domestic security at home, including but not limited to the war on terrorism. Furthermore, it seeks to break down barriers that separate databases in different government agencies, in order to bring together information from counterintelligence investigations of foreign threats and ordinary domestic criminal law enforcement. The view is that borderless threats require borderless law enforcement across organizational entities nationally and internationally, and across categories of citizens and non-citizens.

The U.S. government imagines a global surveillance state. This was symbolized in the Total Information Awareness (TIA) Program logo of an eye at the apex of a pyramid scanning the globe, accompanied by the slogan *Scientia ist potentia*, knowledge is power. The TIA program was housed in the Defense Advance Research Projects Agency (DARPA) and headed by Vice Admiral John Poindexter, infamously known for his involvement in the Iran Contra affair. DARPA's TIA plans for omniscience met with resistance across the political spectrum on the grounds that they signified the end of privacy. The TIA began to backtrack on its more ambitious claims; however, further concern was raised when Poindexter proposed a terrorism risk catastrophe bond market in which investors would speculate on future terrorist activity and profit if a catastrophe did not occur within the period during which the bond was held. The hope was that this futures market in terrorism would extend surveillance capacity because investors would demand better data to predict terrorism futures, and these data could in turn be used in the national security effort. For many, including then Deputy Defense Secretary Donald Rumsfeld, this proposal was the final indicator that the TIA program had become a political liability. Poindexter was dismissed and the program was terminated.

As Whitaker (2006) observes, the termination of the formal TIA program did not in any way stop other TIA-like initiatives. For example, DARPA also created Lifelog "which seeks to amass every conceivable bit of information that can be gathered from every source (including audiovisual sensors and biomedical monitors) about an individual's life, and download it all into a vast, searchable database" (ibid: 158–9). In the spring of 2003, the FBI and CIA jointly created the Terrorist Threat Integration Center to integrate information from all available foreign and domestic sources for possible signs of terrorism.

The effort to connect the surveillance infrastructures of national security and domestic security has led to an organizational and operational blurring between them. For example, in at least seventy-five cases identified by the *Foreign Intelligence Surveillance Act* (FISA) review court, the FBI was said to have misled the court in its justifications for electronic surveillance (Whitaker 2006). In particular, the FBI justified electronic surveillance applications in the name of foreign threats to national security but used intelligence gathered for bringing charges in domestic criminal cases. The U.S. Justice Department appealed this decision to the new Foreign Intelligence Surveillance Court of Review, and this court concluded that amendments to FISA under the USA Patriot Act permit such criminal prosecutions as long as the surveillance also has a significant foreign intelligence purpose. Attorney General Ashcroft declared that this was a new legal permit for criminal investigators and intelligence agents to collaborate, and announced plans to intensify covert surveillance operators through designated intelligence prosecutors in each federal court district as well as a new intelligence warrant unit in the FBI. Ashcroft later "revealed that he had personally authorized secret electronic surveillance and physical searches without immediate court oversight in 170 'emergency' cases since the 9/11 attacks – more than triple the emergency searches authorized by other attorneys general over the past 20 years (Schmidt 2003)" (Whitaker 2006: 151).

There was a simultaneous effort to break down barriers to surveillance between government and private sector organizations, and among private sector organizations themselves. This effort was based on the view that Little Brother collaboration will yield more than the sum of its parts, a Big Brother surveillance infrastructure of total information awareness. The process began with the 9/11 investigation itself, which relied heavily on the data doubles of suspects in credit card, telephone and airmiles databases. It continued with an expansion of enabling regulations and technologies for surveillance in a wide range of private sector contexts. New air transportation information systems and screening procedures were developed to track the movement of people and goods (C. Bennett 2005; Brodeur and Leman-Langlois 2006; see also Sparke, this volume). Money trail surveillance by financial institutions, already in place regarding the drug trade and other forms of organized crime, was enhanced (see de Goede, this volume). With the aid of the USA Patriot Act provisions, financial institutions are enlisted in the government's money trail surveillance program on threat of severe sanction, including seizure of assets, for failure to cooperate. Many other fields of business enterprise have been enlisted, for example in creating surveillant assemblages that might identify financiers of terrorist activity or purveyors of nuclear, biological, and chemical materials.

On a different level, there is an effort to mobilize entire industries because of their key role at the foundation of surveillance infrastructures. One such industry is private security, which, because of its special legal access to private spaces on behalf of property owners, has a unique position as front-line "eyes and ears" in the national security effort.

Private security was a fast growing and substantial part of the U.S. economy prior to 9/11. One estimate of private security spending in the U. S. during the 1990s is US$40 billion annually, with almost half devoted to private police staff and the remainder to preventive security technologies (Anderson 1999). The OECD projected that private security would expand considerably following 9/11, with possible effects on economic growth and productivity: "A doubling of private security might reduce the level of potential output by 0.6 per cent after five years and the level of private sector productivity by 0.8 per cent" (2002: 136). The New York City Comptroller reported that, in 2001, over 1 percent of all workers in New York City were security guards. He observed that, in the four years following the 1993 World Trade Center bombing, there was a 22 percent increase in spending on private security guards. Assuming the same level of growth over four years following 9/11, the additional cost would be about US$1 billion. The Comptroller also noted that some of this post-9/11 increase in private security would be driven by contract stipulations of the insurance industry. "Security-related spending, however, is a cost that may be seen as an investment because it helps to narrow the future property/casualty [insurance] premium between NYC and other cities" (Thompson 2002: 22).

Joh (2004) documents the role of private security operatives in various contexts of terrorism-related security. For example, Disney World in Florida has an 800-member security force attuned to the post-9/11 environment. On the eve of the invasion of Iraq, the Federal Aviation Authority granted Disney World, as well as Disneyland in California, a no-fly zone as a precautionary measure. In an ethnographic study of policing in a large commercial complex in Manhattan, Joh found ongoing relations between city police and private security operatives regarding terrorism-related security threats.

At the same time, private security operatives are sometimes viewed as a source of threat because of their intimate knowledge of, and access to, critical infrastructures, and the fact that they are often ill-trained, poorly equipped, inadequately regulated, and at the margins of the labor market. Private security operatives are said to be in need of intensified surveillance even as they are embraced as essential to surveillance infrastructures.

As indicated in the statement above by the New York City Comptroller, the private insurance industry is also a key player in the development of surveillance infrastructures. It has unique capacities to govern other organizations through contracts which define the meaning of terrorism and specify the security measures the insured must put in place to help preempt terrorism.

In the insurance world, there is a marketplace of definitions of terrorism, open to negotiation depending on how insurers wish to participate in a specific terrorism risk with specific clients. For example, a reinsurance company I studied (Ericson and Doyle 2004b: chap. 5) created a very broad definition of terrorism as an opening position from which to negotiate contracts with primary insurers and in turn their clients. An executive involved in these negotiations said that, "we might throw out these words, then someone else might throw out another set of words to define terrorism, and we work through it ... Everybody usually has a different point of view on things, which are guided maybe by corporate risk appetites and such." A colleague added, "There are as many terrorist exclusions in the marketplace as there are ceding companies. So at last count I think we were above 250 [companies]. So there's probably 250 some-odd wordings for terrorism exclusion in the current marketplace." He stated that the final definition of terrorism settled on for a given insurance contract depends on the other terms of the contract. "There's a lot of negotiation that goes back and forth with the companies depending upon our participation in the program, limits offered, attachment points, whatever, where we may come off some of those [definitions that exclude specific aspects of terrorism] objectives. Sub-limits are one of the ways to obviously reduce your exposures, to reduce your limits, then maybe we can give a little bit on the wording."

Insurance contracts also place terrorism-related preventive security require-ments on the insured, with the capacity for detailed, on-site inspections for compliance. A senior executive of a reinsurance company explained to me how 9/11 changed the commercial risk underwriting environment in this regard.

> It's impacted our whole underwriting process, where, before we renew reinsurance contracts, we ask for a lot more information from our clients ... Stuff that before nobody would care to find out or ask about. Now it's being asked by the reinsurer, and in turn the insurance company needs to find out from the insured and make sure that information is kept up to date ... You are also dealing with a very "live" [hard] market. This [9/11] came at the end of a very soft market. Typically in a soft market people don't dare ask a lot of questions, the client goes some-where else ... [T]he market started turning before 9/11 – 9/11 really pushed it up in a much more dramatic fashion. Now it's OK to ask ten, twenty, thirty questions before you renew your account, and get that information.

Another reinsurance executive said that his company was questioning ceding insurers about their clients' preventive security arrangements with respect to terrorism. This new vigilance was exercised in relation to all commercial reinsurance under consideration, but intensified if the buildings involved were deemed symbolic targets of terrorism.

> One of the first questions we ask our underwriters toward their clients is, "What do your clients do about the terrorism exposure?" ... There's things you can do on an underwriting basis, on a loss prevention basis ... to avoid a terrorist act. For example, you own a building and

you have a security guard at the entrance, that will prevent a lot of unwanted people from wandering around the building. The WTC, the top door to the roof had been locked for some reason. A good loss control person, had he or she done a review, would have noticed the door probably should not have been locked, lives would have been saved ... We have developed a number of detailed questionnaires ... [regarding] accessibility, security, after-event evacuation procedures, those types of things ... And this target-class list ... main targets of terrorism, many of those [questionnaires] have to do with security ... precautions that are taken. We're just trying to limit the accessibility of these targets to outsiders, to people that we don't want in there. Inside concerns, how are you monitoring the inside of your plant?

In direct underwriting situations, some insurers send loss control engineers to field sites with detailed questionnaires addressing terrorism-related security arrangements. This assessment is used to decide whether terrorism coverage should be excluded entirely, or included at particular sub-limits and prices. Agreed levels of surveillance personnel and technologies are negotiated in this process.

Insurance company executives I interviewed offered various examples of increased vigilance about commercial operations. A reinsurance company executive used the example of a trucking company and said that, before 9/11, the drivers' licenses may have been checked annually for authenticity but now "we may come up with a recommendation that if you want us to reinsure your business, we want you to *insist* on having drivers' records checked on a quarterly basis. Because there is turnover and you never know who is going to drive a truck on a particular day. So in those cases, we would make a proactive check that they do so, and we would come back and follow up ... We can certainly get off that business, or break the contract, if we don't like what we see." Another interviewee illustrated the point with "the courier company that couriers packages, or a small airlines company, I wouldn't necessarily exclude terrorism but I would ask questions. 'What have you done since 9/11 to increase your security? Do you check what's in the packages before they board the plane? How are your pilots trained? How do you screen people?'"

There is no doubt that business enterprise became more vigilant after 9/11. In a survey of chief executive officers asking them to identify "post 9/11 precautions," the following were mentioned most frequently: review of disaster plan (90 percent), background checks on contractors (51 percent), background checks on employees (39 percent), limiting staff on a single flight (36 percent), and considering alternative office space (35 percent) (Insurance Information Institute, www.iii.org, 25 April 2002). Organizations were urged to examine building infrastructures regarding their physical security features. With visions of the *Titanic* as *the* infallible technology that failed, it was pointed out that the World Trade Center had been touted as "collapse proof." Those contemplating future high rise construction were implored to take note of total loss risks, while those responsible for existing buildings were asked to address remedial measures that might reduce such risks. On a mundane level, advice flowed on the need for target hardening. "For instance, installing a film across windows can reduce the risk of injuries from flying glass. By putting a barrier around a building, a company can keep potentially dangerous cars and trucks away" (Green 2002).

## Conclusions

Jihadist terrorism is a real threat. Preemptive security efforts to address this threat produce myths. These myths in turn constitute new realities of managing risks through counter law.

The war on terror perpetuates four myths. First, there is a belief that Jihadists are all fearless demons bent on death and destruction, and that their power to create tsunami-like waves of devastation is underpinned by networks that are global in their reach. Second, the entire terrorist movement can be toppled if only the heads of its mastermind monsters can be decapitated. During the 2004 presidential election debates on television, even the Democratic Party candidate John Kerry was scripted to repeat at many junctures "We will *kill* the terrorists. We will *kill* the terrorists. We will *kill* the terrorists." Third, there is a need for preemptive war abroad in the name of preventing attacks at home. National security cannot be separated from global security. Fourth, there is a new doctrine of *parens patriae* regarding homeland security: citizens are children in need of constant protection from danger, precautionary moral lessons, and surveillance.

These myths of the war on terror constitute new realities. There is the reality of counter law I, laws against law, which undermine the principles, standards, and procedures of democratic legal institutions. There is the reality of counter law II, surveillant assemblages that not only counteract democratic legal institutions but also substitute a new basis for governing that is patently undemocratic in its mobilization of categorical suspicion, suspicion by association, discrimination, decreased privacy, and exclusion.

Happily, there has been some democratic resistance. There are mounting court cases and some legal decisions freeing some terrorist suspects and placing some limits on laws against law. There was successful resistance to the original TIA initiatives. But the war on terror continues to use both forms of counter law more or less unabated. Indeed, given U.S. aspirations to be a global Leviathan, its myths of terror – malicious demons, leaders to be decapitated, wars to be fought abroad in the name of security at home, and the need for *parens patriae* – extend around the world, accompanied by the new realities of counter law I and II. Preemptive security trumps justice, and insecurity proves itself.

# Part II

# Crime, deviance, exception

# 4 Choosing our wars, transforming governance

## Cancer, crime, and terror

*Jonathan Simon*

President George W. Bush's "war on terror" is only the latest effort to redefine the scope of the US federal government's power (and especially the executive branch) by invoking the metaphor of war. In the 1950s and 1960s, the idea of a "war on cancer" quietly began to shape a powerful new form of law that came to be known after 1970 as "environmental law."[1] The Johnson Administration launched a "war on poverty" that, combined with federal mandates for school desegregation and open housing, began to transform the governance of cities and states, facilitating the final break-down of the urban party machines that dominated politics. Since the 1960s, a "war on crime" has seen enormous expansions in federal criminal law enforcement and the growth of mass imprisonment at the federal and state levels.

Of course, Americans are not the only people to invoke the metaphor of war; but I think a more careful comparative study of the use of the war metaphor to describe and encourage transformations in the nature and enterprise governance would support my sense that the US usage is rather distinctive. This usage may even have a very specific point of emergency. That moment is January 6, 1941, in President Franklin D. Roosevelt's "State of the Union" speech to Congress. The setting is dramatic. Roosevelt has only just been re-elected to an unprecedented and controversial third term as President. He was very visibly rallying the nation to join escalating wars in Europe and the Pacific at a time when pacifism remained a very popular creed in the country following the unfulfilled promise of American entry into the Second World War.

After summarizing the history of US autonomy from political events outside the Western hemisphere, and the increasingly dire confrontation between what Roosevelt described as "the new order of tyranny" and the "democratic way of life," Roosevelt baldly stated the need for a new singular reconstitution of government around the coming armed conflict with "the aggressor nations."

> That is why this annual message to the Congress is unique in our history. That is why every member of the executive branch of the government and every member of Congress face great responsibility – great accountability.

The need of the moment is that our actions and our policy should be devoted primarily – almost exclusively – to meeting this foreign peril. For all our domestic problems are now part of the great emergency.

Although Roosevelt stops short of a declaration of war,[2] his intent to refocus all of government on one problem – reversing the gains of the Axis nations through a military build-up – is unmistakable and clear. Domestic governance must go on, but with a singular awareness of the "great emergency." If neither cancer, nor poverty, nor crime, nor even terror, has reached the same level of practical mobilization (President Bush famously refused to call for sacrifices and urged Americans early on in the crisis to "go shopping"), they all aspired to precisely that sweep.

In speaking of cancer, drugs, crime, or terrorism, late twentieth- and early twenty-first-century American presidents have invoked both sides of Roosevelt's equation. On the one hand, they have presented an existential threat to the nation from an enemy that is both monstrously abnormal, but capable of penetrating into the very center of normal American life. On the other hand, they have called for the vast expanse of contemporary government to refocus itself on mobilizing against an enemy that can only be defeated through strategies of enormous complexity and integration.

Roosevelt also invoked a term that is now quite familiar in terms of the enemy, but which he directed at government itself. "Every member of the executive branch," and Congress as well, face great responsibility and "great accountability." Accountability for government had certain clarity in the struggle against the Axis powers that none of the other wars has allowed. The portion of the globe under the control of Axis military forces was something that newspaper readers everywhere could track to at least some degree of precision (even if not without delays). In contrast, the clarity with which we can speak of the shrinkage or advance of crime, drugs, cancer, and terrorism tends to be very hard to sustain on any kind of detailed inspection. Rates of all four are notoriously subject to reporting practices. Cancer and terrorism are difficult even to define on the individual level where the staging of tumors and the ferreting out of terrorist "cells" depend a great deal on the specific experts involved and are subject to fundamental challenge.

It would be nice to imagine that such movements to redefine and redeploy governmental strategies could be undertaken without the costly metaphor of war. While our best loved politicians have often invoked American dreams as their guide, it is more accurate to suggest that nightmares have been the driving force in inventing new forms of government. Ronald Reagan may be our most compelling recent example. His popularity was widely associated with his optimism in the face of adversity. He was at his (speech writers') best when he spoke after the Challenger disaster of 1985 of those who break "the surly bonds of earth to touch the face of God." Yet his political base from early on was built on a capacity to speak directly to the fears of many middle-class voters concerning national decline generally and rising insecurity in particular. In the 1980 elections, these were framed not so much in terms of crime as in terms that anticipated crime, inflation, mass immigration, and terrorism.

After exploring some of the salient similarities and differences between recent wars on cancer, crime, and terror, I want to defend the proposal that I have recently made (Simon 2007a) that the "war on cancer" is a preferred war in which to re-imagine a liberal rationality of governance.

## War on cancer

While the war on cancer is often dated to the Nixon Administration, it began much earlier, in the 1950s, when Congress adopted tough standards on carcinogens in the very first modern environmental law, "the Delaney Amendment." In this early and enduring manifestation, the war on cancer became identified with the legal quest to purge the consumption of American products from the danger of causing cancer. In this respect, it was a war directed toward industries, especially those industries stoked by the consumption of highly processed goods (chemicals, processed foods, house paints and products).

Fear of cancer was a growing public concern in the United States throughout the twentieth century (Patterson 1987). The 1950s brought fear of cancer to a new intensity. Many believed that the amazing powers of science demonstrated in the Second World War would yield a cure soon. Science, however, was also yielding new evidence that environmental pollutions associated with technological society itself, especially radiation and petrochemicals, were a significant source of cancer. By the late 1950s, many experts claimed that 60 or 70 percent of cancers were "environmental" (as critics pointed out, the greatest portion of them was probably smoking and diet, but the term environmental had its own power at that point).

This link between cancer and the environment would be enormously productive for the creation of environmentalism for two reasons. First, it brought both science and industrial capitalism into a dangerous association with a uniquely feared disease. Second, cancer was itself a uniquely potent metaphor for one of the most destabilizing aspects of what historian Samuel P. Hays (1987: 173) calls "toxic perception."

> Toxic perception often included the notion of a chemical "time bomb," that a sequence of events begun at one time could remain undetected only to work their effect later. One could suddenly discover cancer caused by much earlier exposures, now coming to light when preventive action would be pointless.

In short, cancer became the first intense public panic in the US over a new kind of risk different from car accidents and tuberculosis. These new risks are catastrophic in their results, irreversible, and invisible. This kind of risk cannot be fought after it has come to fruition; there is no mitigation or spreading of the loss. It can only be prevented and then only with measures aimed at preventing even its precursor events from taking place.

This panic produced its most important legislative result in 1958 with the enactment of the Delaney Amendment (technically an amendment to the appropriations bill for the Food and Drug Administration). The clause provided that:

> No additive shall be deemed safe if it is found to induce cancer when ingested by man or animal, or if it is to be found, after tests which are appropriate for the evaluation of the safety of food additives, to induce cancer in man or animals.

Although the clause does not contain the language of "zero tolerance," it was widely taken to mean that, once a chemical was found to promote cancer, there could no longer be a safe level at which it might be included in food additives. Thus, manufacturers of the additive must take steps to remove any trace of the chemical that can be found. Placing the burden on the regulated industry to prove their adherence to a standard was hardly a novel exercise of governance. It was this space for judgment that nascent environmentalists concerned about pesticides and their effects on humans would focus on in the 1960s. The key text was Rachel Carson's *Silent Spring* (1962). Carson and her colleagues had little trust in the neutrality of the judges that would decide these regulatory questions, regardless of the burdens, given the influence of the chemical industry. It is in light of that distrust that Carson uses the phrase "zero tolerance."

> What is the solution? The first necessity is the elimination of *tolerances* on the chlorinated hydrocarbons, the organic phosphorus groups, and other highly toxic chemicals. It will immediately be objected that this will place an *intolerable* burden on the farmer. But if, as is now the presumable goal, it is possible to use chemicals in such a way that they leave a residue of only 7 parts per million (the *tolerance* for DDT), or of 1 part per million (the *tolerance* for parathion), or even of only 0.1 part per million as is required for dieldrin on a great variety of fruits and vegetables, then why is it not possible, with only a little more care, to prevent the occurrence of any residues at all? This, in fact, is what is required for some chemicals such as heptachlor, endrin, and dieldrin on certain crops. If it is considered practical in these instances, why not for all? But this is not a complete or final solution, for a *zero tolerance* on paper is of little value.
>
> Carson (1962/2002: 183)

Notice that, while Carson is looking for a new mentality or consciousness about life in industrial society, it is not exactly summarized by zero tolerance.

From her perspective, it is more the intolerance of postwar Americans to bugs, dirt, and the labor-intensive house-cleaning methods of earlier times that has to be overcome. The regulation of food and drugs had long deferred to the economic priorities of sustaining agriculture. Zero tolerance was a way of breaking up this corporatist model left over from the Great Depression by creating opportunities for outsiders to use knowledge about carcinogens to compel regulators to act. This aspect of zero tolerance turned out to be an important one in maintaining some pressure on industry once neoconservative forces had recaptured the regulatory agencies themselves in the 1980s and 1990s.

And zero tolerance on paper is all that anyone would see. For most of the 1960s and 1970s, industry successfully tied up enforcement of the Delaney clause in internal agency proceedings. Finally, in the mid-1970s, with increased pressure from a more liberal post-Watergate Congress to do something about pollution, there seemed to be a real likelihood of important consumer chemicals being removed from the market. It was at this point that the term "zero tolerance," used almost reticently by Carson, gets adopted by neoliberal economic critics of environmental regulations.

> Given the *zero-tolerance* philosophy being pushed by some environmentalists, FDA might have been stampeded, acceding to Ralph Nader's Health Research Group and its petition to summarily ban all food-contact uses [of PVC plastic]. It did not. Instead, it took a more selective approach. FDA's basic premise is that "use of vinyl chloride polymers should be prohibited where there is a reasonable expectation of any migration of vinyl chloride into food." Conversely, it would approve such use in the absence of such expectation.
>
> McCurdy (1975: 5)

Zero tolerance toward carcinogens was ultimately a policy of cancer prevention. The specific features of zero tolerance owe a lot to the understanding of cancer that had developed in the US in the postwar period.[3] Cancer had already been a prominent public concern in the US for more than half a century. In the 1950s, it became an explosive political concern. The social policies of the New Deal and the prosperity of the postwar period both contributed to the emergence of cancer fear by reducing successfully many of the more traditional collective pitfalls of working-class life through full employment, union-style benefits, social insurance, and the like. For more Americans, cancer loomed as a unique kind of threat, undiminished, perhaps even intensified, by the governmental and technological prowess of twentieth-century America. The scientific triumphs associated with the war, including atomic weapons, rockets, and sulfa drugs, seemed to project the combination of expertise and discipline necessary to prevail over a threat such as cancer (or the Axis powers).

As a model for what must be "governed," cancer stood out in two important ways from other medical maladies.[4] Compared with other infamous diseases, cancer is a uniquely individualized and individualizing disease. It is not infectious and does not usually strike "communities."[5] Its often long and wasting course also tends to isolate the individual from friends and loved ones. Second, cancer has long been associated with the terrifying tendency to move from the undetectably small to the irreversibly large with only a fleeting possibility of being caught between the two moments.[6] The evident progress of medicine against infectious diseases, progress that government effectively deployed in the war efforts and through the increasing government investment in health care, was cast into doubt by cancer. The most competent medicalized state in the world was of no help to an individual for whom the tiny window of opportunity to stop or catch cancer in its origins had closed.

It is little wonder that, with or without a scientific basis, this principle of cancer should come to apply to those chemicals thought to induce it. If cancer itself was a spectrum from the almost benign to the nearly mortal, would it be possible to say with any certainty just how much of a cancer inducement one can "safely" encounter? It was against this background that one can understand Congress at the end of a mightily conservative decade passing a regulatory standard that would come to be seen as an extremist model of environmentalism. Even in the midst of the Cold War against the Soviet Union, and growing public concern about crime at the state and local level, a politician could rightly fear being tagged as "favoring 'a little bit of cancer'" or, as we might put it today, being "soft on cancer."

The other key element was food. The Delaney Amendment was radical precisely because food is such a radical type of human need. Food presented a potent framework for problematizing governance in a society in which the newly affluent still remembered hunger (and would soon rediscover its presence within "poverty areas" of the social body). The long history of federal involvement with agriculture was all about increasing production and protecting producers. Even the first regimes to deal with pesticides and other chemical risks were developed in the New Deal to protect farmers and farm workers with only a residual concern for consumers (who implicitly were supposed to be lucky to be well fed after the Depression experience). The Delaney Amendment marked the emergence of the vulnerable consumer as the key political subjectivity as the consumer of food replaced the producer.

The nature of the consumer as political subject was highly contested. Rachel Carson in a way had demonstrated that the proud American consumers of the early 1960s were really no more capable than children of protecting themselves from absorbing carcinogenic chemicals from their food, water, and air. Indeed, Carson herself, a nationally prominent science writer even before *Silent Spring*, was battling breast cancer when she wrote the book. Her death two years later, after the book had already become a national bestseller, was widely seen as further confirmation of the danger to which she sought to alert Americans.

As a victim of cancer, Carson might have become the first martyr in a war on environmental cancers in the 1960s and 1970s. Unlike the murder victims of the 1980s and 1990s, mostly children, the cancer victim never became a central focus of governance. Perhaps as an adult, Carson was insufficiently innocent. Her insistence that the obligation to endure requires the right to know constructs something very different from the passive and individualized body of the crime victim. Carson's subjects face the burden of adding a growing body of information to their own management of life and to their political choices. Zero tolerance in that strategy is only a way of playing for time, slowing the entry of new chemicals into population while compelling the government to participate in building a network of knowledge about cancer and food.

In that respect, Carson anticipated the experience of the contemporary cancer victim who (unlike the average patient in Carson's time) is also playing for time often without a paternalistic physician to lead the fight, supported in large part by a government-built network of research centers and online information about cancer diagnosis and treatment.

The 1970s marked the beginning of the end for anything like zero tolerance toward environmental carcinogens (even in the food supply), but not of the problem of governing intolerable risks. The power of the petrochemical industries was great enough to push the problem of cancer politically away from the issue of regulating production decisions and toward individual strategies of prevention. Cancer remains emblematic of the whole field of intolerable risks. The original success of the Delaney clause and its "zero tolerance" policy toward carcinogens reflected a new kind of governance strategy appropriate to a class of risks just becoming apparent in the 1950s, risks that begin as invisible and become irreversible. It was in this context that the whole business of establishing a safe tolerance level for a chemical came to seem unacceptably risky; thus the internally incoherent slogan of "zero tolerance."

The early 1970s saw a second wave of "war on cancer," this time visibly expressed by the President of the United States. Nixon did not use the term precisely, but it was invoked soon enough in the public discussion of Nixon's announcement in his 1971 State of the Union address that he would launch "an intensive campaign against cancer." The National Cancer Act passed later that year created a permanent federal funding stream for medical research into cancer treatment and, through the creation of a National Cancer Institute, placed cancer medicine on a unique footing with near-cabinet level representation in the executive branch.

The war on cancer also has genealogical links with the science-warfare side of the New Deal state, especially the Roosevelt Administration's Manhattan Project and, later, the Kennedy Administration's race to the moon. Indeed, these were precisely the markers Nixon laid down in his speech to the Ninety-Second Congress.

> The time has come in America when the same kind of concentrated effort that split the atom and took man to the moon should be turned

toward conquering this dread disease. Let us make a total national commitment to achieve this goal.

Rather than dispersing money through a broad political network (as did much of the New Deal and the war on poverty and later the war on drugs), the Manhattan Project, the space program, and the war on cancer pumped money into highly centralized research establishments [such as the Los Alamos, Berkeley, and Chicago laboratories during the 1940s; the National Aeronautics and Space Administration (NASA) in the 1960s; and the National Cancer Institute in the 1970s]. Although the war on drugs created a new federal to local network around law enforcement, the war on cancer presupposed and reinforced one that had already become an important component of government since the New Deal: mass media, research science, and big government. Coverage of moon shots, missiles, and presidents was displacing more traditional political circuits that ran vertically through local political machines and news outlets. Rather than threatening industry, this kind of war on cancer would ultimately invest in many of these very same industries as producers of anticancer drugs.

Whatever its future, the war on cancer has already produced dramatic changes within limited spheres. In the world of big medicine, the war on cancer has made cancer king. Prior to the 1970s, cancer was not considered a high-prestige pathway in medicine for either researchers or clinicians. One important reason was the dismal success thus far of the field, and the resulting loss of esteem when virtually all of one's patients died. In addition, cancer had a stigma associated with it, a stigma we must pursue if we are to fully compare crime and cancer as governance pathways. The National Cancer Act changed that by dramatically increasing the portion of federal research money allocated for cancer. As a result of the larger pool for research, many of the brightest and most ambitious researchers have pursued oncology. The same pattern is visible from the air if one were to tour the major medical research centers across America where some of the largest and newest buildings are cancer research and treatment centers.

The war on cancer has also worked a dramatic transformation in the status of cancer patients. First, in both a surface and a deeper way, the National Cancer Act made cancer patients a special subject of concern of the national sovereign (a special favorite of the law, as an earlier age might have put it). Superficially, this is true because the Act made cancer a cabinet-level concern and thus opened up the highest level of federal power to consideration of the needs of cancer patients on a theoretically systematic basis. More deeply, this is true because the Act and its by-products have led to efforts at expanding the pool of cancer subjects through early diagnosis and preventive medicine (in the latter sense, everyone is a cancer subject). The results have worked a truly profound shift in the basic status of the cancer subject.

Increased federal investment in cancer research has transformed the relative status of cancer research and treatment practitioners to among the highest in medicine in pay, prestige, and professional morale. The war on cancer has also influenced discourse, diet, and institutional practices of all sorts. These changes are particularly profound for those afflicted with the disease and their families. Cancer was once a disease with a great deal of hopelessness, embarrassment, and shame associated with it. Much like crime victims, cancer patients today occupy a subject position that has been invested with significant and positive meaning.

## The war on crime

The possibility of a war on crime had been invoked as early as Franklin Roosevelt's first term when he and Attorney General Homer Cummings began to build a high-profile strategy for a federal response to crime (largely directed at bank robbers). Roosevelt ended up fighting a real war against the Axis powers, and the 1950s saw the emergence of a successor war between the US and its former ally, the Soviet Union, a struggle that quickly globalized with the fall of China and the collapse of the French colonial regime in Vietnam. There was little space on the agenda for a new metaphoric war aimed at reshaping governance.

The Kennedy Administration began to define crime as a primary focus of federal action, highlighting criminal justice reform and, to a lesser extent, aggressive moves against organized crime. While Attorney General Robert Kennedy never declared a "war on crime," his vigorous prosecution of Teamster President (and alleged mobster) Jimmy Hoffa merged with his confrontational approach toward segregationist governors to model a certain liberal kind of law and order paradigm (Simon 2007a). President Johnson did speak openly of a war on crime, and his Administration prepared a vast report on the state of American criminal justice. Richard Nixon expounded a conservative discourse of crime as an outgrowth of permissiveness in American society and, when he invoked a war on crime (and drugs), it was one to be directed against deviant and unpopular groups in the American underclass, especially drug sellers and users.

Presidents since Nixon, with the short-lived exceptions created by Nixon's own criminal behavior in the Watergate scandal, have all to varying degrees filled the role of the crime warrior, proclaiming the moral necessity of a broad federal commitment to combat crime, and extending the growth of penal sanctions and severity.

In remarkably short order, just as the Reagan Administration was reversing the potential take-off of zero tolerance as a technology of environmental governance and a significant face of the war on cancer, zero tolerance resurfaced in the Administration's new tough stance on drugs and crime. A number of figures within the Reagan Administration would get credit at various times for "inventing" this policy, including First Lady Nancy Reagan (whose "just say no" is a rough translation of zero tolerance restated as a rule for behavior), White House Chief of Staff and later

Attorney General Edwin Meese, and Customs Commissioner William Von Raab.

The earliest point of emergence seems to have been in the Navy where an aggressive program to drug test recruits and compel abstinence with the threat of expulsion for a second positive test was part of a broad effort in the armed services to overcome a reputation for an underachieving, over-substance-abusing recruit pool (at a time of renewed enthusiasm for military preparedness). Attorney General Edwin Meese promoted zero tolerance as an approach to toughening up the use of civil forfeiture laws to take property linked to drug assets, even in cases of very small quantities of drugs. Von Raab promoted both testing and expulsion for agents in the customs service, and forfeiture for property linked to even small quantities of drugs.[7]

By 1988, zero tolerance as a concept was embraced at the level of the presidency by successful candidate George Bush, who offered in his nomination acceptance speech that year a vision of zero tolerance as an attitude, perhaps a defining one, for both governed and governor; one that could finally win the war on drugs and more.

> I want a drug-free America – and this will not be easy to achieve. But I want to enlist the help of some people who are rarely included. Tonight I challenge the young people of our country to shut down the drug dealers around world. Unite with us; work with us. "Zero tolerance" isn't just a policy, it's an attitude. Tell them what you think of people who underwrite the dealers who put poison in our society. And while you're doing that, my Administration will be telling the dealers: Whatever we have to do, we'll do, but your day is over, you're history.
>
> Associated Press (1988: 6)

The political shift from left to right, from pollution to drugs, was consummated during the 1988 presidential campaign between the confident Republican candidate Bush and the Democratic nominee and former Governor of Massachusetts Michael Dukakis. Bush had already cast Dukakis as being soft on crime when he began to attack the Governor for being soft on polluters in Massachusetts. Deftly reversing the birth order, Bush managed to make his strong *"zero tolerance"* stance appear applicable to wide-ranging issues: "Bush called for a policy of 'zero tolerance ... not only to those who poison our children's minds with drugs, but to those who poison our water with toxic chemicals.'" (Peterson 1988: A1, emphasis added).

The Bush Presidency highlighted the potential for zero tolerance from the highest level. This example has been followed by the application of the concept farther and farther from its original entry point of toxic chemicals and drugs. Its promoters are not shy in taking exactly the view that our framework suggests, i.e., that zero tolerance is not so much a policy as a mentality of governance.

Zero tolerance has even emerged as a new kind of posture in foreign affairs where it purports to be a response to "rogue nations" who both pose a threat to their neighbors and fail to respond to traditional diplomatic and military techniques. Ironically, given the application of the crime model, the description that a country is a rogue nation actually suggests that deterrence, the normal logic of international relations, will not work. [8]

In 2002, Iraq came to be cast in this role by the Bush Administration. Commenting on the US vision for a United Nations policy on Iraq, Bush advisor Condoleezza Rice was quoted in *Time Magazine*:

> The world has to have a *zero tolerance* view on Iraq. "This country is the size of France. You can always hide things in a country that big. So it is not incumbent on the U.N. to find things in a country that big. So it is not incumbent on the U.N. to find things. What we're saying is that it is incumbent on Saddam Hussein to show that he is compliant".
>
> Gibbs and Duffy (2002: 42, 47)

In the months leading up to the recent war between the US and Iraq, President Bush made clear that he considered that previous United Nation's resolutions to have given him the authority to impose a "zero tolerance" policy on the regime of Saddam Hussein. The President explicitly contrasted this policy with the previous inspection regime in which the U.N. inspectors were required to find proof of weapons of mass destruction. According to Bush, the Hussein regime had an affirmative obligation to actively disarm or face punishment. This is a new kind of international legal order in which unreliable nations will be required to provide their own proof of compliance. The inspection regime is just another form of mandatory drug testing.

## Why crime beat cancer

Like crime, cancer enjoys a long history of being particularly alarming to Americans when compared with their economic peers in Europe and Asia. Yet the war on cancer has largely been a flop compared with its sister war on drugs. This is clearly true of the direct financial investment. As a rough measure, the money spent just by the federal government on an annual basis for the war on crime and drugs is equivalent to the total amount invested in the war on cancer in its three decades. [9] It is also true of other ways we govern through crime or cancer. The National Cancer Act of 1971 has rarely been amended, but Congress has enacted many crime bills since then. Drugs and crime have been highly productive subjects for the reformulation of the executive role, supporting the rise of the attorney generals at the state and federal level, and the emergence of the prosecutor as the dominant model of the executive (Simon 2007a). Indeed, one of the first pieces of legislation in the Nixon Administration's war on drugs shifted control over defining the level of threat posed by various controlled drugs from the office of the Surgeon General to that of the Attorney General (Baum 1996: 53).

Nixon added cancer to the cabinet through the elevation of the National Cancer Institute to a plenary role within the National Institutes of Health (Patterson 1987). In contrast, drugs were elevated not simply into the executive branch but into the White House itself through the creation of a Special Action Office for Drug Abuse Prevention to coordinate federal efforts to control addicts (Marion 1994, 83). The Justice Department, second only to the White House within the modern executive branch, was given a parallel agency, the Office of Drug Abuse and Law Enforcement (ODALE) to coordinate federal enforcement efforts including running operations in major cities (Marion 1994).

Today, public officials at every level of government need to have an agenda around crime in general and drugs in particular, but cancer policy affects relatively few officials. Crime has become a major focus of education at all levels. Drugs in particular are a major nexus for pedagogy and discipline in schools. Drug enforcement signs adorn the outside of school buildings. Inside, drugs influence the curriculum in a variety of ways ranging from direct teaching of an anti-drug curriculum by law enforcement officers (the popular DARE program), to substantial treatment of the harms of drugs in science and social studies courses, to a "values curriculum" aimed at building up a strong moral sensibility, in part because students thus armored are thought to be more resistant to drugs. Cancer, in contrast, is a specialty topic for advanced courses at the most pampered high schools. Why? Was this the result of political strategy, popular resonance, or governmental capacity? In fact, all three seem to be part of the explanation.

## Politics

The Nixon Administration, and virtually every subsequent one, has chosen to avoid a major showdown with industrial chemistry over the cancers and other risks caused by the proliferation of industrially produced chemical compounds both as waste products in nature and as commodities in the home and work environments. As a result, the war on cancer has been limited largely to funding scientific research on cancer remedies, diagnostics, and preventives. An expanded war on cancer would almost inevitably turn to chemical pollution as a major vector of prevention, leading to an unwanted political confrontation with some of the most powerful and influential economic interests in America.

Perhaps the most important blame targets of crime fear are minorities, particularly African Americans. Katherine Beckett (1997) has traced the route by which segregationists in the American South translated their resistance to integration by characterizing civil rights groups as criminal. Northern opponents of integration who focused on the crime threat of desegregated schools and from scattered site housing projects picked up the same theme. Politicians seeking to mobilize support from these groups, such as Richard Nixon and Ronald Reagan, made crime a major focus of their campaign rhetoric. In the 1990s, immigrants also became the targets of blame for crime.

Crime fear also points back at the government itself. Government is blamed for failing to adequately punish criminals and thus deter future crime. This does not strike all of government. Police, for example, are generally viewed as doing a good job. It is certain aspects of government, particularly the courts, that are painted as undermining social control. Government social programs have been special targets of this fear-based outrage. Welfare in particular has been blamed as a source of crime since at least the Goldwater campaign of 1964. A closely related target has been the so-called liberal establishment. Liberals have been blamed for weakening the resolve of government to fight crime. Academics, sociologists in particular, have been seen as corrupting both government and society by spreading the idea that crimes are the fault of social failures and that individual criminals should be coddled rather than scorned and punished (Wilson 1997). Large cities have also emerged as a central target of crime criticism. While cities might be seen as victims of crime, contemporary rhetoric tends to portray the city as a source of crime. From the early twentieth century, the great cities, with their poverty, immigration, and industrial problems, were blamed by social scientists for facilitating and creating crime and for the spread of demoralizing commodities such as pornography and drugs (Park, Burgess and McKensie 1925; Banfield 1970). City governments have been particularly castigated. As they have been associated in recent years with both minority groups and liberals, this also channels the previously noted blaming preferences.

Crime fear is also important for what and whom it allows to be valorized. The logic of media panics about crime points to the children of white suburban families as the ideal-type victim. Although these families are statistically unlikely to suffer from violent crime, they are clearly the preferred models of what victims need as political subjects, held up by the mirror of crime. A series of murders, kidnappings, and sexual crimes against young white females, including Megan Kanka in New Jersey and Polly Klass in California, led to major moral panics in the 1990s and a wide range of legislative changes, making criminal punishment more severe and extending new forms of post-prison control including community notification and in some cases preventive detention under civil commitment.

Prioritizing the need for government to punish crime also serves to valorize personal responsibility. Anti-crime rhetoric since the early 1960s has emphasized the importance of individual moral integrity as the virtue whose decline was manifest in crime. Violent criminals are taken as examples of how crime reflects not social pathologies but failures in the ability of individuals to hold their desires in check. The mirror images of these monsters are people who practice moral discipline and do not expose themselves to drugs and pornography. The popularity of the "just say no" slogan in the 1980s captures this moral valence perfectly.

## *Public opinion*

Assuming that careful disaggregating of political stimulation and public opinion showed that drugs and crime have been more resonant issues for Americans than cancer (and I'm not sure it would show that), it may be a function in part of the demographics of the American population from the 1960s to the present. During the 1960s and through the 1980s, American social policy was in many ways preoccupied with concerns about youth deviance and violence primarily because of the social unrest associated with the huge baby boom set of cohorts that passed through their crime- and violence-prone years from 1964 through 1984. Because the baby boom wave itself involves many cohorts, older boomers were already raising children in the 1970s and 1980s, and their own parental fears for their kids were raising the salience of crime and drugs as it had for their parents who began moving away from crime-prone cities as early as the 1950s.

This youth-centered fear raised the salience of drugs and crime for several reasons. First, youth are more prone to violence and criminal risk taking of various sorts. The large baby boom cohorts certainly helped raise the rates of reported crime and contributed to a sense that crime control was a priority challenge for American governance after the Second World War. Second, parents of children feel unique vulnerabilities and especially in the culture of affluence that has become normal and normative in America since the 1960s. Fear of children being harmed by criminal violence and/or by drugs has been a powerful obsession for American parents since at least the 1950s. In the 1980s, baby boomer parents found themselves particularly concerned about drugs because of fears that their children would face educational disadvantages or even exclusion as a result of exposure to and involvement with illegal drugs, a fear highlighted by Nancy Reagan's "just say no" campaign and the spread of school drug testing. As David Garland has argued, these cohorts have also experienced significant change in the social organization of home and work life driven by the entry of women into the workforce at increasingly high levels from the 1960s on.

## *Governmental capacity*

Crime and drugs may also have prevailed because they represented forms of governance that were relatively easy to produce. We had police, prisons, and courts. The wars on crime and drugs have involved increased spending on existing state and local agencies as well as the creation of extensive new federal agencies to support state agencies as well as to compete with them in enforcing an expanding range of federal crimes. The channeling of the war on drugs into institutions such as workplaces, schools, and the military has perpetuated technologies such as drug testing to reinforce existing bureaucratic mechanisms of discipline.

In contrast, a war on cancer, particularly one that moved beyond funding research for cancer therapies, fed no obvious group of existing institutions. Universities and medical centers existed to compete for research funds and have done so. An effort to govern through cancer in lifestyles, environmental management, and education would have required the creation of new institutions or significant modification of existing ones. Notwithstanding its power as a cultural icon of dread, cancer hardly touches the curriculum of students from kindergarten through college, plays a minimal role in shaping the routines of the workplace, and is only marginally inscribed in the way families consume and govern through consumption.

The National Cancer Act of 1971, combined with sweeping environmental legislation of that era, might have led to a focus on carcinogenic chemicals in everyday life and far-reaching regulation of work and consumption exposure to toxic chemicals, as well as more aggressive moves against tobacco and other toxic consumption patterns (Patterson 1987, 285). Symbolically, cancer fits closely with the moral universe described by environmentalists, for whom a natural harmony was being violated by something insidious, alien, and associated with excess. Indeed, the concept of zero tolerance, which has come to epitomize a whole approach to governing strongly associated with crime control and the war on drugs in particular, originated in the 1970s over concern with human exposure to carcinogens. Zero tolerance was supposed to be a goal for regulating the chemical industry. Instead, it has become a norm for regulating school children and welfare recipients.

## From war on crime to war on terror

The war on crime as a panoply of political technologies and mentalities has profoundly shaped the strategic context of the war on terror. The Bush Administration has made a political theme of claiming that a war on terror is an alternative to a law enforcement approach, a tag it tried, with some success, to hang on Democratic candidate John Kerry during the 2004 election campaign. Yet the Administration's approach to that war has been in large part a continuation of the war on crime, as seen in the arrest of suspected militants, both citizens and aliens; the use of harsh methods to extract confessions; and mass incarceration of a class defined by race and religion as "dangerous" in a global archipelago of prisons. Many of the deformations in American institutions produced by the war on crime, developments that have made our society less democratic, are being publicly rejustified as responses to the threat of terror.

This metaphoric transfer between the war on crime and the war on terror has remained beneath the radar for the most part, emerging only obliquely during the 2004 presidential campaign between President George W. Bush and Senator John Kerry in the form of a subdued debate over whether the war on terror could be handled through criminal justice strategies or needed to be handled exclusively at the level of military strategy and foreign relations. President Bush and his supporters argued that Kerry – a former prosecutor and proponent in the 1990s of greater federal attention to global criminal organizations – was locked into a law enforcement model of how to fight terrorism, a strategy they denounced as unrealistic and undesirable for, among other reasons, the fact that it might involve too much deference to international law and cooperation. Senator Kerry likewise attacked the President for being locked into an overreliance on unilateral US military power. Kerry embraced the organized crime model, stating at the height of the campaign that he expected that terrorism would not be eliminated but rather reduced like organized crime to a tolerable problem. Bush supporters leaped to criticize Kerry for accepting something far less than total victory in the war on terror.

These rather tepid exchanges between the candidates revealed more about how porous the boundaries between war and crime control have become than about any difference in principles between the candidates. Having criticized Kerry's law enforcement strategies for fighting terror, Bush moved after his re-election to appoint Michael Chertoff, a veteran federal prosecutor and former deputy attorney general for criminal prosecutions, to lead the Department of Homeland Security. Indeed, other than the short weeks of direct military campaigning in Afghanistan and ongoing bloodshed in Iraq, much of both wars and the global pursuit of Al Qaeda has come to look much like a particularly grim war on crime: heavy reliance on a strategy of arrest, incarcerate, or kill, in which the dominant symbols have become not huge tank battles but prisons, including Guantánamo Bay in Cuba and Abu Ghraib in Iraq. For Kerry, the argument that Al Qaeda be pursued as an international cartel of criminals emerged from his earlier focus on international criminal organizations as the growing international threat to US security in a post-Cold War world.

Inside the US, the "war on terror" has consisted of extensions of executive power that are both fully consistent with the structural logics of the war on crime and utilize the same basic techniques and practices. The Patriot Act, enacted less than a month after the terror attacks, consisted of a large list of advantages sought by prosecutors and federal law enforcement agencies, most having little or no connection to the problems that prevented the 9/11 plot from being uncovered. One provision, for example, aims at speeding up executions of death row inmates by giving the Attorney General power to certify that states are eligible to move to a faster method of appeals. While the death penalty has no imaginable relevance in stopping suicide-based terrorism, it does have enormous salience in the war on crime. Likewise, the shift of authority to certify states from judges to the Attorney General tracks both the decline of the judiciary and the rise of the Attorney General, both central features of the war on crime (Simon 2007a).

## Conclusion: back to the war on cancer

In perhaps the most famous sound-bite of recent presidential history, television journalist Bernard Shaw asked Michael Dukakis, the Democratic Party's nominee in 1988, what he would want done in the hypothetical case of a criminal who had raped and murdered his wife. Dukakis' bland and technocratic response is widely believed to have fatally injured his campaign for President that year against then-Vice President George H.W. Bush. His apparent inability to identify with a crime victim – even when asked to imagine that it was his wife – and his reluctance to demand the harshest possible punishment in her name defined him as an unreliable protector of American values and interests.

Americans in that era were in the midst of re-imagining their institutions, political as well as household, around the problem of violent crime and its corollaries (drugs, homelessness, gangs). Fairly or not, Dukakis' response to Bernard Shaw revealed something central about his disposition as a leader in a time of governing through crime. Successful politicians since then, from Bill Clinton to George W. Bush, have been effective at expressing deep concern for crime victims and pursuing policies that resonate with harsh criminal justice. This leadership style has left its mark on our national institutions and has been carried forward into the war on terror (talk of evildoers, endless imprisonment, etc.).

Senator John Edwards' emotional *and* thoughtful response in the spring of 2007 to questions raised by reporters about his wife Elizabeth's cancer may be remembered as the inverse Dukakis moment. This time, the presidential candidate, a skilled courtroom lawyer who has spoken of tragic accidents and bottom-line needs to juries on numerous occasions, was able to express compassion for his spouse and family, as well as an informed and realistic sense of both treatment and campaign.

Questions will continue to persist as to whether the Edwards are making the right choice for themselves, their family, and for the country. But if they are able to demonstrate their ability to keep treatment and campaign on course, they may have an opportunity to do something even bigger than win a presidential election; they could help define a new model question against which leaders of all kinds might be tested, one that could replace that now tired and dangerously misleading metaphor of crime. Imagine if presidential candidates in debates this year are asked the following question: What would you do if your closest life companion was found to have an incurable but treatable cancer?

No single threat should rule the imagination of our leaders. The needs of our great and diverse land cannot be condensed into the figure of any particular kind of victim and the hearts of our leaders must be open to many narratives of distress. But, if some threats are to become leading metaphors for our national needs, cancer may be a much better model threat than crime. Cancer, especially recurrent cancer, is a disease beyond simple explanations or solutions. It is a disease of complexity in which our history, our behavioral patterns, our treatment, our environment, and the behavioral patterns of others may all be involved. The same is, of course, true for much of crime as well, but politically we have long professed to being satisfied with simple sound-bite solutions: "three strikes and you're out," "Saddam has been held accountable," etc. Few who face recurrent cancer, or have a loved one facing such a cancer, would be satisfied with similar bromides.

How might an expanded war on cancer provide a model for governing other risks such as terrorism? A cancer approach to terror would follow three basic principles. First, a holistic examination of our relationship with the populations engaged in terrorism should be undertaken with an aim of identifying what the major grievances are and changing the behavior that encourages terrorists to gain influence. As much as possible, if consistent with our other national values and objectives, we should cease engaging in the conduct that seems to lead to the mutation of terror. Second, we should identify existing terrorist cells and seek to isolate and destroy them, but only through methods that do not violate the first principle. Third, we should foster social and political developments that encourage the strengthening of alternatives to terrorism among the populations most attracted to terror.

## Notes

1 President Nixon spoke of a war on cancer in 1971, but the idea and the phrase had been circulating since the 1950s.
2 That would come almost eleven months later after Japan's attack on Pearl Harbor.
3 Europe, with its devastation and poverty, would take decades to become as culturally concerned with cancer as the U.S., a gap that remains significant even today.
4 Disease of course has a long history as a stimulus to governance (see McNeill 1977).
5 An earlier wave of cancer research and governmental effort during the New Deal was focused on industrial cancers, something far closer to the community model of traditional public health analysis.
6 Cancer has had enormous potential as a defining problem for government during the post-Second World War period. Its failure to become a dominant problem for government in competition first with the Cold War and later with crime is a question I plan to pursue further in my next book project.
7 According to journalist Dan Baum, Van Raab called his policy "zero tolerance" which he took from Nixon chief of staff Bob Haldeman who called one of his administrative policies "zero defect" (Baum 1996: 244).
8 Ironic, because this is one area where deterrence, which is generally associated with the model of crime, was already in independent use, and the language of crime, rogue nations, actually signals the breakdown of that logic. To be sure, modern criminal policy has also abandoned deterrence.
9 It is difficult to put together a precise comparison. Should one consider just federal spending or also that of the other levels of government? What about private spending on cancer and crime?

# 5 Risk, preemption and exception in the war on terrorist financing[1]

*Marieke de Goede*

The car being clean, they now turned to my life, which was far harder to search. They questioned me about my identity, activities, exchanges and purchases, friends, travels and above all what made me different from the men and women allowed to zip across the border without question or a thought. Every card, every piece of paper in my wallet was checked. I was asked to explain my credit card receipts. A bill for $500 from a small-town garage for the purchase of four new tyres aroused suspicion and led to more questions. A receipt for an airline ticket to Atlanta raised alarm. 'What was the purpose of your trip to Atlanta?' asked the officer. 'A book I had written was featured at a conference,' I replied. What, he asked suspiciously, was the subject of that book?

Behzad Yaghmaian (2006)

## Introduction: financial intelligence

As the experiences of Iranian-born US college professor Behzad Yaghmaian at the US–Canada border in the wake of 9/11 demonstrate, financial data have assumed a crucial role in practices of searching, profiling and questioning deployed at the border and elsewhere. It is through his purchases and credit card receipts that security authorities expect to uncover Yaghmaian's movements and networks, and to determine his trustworthiness. Credit card purchases, wire transfers and automated teller machine (ATM) transactions are increasingly regarded as a mine of information in the context of the war on terror. As journalist Robert O'Harrow (2005: 260) puts it, "there is no overstating the value government investigators place on financial activity. It's considered almost like a fuel for their intelligence engine" (see also Shields 2004). It is partly through financial data mining, then, that current practice endeavours to "thwart a terrorist who has not yet been identified" (Michael Chertoff 2006, quoted in the Introduction to this volume). Financial data are considered vital to the process of "connecting the dots" of potential terrorists and plots *before* they strike.

Seemingly American led, it should be emphasized that the European Union has largely embraced the "financial war on terror", as it is regarded as a non-violent and technologically sophisticated aspect of the war on terror, more befitting the European approach to security than military intervention (de Goede 2008). In fact, one of the main proponents of the deployment of financial data in the context of the war on terror is UK Prime Minister Gordon Brown (2006), who recently announced the creation of a modern-day "Bletchley Park" in the UK, in which financial information is to be a key asset in "breaking" the contemporary "code" of international terrorism. Brown's assertions parallel those of US governmental officials, such as David Aufhauser and John B. Taylor, who have repeatedly argued that "money trails don't lie", and that following the money has the ability to reveal the structure of terrorist networks. For example, according to Aufhauser,

> The evidence that the financial system coughs up is actually true and correct; it doesn't lie. There's not much room, wiggle room for it being false or suspect, as opposed to the kind of evidence you might get out of extreme measures in interrogation rooms.
>
> Council on Foreign Relations (2007); cf. Taylor (2007)

Brown (2006) concludes that the *Treasury itself* has become "a department for security", and he recommends the deployment of "imaginative and pathbreaking methods" in the war on terror. Such imaginative methods now include the Treasury's powers to freeze the assets of and flows to anyone in the UK "suspected of planning terror or engagement with terror" on the basis of secret source evidence (Elliot 2006).

If this manifestation of new "financial borders" signifies a return of sovereign power over deterritorialized financial flows, as some have argued (Biersteker 2002, 2004), it is a power that should be understood to operate not as a centrally (state-) directed subjugation of market forces, but as one that works as a complex and mobile "dividing practice" (Dillon 2004a: 55, quoted in Gregory 2006: 407; cf. Campbell 2005). For Jenny Edkins and Véronique Pin-Fat (2004: 3), "the notion of sovereign power as opposed to sovereignty is crucial here". So, although Edkins and Pin-Fat argue that "sovereign power is far from dead", this should not be taken to mean that they observe the unproblematic "survival ... of sovereign statehood" (2004: 3). Instead, it is necessary to explore the "relations or grammars" of power that deploy "sovereignty" as their rationale, and how these are productive of "particular forms of life (or lives lived)" (Edkins and Pin-Fat, 2004: 4; see also Sparke, this volume). Sovereign power, for Edkins and Pin-Fat (drawing on Agamben) is defined through the right to draw lines, "between *zoe* and *bios*, inside and outside, human and inhuman" (2004: 13). Indeed, as Dillon (2004a: 55) puts it, the "dividing practices" that animate such power "constitute inclusions and exclusions but ... also modulate intelligibilities, eligibilities, liabilities, and legibilities for populations and individuals alike". Yaghmaian's story clearly illustrates the intelligibilities and elig-ibilities produced through the examination of financial data, as it is pre-cisely *his* questioning and detaining that facilitates others "zipping across the border" (2006).

This chapter analyses the new mobile dividing practices of financial (re) bordering that work through delineations of suspect and terrorist money flows. *Risk* is central to the dividing practices of terrorist finance – for risk becomes the automated means through which the "suspect" is sorted from the "legitimate", the "abnormal" is separated from the "normal" (Amoore and de Goede 2005; Coward 2006). However, and as is discussed in this volume by Mark Salter among others, the deployment of risk in anti-ter-rorist finance practice exceeds established methodologies of risk calculation, and entails a self-conscious deployment of imagination. Thus, according to Aufhauser, financial data are "extremely useful in tracing and investigating *mere suspicions* so that you might also similarly prevent a calamity that *you don't yet have definition on*" (in Council on Foreign Relations 2007; emphases added). As will be explored in this chapter, social network analysis is one such imaginative method, couched in the language of risk while exceeding its technologies, which works through creatively mining and mapping "terrorist networks". Thus, the practices enabled in the name of the war on terrorist finance now far exceed its stated objectives, and produce extra-jur-idical security actions, such as the closing down of Islamic charities (Atia 2007), the persecution of informal money remitters (de Goede 2003) and, in fact, have come to decide who is to be a suspect in the war on terror. In the administrative appearance of such dividing practices, moreover, the violence of its sovereign decision-making has become all but invisible.

It is in this sense, then, that targeting terrorist finances can be seen as exemplary of what Aradau and van Munster in this volume call a *dispositif of precautionary risk*, in which a vision of a disastrous future about to unfold produces the depoliticized imperative of present action. This chapter argues that pursuing terrorist finances enables the production of everyday "spaces of exception" in which not just particular money flows, but also particular (groups of) people can be preemptively targeted and disrupted (Agamben 1998, 2005; see also Ericson, this volume). Not unlike the *Schutzhaft*, ana-lysed by Agamben (1998: 167), that "allowed individuals to be 'taken into custody' independently of any criminal behaviour", the objective of the financial war on terror is to enable disruptive action against those who are not necessarily guilty of criminal behaviour, and could not be tried in court, but are thought to pose a possible danger in the future. Asset freezing is designed explicitly to enable security action outside the courts, and is used by most countries *instead of* trial (Cameron 2006). Thus, listed individuals become subject to a "temporary" and pre-legal measure that, in practice, can last indefinitely, and to which they have no legal recourse (Vlcek 2006: 505–6). As former US Treasury Secretary Paul O'Neill recounts the rationale of asset freezing in the wake of 9/11:

> Because the funds would be frozen, not seized, the threshold of evidence
> could be lower and the net wider. Yet 'freeze' is something of a legal
> misnomer – funds of Communist Cuba have been frozen in various US
> banks for forty years.
>
> Quoted in Suskind (2004: 192)

The Netherlands, for example, froze the assets not only of the convicted members of the alleged Dutch terrorist network the "Hofstadgroep", but also of those acquitted at trials and released after serving their sentences. When it was pointed out that some of those sanctioned were still in appeal procedures, the Foreign Ministry emphasized that the measure exceeds criminal procedural standards, and stated: "Being released does not mean that they are no longer terrorists".[2] The ministry, in other words, suggested that the decision about whether these persons were terrorists had been taken *in advance of*, or at least *in a different space than*, the court's deliberations.

It is not just the practice of freezing itself, but also the prior sorting of suspicious from normal money flows through automated risk modelling, and the designation of suspect financial relationships through social network analysis, that concerns this chapter. As will be argued, such sovereign designations are productive of particular "lives lived", in which financial narratives are seen to anchor the contemporary "normal" citizen. As in Bletchley Park, however, to which Brown appealed in order to associate the pursuit of terrorist financing with the arcane work of accountants, rather than the brutal work of military battle, the violence of such productions remains implicit.

## Complex assemblages of risk and regulation

Edkins and Pin-Fat (2004: 2) emphasize that the sovereign power they seek to analyse is to be understood as "dispersed, not centralised" (cf. Raley 2004; de Goede 2007). In other words, and as explored by William Connolly (2004: 35), the sovereign decision is not handed down, once and for all, through the "single will of a people, a king, or a dictator", but works through a "complex assemblage" (see also J. Bennett 2005). Such a complex assemblage is composed of a "plurality of forces" that circulate "through and under the positional sovereignty of the official arbitrating body" (Connolly 2005: 145). The new financial borders are best understood as such a complex assemblage, in which private financial institutions are newly authorized to make security decisions, and in which commercial data are newly inscribed with public security meanings. The plurality of forces at work here includes both the risk analysts and the models they build, both the security experts and the imagination they deploy, both the mid-level bureaucrat and the law they exceed. Thus understood, spaces of exception are not so much the "outcome of law's suspension" than they are the outcome of, in Fleur Johns' (2005: 614) words, "elaborate regulatory efforts by a range of … authorities".

Current approaches to financial regulation are productive of this complex assemblage of governing in Connolly's sense. Through what is called the "risk-based approach" to financial regulation, financial institutions are authorized to deploy their own models of financial suspicion and abnormality. Simply put, risk-based regulation demands that banks be compliant, but does not stipulate exactly how a bank achieves this, and has abandoned the rules that specify which transactions need to be reported. According to the UK Treasury (2007: 13), a leading proponent, the risk-based approach enlists the private sector to target resources to the most risky clients or products, in contrast to what they call "prescriptive 'tick-box' approaches". Accordingly, the European Third Money Laundering Directive (3rd Directive), which was designed specifically to bring the new terrorist financing provisions of the Financial Action Task Force (FATF) into the European *acquis*, stipulates that institutions need to scrutinize

> any activity which they regard as particularly likely, by its nature, to be related to money laundering and terrorist financing and in particular complex or unusually large transactions and all *unusual patterns of transactions which have no apparent economic or visible lawful purpose.*[3]

By comparison, Title III of the Patriot Act requires financial institutions (not just banks, but also insurance companies, brokerage firms, jewellers and many other businesses) to report "any transaction that has no business or apparent lawful purpose or is not the sort in which a particular customer would normally be expected to engage" (quoted in Naylor 2006: 144). Accordingly, it becomes the responsibility of private institutions to determine usual and unusual transactions patterns, to model economic purpose and normality and to determine and report deviations. As R. T. Naylor (2006: 144) explains, these regulatory changes shift "institutional obligations from passive to reactive–proactive", whereby banks are authorized to determine what is and what is not suspicious, and to freeze and arrest transactions (also Pieth and Aiolfi 2005: 6). This fosters new assemblages of governing between regulator, private institutions, risk assessors and software programs. In fact, as Sue Eckert of the Watson Institute explains, "no government freezes assets. It's the banks. It's the financial institutions that take the specific actions to implement the terrorist financing program" (in Council on Foreign Relations 2007).

Risk-based regulation, then, actively produces what Louise Amoore in this volume calls the "proxy sovereignty" of private (financial) institutions. Judith Butler coins the term "petty sovereigns" to analyse the bureaucratic and institutional reign in which decisions to detain, arrest and freeze are rendered possible without legal recourse. It is here that sovereignty and governmentality merge into each other in complex ways – rather than being mutually exclusive or historically successive. Butler (2004: 59) writes of petty sovereigns:

> they are ... part of the apparatus of governmentality; their decision, the power they wield to 'deem' someone dangerous and constitute them effectively as such, is a sovereign power, a ghostly and forceful resurgence of sovereignty in the midst of governmentality.

Because banks are best placed to know whether a transaction "smells wrong" or "looks bad", it is they who need to engage in disruptive actions, so it is reasoned. Thus, regulators no longer set out indicators of suspicion (with a few exceptions) but appeal specifically to the judgement, suppleness and imagination of financial institutions in deciding what transactions to report or freeze. As the UK Treasury (2007: 13) puts it, "criminal and terrorist finance threats change constantly ... This means that the response to crime and terrorism needs to be as *supple* as the criminals and terrorists themselves" (emphasis added). The bank, in other words, needs to become like the terrorist: being able to strike, unexpectedly and unfoundedly, at those thought to pose a risk. At the same time as this appeal to suppleness, however, the Third Money Laundering Directive and the Patriot Act endeavour to provide lawful foundations to the bank's strike, by stipulating that it is transactions *without apparent lawful purpose* that are singled out for report and freezing. It is precisely this explicit exceeding of the law (to enable "supple" decision-making) in the name of lawfulness that, to Agamben, characterizes the state of exception (cf. Johns 2005).

While risk-based regulation is particular to the financial sector, the authorization of all kinds of societal groups to make security decisions fits into an established pattern in the war on terror. Campaigns that ask the public to "be vigilant" authorize truck drivers, workers, airplane passengers, supermarket personnel as well as citizens in general to report suspicious activity or unusual behaviour (see Amoore, this volume; also Amoore 2006, 2007a; Hay and Andrejevic 2006; Ericson 2007: 61–70). The definition of "what to look for", however, can *never* be fully articulated, because it is thought to inform terrorists about what to avoid, and because it leaves authorities vulnerable to charges of discrimination. Instead, vague notions of abnormality are articulated, encouraging citizens to identify, for example, "anyone who does not appear to belong" (Maryland State Police flyer, quoted in Stanley 2004: 7). While deploying the language of risk and measurable deviation from the norm, such campaigns clearly exceed the limits of calculation and encourage the deployment of citizen's imagination (see Salter, this volume). Such precautionary imagination, in turn, is still thought to be actionable, and public tip-offs have led to controversial security decisions, including the arrest of two traditionally clothed Muslim men on the Frankfurt–Amsterdam train in November 2005, whose suspicious behaviour turned out to be a ritual cleaning in the train's washroom in advance of prayer; and the six American Imams who were removed from a US Airways flight after public complaints in 2006.[4]

## Lived financial lives

For Edkins and Pin-Fat (2004: 4), the petty sovereign's power is productive of "particular forms of life (or lives lived)". It is possible to argue that financial transactions are now among the most important anchor of "normal" contemporary lives. The mapping and modelling of financial normality increasingly demands of citizens that they leave tracks of "normal" financial records throughout their daily lives. As financial institutions are themselves partly outsourcing their proxy sovereign power to software companies, algorithmic articulations of normal financial lives become ever more tightly drawn. One thing that is remarkable about the risk-based compliance models developed by software companies such as Mantas and NetEconomy, which promise to be able to flag financial abnormalities in the millions of daily transactions conducted by banks, is how they increasingly entail software modelling of *normal* behaviour. If risk assessment has traditionally depended upon articulations of deviant or risky behaviour, leaving the "norm" of behaviour implicit (e.g. Hacking 1990; Ericson and Haggerty 2002; de Goede 2005), financial modelling is now making a turn towards profiling the standard against which deviance is to be measured. As one company brochure puts it:

> The purpose of monitoring is for financial institutions to understand the normal and reasonable account activity of their customers, so that they can quickly detect any unexpected and unexplained changes or inconsistencies in the behaviour of an account.
>
> NetEconomy (2005: 24)

But what, more precisely, happens inside the software as the program "runs overnight"? How does anti-money laundering software "continuously and invisibly classify, standardize, and demarcate rights, privileges, inclusions, exclusions" (Graham 2005: 563)? In order to make predictions concerning the kind of business the customer would normally engage in, financial institutions collect customer information "over and above basic identity information", including the purpose of opening the account, sources of wealth, details of employment, anticipated level of account activity and the relationship between signatories (NetEconomy 2005: 16). As one representative of the American Banking Association (ABA) explains it: "You want to find out what kind of business [the new client] wants to conduct with the bank and the bank has to make an evaluation: is that the kind of business I would expect this kind of a customer to engage in?"[5] For example, one software sales manager explained to me that he knows the profile of doctors in the area: how much they earn, when they are paid, what their spending patterns are. As another software developer explains:

> The system . . . takes into consideration use of cash machines, cheques, loans and all other accounts to pull together a view of what the customer

looks like and how they behave each day ... It looks at how you compare to your peers, for example, you will have an industry code and we will profile you against every other person of the same occupation that banks in your institution. We know the profile of every dairy producer, every butcher, every teacher.

Mantas (2003)

Indeed, it is believed that preemptive disruption *is* possible through such data mining, as it is inscribed with potential to "identify useful patterns that can predict an extremely rare activity – terrorist planning and attacks" (DeRosa 2004: 8).

In is in this sense, then, that we can argue that financial risk assessment is productive of a particular "way of life" (Johnson 2002; Amoore, this volume). Not only is it expected that individual financial customers fit into a peer group pattern, more important still is the fact that all citizens are expected to produce an electronic financial record throughout their daily lives. This depends upon what Michael Curry (2004: 496–7) calls an "appeal to narrative", where it is imagined that, "in his or her life a person *must* have done certain things, and *must* have created certain trails of information; not to have fit within these imagined narratives is to raise suspicions" (emphasis in original). The narratives of normal financial lives revolve around the normal person's use of direct debits, cash machines, loans, salary, mortgage and – importantly – proper use of cash and proper frequency of overseas transactions. As a consequence, the *absence* of information, as Curry (2004: 496) rightly notes, becomes regarded as suspicious in itself. So, for example, the absence of an electronic transaction trail of a wrongly suspected British Muslim family who preferred to keep their savings in cash because of religious beliefs became grounds for suspicion and speculation that the family must have been criminally involved (see Amoore and de Goede 2008, in press). It is in this context, then, that financial networks that are perceived as *not* accumulating (accessible) transactions records, such as *hawala* and charities, have become suspect in themselves in the post-9/11 security environment (de Goede 2003; Atia 2007).

The liveable lives produced through the modes of seeing, recording and analysing at work in financial data mining, according to Jordan Crandall (2005: 20), constitute "not only a form of control" but pivot on modes of "self-reflection and self-awareness" that can be experienced as offering recognition and even pleasure to contemporary citizen/consumers. Financial data mining, in Crandall's analysis, is not a technique that most of us would necessarily object to; instead, it is a comforting gaze, which construes our identity and makes possible our participation in society. "Being-seen is an ontological necessity", writes Crandall (2005: 21),

we strive to be accounted for within the dominant representational matrices of our time. We are not only talking about a gaze that is intrusive and controlling. We are talking about a gaze that provides the condition for action – the gaze for which one acts.

Intimately connected to our "buying patterns" and "lifestyle choices", the power and technology at work here fuse security action with commercial opportunity (Crandall 2005; Le Billon 2006). It is no coincidence, then, that much of the software modelling now deployed with regard to terrorist finance was first developed in the context of financial marketing and relationship management. For example, algorithmic financial peer grouping was first deployed to develop "customized propositions" – including special offers, better service or, alternatively, reduced service and longer call centre waiting time – for financial customers, and enabled "unbundled service and access packages" to maximize the bank's profitability (Graham 2005: 566; also Peppard 2000; Danna and Gandy 2002; Graham and Wood 2003). The expanded information collected about financial clients in the context of new terrorist finance regulations does not only draw on marketing technology, but also offers new opportunities in this respect: the integration of customer relationships management with anti-money laundering databases, according to one interviewee, is the future of financial business practice.[6]

## SWIFT and social network analysis

I have argued that the war on terrorist finance exceeds its stated objective and, in practice, creates spaces in which exceptional security decisions are enabled on the basis of a mobile articulation or normal/abnormal financial lives. As they evolved in the years after 9/11, the practices enabled in the name of "targeting terrorist finances" themselves became a moving target. From cutting off financial resources to terrorists, the purpose of the exercise became the registering and mining of financial data. Nowhere is this clearer than in the ways in which financial data are increasingly mined for suspects' associations, and their associations. Such "social network analysis" starts from a suspect name, phone number or credit card number, in order to preemptively arrest, detain and disrupt those thought to pose a future danger. In this manner, "following the money" becomes a way of determining who is to be a suspect in the war on terror. As one Department of Justice official puts it in a recent interview,

> In the game of prevention . . . it is not enough to expect law enforcement [to] uncover the bomber before he detonates the bomb. The goal of pursuing terrorism financing as a crime is to *widen the universe of possible criminal defendants so that we can prosecute before the terrorist act occurs.*
> Breinholt, quoted in Chediak (2005, emphasis added)

Social network analysis is perceived to be an imaginative and innovative risk technique in the war on terror that enables the preemptive identification and disruption of potential suspects. Despite its blanking out of particular phrases, for example, the following conclusion from the British Intelligence and Security Committee enquiry into the 2005 London bombings reveals quite clearly its vision of social network analysis:

> The main lesson learned from the July attacks was the need to get into 'the unknowns' – to find ways of broadening coverage to pick up currently unknown terrorist activity or plots ... Steps are now being taken to develop a more proactive approach to identifying threats in the UK ... The potential value of *** and *** as a means for identifying new threats has been highlighted to the Committee. The fact that the 7 July group was in contact with others under Security Service investigation has emphasised *the potential for new threats to be identified through the examination of information and contact networks relating to existing targets.*
>
> Intelligence and Security Committee (2006: 35–6, emphasis added)

Here, the Committee appeals to precisely those "unknowns" that, as Aradau and van Munster argue in this volume, underpin a politics of precaution. A preemptive vision is being deployed, where it is imagined that those with financial associations with suspects are themselves about to enact the worst. For example, in the vision of the UK Treasury (2007: 10), financial data analysis makes it possible not just to "look backwards" in the context of a criminal investigation, but also to

- *look sideways*, by identifying and confirming associations between individuals and activities linked to conspiracies, even if overseas ...; and
- *look forward*, by identifying the warning signs of criminal or terrorist activity in preparation.

It is the conceptualization of the terrorist threat as diffuse, global and networked that has propelled social network analysis to the top of intelligence agendas. As Wendy Larner discusses in this volume, contemporary security analysts assert that terrorism "has no headquarters, no military base, no barracks to be bombed" (Bauman and Galecki 2005, quoted by Larner; see also Raley, this volume; Der Derian 2001; Weber 2005: 90–108). Instead, transnational terrorism is represented as a "new, adaptable and complex form of 'networked' asymmetric adversary" that has a "polymorphic structure or design with a multiplicity of nods" (Ranstorp 2007: 1, 7; see also Knorr Cetina 2005). Visualizations of the networks and associations of the 9/11 perpetrators as well as the Madrid bombers have been influential in both supporting such securitizations and in articulating (and selling) social network analytical software "solutions". As management consultant and software designer Valdis Krebs puts it in his article that attempts to visualize the 9/11 network:

My aim was to uncover network patterns that would reveal Al Qaeda's preferred methods of stealth organization. If we know what patterns of organization they prefer, we may know what to look for as we search them out in countries across the world.

Krebs (2002); see also Rodríguez (2005)

The key question in social network analyses becomes the identification and measurement of the *nodes* in the network. Writes one journalist: "maybe we can't cut off terror's head, but we can take out its nodes" (Garreau 2001). Mathematical concepts and methods, as well as specialized software packages, have emerged in the domain of social network analysis to claim scientific precision in their ability to map and measure network hubs and nodes – for example, by measuring the number of connections of a network member, their centrality or their closeness (Knox, Savage and Harvey 2005: 4). Through this representation, a policy whereby these supposed nodes are targeted and whereby, "via snowball sampling" (Krebs 2002: 14), a suspect's associates (and *their* associates) are targeted, becomes seemingly logical. As Samuel Weber (2005: 101) puts it, "However acephalous or Janus-faced netwar may be, there must still be an *enemy* to be *targeted*, which is to say, located and subdued, either by being killed, destroyed, or rendered dysfunctional or dependent" (emphases in original). Such targeting can be financial: in the absence of (criminal) evidence, blacklisting and asset freezing become a preferred means of rendering a suspect dysfunctional or dependent (as well as destroying their reputation and livelihoods).

In the process of social network analysis, financial data are not just a primary data source for network mapping, but become more specifically the means through which to determine *the wider network* of "direct and indirect associates" (Krebs 2002: 7). Thus, if the strongest network links are calculated through family contacts, meetings and time spent together, the wider links are thought to be identifiable through financial transactions records, such as wire transfer records. Deducting such links and associations may entail the deployment of non-obvious relationship awareness (NORA) software, which was pioneered (like many security technologies deployed in the war on terror) to govern access to Las Vegas casinos. Such software is able to search through different databases and lists in order to, as one journalist puts it, "figure out if people are connected with unsavory characters" (Levy 2007; see also DeRosa 2004: 4). Such connections may be "non-obvious", so, in addition to determining whether persons share an address or credit card number, the software may be able to identify connections through addresses that have bordering backyards, or names that are *similar* rather than the same.

The most (in)famous instance whereby financial data were deployed for social network analysis was, of course, when the US Treasury subpoenaed millions of records from the Belgian-based banking cooperative Society for Worldwide Interbank Financial Telecommunication (SWIFT). As one of the architects of the SWIFT data mining program, John B. Taylor (2007: 19–20) wrote, "there is a huge amount of information in SWIFT ... Using [that] information ... intelligence experts could then map out terrorist networks and fill in missing links in chains of terrorists". Indeed, while controversy over both the disclosure of the program by two major US newspapers, as well as over its privacy implications continues (see, for example, Belgian Privacy Commission 2006), the ambition to retain, map and mine wire transfer data continues unabated (and, in fact, largely untouched by the controversies). In a "feasibility study" published in October 2006, the Financial Crimes Enforcement Network (FinCen) of the US Treasury explores the possibility of creating a real-time accessible database of all wire transfers in and out of the US, collected in a "federated data warehouse architecture", the management of which would be subcontracted. The database would be used, among other things, for what the US Treasury calls "link analysis," which, it is envisaged, "provides a way of combining ... different records so that analysts can detect the patterns and relationships between different sets of data" (FinCen 2006: 10). Thus, from the basis of particular suspects, a financial data "string" may be "pulled" in order to associate names, phone numbers, social security numbers, credit card numbers and addresses from different databases. Clad in the required privacy safeguards, FinCen's financial warehouse is expected to be operational within three years. And lest we think this is a specifically American objective, it is important to note that both Canada and Australia already have such wire transfer databases in place.

Although the precise deployment and yields of the SWIFT data mining program are classified, officials are keen to assert, as an "article of faith", that "what it produced was remarkable and saved lives and enhanced the national security of nations across the world" (Aufhauser, in Council on Foreign Relations 2007: 7). However, the emerging evidence of financial links detected and pursued in the context of the war on terror raises substantial questions. For example, American research group OMB Watch (2006: 11), in their work on the pursuit of Muslim charities in the wake of 9/11, notes with concern how "government suspicion and scrutiny" has expanded to those with past and sometimes loose links to suspect charities. OMB Watch (2006: 11) documents one case of a naturalized American citizen of Bangladeshi descent, whose house was raided in 2004 and who remains on a no-fly list for having donated money to a suspect charity "years before it was accused of supporting terrorism". In the case of another charity, the Treasury's accusations focused almost entirely on "the group's ties with other suspect individuals and organizations" rather than on any actions taken by the charity itself (OMB Watch 2006: 13).[7] Indeed, many cases of suspect, blacklisted and deported persons in the wake of 9/11 hinge on allegations of having *links to*, or *connections with*, known suspects (Naylor 2006; see also Ericson, this volume). As a 2005 Human Rights Watch report on the misuse of the material witness law in the US states:

Many of the seventy material witnesses whose cases are addressed in this report were arrested and incarcerated on the basis of evidence that would never have sufficed for criminal arrest and pre-trial detention. The evidence often consisted of little more than the fact that the person was a Muslim of Middle Eastern or South Asian descent, in combination with *having worked in the same place* or *attended the same mosque as* a September 11 hijacker, [or] *gone to college parties with* an accused terrorism suspect.

*Human Rights Watch* (2005: 4–5, emphases added)

Often, such links and connections remain unexamined in courts of law, either because, in the case of charities, authorities decline to prosecute as the accusations and freezing orders succeeded in making the organizations defunct, or because, in the case of blacklisting, criminal standard evidence is neither available nor required as prosecution does not follow the listing procedure. In this way, the "association rules" governing the mathematical logics of social network analysis produce guilt *by association* – destroying organizations and individual reputations, without, in many instances, juridical recourse (Cameron 2003, 2006; Donohue 2006). Like the *Schutzhaft*, financial targeting enables security action, and even criminal prosecution, without a link to crime. As legal scholar Iain Cameron argues in his report to the Council of Europe, the relationship between asset freezing and criminal prosecution is tenuous, to say the least. Cameron (2006: 10) writes: "blacklisting is a strange type of criminal charge. The Security Council decrees lay down no prohibited activity against which the named individuals' actions or omissions are to be measured. And where there is no norm laid down, the individual cannot breach it". Indeed, as William Vlcek (2006: 506) argues, sanctioned persons, "in the absence of any means to rectify their situation ... and [having] no avenue to recover their presence in society", have become akin to Agamben's *homo sacer*, or "bare life". At the same time, however, the elaborately compiled, regulated and published blacklists of various authorities, including the UN and the EU, which contain hundreds of names, demonstrate that the exceptionality embodied in them requires not so much legal suspension, but more "the painstaking work of legal classification" (Johns 2005: 617).[8]

Indeed, one of the most important political issues surrounding social network analysis, mentioned but not pursued by Krebs (2002: 2), is the problem of "fuzzy boundaries" or the "difficulty of deciding who to include and who not to include". The political pressures of taking preemptive disruptive action against terrorist associates mean that ever further degrees of separation of actual perpetrators or legitimate suspects become targeted. But who decides where the boundaries of a network are? Who decides which network member is to be pursued, targeted, blacklisted, and which network member is judged to be falsely ensnared? The social network art of Mark Lombardi, which was taken seriously enough by the Federal Bureau of

Investigation (FBI) for them to study one of his drawings at the Whitney Museum in the wake of 9/11, shows Bush and Bin Laden themselves to be only three degrees separated, thus illustrating the poignancy of these questions (NPR 2003). Moreover, the problem with the boundaries reflects back on a wider problematic concerning network analysis itself. As Weber (2005: 101) asks, "What holds networks together? ... Is *targeting* something that occurs independently of the network or is it part and parcel of how the 'net' works?" (emphasis in original). Put simply, the network may be a performative, constituted through the act of mapping and measuring itself (Knox, Savage and Harvey 2005: 11). And selecting the target, in Weber's (2005: 105) reading, is in itself an act of violence: "Since ... the place targeted is always enmeshed in a net of relations that is intrinsically inexhaustible and unlimited ... the act of targeting is an act of violence even before any shot is fired".

## Conclusions: violence and resistance

This chapter has argued that the "war on terrorist finance" produces everyday spaces of exception, in which specific transactions and specific persons are preemptively targeted. This everyday space of exception works as a dividing practice, often on the basis of a risk assessment in which the expert and the imaginative are subtly combined, that is able to negate its violence through its administrative appearance. Brown's appeal to a modern-day Bletchley Park, where British code breakers worked to crack the encryption of German military communications during the Second World War, is revealing here. The 2001 film *Enigma*, a suspense story which simultaneously attempts to give a representative historical account of the work at Bletchley Park, portrays the geeky and mathematically obsessed code breakers in stark contrast to the parallel violence of the "real" military battlefield (Apted 2001). It was perhaps precisely this mathematical, administrative and non-violent image, in contrast to the violent battlefields in Iraq and Afghanistan, that Brown wished to appeal to in order to carve out his own approach to the war on terror. What Brown does not acknowledge, however, and what *Enigma* clearly portrays, is the violence enacted by the code breakers *themselves*. In the film, the geeky code breakers decide to let a German attack on British submarines proceed unreported and undisturbed, so that they can intercept more communication signals – right up until the firing of the first shot after which eighty lives are lost in a matter of minutes. The code breakers' obsession with their target – the Enigma Code – renders the lives lost visible only as "collateral damage". Similarly, we can argue that a barely visible but pervasive violence takes place through the apparently administrative articulations of new powerful definitions of normality and abnormality in transactions monitoring. As minute models of normality become increasingly important for societal participation, those who are wrongly targeted and economically disabled are only able to appear as collateral damage, at best.

At the same time, however, and as further explored in other contributions to this volume, it is important to render visible the *space*, the room for manoeuvre, in the space of exception (see especially the chapters by Amoore, Raley and Coutin in this volume). If the sovereign decision is conceived as being made up of a plurality of forces – instead of a "single will" – this has the advantage, according to Connolly (2005: 145), of rendering visible "strategic issues and sites to address for those who seek to introduce a robust pluralism into the ethos of sovereignty". One such strategic site is explored by Coutin in her contribution to this volume, where she notes how US banks offer financial products to the unbanked and undocumented. Despite the tightly drawn dividing practices increasingly at work in the name of pursuing terrorist finance, some American banks appear to search for the possibility of different choices *vis à vis* undocumented migrants. To be sure, not a vision of resistance, but a vision of profit seems to motivate the banks' decisions: the new financial products offered to undocumented migrants are innovative in the sense of the high charges they incur, if nothing else. However, the Bank of America's resistance to be enlisted in the proxy sovereignty of border control (Staps 2007) offers a sharp contrast to current practice in The Netherlands, where a wholesale drive is currently under way for all *existing* financial customers to have their identity documents checked and registered by their financial institutions. Dutch banks have done little to contest their sovereign enlistment here, and have sent out notice to all customers that failure to identify themselves can lead to a closing of their accounts and/or freezing of their assets. In contrast, (some) American banks' reinterpretation of the legal identity requirements demonstrates the potential mobility of the lines drawn in the name of sovereignty, a mobility that can function to (temporarily) resist sovereignty's logic.

## Notes

1 Earlier drafts of this chapter were presented to the International Studies Association Workshop "Governing by Risk in the War on Terror" in San Diego in March 2006 and to the Open University's Geography Seminar Series in November 2006. Many thanks to participants at both events for their helpful comments on this paper. Special thanks to Louise Amoore for her very insightful comments on different versions of this chapter.
2 "vrij zijn betekent niet dat ze terrorist af zijn", cited in Olgun (2006), my translation.
3 EU Third Money Laundering Directive, 2005, article 20, emphasis added.
4 These imams are now suing both the airline and the passengers who reported them, leading some to worry that this will have "a chilling effect on the willingness of people to provide information that authorities need to act when people are engaged in wrongdoing". Mark Behrens, defence lawyer, quoted in *The Washington Times* (2007).
5 Buchanan (2006), quote at 6–7 minutes.
6 Confidential interview with a sales representative from NetEconomy, commercial data mining firm, Amsterdam, January 18, 2006.
7 See further OMB Watch (2005); Naylor (2006); Atia (2007) for the documentation of many other problematic cases in relation to the pursuit of Muslim charities.
8 See, for example, the searchable European Union online sanctions list at http://ec.europa.eu/external_relations/cfsp/sanctions/list/consol-list.htm (accessed October 8, 2007).

# 6  Consulting, culture, the camp

## On the economies of the exception[1]

*Louise Amoore*

Imagine people going about their everyday lives – enjoying their families and friends, engaging in productive pursuits in thriving communities, travelling to and from home, school and work – with the self-assurance that stems from being informed, alert, and aware of their surroundings. The threat of a terrorist attack does not deter us from living life to the full.

> Department of Homeland Security (2004)

A culture, while it is being lived, is always in part unknown, in part unrealized.

> Raymond Williams (1962: 320)

## Living life to the full: welcome to the homeland security enterprise[2]

In September 2003, the then US Secretary for Homeland Security, Tom Ridge, toured the town halls of America in a bid to "make the citizens' homeland security vision a national reality". Accompanied in his mission by management consultants Accenture and Deloitte, and by IT and software companies IBM, Microsoft, Hewlett Packard and Ascential, Secretary Ridge urged that "in the war against terrorism, citizens are just as important to fighting the war as soldiers on the battlefield" (Department of Homeland Security 2003: 5). From Massachusetts and Virginia to Florida, California, Texas and Missouri, the self-styled homeland security enterprise rolled out a programme of civil society workshops (broadcast on *NBC* and *Fox*) designed to create a "culture of homeland security in every city, every neighbourhood, every state, and every home across America" (Department of Homeland Security 2003: 4). The spectre of 9/11 haunts and rallies the call to arms of the homeland security citizens: "our lives were forever changed"; "our belief in America as an impenetrable stronghold was shattered, gone"; "terrorism becomes palpably real" as we "shift to a new normalcy shadowed by the threat of global terrorism" (Department of Homeland Security 2003: 2).

Just as "citizens rushed the cockpit of Flight 93", the gathered people are told, so citizens must now "harness the spirit of Americans in the wake of 9/11" in schools, on public transportation systems, in workplaces and neighbourhoods and in the home.

The incorporation of the citizen into the homeland security enterprise is suggestive of what I see as a pervasive and politically troubling move to deploy the idea of culture as a governmental domain for times of exception, necessity or crisis. Understood in Raymond Williams' terms as "ways of life" (1962: 312; 1965: 12), and as Richard Johnson proposes in his discussion of the Bush–Blair rhetoric (2002), culture is invoked on a number of registers as a call to arms in the war on terror. First, way of life (*singular*) appears as a gesture of defiance in the face of risk and threat. As in my opening extract, the everyday activities of fun with family and friends, productive work, education, consumption and so on become designated resources to the war on terror. As Susan Willis comments on the immediate days following the events of 9/11: "we were told to shop. Shop to show we are patriotic Americans. Shop to show our resilience over death and destruction" (2003: 122). The practices of daily life are thus framed as essentially sustaining, defiant and indefatigable, in their very ordinariness and familiarity in the face of other ways of life that are beyond comprehension.

In the days following the London bombings of July 7, 2005, a similar deployment of ways of life was at work. Addressing Parliament four days after the bombings, the Prime Minister depicts "something wonderfully familiar" as the city defiantly returns to its normality: "just four days later, London's buses, trains and as much of the underground as possible, are back on normal schedules; its businesses, shops and schools are open; its millions of people are coming to work with a steely determination that is genuinely remarkable" (Blair 2005). This calling up of a singular and unified/unifying urban way of life, then, takes place as the authorities simultaneously request the residue of everyday commuter life (text messages, video clips, digital photographs, CCTV footage ... ) to help locate the source of such a violent transgression of normal events. The settling out of a normalized economy (via an economy of normalcy) simultaneously performs and exposes the exception.

In this way, ways of life are framed in terms of securing normality, but also – and this is my second point – as somehow indicative of threat or danger, or delineating an exception to the normal run of things. The overwhelming emphasis of the homeland security citizenship programme, for example, is on being "informed, alert and aware of surroundings" and "reporting questionable incidents and circumstances" (Department of Homeland Security 2004: 12). The routines of the commute, the office, the city street, the shopping mall, the neighbourhood, not only become sites of defiance and resilience – as in the UK's "London Resilience Partnership", for example – but are also positioned as settled contexts against which suspicious or unusual behaviour can be identified and punished. The production of a culture of homeland security, then, precisely implies also the identification and visualization of a deviant other who is seen not to share the designated way of life.

Italian philosopher, Giorgio Agamben, offers the bare life (*zoe*) political life (*bios*) distinction as the "fundamental categorical pair of Western politics" (1998: 8). Although we are "all potentially exposed" to the condition of bare life, to the stripped down vulnerability of life as shared by humans and animals, the modern democracy, as Agamben has it, "is constantly trying to transform its own bare life into a way of life", to find the civility of political life (1998: 9). When a state of emergency is invoked, or in Agamben's reading, a Schmittian state of exception that increasingly appears "as the dominant paradigm of government in contemporary politics", certain categorised people experience the suspension of their political life and the reduction of their existence to the bare life of *homo sacer* (Agamben 2005: 2). As his life is devoid of value in law, the very existence of a life that matters being suspended with the annulment of the juridical norm, *homo sacer* cannot be sacrificed and his killing must go unpunished.

What is at stake, then, in thinking through the sorting of safe liveable ways of life from risky unliveable ways of life as a mode of risk calculation? Agamben's compelling insight is that the state of exception has biopolitical significance precisely because it incorporates living beings "by means of its own suspension" (2005: 3). The sovereign power "who can decide on the state of exception" thus produces a central paradox. The annulment of the norm is declared at the same time as the state "guarantees its anchorage to the juridical order" (Agamben 2005: 35). In this way, the force of law becomes indeterminate and amorphous as acts proliferate "that do not have the value of law but acquire its force" (Agamben 2005: 38). For Agamben, the contemporary state of exception is not defined by the acquisition of new powers, or by the "fullness of powers", but rather as a "kenomatic state, an emptiness and a standstill of the law" (Agamben 2005: 48). The archetypal embodiment of this emptiness, or zone of indistinction, is Agamben's "camp":

> The paradoxical status of the camp as a space of exception must be considered. The camp is a piece of land placed outside the normal juridical order, but it is nevertheless not simply an external space. What is excluded in the camp is, according to the etymological sense of the term 'exception' (*ex capere*), *taken outside*, included through its own exclusion. But what is first of all taken into the juridical order is the state of exception itself ... it inaugurates a new juridico-political paradigm in which the norm becomes indistinguishable from the exception. The camp is thus the structure in which the state of exception – the possibility of deciding on which founds sovereign power – is realized *normally*.
>
> Agamben (1998: 170)

While Agamben's camp does speak to contemporary exceptional spaces that are, quite literally, "taken outside" – as in the works of those who consider Abu Ghraib, Guantánamo Bay or the practices of extraordinary rendition (see Butler 2004; Edkins, Pin-Fat and Shapiro 2004; Minca 2005) – it clearly also suggests the ubiquity of the camp in everyday life. As Bülent Diken and Carsten Bagge Lautsen argue compellingly, the camp extends beyond Agamben's "piece of land" and "beyond the walls of the concentration camp". "Today", they write, "the logic of the camp is generalized; the exception is normalized" (2005: 5). Social theories that have long understood the camp as an anomalous space, a means of situating society's excluded beyond the borders, precisely as "encampment", now suggest that the camp enables the inclusion of the excluded via their very exclusion. Hence, the voucher systems that incorporate asylum seekers by their exclusion from normal work and consumption, or the export processing zones that incorporate new forms of slavery via the annulment of regulation. For those concerned with the proliferation of camps within the war on terror, it is this incorporation by exception that stages the risk profiling of people at international borders, airports and in the financial system (see Lyon 2003; van Munster 2004; Amoore and de Goede 2005; O'Harrow 2005; Sparke 2006). Agamben's space of exception has, then, come to capture something of the conditions within which contemporary sovereignty is constituted, as well as the general mood in which geographers, international relations scholars, sociologists and philosophers find themselves writing.

Yet, confronted by scenarios such as the advance of homeland security citizenship as a technique in the war on terror, I see an economy of exception that does not sit easily within Agamben's sense of "an emptiness" or "anomic space" (2005: 39). What is it that is at work *within* the state of exception? Does the sovereign invocation of the state of exception exceed Agamben's paradox because it opens the space for the proliferation of new proxy sovereignties that are designated to act with the force of the law? As Judith Butler describes it, "a contemporary version of sovereignty" is produced with the suspension of the norm, "at the moment of withdrawal" (2004: 61). I will concern myself here with the consultants, companies and citizens whose actions I see as both *designated by* the state of exception and *continually designating* exceptional circumstances. Understanding the emergence of economies of exception, I will argue, has become critical to our sense of how sovereignty is manifested and how exception is concretely materialized.

Agamben brings a tightly drawn finality to the intersection of biopolitics and culture. As William Connolly suggests, Agamben "encloses political culture within a tight logic" such that "nowhere in the book is a way out actually proposed" (2005: 137). Connolly calls up a world of ambiguities and ambivalences that are "more littered, layered and complex" than Agamben allows. "If you loosen Agamben's logic of paradox without eliminating it altogether", he writes, "you express more appreciation for the materialization of culture and locate more space to manoeuvre within the paradoxes he delineates" (2005: 140). For Connolly, within the state of exception, there is a perpetual and contingent interplay between the authorities "that decide the exception" and the plural "cultural forces that insert themselves irresistibly into the outcome" (2005: 141). Governing via, through and against ways of life, then, is a significant feature of contemporary micropolitics. But the outcome is not entirely, perhaps not even partially, knowable – there are spaces within the state of exception precisely because it is declared, sustained and contested by multiple forces. The designation of exception deploys a singular way of life as its means of recuperating civil political life but, as it does so, it confronts plural ways of life in the sense intended by Raymond Williams, as a lived culture that is "always in part unknown, in part unrealized" (1962: 320).

## "Let the consuls see to it": deferred decisions

If the conditions of the exception are decided, if there is a decision, then who takes it and how is it to be taken? As Claudia Aradau and Rens van Munster argue in this volume, the contemporary risk *dispositif* is preemptive, it takes anticipatory decisions. "Rather than acting in the present to avoid an occurrence in the future", writes Brian Massumi, "pre-emption brings the future into the present. It makes present the future consequences of an eventuality that may or may not occur, indifferent to its actual occurrence" (2005: 7–8). The temporality of the decision, then, is anticipatory – it folds the uncertain future into immediate risk calculation. For Massumi, the preemptive decision is a "lightening strike" of sovereign power that cannot "admit to discussing, studying, consulting, analyzing" for fear of admitting "to having been in a state of indecision" (2005: 5–6). In fact, contemporary risk practices do engage deeply in forms of protracted calculation, consultation and analysis, but of types that defer the decision itself into a seemingly limitless series of authorizations. Thus, practices of data mining, social network analysis, risk profiling, identity management and so on diffuse security decisions into algorithmic calculation.

In contrast to Massumi's observation of analysis and consultation characterizing sovereign decisions, it is precisely the modern state's consultation with mobile expert/inexpert knowledges that eradicates the possibility of a decision, rendering the decision perennially deferred. As Jacques Derrida reminds us, "the decision, if there is to be one, must advance towards a future which is not known, which cannot be anticipated" (1994: 57). A decision that simply invokes a risk calculation – this person to be placed on a "no-fly" list; that individual's assets to be frozen; that call to an "anti-terror hotline" to be prioritized – is in these terms not a decision at all, but merely the "application of a body of knowledge" (1994: 37). Of course, decisions to intervene are made all the time, but they do not eschew the mere enactment of a calculation, nor take responsibility for confronting the political difficulties of indecision.

Although contemporary modalities of risk mobilize ways of life in various ways, then, they categorically avoid confrontation with the agonistic difficulty of life as it is lived. As the practices of contemporary security are dispersed into mundane and prosaic settings – the "normal" subway at 8.30am; the "trusted" traveller; the "suspicious" transaction (see Sparke, this volume; de Goede, this volume) – we may never know when a decision is a decision, made in the context of difficulty and uncertainty, and when it is a programmed risk calculation. The exception appears as a designation and not a decision, it acts and delineates, it does not meaningfully decide. It *is* consultative, it *does* deliberate, but yet it appears as a "lightning strike" of sovereign power because it defers to mathematical formulae and integrated software that give immediately actionable data. It does not entangle itself with political difficulty because the risk calculation is always already made.

What is this practice of consultation and deliberation that draws on the prosaic and ordinary settings of daily life? What we have come to know as consulting finds its roots in the Latin *consulto*, meaning to ask the advice of, and *consultum*, meaning to decree [having taken advice]. There can be little doubt that consulting as a business practice is proliferating in the war on terror: Accenture have the major US borders contract; IBM Consulting are leading the UK's e-borders trials; BearingPoint lead the UK's identity/security programmes; Deloitte lead many of the "smart chip" security technologies. Yet, it is not simply that the state outsources or defers its security decisions to private consulting "expertise", but rather that there is a proliferation of *consulting* – a way of thinking, ordering, calculating and acting on the world – and not simply the actions of *consultants* as identifiable agents. In his search for a paradigmatic model of the state of exception, Agamben offers an institution of Roman law: the *iustitium* or suspension of the law. What is interesting for my discussion here is the processes of authorization that are produced within the *iustitium* when a *tumultus* [emergency situation] is decreed. In the Roman Republic, the *consuls* acted as something akin to chief magistrates who convened the Senate, served as generals in military campaigns and appointed or acted as dictator for lengthy periods in times of emergency when the constitution was suspended. As Agamben outlines, "*a senatus consultum ultimum* [final decree of the Senate]" would be enacted to declare an emergency situation, calling upon "the consuls, the tribunes of the people, and even, in extreme cases, all citizens, to take whatever measures they considered necessary for the salvation of the state" (2005: 41).

Within the designation of exception, then, the advice of the consuls would be pivotal to the act of declaring an emergency and, at the same time, the decree itself confers upon the consuls and citizens the authority to take necessary measures. Citizens acquire the right of self-defence by command of the consuls and, indeed, are called to act in their stead, while also assuming proxy responsibility for the self-defence of the state. There is thus no creation of a singular new locus of authority but, rather, "every citizen seems to be invested with a floating and anomalous *imperium* that resists definition within the terms of the normal order" (Agamben 2005: 43). Neither consul nor citizen, acting within the decree, can be said to create, decide or break the law because, in effect, law is annulled. They do, however, act with the force equivalent to law by the authority invested by the sovereign decree. Indeed, in Agamben's reading, "the consuls are reduced to the condition of private citizens, while every private citizen acts as if he were invested with an *imperium*" (2005: 79). The distinction between the public and private spheres of action is broken down, and consuls and citizens are free to act as they see fit: *"videant consules* [let the consuls see to it]" (Agamben 2005: 50).

I should make it clear here that I am not arguing that the management consultants are the modern-day consuls in a contemporary *iustitium*, although "let the consuls see to it" is an increasingly common refrain in the designation of many of today's spaces of exception, from "free zone" offshore production sites to biometric border controls (Amoore 2006). But the roles of the *consuls*, understood as those who authorize and are authorized to designate, do illuminate what I see as significant and worrisome moves within a broader emerging economy of exception. There are three aspects that I will highlight in my discussion of the homeland security enterprise: (1) a declaring of emergency that is amorphous, that circulates and defies ascribed boundaries of state/civil society; public/private; expert/lay; (2) the call to the consuls to "see to it" and take necessary measures to identify dangerous ways of life in order that "our" way of life might be secured; and (3) the apparently unpunishable actions of citizens defending their way of life within the decree.

In effect, the homeland security citizenship project is but one example of the complex array of authorities implicated in designating a state of exception within the war on terror. Rather than appearing as a single sovereign declaration, in this instance, the state consults with "experts" and citizens, takes advice and then confers proxy authority on the "consuls", comprising experts and citizens. In this sense, the homeland security citizen becomes emblematic of the interpenetration of "external" and "internal" security that Didier Bigo describes as the Möbius ribbon, where one does not know "on which face of the strip one is located" (2001: 115). The preface to the Department of Homeland Security's report from the workshops, for example, acknowledges the public and private authorities who "listened to citizens' concerns and provided guidance about approaches and solutions to achieve the safety and freedom that citizens want" (US Department of Homeland Security 2004). It is, however, the report concludes, "the countless citizens across the country" who are the "true authors of this document, and the architects of the changes to come". The true *authors*, then, are precisely those who *author*ize the continued deferral of decision.

Viewing the broadcasts and webcasts of the town hall events, one is struck by the emphasis on vigilance, information sharing, data gathering and communications as the key to the war on terror.[3] The final report concludes that citizens are overwhelmingly in support of the US Patriot Act and willing to sacrifice a degree of privacy and liberty to the cause of enhanced security (ibid 2004: 17). New systems of data sharing, downloadable smart phone emergency numbers and personal safety advice, new biometric identity cards at borders and increased workplace and neighbourhood surveillance: all are flagged as having the support of citizens or, indeed, as being "truly authored" by citizens.

At the same time as the Department of Homeland Security and twelve major multinational corporations are consulting the town hall citizenry, the US government is consulting Accenture, IBM and other companies on how to put private sector methods of surveillance at the service of state security. "Had information coordination technology been properly in place before September 11", reported the findings of one expert panel to a House Subcommittee hearing on technology procurement, "the preattack activities of the hijackers could have been identified and prevented" (cited in Kestelyn 2002). The vision is a system that classifies safe/normal and unsafe/dangerous ways of life based on data mining and risk profiling. It is a "dream", say Mariana Valverde and Michael Mopas, of a "'smart', specific, side-effects free, information-driven utopia of governance" (2004: 239). A closer look at the experts on the homeland security citizenship advisory panels reveals an interesting picture of what is at stake in this dream: business consultants Deloitte, specialists in radio frequency identity (RFID) research, trialled in smart cards at six US–Mexico border crossings and in I-94 visa waiver forms; software giants Microsoft and IBM (now also the world's largest management consultancy), who at the time were part of the "Secure Border Partnership" bidding for Department of Homeland Security contracts; data warehousing companies SAP and EMC, specialists in the storage, management and integration of personal and corporate data; data interfacing multinationals CGI AMS and Ascential; personal computing, digital wireless and mobile phone companies including Hewlett Packard, SBC, Nextel, Motorola and Dell; and biometrics and identity management specialists Oracle.

Global management consultants Accenture, the major sponsor of the workshops, have been named subsequently by the Department of Homeland Security as the prime contractors for US VISIT,[4] a US$10 billion project to introduce "virtual" borders at all US air, land and sea ports of entry. As the Smart Borders Alliance, Accenture's team – which includes Deloitte, Dell and Oracle among others – deploys biometric identifiers, data integration technologies, RFID and other techniques to "assess the security risks of all US-bound travellers and prevent potential threats from reaching US borders" (Accenture Digital Forum 2004: 1). As one consultant put it: "the old systems could really only check the person. Accenture's system will check your associates. It will ask if you have made international phone calls to Afghanistan, taken flying lessons, or purchased 1000 pounds of fertilizer" (cited in

*Business Week* 2001: 1). I will not concern myself here with a lengthy analysis of Smart Borders, although I do so elsewhere (Amoore and de Goede
2005; Amoore 2006). Rather, my concern here is with how these practices
of sorting and profiling the electronic imprints of ways of life are both
designated by, and continually designating, a state of exception. Just as the
US VISIT programme is predicated on using integrated databases across
banking records, airline passenger manifests, health and social security,
criminal records and so on in order to identify patterns of daily life that
deviate from the "norm", so homeland security citizenship encourages
watchfulness for that which transgresses the everyday run of things (Amoore
2007a). Indeed, the very same technologies deployed at the smart border at
the service of governing in a state of exception are proffered as "trusted
partners" in the homeland security household: digital wireless technologies
that enable what is being called a "global neighbourhood watch" (US
Department of Homeland Security 2004: 14).

The spaces of exception emerging within the homeland security project,
then, are complex and highly mobile, ever shifting, circulating and drawing
in new subjects and calling up new subjectivities. As William Connolly
elucidates in his reading of Agamben:

> The sovereign is not simply (as Agamben and Schmitt tend to say) *he*
> (or *she*) who first decides that there is an exception and then decides
> how to resolve it. Sovereign is *that* which decides an exception exists
> and how to decide it, with the that composed of a plurality of forces
> circulating through and under the positional sovereignty of the official
> arbitrating body.
>
> Connolly (2005: 145)

If, for example, we take the US Patriot Act[5] as indicative of a declared state
of exception – as do, it is fair to say, both Judith Butler (2004: xvi) and
Giorgio Agamben (2005: 3),[6] we can re-read it through Connolly's insight
of a plurality of forces within and beneath the sovereign author of the
exception. The Act explicitly opens up the possibilities for multiple authorities to decide the nature and limits of exception, laying out rights of
access to personal data and information, for example, to all agencies charged
with "investigating and identifying aliens".[7] In Connolly's terms, then, the
sovereign authorities of the state of exception extend beyond the initial
authorship of the Act itself. The US Patriot Act actively decentres the
power to designate civil life from bare life, bundling together the categories
of immigrant and terrorist, and annulling laws governing periods of detention and rights to privacy.

Indeed, it is just such diffusion of the power to enact exception that is
expressed in the concerns of civil liberties and privacy organizations and
immigration lawyers. In April 2004, a coalition including the Arab-American
Discrimination Committee, National Immigration Law Center, Electronic

Privacy Information Center (EPIC) and American Civil Liberties Union (ACLU) wrote to the Department of Homeland Security (DHS), expressing concern at "the enormous potential for error and violation of human rights standards".[8] The US Patriot Act provided the legal framework, or perhaps more accurately, the conditions for the suspension of the normal legal framework that established the US VISIT "smart borders" system. Under the Act, Congress fast tracked the biometrics frameworks for US VISIT and extended the powers of the DHS to determine the expertise and authorities required to implement the programme. As one EPIC lawyer put it: "the expansive purpose of 'investigate and identify' in the [Patriot] Act leaves open serious questions as to whether US Visit, a border control system, will be used routinely on the streets of America".[9] Certainly, the architects of the system, Accenture, have the hope that their systems will be used routinely on the streets. During the bid for the government contract, for example, they reputedly "wowed government officials with a demo that included wireless tags that tracked immigrants' whereabouts" (*Business Week* 2004: 74). Interviewed in the business press, Accenture's head of government services, Eric Stange, called for a "cultural change" in the war on terror, an emphasis on the "individual citizen's perceptions and responsibilities" (*CIO Insight* 2004). Thus, although as a declaration of necessary measures in a state of emergency, the Patriot Act may appear to embody the kenomatic space Agamben suggests, in fact it is swiftly colonized by consultants, IT companies, immigration authorities, vehicle licensing agencies, passengers, tourists, workers, citizens and so on and on.

Perhaps there should not be surprise, then, that just as the state of exception is producing new "camps" such as Guantánamo Bay, it is also making homeland security citizens who, as "well intentioned Americans", are willing to "volunteer to help fight the war on terror" (Department of Homeland Security 2004: 11). In this sense, Claudio Minca is correct to assert that "the return of the Camp has been simply metabolized by a significant part of the electorate in the world's most important democracy" (2005: 405). In Minca's reading of Agamben, the zone of indistinction represented by the camp "allows for the decision of what is human and what is not", so that "Guantánamo represents just the most visible and symptomatic expression" of the camp (2005: 405–9). Indeed, the actual tangible spaces of exception represented by Guantánamo or Abu Ghraib are so tightly interwoven with the everyday production of the camp as to be almost inseparable.

Certainly, the Homeland Security workshops did not discuss with citizens the racial profiling that might be implicated in their vigilant watchfulness for the unusual or the out of the ordinary (see Nagel 2002; Edley 2003). Nor do they reveal that the border security they report to be "a top priority of citizens" is, in part, provided by the Titan Corporation, suppliers of interrogators and interpreters to the Abu Ghraib prison in Iraq, and Raytheon, manufacturers of cluster bombs. The visceral violences of Iraq and

Afghanistan, then, are tightly interwoven with the more prosaic prejudices of homeland security practices. "When the alert goes out", writes Judith Butler, "every member of the population is asked to become a 'foot soldier' in the war on terror", observing the behaviour of fellow passengers on a train, new neighbours in town and "anyone who looks vaguely Arab in the dominant racial imaginary" (2004: 39). In the wake of London's July 7 bombings, for example, the Chief Constable of London's transport police called for commuters and tourists to "be vigilant" and for his officers to "target" stop and search on "risky groups" rather than "waste time on white old ladies" (*The Guardian* 2005a).

"Let the consuls see to it", then, serves as a call that potentially authorizes citizens to act without fear of reprisals, and actively blurs the distinction between public and private authority. At the time of writing, the British Metropolitan Police Commissioner Ian Blair has explicitly conveyed the indistinguishability of public and private envisaged in Agamben's *iustitium*: "the police are the public and the public are the police. You and we are one: A new giant has arisen", he argues in the annual Dimbleby lecture (BBC 2005). He contrasts the way of life of the Olympic bid (announced on July 6 – the day before the bombings), which he depicts as an unarmed police force in a diverse and multicultural society, with the new way of life post July 7, where "6th July represents an aspiration" and "7th July represents a fact". As Agamben's *iustitium* invests "every citizen with a floating and anomalous *imperium*" (2005: 43), and the US homeland security project seeks to make the citizen author and architect of the changes to come, so Ian Blair demands "the citizens of Britain now have to articulate what they want" and "it should be you, not me who decides". The implication of this moment of decision is writ large. The state of emergency designated by the London bombings risks the unpunishable killing of *homo sacer*, the indistinguishability of bare life from political life. "I believe", says Blair, "that we can't now have either 7th July or 6th July without risks like that of 22nd July, when officers of my service shot dead an innocent man" (BBC 2005). The speech implicates citizens in the declaring of measures that may risk the killing of *homo sacer* in the name of security.

On July 22, 2005, Brazilian immigrant Jean Charles De Menezes was shot dead on London's Stockwell underground station by police officers and soldiers engaged in anti-terrorist operations. In the aftermath of De Menezes' death, there was a struggle by the authorities to somehow position his life outside of civilized ways of life and in the realm of bare life. Disputes emerged as to whether or not he had legal status in the UK; whether his student visa had expired two years previously; or whether he exhibited suspicious "out of the ordinary" behaviour – was he "wearing a bulky jacket" or "jumping the ticket barrier" (*The Guardian* 2005b). The profiling of such outward appearances of a way of life, if we follow the logic of the homeland security project, becomes essential to the fighting of the war on terror. In his discussion of "accidental citizenship" in the US – "birthright" citizenship that denies full political citizenship – Peter Nyers reveals how discourses of accidental citizenship enable inclusion via exclusion. "Accidental citizenship is nominal (not necessary), ephemeral (not essential), and dangerous (not desirable) ... a potentially catastrophic exception to the norm" (2006: 24). The designation of a category of citizen that is "dangerous to the body politic", then, makes it possible to securitize the suspicious accidental citizen under "exceptional measures", while simultaneously shoring up the "desirable citizen" who is a true "citizen of substance" (ibid 24–6).

We can extend Nyers' insight into the performance of citizenship by accidents of birth to the "accident" of De Menezes death. The economies of exception that work through homeland security citizenship designate migrants such as De Menezes either as non-citizen illegals or as undesirable citizens (another zone of indistinction in which difference scarcely matters). Via the "accident" of his death, the desirable and essential citizen is secured and shored up; indeed, he is called upon to designate the exception. The Metropolitan Police Commissioner leaves us in little doubt as to the intimacy between the killing of *homo sacer* and the safety of our neighbourhoods. "The dreadful death of Mr Menezes is a watershed", he said, a recognition of the exceptional times "after New York, Madrid and London, after Bali, Casablanca, Istanbul, Delhi and Jordan" (BBC 2005). The places are chained together, listed in his speech in such a way that they can be read only together, as the grounds for the "fears for personal and communal safety that are inextricably part of contemporary life" (BBC 2005). This is a state of exception acting on and through people's ways of life, reminding us of our reducibility to bare life, and establishing the boundaries of political life by appealing to a happy but vigilant/fearful public civility.

## Finding space(s) in the state of exception

One of the questions that emerges in thinking through the emergence of modalities of risk that operate on and through "norms" and ways of life is how one might loosen Agamben's tight drawing of the state of exception around the *sovereign state*. "In modernity", writes Agamben, "life is more and more clearly placed at the centre of state politics", so that "all citizens can be said to appear virtually as *homines sacri*". It is this essence of biopolitics – the capacity to determine the limits of the "camp" – that constitutes "the essential structure of sovereign power" (1998: 111). In part, the teasing out of what William Connolly calls Agamben's "tight logic of political culture" (2005: 140) is important because it questions precisely the enclosure of the designation of exception from the circulatory, ambiguous and uncertain nature of its making. As I have argued, we need to be able to think also about the proliferation of new proxy sovereignties that colonize and constitute spaces of exception. Yet, prising open the state of exception and its sovereign logic also has political implications in terms of locating space within spaces of exception. Making the camp a ubiquitous spectre of contemporary life, the ever present manifestation of biopolitics, implies always acting on, through and against ways of life. But, what are these ways of life? Are they knowable, can they be reduced to a calculated and calculable mode of citizenship such as that in the homeland security project? If, following Raymond Williams, the living and experiencing of culture is always mobile, never fixed, always "in part unknown, in part unrealized" (1962: 320), then the making of the camp is more ambivalent and uncertain than the world the *consuls* thought they were inhabiting.

The making of a culture of consulting whereby every citizen is invested with an authority to watch, to report, to decide, powerful though it is, inescapably works with an unstable referent point. When the Department of Homeland Security declares that "*these* are the voices of Americans living on the front line of homeland security", or that "*we* the people are the nation's most important resource in the homeland security enterprise" (2004: 7), can they be sure of the identity of the "we" for whom they speak? How does the invocation of the "we" simultaneously summon, acknowledge and deny a "they" whose story is not told, whose voice is unheard? And in what ways does the declaration of the "we" create a feigned invulnerability to, and disavowed culpability in, the lives of "they"? In Homi Bhabha's terms: "symbolic citizenship is now principally defined by a surveillant culture of 'security' – how do we tell the good migrant from the bad migrant? Which cultures are safe? Which unsafe?" (1994a/2004: xvii).

The project of symbolic citizenship that Bhabha denotes, in its framing of good and evil, civil and uncivil, safe and dangerous, encounters just the kind of plural forces envisaged by Connolly in his critique of Agamben. The possibility of "we the people" against "they" – the terrorists or illegal migrants – writ large in the Patriot Act and in US VISIT, and in the UK policing response to 7/7 – is more thoroughly ambivalent than it may first appear. As Bhabha has it, "the disavowal of the Other always exacerbates the edge of identification, reveals that dangerous place where identity and aggressivity are twinned. For denial is always a retroactive process; a half acknowledgement of that otherness has left its traumatic mark" (1994a/2004: 88). In this uncertainty of identification, for Bhabha, lies the possibility of political subversion. The authorities that declare and designate an exception, understood in these terms, cannot avoid encounter with the borderlands and margins that they partially acknowledge.[10] "The demand of authority", writes Bhabha, "cannot unify its message nor simply identify its subjects" (1994a/2004: 89). The assertion of a unity of homeland security citizens, to return to our example, is extraordinarily dependent on representational practices that identify safe and secure ways of life and subjectivities in relation to suspicious and dangerous ways of life and subjectivities. The spaces of vigilance invoked by the discourses of homeland security citizenship – neighbourhoods, borders (virtual and physical), workplaces, city streets, subways and shopping malls – are peculiarly both the potential spaces of exception and the ghosts that haunt the production of bare life.

Consider, by way of example, Max Stafford-Clark's staging of Robin Soans' play *Talking to Terrorists*. We can read this piece of theatre as, at least in part, capturing Bhabha's sense of ambivalence in the binaries that define symbolic citizenship: citizen/terrorist, homeland/strangeland, civil/uncivil and so on. Soans' script, derived from dialogue with resistance fighters (from the PKK to Al Aqsa and the IRA), peace activists and politicians, conveys the idea that "the difference between terrorists and the rest of us is not that great" (Soans, cited in *The Guardian* 2005c). Told through interwoven oral testimonies, the play juxtaposes, for example, witness accounts of British government-backed torture in Iraq with the experiences of a 13-year-old Ugandan child soldier who has supervised torture. The play powerfully unsettles the categories of "we" and "they", suggesting that the disavowed distancing of the terrorist is a partial acknowledgement of the proximity of "their" practices to "ours". As in Niza Young's use of Bhabha's work to explore Jewish and Palestinian experiences of hatred, *Talking to Terrorists* acknowledges the "split recognition of similarity and difference" that works as a "point of identity for both sides of the relation" (2002: 74). Soans' play, in its presentation of the domestic, household, urban, national and global contexts of terror, powerfully disrupts the settled categories of "same" and "different" that are deployed in the exceptional economy of the homeland security enterprise.

The subjectivities and identities produced within spaces of exception, then, render the outcome of the declared state of emergency far from certain. Although it may be difficult to conceive of resisting the designation of exception *per se*, it is potentially useful to think about how we might (to paraphrase Foucault) resist what it "makes of us" (Foucault: 1983: 216). Thinking for a moment, then, about the making of the identities and subjectivities of watchful security citizens, we might reflect on what Agamben's "floating *imperium*" makes of us, or on what Michael Dillon frames as a new set of security questions. For Dillon, the task begins:

> Not by asking what is dangerous? But by asking what does a representation of danger make of 'us' and those who are not 'us' … Not by asking what are we endangered by? But by asking how does a representation of danger make 'us' what we are? … And finally, not by asking how to secure security? But, by enquiring about what is lost and forgotten, and who or what pays the inevitable price, for the way that 'we' are thus habited in fear?
>
> Dillon (1996: 35)

Dillon does not explicitly intend this to suggest a potential opening of interstitial spaces of dissent; indeed, in later work, there is arguably less space in his framing of biopolitics (2004b). However, the notion that discourses of risk and danger act on and through us and our lives does reveal precisely such gaps in the designation of states of exception. "[I]f biopolitics increasingly penetrates all of our bodies", argues Claudio Minca, "we should not forget that it also needs *our* bodies for its very reproduction, and very often *our consensus*" (2005: 411). Life as politics, and culture as a domain of governing, assumes an identifiable and stable body through which to act. The subjectivity of the homeland security citizen is erupting in very many different ways, few of them predictable or strictly manageable. April 2005, for example, saw hundreds of self-styled "Minutemen", armed and uniformed volunteers/vigilantes "assisting the government in the dangerous task" of policing the Arizona stretch of the US–Mexico border (cited in *The Guardian* 2005d). Although the US government professed not to support the actions of the Minutemen, one does not have to look very far to find the elision of vigilance with vigilantism in the Citizencorps, USAonwatch and the Freedom Corps.[11] The Citizencorps neighbourhood watch programme, for example, summons up a history of American suburban watchfulness, a "critical element in community safety – not through vigilantism, but simply through a willingness to look out for suspicious activity in their neighbourhood". The "aftermath of September 11" has, the Citizencorps tell us, lent "greater significance to watch groups".[12]

The political challenging of these kinds of manifestations of homeland security citizenship, it seems to me, requires us to at least make it possible to think that things could be different, that the work of the homeland projects will never be complete. As Homi Bhabha sees it, what is "politically crucial" is the necessity of thinking beyond "initial categories and initiatory subjects" – whether "homeland" or "citizen" or "enterprise" or "nation" or "the people" – and focusing instead "on those interstitial movements or processes that are produced in the articulation of difference" (1994b: 269). For Bhabha, the interstices that emerge at the frontiers and borderlands of the contemporary world have particular significance. The struggles, negotiations and accommodations of migrants, refugees and minorities, "against the authorities" that would seek to define their identities in particular ways become central to "rethinking collective, communal concepts like homeland, the people, cultural exile, national cultures" (1994b: 270–1). The identification of "homeland", together with what Bhabha calls "the unhomely inhabitants of the contemporary world", abound in current designations of the state of exception. Bhabha gives us the sense, though, that the invocation of homeland cannot avoid engagement with the borderland: with hybrid and shifting experiences of belonging, place and displacement.

To illustrate my point, we can return to the case of the killing of Brazilian migrant Jean Charles De Menezes on London's Stockwell underground station. Although, as I have argued, it is possible to think about De Menezes as one possible figure of *homo sacer*, he who can be killed and yet not sacrificed, his life and death also reveal something of Bhabha's interstices that are produced in the articulation of sameness and difference. Although the authorities and the news media reports were quick to point to difference – a different way of dressing, behaving, a different lifestyle, a different legal status – they also revealed gaps in identification. Hidden in the back-ground details of the news reports was the residue of a life lived at the borderlands, in the liminal spaces between two worlds. De Menezes worked as a contract electrician, fitting fire alarms and security devices. The night before the shooting, he had been helping out a friend, working as a night porter at a hotel in Charing Cross. Rather as Okwe, the Nigerian night porter in Stephen Frears' film *Dirty Pretty Things*, who says "we are the people you do not see. We clean your rooms, drive your cabs" (Frears 2002), De Menezes lived something of culture's "in-between" (Bhabha 1993). Not quite here and not quite there, De Menezes' life and death defy a clear delineation of civilized, safe and secure neighbourhoods from dangerous transgressions of civility. We are reminded, as Judith Butler puts the pro-blem, of the "many ways in which our lives are profoundly implicated in the lives of others" (2004: 7), or the ways in which a "safe" neighbourhood cosmetically covers the risks and dangers of the migrant worker who makes that idea of safety possible. On the one hand, the borderlands have become a key terrain in the war on terror (Zureik and Salter 2005; Sparke 2006). On the other, they are reopened as potential sites of everyday questioning and challenging of the apparent logics of homeland security citizenship. What does the idea of the dangerous border between the homeland and the strangeland make of us and those who are not us?

## Concluding remarks: running with risk

A world of imminent emergency, ever present alarm bells and perpetual crisis has dominated commercial risk imaginaries for a very long time. Just as economist Frank Knight (1921) saw the source of commercial profit in "living with uncertainty", and in the incorporation of uncertainty via entrepreneurial risk practices, so contemporary management thinking also actively "embraces risk" (Baker and Simon 2002). The very business con-sultants we now see dominating the homeland security enterprise also trade profitably in ideas for learning to live with risk: "you have to embrace risk in order to master it and thrive"; "when the future is truly uncertain, pre-diction is downright dangerous" (Anderson Consulting; McKinsey & Co., cited in Amoore 2004). It is precisely this modality of running with risk, making it one's constant companion, that saturates programmes of home-land security citizenship. "While the law wants to prevent and prescribe", writes Agamben, the "physiocrats' security wants to intervene in ongoing processes to direct them" (2002: 2). In the war on terror, risk practices do not seek prevention, but preemption; they do not seek to reduce or limit risk, but to run with it; they are not designed to render safe or secure, but instead to give the appearance of securability.

As the designation of multiple exceptions draws in proxy sovereigns, from consultants to citizens, running with risk implies the deferral of political decisions into expert calculations. As Jenny Edkins has put the problem, "the room for real political change has been displaced by a technology of expertise" (1999: xii). The depoliticizing effects of "letting the experts see to it" (whether "it" is private security, border controls, biometric techniques, community "preparedness" ... ) loom large in the making of the homeland security project. Slavoj Žižek depicts a world of "anonymous experts whose merchandise is sold to us in a brightly coloured liberal–multiculturalist package", where the "depoliticized Real" of expert knowledge pushes the "unconditional demand that things should return to normal" (1998: 61; 2005: 26). The making of homeland security citizenship crucially hinges on the setting of this "normal" against which exceptions to the norm and deviations from the norm can be established. The return to normality that was so celebrated in the aftermath of 9/11 and 7/7 – shopping, taking the bus or subway, the daily commute to work, the quotidian practices of business and leisure – appeals to a singular way of life that represents the normal run of things, and simultaneously forecloses the possibility of other interpretations of the event.

The culture of homeland security that has become so central to the ideas bought and sold by the "experts", however, can never avoid entirely the entanglements and encounters that are Homi Bhabha's "culture's in-between". The story we tell of ourselves (as citizens, the people, a community and so on) and our place in the world (homeland, neighbourhood, city ... ) is always also bound up with the stories of others. It is the "other" way of life, art historian Jonathan Crary tells us, that we are "taught to fear most". Despite the ambivalent presence of violence in American culture, Crary suggests – the high school massacres, the cult mass suicides, the ever present mundanity of urban homicide – the aberrant, the unexplained and the uncertain are only tolerated in "domestic" contexts. There is a "collective inability", as Crary sees it, to directly confront the presence of our "own" secular rage and violence in what we have decided is a "monster from elsewhere" (2004: 428–9).

As Tijuana artist Marcos Ramirez (aka ERRE) illustrates with his artistic interventions at the US–Mexico border, the borderlands "in-between" cultures are agitative and provocative sites that defy the clear drawing of "our" place and "theirs". In the autumn of 1997, as part of the binational InSite border art project, Ramirez constructed a Janus-headed Trojan horse at the San Ysidro section of the border. The dual-faced wooden structure, positioned across the borderline at the checkpoint, insists on the double reading of homeland/homely and strangeland/stranger. "The bi-directionality of its gaze", writes Jo-Anne Berelowitz in her essay on Ramirez, suggests "that the cultures on either side penetrate one another in ways and to degrees that are both evident and not yet known, that this traffic is both a 'gift' and a way of profoundly disturbing the other's social fabric" (2005: 344). Ramirez's horse can be seen not only as a reminder of the hybridity of the actual physical borderlands, but also as a metaphor for the plurality of forces within and between all aspects of the contemporary drawing up of borders between ways of life and bare life: the figure of the Janus-faced horse can be seen at the gates of many current manifestations of Agamben's "camp".

## Notes

1 An early draft of this paper was presented at the International Studies Association workshop "Governing by Risk in the War on Terror", San Diego, March 21, 2006. I thank the participants for their comments and, particularly, Marieke de Goede, Richard Beardsworth and Mark Salter for their suggestions. Sincere thanks to the immigration lawyers and consultants who have given so generously of their time. I acknowledge the financial support of the ESRC (RES155250087), British Academy and the ISA in the preparation of this work and the funding of the workshop of which it was part.

2 The homeland security enterprise defines itself as "all those who have responsibility related to preventing, preparing for, or responding to terrorist attacks, including people from federal, state, and local governments; the private sector; civic organisations; and citizens" (Department of Homeland Security 2004: 7).

3 See the opening town hall event at http://www.fednet.net/ram/ceig/ceig110303.ram (accessed November 2005).

4 United States Visitor and Immigrant Status Indicator Technology.

5 The contrived acronym for Uniting and Strengthening America by Providing Appropriate Tools Required to Intercept and Obstruct Terrorism, hastily signed into law on October 26, 2001.

6 For Butler, the Patriot Act "constitutes another effort to suspend civil liberties in the name of security" (2004: xvi). For Agamben, it signalled the Attorney General's power to detain "any alien suspected of activities that endangered the national security of the United States" (2005: 3). See also Ericson, this volume.

7 For a full text version of the US Patriot Act, see http://www.epic.org/privacy/terrorism/hr3162.htm

8 For the full text of the letter, see http://www.epic.org/privacy/usvisit/redress_letter.pdf

9 Interviews conducted at EPIC, Washington, DC, November 9, 2004.

10 Rita Raley's "Wanted" road signs, discussed in this volume, explore just such an ambivalence in the disavowal and acknowledgement of people at the edge. The migrants at the US–Mexico border are simultaneously "wanted" by the US economy and "wanted"/hunted down by the homeland security enterprise.

11 See http://www.citizencorps.gov; www.usaonwatch.org and http://www.freedomcorps.gov

12 See http://www.citizencorps.gov/programs/watch.shtm

Part III

# Biopolitics, biometrics, borders

# 7 Fast capitalism/slow terror

## Cushy cosmopolitanism and its extraordinary others

*Matthew Sparke*

"Cross often?" asks the Canadian Border Services Agency website: "Make it simple, use NEXUS." It almost sounds like an advert from an online travel agency, and the very name of the Canadian government's new border management agency would likewise seem to signal a revisioning of travelers as customers consuming services. But the invitation here to "Make it simple, use NEXUS" is nevertheless an invitation to enroll in a government program, and the agency that runs the program – notwithstanding its titular tilt towards "Border Services" – remains a governmental institution charged with managing Canada's borders by administering over ninety different Canadian laws. The NEXUS program, which is designed to reduce delays for pre-cleared frequent travelers across the US–Canadian border, is not a particularly significant program in and of itself (by the summer of 2005, it only had about 45,000 enrollees).[1] It builds on a number of prior programs designed to expedite border crossing between Canada and the US, and it will no doubt be revised and replaced in its own turn. However, it is a revealing example of contemporary border developments because of the way it has been jointly developed by Canada and the US in line with a so-called Smart Border Declaration made by the two countries on December 12, 2001 in the immediate aftermath of 9/11.

In this chapter, I will explore how, as an illustration of Smart Border management practice, the development of NEXUS and related programs also reveals a great deal about the changing meanings of citizenship in contemporary North America. Following many other political geographers (e.g., Paasi 1996; Newman and Paasi 1998; Van Houtum and Van Naerssen 2002; Fall 2005; Hyndman 2005), the premise in this respect is that borders are consequential condensation points where wider changes in statemaking and the nature of citizenship are worked out on the ground.

What makes NEXUS an especially worthwhile focus for analysis is the way in which its development as a border management program has taken shape as a technological fix mediating two extremely significant and contradictory sets of contemporary social forces in North America (cf. Larner, this volume). On the one side are the economic forces that continue to generate pressures for liberalized cross-border business movement in the context of the North American Free Trade Agreement (NAFTA). On the other side are the political and cultural forces that are leading to heightened border surveillance and more militarized border enforcement in the context of the US "war on terror," cultural and political forces that are also based on more longstanding raciological and class preoccupations with restricting access for non-white non-professionals. While the agents of the economic imperatives employ a geo-economic rhetoric of economic facilitation and urge border softening measures, the advocates of intensified border policing make a geopolitical case for a harder border that combines an older, often ethnically exclusivist, xenophobia with the post-9/11 security script of fighting terror and (at least in the US) defending "homeland security." Clearly, the borderlands between these contradictory social forces are fraught with tension, and yet the promoters of NEXUS see it as a high-tech bridge that can span the tensions and facilitate economic development while improving homeland security. The questions that I would therefore like to pose in what follows are: Who is being developed and secured by this bridging exercise? What kinds of people are they? What new forms of citizenship might they be argued to embody? And, lastly, what new forms of sub-citizenship and subordination are emerging as the underside of expedited border crossing privilege? Answering such questions, I want to suggest, should take us much further than a narrow focus on the national credentials required by the US and Canadian authorities administering programs such as NEXUS. It also requires us to move beyond the anachronistic methodological nationalism of arguments that posit the protection of propertied citizens and the defense of national borders as two defining features of liberal state-making. The deeper and more complexly inter-scalar issues raised by the intersection of homeland securitization and economic facilitation at the border concern the transformation of citizenship on a continent shaped by a notably *neo*liberal nexus of *securitized nationalism* and *free market transnationalism*.

By securitized nationalism, I am referring to the cultural–political forces that lead to the imagining, surveillance and policing of the nation-state in especially exclusionary but economically discerning ways. The increasingly market-mediated methods of such securitization often involve commercial risk management and "dataveillance" strategies but, with securitized nationalism, they are combined with longstanding nationalistic traditions of imagining the homeland, encoding bodies, and – in David Campbell's (1998) terms – "writing security" through identity-based exclusions of people deemed to be untrustworthy aliens. By free market transnationalism, in contrast, I am referring to distinctively incorporative economic imperatives that involve increasing transnational capitalist interdependencies and the associated entrenchment of transnational capitalist mobility rights through various forms of free market re-regulation. Such a regime of free market transnationalism may well be considered by many readers to be a rough synonym for neoliberalism. But here I am proposing a more conjunctural approach to theorizing neoliberalism as a contextually contingent *articulation* of free market governmental practices *with* varied and often quite illiberal forms of social and political rule (see also Sparke 2004a, 2006a). This context-contingent definition of neoliberalism should not be taken to imply that it is a form of rule that is all inclusive or simply continuous with the long history and heterogeneity of capitalism itself. The "neo" does mark something discrete and new historically, including, not least of all, the transnationalism of today's liberalized market regimes. While neoliberalism certainly represents a revival of classical nineteenth-century free market liberalism, it is also clearly a new kind of capitalist liberalization that is distinct insofar as it has been imagined and implemented *after* and *in opposition to* the state-regulated national economies of the twentieth century. It is because such imagination and implementation has been worked out in different ways in different places that neoliberalism needs to be examined conjuncturally.

A conjunctural approach, it needs underlining, does not foreclose the possibility of making more general claims about neoliberalism and its reterritorialization of social and political life. Thus, while explaining the emergence and significance of the NEXUS program as a context-contingent response to the contradictory imperatives of national securitization and economic facilitation, the article still makes a claim that the program exemplifies broader changes to citizenship – most notably, new transnational mobility rights for some and new exclusions for others – under a combination of macroscale neoliberal governance and microscale neoliberal governmentality. In order to clarify this argument, I begin by explaining what I mean by neoliberal governance and governmentality and why border management can be viewed as a useful window on to the neoliberal remaking of citizenship. Subsequently, I will chart the contradictory story of the development of the NEXUS program and consider the ways in which it exemplifies both the inclusions and the exclusions of neoliberal citizenship.

## Neoliberalism and citizenship

Neoliberalism as a regime of *governance* is easy enough to describe in the abstract. Ideologically, it is organized around the twin ideas of liberalizing the capitalist market from state control and refashioning state practices in the idealized image of the free market. At the macroscale of government policy, these ideas have inspired and informed the promotion and entrenchment of the now familiar neoliberal approach to governance that includes free trade, privatization, financial deregulation, monetarism, fiscal austerity, welfare reform, and the punitive policing of the poor. At the level of the more micropractices that Foucault's followers have called *governmentality* (see Burchell, Gordon and Miller 1991), neoliberalism is also commonly associated with the remaking of state regulation through the market-based mentalities and techniques associated with audits, performance assessments, benchmarking, risk ratings, and, at a still more personal level, the educational and cultural cultivation of a new kind of self-promoting and self-policing entrepreneurial individualism. Whether macro or micro, all these innovations in governmental policy and practice represent transformed patterns of state-making and rule. Even in the abstract, therefore, it is clear that, despite the common sense cant about "deregulation" in neoliberal rhetoric, neoliberalism leads in practice to *re*-regulation. However, when such context-contingent neoliberal re-regulations are examined in detail, the contradictions and resulting theoretical complications expand exponentially (Sparke 2006a).

As I have argued elsewhere (Sparke 2006b), a combination of abilities and attitudes associated with transnational corporate mobility underpins what I describe as the transnational rescaling of civil citizenship. Through a whole set of governmental practices – from the formal and most obvious acts of remaking national law in accordance with transnational trade law (Wallach and Woodall 2004) to the most informal and often unnoticed developments in education and popular culture (Hillis, Petit and Cravey 2001; Roberts 2004) – we are witnessing an emergence, albeit an extremely uneven emergence, of a new kind of transnationally envisioned, transnationally protected and transnationally mobile citizen-subject. However, the big challenge for scholars – not to mention for transnational business class entrepreneurs themselves – involves coming to terms with how such transnational trans-formations of citizenship are worked out on the ground in the context of all sorts of countervailing imperatives, including not least of all the sorts of intensified border securitization we have seen in North America in the after-math of 9/11.

Taking my cue from Foucault's own work on the so-called biopolitical production of self-governing citizen-subjects in modern prisons, clinics, classrooms, and so on, my suggestion in what follows is that we can usefully examine the context-contingent transnationalization of civil citizenship – including how it is shaped by countervailing nationalistic forces – by focusing on the particular spaces of border management technologies. The jargon of biopolitics is useful in this respect because it points to what the recoding of citizenship through border discipline can tell us about the assumptions, attitudes, and abilities associated with the more general neo-liberal refashioning of civil citizenship. Biopolitics for Foucault included both discourses about the self-governing subject *and* the actual production of self-governed life within particular modern spaces. Some of the govern-mentality literature that supposedly follows in his footsteps has not always addressed both these aspects of biopolitics. Nikolas Rose's depiction of "advanced liberalism," for example, offers such an abstract discursive account of the self-government of the entrepreneurial subject that the nitty-gritty activities of biopolitical production under neoliberalism disappear from view. Partly, this is because he associates neoliberalism more with ideology than with government practices, and partly this appears to be because he wants to avoid an epochal account of historical transition from an age of liberalism to an age of neoliberalism. However, his disembodied account is also ironically indicative of a structuralism that he disavows. Thus, as Wendy Larner cautions, "without analyses of the 'messy actualities' of particular neo-liberal projects, those working within this analytic run the risk of precisely the problem they wish to avoid – that of producing generalized accounts of historical epochs" (Larner 2000: 14). Here, therefore, I want to explore the messy actualities of the development of the NEXUS lane as a way of examining in a more grounded way the convolutions, contradictions, and countervailing forces surrounding the neoliberalization of citizenship in contemporary North America. In underlining the reterritorialization of the resulting civil citizenship and by therefore highlighting how the "new normal" – as Davina Bhandar (2004) calls it – of this neoliberalized citizenship is distinctively transnational in scope, I also want to point toward the parallel transnationalization of the new abnormal. As a result, I complement and conclude this study by exploring how NAFTA region neoliberalization also entails new forms of exceptionalism: new exclusionary exceptions from citizenship that are based upon older raciological imaginations of nation, but which work through new techniques of expedited and transnationalized alienation that expel so-called "aliens" as quickly as business travelers can now buy fast passage across the NAFTA region's internal borders.

## The NEXUS of neoliberalization (and its others)

### From economic integration to expedited crossing lanes

In order to understand the rocky road from NAFTA to NEXUS, it is important to stress from the start that the difficulties for business promoters of border softening, did not simply begin in 2001 after 9/11. Some of their problems actually related to other neoliberal reforms in Washington, DC. And yet others represented a relay of NAFTA's very own transnational state-making, including in particular the way in which the agreement connected Canada–US border management practices with developments on the Mexico–US border (see Gilbert 2007). At the very same time as they were issuing their appeals for border bulldozing, therefore, the business visionaries of post-national citizenship were already approaching roadblocks. The intensified border control measures that followed 9/11 obviously added to these challenges. But, as we shall now see, neoliberal contradictions were already complicating the glocalized neoliberal visions of fast cross-border movement and free trade led cross-border development.

One of the expedited crossing programs in which West Coast business visionaries placed much pride and hope in the early 1990s was called the PACE lane. The acronym initially stood for Peace Arch Crossing Entry, a reference to the crossing on the Pacific coast between the US state of Washington and the Canadian province of British Columbia. Subsequently, other PACE lanes were developed at a number of other sites along the US–Canada border, all of them underpinned by the basic idea of expediting the transit of frequent travelers across the border and thereby picking up the pace, as it were, of cross-border travel for local business. The way in which the PACE and CANPASS lanes worked was quite simple. Applicants were screened, and then, if they passed, they were issued with a decal for their car that showed they were entitled to drive in the PACE lane when they came to the US border or the CANPASS lane when they came to the Canadian border. Being reserved only for pre-cleared travelers with the designated decals, these dedicated commuter lanes had much shorter wait times than other lanes, and the likelihood of a long verbal interrogation by the border guard was also considerably reduced. Thus, as long as applicants were American or Canadian citizens, and as long as they were prepared to pay the relatively small fee to purchase fast lane memberships, the application process was not especially burdensome. It was precisely this model that so excited the business visionaries as something that "should be more widely promoted and expanded, eventually leading to even more open borders between the United States and Canada" (Schell and Hamer 1995: 148).

As a technique of border management, the PACE and CANPASS lanes encoded a division already long used by border agents to distinguish between, on the one hand, supposedly safe travelers deemed fit for high-speed "primary" processing and, on the other hand, questionable travelers made subject to the slower ordeals of "secondary" processing. The dedicated commuter lanes simply gave "primary" travelers who crossed the border frequently the chance to buy the additional flexibility they needed to cross the border fast, all the while guaranteeing them a certain degree of protection from the likelihood of being trapped by delays or erroneous assignments to "secondary." In a sense, then, the programs merely stripped away the superficial sense of equality that used to emerge from the common experience shared by primary and secondary populations alike of waiting in line to be interviewed at the checkpoints. Like the SUV citizenship that Mitchell (2005) finds in the atomized-cum-cocooned citizenship ideals running through recent US court decisions, PACE and CANPASS citizenship would seem in this sense to have embodied – or, more precisely, encoded on to the bodies of primary travelers – the private mobility rights so cherished by neoliberal visionaries. With rarely a line-up at all in the PACE and CANPASS lanes, those who signed up as members could follow the equivalent of a red carpet up to the border and proceed onwards with almost as little trouble as crossing a line between two provinces or two states. This was a form of flexibility much appreciated by local business groups and, as such, it seemed for a short period to bear out Aiwha Ong's characterization of a flexible citizenship based on "the cultural logics of capitalist accumulation, travel, and displacement that induce subjects to respond fluidly and opportunistically to changing political–economic conditions" (Ong 1999: 6). But this flexibility was not to last.

*Neoliberal ideals versus neoliberal and nationalist practices*

In 1996 in Washington, DC, the US Congress passed the Immigrant Responsibility and Illegal Immigration Reform Act (IRIIRA). Leading Republicans such as then House Leader Newt Gingrich boasted that the legislation made good on a key immigration control pledge of the 1994 "Contract with America" and, in many ways, it did. Like "The Contract" with its neoliberal emphases on personal responsibility and government accountability, the 1996 IRIIRA combined a traditionally conservative restrictionist approach to immigration with a radically individualizing contractualism. Just like the contractualism that Sanford Schram has traced from "The Contract" into the atomization of citizenship enacted in the 1996 welfare reform act (Schram 2000), the contractualism of IRIIRA represented a notably neoliberal roll-back of social and political citizenship rights. Counterintuitively, however, it also was this very same neoliberal contractualism with its repeated emphasis on personal responsibility and individual accountability that was ultimately to create so many difficulties for the neoliberal promoters of expedited border crossing. IRIIRA had actually been intended to facilitate cross-border business flows while interdicting illegitimate flows, and the aim was to implement this double-pronged strategy using high-technology applications at the border. But when combined with the legislation's underlying embrace of individualizing contractualism, the implications of the act for programs such as PACE and CANPASS seemed nothing short of disastrous. "It's more than a slap in the face," one cross-border business booster told a reporter. "It would bring business between Canada and the United States to a grinding halt" (Pynn 1997). The reason why was that Section 110 of IRIIRA had massively overextended the neoliberal idea of personal accountability without fully acknowledging its practical consequences. Based on the fact that most unauthorized immigration into the US begins with visa overstays, Section 110 had sought to implement an automated entry and exit recording system for all "aliens" including, although some house members did not seem to realize this when they voted for the act, both Canadians and Mexicans (see Wilhelm 1997). The Immigration and Naturalization Service (INS) was mandated by IRIIRA to put this system quickly into place, thereby immediately obliging all Canadians and all Mexicans entering *and* exiting the US to file the necessary information so that by matching up entry and exit data officials could start tracking overstays. When the huge delays this system would create on US borders became clear to officials, when it became obvious that such delays would create lines stretching back so far that it would not even be possible to *access* PACE and CANPASS lanes, and when it was also noticed that Congress had mandated the whole of the Section 110 system without providing for any additional funding, the business community went into uproar and immediately began to lobby for change, creating a group called Americans For Better Borders (Cohn 1999). Joining the business lobbying against Section 110, the Canadian government went into a high-gear effort to have Canadians exempted from the system. To this, the Mexican government – now a NAFTA signatory like Canada – added its own criticisms of Section 110, arguing in a way that was to become significant for subsequent rounds of re-regulation that one NAFTA signatory should not be treated any differently from another. As a result of all these lobbying efforts across the length and breadth of the whole NAFTA region, it was not long before legislative amendment ensued. Section 110 was first put on hold, and then finally, in the early summer of 2000, it was effectively annulled. However, just as PACE lane promoters were celebrating their victory over Section 110, federal action struck again. Initially, it was just new neoliberal budget cuts affecting PACE lane funding that had to be dodged, but then came the terrorist attacks, the intense ensuing governmental interest in homeland security, and among other militarized responses, the deployment of over 1,600 US military personnel to border control duties.

The instant results of the militarization of border security after 9/11 were monumental cross-border traffic delays. Border control agents implemented Level 1 Code Red anti-terrorism operations that involved inspecting individually all private vehicles, trucks, and buses. Overnight, there were sixteen-hour wait times being reported on the major crossings from Canada into Michigan and New York, and elsewhere on the US–Mexico border nine-hour delays were common (quoted in Flynn 2003: 115; and dePalma 2001). It was also not long before the economic impacts of these delays began to be felt in border regions. In Washington State border areas, businesses complained that they were facing "an economic disaster" (Stark 2001). And on the Ontario–Michigan border between Detroit and Windsor, the economic consequences of the delays were still more significant because of the "just-in-time" production systems run by the auto companies moving parts and vehicles across the border. Stephen Flynn, one of the leading Republican policy specialists on border issues, notes that, in this respect, the economic impacts were immediate and immense:

> By September 13, Daimler Chrysler announced they would have to close an assembly plant ... because their supplies were stuck on the north side of the border. On September 14, Ford announced they would have to close five plants the following week.
>
> Flynn (2003: 115)

Flynn himself depicts such economic costs of border hardening as intolerable, and, as we shall see, he has therefore allied his influential voice with others who have called for technological solutions such as NEXUS that can supposedly bridge the demands of transnational economic integration and national homeland security. Yet, while these voices are now in the ascendancy, back in the immediate aftermath of 9/11, it was the border control restrictionists who held sway. The conservative Congressional Immigration Reform Caucus declared that: "The time is right to call for troops on the border in order to protect our national security interests" (quoted in Ackelson 2005: 177). And, as Jason Ackleson describes in more detail, numerous federal politicians joined the call for stronger border enforcement, arguing like Tom Tancredo, a Republican from Colorado, that: "The defense of the nation begins with the defense of its borders" (quoted in Ackelson 2005: 177). As a result of this congressional preoccupation with defending "homeland security," new immigration and border control measures were passed as part of both the Patriot Act and the Enhanced Border Security Act, and, among their many other impacts, these new laws officially ended low-tech fast lanes such as PACE. Meanwhile, anti-immigration think-tanks such as the Center for Immigration Studies (CIS) had a field day, claiming that the terrorist attacks vindicated their long-held suspicions about both foreigners and the business boosters of a "borderless world" (Center for Immigration Studies 2005).

Insofar as anti-immigration groups found vindication in the new preoccupations with homeland security, their arguments should also remind us that the border securitization initiatives that followed in the wake of 9/11 did not spring out of thin air. As Matt Coleman usefully underlines, they grew out of longstanding links between anti-immigration discourse and associated border control measures. "[T]he PATRIOT Act and the Enhanced Border Security Act," he explains thus, "built on already well-established grounds for immigration inadmissibility and previously legislated policing solutions." Tracing these established practices back to the 1986 Immigration and Reform Control Act (which increased funding for detention facilities, surveillance equipment, fencing, and roads), the 1994 Violent Crime Control and Law Enforcement Act (which provided money for a "criminal alien" tracking center and expedited removal for aliens convicted of felonies), as well as to IRIIRA, Coleman makes a compelling case that the Patriot Act and Enhanced Border Security Act were therefore "part of a long-standing geopolitical frontier regime rooted in congressional immigration law" (Coleman 2005: 194). This same geopolitical frontier regime was in turn also clearly buttressed after 9/11 by the wider burgeoning discourse on "homeland security." Following the critically questioning approach of intellectual historian Amy Kaplan, we might therefore further ask: "Does the word *homeland* itself do some of the cultural work of securing national borders?" (Kaplan 2003: 85). Answering her own question in the affirmative, Kaplan clearly suggests that it does: "[T]he meaning of *homeland*," she says, "has an exclusionary effect that underwrites a resurgent nativism and anti-immigrant sentiment and policy" (Kaplan 2003: 87).

Yet, while the geopolitics of border securitization built on longstanding legislation and the resurgence of anti-immigrant nativism, there was also something novel, indeed something neoliberal, about the ways in which "homeland security" discourse became translated into biopolitical practice at the border. As Coleman himself suggests, there was a notable geo-economic influence on this translation exercise, and, following a definition of geo-economics I have developed elsewhere (Sparke 2002; 2005), I would also argue thus that a whole set of geo-economic preoccupations – including a subordination of frontiers and place to spatial metaphors fetishizing networks and space – informed the redevelopment of border management practices that ensued. It was true, programs such as the PACE lane were no longer considered acceptable (Olson 2001). However, the basic idea of using computer-based systems to separate pre-cleared "primary" travelers from more suspect "secondary" travelers remained the starting point for the new "smart border" management technologies. Such systems, it was effectively argued, could provide a solution to the competing geopolitical and geo-economic concerns: delivering economic liberty and homeland security with a high-tech fix. Moreover, unlike 1996, when there were no federal monies made available for implementing the automated entry–exit data tracking system envisioned in Section 110 of IIRIRA, now there was almost no limit to the amount of funding the federal government was prepared to invest. Thus, when the Canadian and Mexican governments and the US border business communities began their inevitable complaints about the restrictionist border control regime put in place after 9/11, both the funding for a high-tech border management solution and the rationale for a free trade facilitative approach were already in place.

## Homeland security and economic security

In addition to an open public purse, the main reason why significant new investments in high-tech border management were quickly proposed was that the massive scale of the NAFTA-based economic interdependencies made the economic costs of slowing cross-border traffic both huge and obvious. These costs forced even conservative "homeland security"-minded politicians and commentators to turn from geopolitical angst about border insecurity to geo-economic worries about damage to the networks beyond the borders. Flynn, for example, described the likely economic impact with typical geo-economic metaphors about the vulnerability of commercial networks. "[H]owever compelling the homeland security imperative may be," he said, "it should not mean a derailment of the continental engine of free trade and travel. U.S. prosperity – and much of its power – relies on its ready access to North American and global networks of transport, energy, information, finance, and labor. It is self-defeating for the United States to embrace security measures that isolate it from those networks" (Flynn 2003: 111).

In statements such as these, a geo-economic argument about America's economic interdependencies effectively came to trump geopolitical imaginations of homeland fortification. An isolationist border-hardening approach to security was thus made to seem like a backward, pre-network-world strategy. Not surprisingly, therefore, border region politicians, both Democrats and

Republicans alike, turned repeatedly to similar geo-economic scripts as they sought to address the perils of border hardening. They did so cautiously, being careful not to offend the geopolitical sensibilities of those with more fortification fancies about homeland security. But, at the same time, they nevertheless demanded geo-economic security too.

In the subsequent period, the dualistic call for a combination of homeland security and economic liberty multiplied across US political speech, quickly metamorphosing into a new governmental discourse on the so-called Smart Border of the Future. By December 12th, 2001, the Canadian government had also found common cause in the same combinatory rhetoric, developing the "Smart Border Declaration" in concert with the offices of the new US Homeland Security chief, Tom Ridge. In the declaration, the two governments committed themselves to "collaborate in identifying and addressing security risks while efficiently and effectively expediting the legitimate flow of people and goods across the Canada–U.S. border" (Smart Border Declaration 2001). John Manley, the Canadian Minister of Foreign Affairs, made clear that, from his perspective, security and efficiency would thereby somehow become one. "We have agreed to an aggressive action plan that will allow the safest, most efficient passage of people and goods between our two countries, as part of our ongoing commitment to the creation of a Smart Border." Emphasizing the technological sophistication of the new plans, Manley went on, "[t]his action plan will enhance the technology, coordination and information sharing that are essential to safeguard our mutual security and strengthen cross-border commerce for the world's largest binational trading relationship" (Smart Border Declaration 2001: 1). Tom Ridge echoed the exact same mantra of combining efficiency and security with his own supporting comments on the declaration. "On behalf of President Bush," he said, "I was pleased to visit Canada to meet with Minister Manley and senior Canadian officials to discuss how to build a smart and secure border that allows the free flow of people and goods between our two countries. We look forward to working together to achieve real time real solutions as quickly as possible" (Smart Border Declaration 2001: 1). Soon thereafter, the White House made a press release on January 25th, 2002, that further explained what the resulting "Smart Border of the Future" was actually supposed to look like from the perspective of the administration. It would be, said the press release, "a border management system that keeps pace with expanding trade while protecting the United States and its territories from the threats of terrorist attack, illegal migration, illegal drugs, and other contraband" (Office of the President of the United States 2002a,b). It was precisely this high-tech smart border fix to the contradictions of economy and security that Congress proceeded to turn into funded legislation in the form of the Enhanced Border Security and Visa Entry Reform Act (EBSVRA) of 2002. When President Bush signed this act into law, he therefore again not surprisingly emphasized its double purpose with the by now familiar dualistic discourse. "I'm honored today," he said, "to sign a bill that is an important step in an effort to secure our border, while promoting trade and commerce" (Bush 2002a).

The idea of bolstering both the economy and security at the same time was clearly becoming more than just a predictable political script. It certainly was and remains a script that we can examine in terms of the intersection of geopolitics and geo-economics. But, more than this, with the implementation of EBSVRA and the establishment later in 2002 of the new Department of Homeland Security (DHS), it also became a complex suite of governmental practices. NEXUS is just one of these smart border practices, and there are many others including FAST (free and secure trade) for cross-border freight traffic, as well as the ambitious overarching entry and exit program known as US VISIT (United States Visitor and Immigrant Status Indicator) (cf. Epstein, this volume). Before we turn to the specifics of NEXUS itself, it is worth noting that, in addition to signaling the neoliberal recoding of citizenship at the border, the development of all of these programs has itself been fundamentally organized by a neoliberal embrace of private sector initiatives and services. The annual homeland security conference, for example, has become a huge corporate lobbying effort in which companies compete to win profitable government contracts. Private firms have been invited to offer bids on developing much of the technology to be used in the programs (see also Lyon 2003: 84; *Equity International* 2005). Most notably, Accenture won and retained a US$10 billion DHS contract to set up US VISIT's biometric system despite congressional complaints that a transnational corporation that is headquartered in Bermuda for tax purposes should not be a recipient of US national tax revenues (see Accenture 2004; Bowe 2004; Wired 2004; see also Amoore, this volume).

*The Economist* magazine has raised concerns for its business class readers about the tremendous bureaucratic hurdles (and possible delays for business class travelers) attending the introduction of the US VISIT program plans for biometric and RFID-based passports (*The Economist* 2005). However, in this context, the simplicity of the NEXUS expedited crossing program has been seen as a much more promising development in smart border technology. Visiting the NEXUS enrollment center on July 1, 2002, Representative Larsen explained thus that "NEXUS is going to help us insure a more secure border while insuring trade and tourism can continue" (Olson 2002). And likewise, standing in front of the world's busiest commercial crossing, the Ambassador Bridge between Windsor and Detroit, President Bush declared that NEXUS – combined with the parallel pre-clearance program for goods – offered a way to enhance business and security at the same time. "With these two initiatives," he said, "we'll ensure faster movement of legal, low-risk goods, and faster travel for people crossing our borders, and we'll be able to better enhance security. Our inspectors will spend less time inspecting law-abiding citizens and more time inspecting those who intend to harm us" (quoted in Flynn 2003: 122). These grand promises obviously raise in turn the question of how NEXUS actually works now it has been implemented.

### *Cushy Cosmopolitanism ?*

Like the PACE and CANPASS systems, and yet joined together as a bureaucratic bridge between Canadian and United States governmental functions, NEXUS basically allows for the former fast track border crossing experience with little of the normal customs and immigration questioning. It is also based on pre-clearance but, unlike the prior systems, it operates on the basis of photo-ID and biometric "proximity cards." NEXUS members crossing into the United States on the dedicated lane carry the card in their car and, as they approach the border, it relays all their enrollment data – including finger prints, photo ID, name, date of birth, and so on – to an antenna and from there to a border guard's computer screen. As President Bush's comments suggested, NEXUS therefore also illustrates the ways in which the dual track, "primary" and "secondary" partitioning of cross-border traffic lives on after the PACE lane. As such, it persists not just in terms of the dualistic smart border discourse, but also very practically in the new hardware of border checkpoint policing. Pre-cleared NEXUS participants are thus able to access a fast lane across the border for a fee (a relatively small fee at the time of writing of US$50).

There is also a NEXUS AIR lane being implemented now in Canadian airports with flights into the US. This program similarly allows pre-screened, low-risk travelers to be processed with little or no delay but adds a further biometric technology by using iris scans. As Vancouver International Airport explains on its own website, the goal of the program is just like the road border NEXUS lane, namely to expedite the border crossing experience for the fee-paying, pre-cleared clients. "Members of the NEXUS program," it underlines,

> bypass border line-ups by simply inserting a membership card in designated automated kiosks with touch screens to answer questions similar to those an inspection officer would ask. A camera on the kiosk takes a harmless snapshot of the user's iris (colored part of the eye) to verify identity. Members also have access to the priority lane at YVR's pre-board screening checkpoints, giving them expedited access to the security screening process for domestic or international departures.
>
> YVR (2005)

Such commercial-sounding advertisements for the fast track crossings point in turn to the imagined audience of the NEXUS lane hype. Just as with the "Make it simple, use NEXUS" appeal, the working assumption of the program's promoters would seem to be that the most likely enrollees in NEXUS are business-class travelers who cross the border frequently and who want as much expedited access and fast track screening as possible. Certainly business-oriented writers tend to applaud the program (e.g., Condon and Sinha 2003), and an article on NEXUS published in the Canadian *Vancouver Sun* (and reprinted significantly on the website of the Vancouver Board of Trade) provides further confirmation of the business clientele. "A regular commuter like Jim Pettinger, a Richmond man with a business in Bellingham, is looking forward to getting his NEXUS card," noted the reporter. He quotes Pettinger as saying: "Right now I have to allow an hour to get from my door to my office. When I had a PACE card, my commute time was 40 minutes" (Ward 2002). Later in the same article, we hear from another apparently typical NEXUS citizen Rick Turner, president of International Aviation Terminals, who told the reporter that he looked forward to quick implementation of the NEXUS system. "'The lack of a fast-lane system has made travel between the Lower Mainland and Washington state quite inconvenient, time consuming and costly,' he said" (Ward 2002). These examples of NEXUS lane applicants are telling enough, but a still more illustrative popular culture example of what life in the expedited crossing lane might be like comes from the online journal *Mobile Enterprise Magazine*. Entitled "Life in the Fast Lane," the article hymns the potential of the mobile RFID devices used in the NEXUS lane, all the while fleshing out an image of the sort of entrepreneurial subject who might enroll.

> Next time you're sitting in your car waiting in line to cross the U.S.– Canadian border, take a look around you. While you're fiddling with your radio dials, leafing through a magazine or playing with your PDA, cars in the NEXUS lane next to you likely are proceeding rapidly across the border and on to their business. Become a member of the NEXUS program, and you too could find yourself in the fast lane. … "We have thousands of low-risk travelers who cross the border frequently," says Tom Campbell, NEXUS program manager for the new U.S. Department of Homeland Security. "We know them. They know us." … The result is a system that is of benefit to both border inspectors and NEXUS participants. Because the fast lane is where you want to be.
>
> Moss (2005)

This exuberant account captures some of the more ambient cultural assumptions about NEXUS enrollees. The DHS knows them, and they apparently know the DHS. They are people who proceed rapidly across the border and on to their business. They are not a security threat. And they are in the fast lane because, as the author avers, the fast lane is where you want to be.

The banality of the assertion about life in the fast lane is hardly surprising given that Moss' account is presented on a commercial webpage designed to appeal to entrepreneurs invested in mobile wireless technology. But nonetheless, it provides a picture of NEXUS lane participants as desirous and self-motivated embodiments of business mobility. Here, I think we come face to face with Foucault's entrepreneurial neoliberal subject: the *homo economicus*, who is "not just an enterprise, but the entrepreneur of himself or herself." Whether it is the car driver with a RFID device reporting personal biometric data to a border agent, or whether it is the airline passenger submitting to an iris scan, there is clearly an element of self-policing and self-coding involved in winning access to the fast lane. As self-managing subjects of the systems, enrollees would seem in this sense to turn themselves into what Emily Martin (1994) calls "flexible bodies" in order to win the flexible citizenship, a form of citizenship, then, that could also be theorized after Martin as a form of economically engineered immunity from delay at the border. What is additionally notable about the way the NEXUS enrollees make entrepreneurs of themselves is that they do so in order to secure the specific flexibility of expedited *transnational* mobility, to share, in other words, the same fast border crossing mobility as the commodities their businesses produce. In gaining this fast transnational mobility, they become something a little distinct from the traditional liberal subjects who self-discipline simply as citizens of territorialized nation-states. They may still carry national passports, but what enables them to transcend territory quickly is their pre-clearance as NEXUS subjects: citizens of nation-states, yes, but with an all-important new kind of transnational para-citizenship in a fast lane designed for business-class frequent travelers.

It would be a mistake to exaggerate the transnationalism of NEXUS lane enrollees. Theirs would not appear to be a particularly challenging or worldly cosmopolitanism, but rather what can be called a "cushy cosmopolitanism" undisturbed by having to leave a country behind, let alone by intercultural negotiations with communities of difference. "Aided by the frequent flyer lounges (and their extensions in international standard hotels)," Craig Calhoun argues that such cushy cosmopolitans "meet others of different backgrounds in spaces that retain familiarity" (Calhoun 2003: 106–7). The familiarity of the NEXUS lane space for its enrollees seems especially convenient and economical. They do not even have to meet others and can simply stay in their cars or move unmolested through the airport. Moreover, while the lane reinstates the fast border crossing movements once afforded by the PACE lane, it is also obviously more deeply integrated with the many other familiar features associated with the fast track lifeworlds of what Peter Adey usefully describes as today's "kinetic elites" (Adey 2004, 2006). Expedited airport screening for upper-class frequent fliers, shorter check-in lines, valet parking, pay as you go highway express lanes, and the multiple privileges and protections for owners of premier status credit cards would all appear to share a deep affinity with the sort of fast lane transnational civil citizenship rights provided by NEXUS. At the very same time, however, it needs noting that all the border biometric developments can also be reconsidered from a more skeptical position as part and parcel of a more restrictionist regime. Alongside the NEXUS lane, after all, the US government has been simultaneously preparing to send military drones, so-called unmanned aerial vehicles (UAVs), to patrol the borders, and in the Pacific Northwest, where the business boosters once called for border bulldozing, the Pentagon has already deployed a sensor-laden aircraft, a Blackhawk helicopter, and boats that will operate out of a new command center in Bellingham, Washington (Biesecker 2004; United Press International 2004). And meanwhile, even the Canadian authorities who have been most keen to push the economic facilitation side of the smart border developments remain keen to underline the security side on the NEXUS webpage. Thus, after the invitation to "Cross Often? Make it simple, use NEXUS," the Canada Border Services Agency (CBSA) website goes on to stress: "The NEXUS programs enable Canadian and Unites States customs and immigration authorities to concentrate their efforts on potentially high-risk travelers and goods, thereby upholding security and protection standards at the border."

Given the all-encompassing imagined geographies of a borderless world that often underlie the geo-economic scripts deployed by neoliberal commentators, such ongoing emphases on border control would hardly seem to betoken the wholesale neoliberalization of citizenship. Surely, critics might suggest, we are seeing a much more contradictory set of phenomena? In part, the developments I have charted thus far in this chapter lead me to concur that we are indeed seeing contradictory imperatives worked out at the border. I agree in this sense with Coleman's careful argument that "the border as security/economy nexus is literally a strategic terrain where countervailing projects of statecraft come to bear on one another" (2005: 200). Likewise, it seems that the fraught stop and go development of expedited crossing lanes further illustrates Coleman's point that, "U.S. statecraft in the borderlands can be read as a fraught bundle of geopolitical and geo-economic 'storylines' rather than as a coherent sovereign 'script'" (2005: 201). However, to this I would also add the further point that not all of the contradictions are about neoliberal dynamics clashing with others that are fully external to neoliberal power relations. In other words, while the geopolitical story line of border securitization certainly clashes with the geo-economic storyline of cross-border economic facilitation, the resulting conflicts and convulsions in policy development need also to be interpreted in terms of contradictions that are also in part actually internal to neoliberal power relations themselves. This does not mean that neoliberalism provides an underlining sovereign "script" after all. More complicatedly, what I think we are seeing are some of the contradictions of a neoliberalization dynamic that, while creating transnationalizing liberal state practices on the one side, simultaneously creates all sorts of new exclusions on the other. In this respect, an important question asked by passport scholar Mark Salter takes on an added urgency: "who pays the cost of freedom for the mobility of others?" (Salter 2004: 86).

## The underside of expedited border crossing: extraordinary others?

One obvious underside to the transnational citizenship of expedited crossing lanes is the slowed down border crossing experience imposed on ordinary travelers who cannot afford to purchase or do not have the organizational capacity or the desire to acquire membership in the fast lane. In his analysis of the code spaces of contemporary airports, Adey suggests in this way that there are also emerging kinetic underclasses moving alongside – but much more slowly than – the fast lane kinetic elites (Adey 2004: 1376). Such an argument in turn begs questions about the different speeds allotted to different kinetic underclasses. Coach class delays and secondary processing may be frustrating for many ordinary travelers today, including many academics, but they are largely just minor annoyances for the traveling middle classes. Unless such travelers are vulnerable to racial coding as supposed "security risks," these club-class passengers still move with significant speed in the cushy cosmopolitan circuits created by international conference trips, international tourism, and international family get-togethers. For the world's working classes and for those subject to "security risk" codification, in contrast, being in the kinetic underclasses has altogether more oppressive and more unpredictable outcomes – including, not least of all, much more volatile mixes of movement and immobility. The experience of immobility in these cases means something entirely different to the petty class resentments that come with seeing business suits and Lexus cars speed by in NEXUS lanes. Immobility for the really subaltern underclasses means incarceration and, as Joe Nevins underlines in his important work on the experiences of working-class Mexican migrants crossing into America, sometimes death too (Nevins 2002; see also Walters, this volume; Coutin, this volume).

It should also be noted that, as well as representing ever more appalling exclusions from the privileges of citizenship and civil rights, those surviving on this bleak underside of NEXUS lane privilege also sometimes ironically experience very rapid movement too: rapid movement into detention centers, rapid movement between detention centers, and, ultimately, rapid transnational movement out of America, sometimes into incarceration elsewhere. The result is a kind of *carceral cosmopolitanism* that underlines the value of arguments by scholars such as Pheng Cheah, James Clifford, and Bruce Robbins that we must distinguish between different forms – "discrepant" forms, as Clifford calls them – of cosmopolitanism (Cheah 1998; Clifford 1998; Robbins 1998). Two North American examples of such carceral cosmopolitanism stand out as especially disturbing parallels-cum-contrasts with the cushy cosmopolitanism of expedited crossing lanes. The first, called "expedited removal," began in the mid-1990s as an another outcome – like Section 110 – of the new immigration controls of IIRIRA; and the second, called "extraordinary rendition," has developed most explicitly in the context of the "war on terror" as a way of offshoring US terror suspects for what one critic has called the "outsourcing of torture" (Mayer 2005). By considering both of these radical forms of expulsion from citizenship and civil rights, I want to end this chapter by asking how the harsh kinds of oppressed and brutalized cosmopolitanism they represent actually might relate to the cushy cosmopolitanism of the NEXUS lane.

In 1996, the very same year that credit cards were being invoked by immigration officials as the passports of a cushy cosmopolitan future, the IIRIRA simultaneously put in place draconian new rules mandating the INS to expedite the removal of so-called aliens petitioning the US for asylum. This was the same IIRIRA that had created with Section 110 such a crisis for PACE lane advocates. However, while the problems of Section 110 were quickly overcome by a mixture of business-class lobbying and, ultimately, the introduction of a funded technological fix through NEXUS, the restrictionism of the new expedited removal rules has only grown in the years that have followed. Before President Clinton signed IIRIRA into law, US INS agents could not compel foreigners with improper documents to depart the US immediately. They could be asked to withdraw their applications for admission but, if they refused to do so, INS agents were obliged to refer such foreigners to an immigration judge for asylum hearings. Detention during the wait for a hearing was always possible, but not common because of a shortage of bed space in detention centers. All this changed with the implementation of IIRIRA. Immigration inspectors were given new powers to summarily remove aliens without appropriate documents. As a consequence, low-level INS agents were freshly empowered as sovereign subjects – indeed, as quasi-sovereigns – able to make final decisions about admission, decisions that could not be contested by asylum seekers who possessed invalid or inadequate travel documents (see also Amoore, this volume).

Reviewing the curtailment of human rights by the new expedited removal laws, legal scholar Erin O'Callaghan argued that:

> In addition to possible violations of international law, IIRIRA gives too much power to immigration officials. . . . The expedited removal system allows both INS officials individually and the INS as a whole to grant or withhold asylum on a discriminatory basis with no real checks on this power.
>
> O'Callaghan (2004: 1748)

As Lisa Laplante, another legal scholar, complained in an earlier article, expedited removal thereby also created another world underneath that of unchecked INS control, "a world without a constitution" (Laplante 1999). This world without a constitution has created in turn a new hybrid political geography of incarceration and expulsion for migrants seeking asylum. As such, it would seem to represent yet another one of the "spaces of exception" described by Derek Gregory (2004) in his critique of the colonial present. But, while Gregory theorizes such spaces through the analytical vocabulary of Italian philosopher Georgio Agamben (1998), and while Agamben's account of "sovereign power" and "bare life" certainly seems to map on to the totalitarian sovereignty exercised over asylum seekers by US border agents, we do not have to turn to his abstract invocation of *homer sacer* in order to come to biopolitical terms with the denial of civil rights to those expedited into the removal system under IIRIRA. Instead, we need only turn to the recent findings of a report by the United States Commission on International Religious Freedom (USCIRF 2005), findings that were also made public before the US Congress in a House judiciary subcommittee meeting on March 10th, 2005 (Haney 2005). Two aspects of the political geography of expedited removal become especially clear in this reporting.

First, there is the way in which the application of IIRIRA's expedited removal laws have been increasingly extended geographically away from just ports of entry to become a much more panoptic system for apprehending, incarcerating, and expeditiously expelling undocumented aliens from anywhere in America. "Expedited Removal is mandatory for aliens arriving at ports of entry," the USCIRF report notes, but continues: "Congress, however, also authorized the Attorney General to exercise discretion in applying Expedited Removal in the interior of the United States to undocumented aliens apprehended within two years after entry" (USCIRF 2005). This extension was then implemented practically when: "On November 13, 2002, Expedited Removal was expanded by the INS to apply to undocumented non-Cubans who entered the United States by sea within the prior two years" (USCIRF 2005). And subsequently further extensions have ensued when:

> On August 11, 2004, the Department of Homeland Security announced that, effective immediately, it was exercising its discretion to further expand Expedited Removal authority to the Border Patrol for undocumented aliens apprehended within 14 days after entry and within 100 miles of the border, in the Tucson and Laredo Border Patrol sectors.
>
> USCIRF (2005)

These expansions of expedited removal into the American interior can no doubt be largely explained in terms of the exclusionary nationalism that has turned "homeland security" into a synonym for homeland *in*security for immigrants. As Amy Kaplan argues:

> The notion of the homeland contributes to making the life of immigrants terribly insecure. It plays a role in policing and shoring up the boundaries between the domestic and the foreign. Yet it does this not simply by stopping foreigners at the borders, but by continually redrawing those boundaries everywhere throughout the nation, between

Americans who can somehow claim the United States as their native land, their birthright, and immigrants and those who look to home-lands elsewhere, who can be rendered inexorably foreign.

Kaplan (2003: 87)

As well as exemplifying the ability of an ethnically coded nationalism to exclude certain subjects from transnational civil rights, the expansion of expedited removal is at the same time notably neoliberal because of the way the law's application has had both transnational and market-mediated fea-tures. The managerial transnationalism of these (and their emplacement within NAFTA's own neoliberal political–economic geography) became clear, for example, in April, 2005, when Michael Chertoff, the Secretary of DHS, was testifying before the Homeland Security Subcommittee of the Senate Appropriations Committee. Describing the need for a comprehensive approach to what he termed "managing illegal migration," Chertoff emphasized that:

We have to be able to have more people at the border, better technology at the border, all of which we are now pushing forward; better investi-gative capabilities, better and more available use of detention beds. And we're doing some additional things as well to free up beds. For exam-ple, we are working with the Mexicans to begin the internal repatria-tion program in the next couple weeks, whereby we transport Mexicans who come in back to interior locations so that they don't simply go back across the border, connect up with the same trafficking organiza-tions and then come back a couple of days later. We're using other kinds of techniques in terms of expediting removal to try to expedite the process of getting people that we do apprehend, moving them, again, across the border back to Mexico.

Chertoff (2005)

Amidst all this expedited effort, the specific connection drawn by Chertoff between expediting removal through transnational risk management and the need to free up bed space is related in turn to a second political geo-graphy of exception highlighted in the USCIRF report: namely, the actual spaces of detention used by the Department of Homeland Security (DHS) to incarcerate asylum seekers while they await expulsion.

Craig Haney, a prison specialist involved in preparing the USCIRF report, informed Congress that, because of the increased need for detention space created by the expansion of expedited removal, the DHS actually had to *rent* space in order to accommodate the new numbers of detainees. "[O]ne third of asylum seekers", he explained,

are detained not merely in jail-like facilities, but are in actual jails and prisons, in which DHS rents "beds." Even though it is a violation of

DHS's own detention standards, asylum seekers in such facilities are often intermingled with criminal aliens, and even with inmates who are still serving criminal sentences.

Haney (2005)

As Haney proceeded to underline in his account of the "inappropriate, [and] unnecessarily severe" treatment of asylum seekers in such rented facilities, a significant result of subcontracting their detention to the sprawling public–private partnership of the American prison system is that DHS detainees have been made subject to the same unpredictable mix of curtailed rights and harsh treatment suffered by criminal prisoners detained in for-profit prisons (USCIRF 2005).

Thus, there is a terrible irony in the carceral cosmopolitanism created by expedited removal: namely, that the so-called "land of the free", so fetishized in neoliberal nostrums about America embodying free market freedoms, has managed now to combine expedited exceptions to human rights for asylum seekers with the expedited border crossing rights for business elites. This awful innovation and combination has been carried yet one step further in the development of "extraordinary rendition": another penal development using subcontracting, but one that deliberately outsources overseas so that, in the words of an unnamed US intelligence official: "We don't kick the shit out of them. We send them to other countries so they can kick the shit out of them" (quoted in Pred 2005: 373). Here then, the carceral cosmopolitanism of expedited removal has been more radically transnationalized, and, in using privately rented corporate jets to speed the outcasts out of the US, extraordinary rendition has created spaces of exception that are still more clearly coeval with the development of the transnationalized citizenship of neoliberal business elites. I suggested above that perhaps the apogee of such transnational elite citizenship might be called, following Don Mitchell's argument about SUV citizenship, *Gulfstream citizenship*. Adverts for Gulfstream jets and fractional jet shares are replete with appeals to the transnational freedoms and enhanced visions of the earth afforded to owners of these elite business-class status symbols. They are without doubt the ultimate badge of belonging and citizenship in the borderless world of neoliberal fantasy–reality. For the same reason, therefore, it seems especially important to reflect on the ways in which they have also featured in recent exposés of the abduction of individuals through extraordinary rendition.

"Detainee's Suit Gains Support From Jet's Log," ran the *New York Times* headline in an article detailing the American government's extraordinary rendition of Maher Arar (Shane, Grey and Fesenden 2005). Apprehended by DHS officials at Kennedy International Airport, this Syrian-born Canadian citizen was flown on a Gulfstream III jet first to an airport near Washington, DC, then to Maine, then to Rome and then to Amman, Jordan, from where he was then driven across the border to Syria and thrown into a windowless underground cell, incarcerated for ten months and brutally beaten with two-inch-thick electrical cables. During the flight on the Gulfstream, the American guards from the "Special Removal Unit" watched movies on the corporate audiovisual system all the while Mr. Arar sat chained to the jet's luxury leather seats. The same jet, it has subsequently transpired, was previously rented by the US government in December, 2003, for a trip to Guantánamo Bay, and reporters tracking these and other extraordinary renditions have so far identified three other Gulfstreams used in this way, including one "also used by the Boston Red Sox manager between missions ferrying detainees and their guards to Guantánamo, with the Red Sox logo attached to the fuselage or removed depending on who was aboard" (Shane, Grey and Fesenden 2005: A9). In all these cases, the gap between the carceral cosmopolitanism of the subaltern and the cushy cosmopolitanism of the global elite seems at once incredibly narrowed and unimaginably vast. Mr. Arar's jet was rented from a Florida company called Presidential Aviation whose manager is reported as saying: "It's a very select group of people that we fly, from entertainers to foreign heads of state, a whole gamut of customers that we fly" (Shane, Grey and Fesenden 2005: A9). A "whole gamut of customers" would seem to be a nicely neoliberal euphemism for the sorts of very select people introduced into Gulfstream sub-citizenship by extraordinary rendition.

For Mr. Arar, the identification of the Gulfstream III that was used to transport him to Jordan turned out to be useful in his lawsuit against the US government. "Finding this plane is really going to help me," he said. "It does remind me of this trip, which is painful, but it should make people understand that this is for real and everything happened the way I said. I hope people will now stop for a moment and think about the morality of this" (Shane, Grey and Fesenden 2005: A9). By the same token, it also seems clear that the double standards of Gulfstream citizenship – videos and leather seats for the elite, chains and beatings for the subaltern – just like the double standards of expedited border processing – NEXUS lanes for the elite and subcontracted prisons for the subaltern – also signal a deeply authoritarian underside of contemporary neoliberalism. The obvious question I want to turn to in conclusion concerns whether or not this authoritarian underside is a *necessary* corollary, a wholly *contingent* corollary, or some more complexly interrelated counterpart to the emergence of elite transnational citizenship under neoliberalism.

## Conclusion

The main argument made in this chapter about NEXUS concerns the ways in which this little known expedited border crossing program and its development are symptomatic of the neoliberalization of citizenship in today's North American context. This is a context, as I have explained, shaped at once by the transnational entrenchment of free market rights and the increasingly oppressive impact of securitized nationalism. NEXUS lane participants – the people who "cross often" and want to "make it simple," the people who are prepared to buy flexible citizenship because "the fast lane is where you want to be" – would seem to represent the paradigmatic neo-liberal citizen-players on the transnational level playing field of free trade, neoliberal citizens for whom transnational mobility rights are part of the more general transnational business-class privilege that continues to be expanded and entrenched globally through the "new constitutionalism" of free trade and related laws. As such, the kinetic elites of the NEXUS lane appear to be able to buy for themselves at least a little of the borderless world fantasy life whose most transcendently transnational subjects can rise above it all as Gulfstream citizens of the world, the world of transnational property rights and mobility rights seen best through the Enhanced Vision System of a Gulfstream jet. But then we have the kinetic underclasses of expedited removal and extraordinary rendition whose borderless world is, in contrast, a world without a constitution, a world that may well extend transnationally via Gulfstream jets across borders, but only so as to better cast out its dehumanized and rights-deprived subjects into the spaces of exception that now increasingly seem to form a transnational gulag of incarceration and outsourced torture.

The violence of extraordinary rendition may seem especially context contingent, in this regard, not a neoliberal or otherwise economically induced outcome, but a result of an exceptional American ability to combine free market fundamentalism with an inhuman disregard for foreigners deemed unfit (often because of orientalist codes) for business. Consider in this regard what happened when Edward Markey, a Democratic congressman from Massachusetts, introduced legislation to ban extraordinary rendition in 2005. Republican House speaker Dennis Hastert said the legislation was going nowhere, and, when Bob Herbert, a columnist from the *New York Times*, asked why, he was told: "The speaker does not support the Markey proposal. He believes that suspected terrorists should be sent to their home countries" (Herbert 2005: A25). Then, when Herbert asked why they should not be held and prosecuted in the US, Pete Jeffries from the Speaker's office replied: "Because U.S. taxpayers should not necessarily be on the hook for their judicial and incarceration costs" (Herbert 2005: A25). This response seems a telling illustration of the white Americans-first exceptionalism that has led many in US government to think that creating spaces of exception to human rights laws is just fine. But it is also, I think, an extraordinarily telling indictment of the neoliberal logic through which extraordinary rendition has been thought out and justified by its perpetrators. American taxpayers, Jeffries seemed to be saying, should not have to pay for government services (whether they be torture or its prevention) when they are being "consumed" by those who do not pay taxes in America. Also overdetermined by economic codes, expedited removal seems to reflect a similarly consumerist neoliberal revisioning of citizenship and security, being imagined by the 1996 legislative promoters of IIRIRA as part of the same individualized contractualism that turned welfare into workfare and recoded American citizenship more generally in the terms of the payments and debts of private commercial contracts. In other words, while both extraordinary rendition and expedited removal both clearly need to be understood in terms of the extra-capitalistic imperatives associated with virulently nationalistic (and thus racist and masculinist) imperatives, they also appear to reflect some of the same economic hallmarks of a neoliberal-ism that, as Foucault once argued, turns citizens into entrepreneurs of their selves. Thus, while asylum seekers thrown into subcontracted prison space by DHS and carceral cosmopolitans such as Maher Arar are completely deprived of agency and choice, their plight needs nonetheless to be under-stood in relation to the ways in which the normative citizen of North America has meanwhile been "re-specified as an active agent both able and obliged to exercise autonomous choices" (Larner 2000: 13).

The implication of the argument that neoliberal ideas and imperatives overdetermine extraordinary rendition and expedited removal is not that these appallingly inhuman state practices are an inevitable outcome of the same neoliberalism that has extended the freedom and choice of economic elites across transnational space (far more intrinsically interconnected, it seems, are the unfree flows of undocumented Mexican workers into the US economy). But nor are the spaces of exception created by rendition and removal entirely disconnected from neoliberalism either. They are not just a contingent outcome of the exceptional American context with its history of free market capitalism rooted in that most profitable as well as paradigmatic space of exception: the slave plantation. There is instead a more complexly interrelated relationship between the neoliberal dynamics and the violence of expedited removal and rendition, a relationship in which neoliberalism provides both the capitalistic context and some of the structuring order too. Private sector promoters of programs such as NEXUS and US VISIT some-times note that the systems offer an alternative to racist border agents and a way of introducing a neutral kind of third-party technical administration that keeps the agents themselves as much as the travelers accountable to the formal protocols of the law. Yet, as we have seen, expedited removal rules like expedited crossing lanes have also been implemented through the mediation of privately procured services. Extraordinary rendition relies in its own turn on the very vehicles used to transport business elites around their borderless world. But, more than this private sector context and mediation, both practices would seem to be structured by a neoliberal double standard: a double standard that is like liberalism's own inaugural double standards – with rights for whites in Europe and often utter inhumanity in the colonies (Mehta 2000) – but which is also significantly reterritorialized and reorga-nized by contemporary transnational business-class power. The result is a recodification of the normative citizen-subject as a *transnationally* mobile cushy cosmopolitan with heightened human capital *vis à vis* all the kinetic underclasses: some of the latter being merely marooned in national-state spaces with weakened political and social citizenship rights; others being expedited into the "world without a constitution" of carceral cosmopolitanism. Examples of such reterritorialized and reorganized neoliberal double standards are by no means exceptional to America (see Rajaram 2003; Hyndman 2005). For example, the neoliberalization of EU citizenship has not happened without the creation of its own spaces of exception. This is what William Walters argues in his account of the partial transnationalization of EU citizenship, a transnationalization which he notes is a "neoliberal project which focuses on enhancing mobility and freedom across an extended European space." Tracking this extension of mobilities and freedoms – in which business has also enjoyed the major benefits – Walter's also notes that "from the perspective of those now named and shunned as 'asylumseekers,' European governance might invoke the renewal of a much older art of government – that of police – but now on a transnational basis" (Walters 2004a: 170). EU Schengen policing may not yet have created the same record of abuse recorded by the critics of expedited removal and extraordinary rendition, but it does suggest that the neoliberal advance of transnational citizenship rights is repeatedly related to the redrawing of lines that shut out and imprison diverse others – sometimes using biometrics to do so (Van der Ploeg 1999). For such transnationals who are expedited into otherness, the invitation to cross often and make it simple seems at once barbed and barred forever.

## Note

1 Data provided verbally by Hugh Conroy of the International Mobility and Trade Corridor (IMTC) project of the Whatcom Council of Governments.

# 8 Putting the migration–security complex in its place[1]

*William Walters*

> we [should] not allow ourselves the facile, rather theatrical declaration
> that this moment in which we exist is one of total perdition, in the
> abyss of darkness, or a triumphant daybreak, etc. It is a time like any
> other, or rather, a time which is never quite like any other.
>
> Foucault (1994: 126)

## Securitization or problematization?

For many commentators on immigration, the September 11, 2001 attacks on
New York and Washington signalled a profound and unprecedented turning
point. Observing that a critical aspect of the political response to the attacks
has been the creation of an entire migration–security complex, John Tirman's (2004) introduction to a recent collection on migration and security
is typical in this respect. Writing about the response taken within the
American homeland itself, he has documented some of the more immediate
ways in which this complex was forged. Based on the widespread perception
that the culprits for the attacks were "porous borders, generous entry policies, violations of the terms of entry, and the entry of immigrants from the
Middle East more generally" (Tirman 2004: 2), a widespread public anxiety
about immigration has been intensified. At the level of the law, this has
sanctioned certain dramatic moves, not least the rapid expansion of state
powers under the USA Patriot Act to detain aliens without due process. But
there have also been developments changing the very structure of the state
and the organization of sovereign power. For instance, Tirman points to the
bureaucratic fusion of migration and security. The most immediate institutional
expression of this fusion is surely the abolition of the Immigration and Naturalization Service (INS) and the transfer of its functions and units into the
Department of Homeland Security whose mandate it is to "prevent and deter
terrorist attacks and protect against and respond to threats a hazards to the
Nation" (Department of Homeland Security 2004; quoted in Inda 2006: 153).

According to Tirman, the forging of this nexus of migration and security
is not limited to the US homeland. In one country after another, he notes,

the pursuit of al Qaeda cells, conducted by various security agencies, has uncovered not only their money-laundering activities, their brief alliances with organized crime or the geographical expanse of the network. This international "war on terror", a campaign that forms the global counterpart to the project of homeland security, has also revealed that:

> Virtually all of this illegal activity, designed to support a large, dispersed network of political violence, was conducted by migrants, underscoring along with the US military and police campaign to destroy or disrupt their actions, the newly minted connection between security and migration, or, to use an unwieldy term, the 'securitization of migration'.
>
> Tirman (2004: 3)

While many Europe-focused scholars would not dispute Tirman's depiction of September 11 as a catalyst in accelerating the securitization of migration, they would probably want to insist that this nexus is not quite as "newly minted" as he suggests. More specifically, they would perhaps point out that his is a somewhat partial and rather US-centric view of a much wider process. For the fact is that scholarship in Europe has for quite some time found itself debating the origins, tendencies, dynamics and consequences of the securitization of migration (Heisler and Layton 1993; Huysmans 1995, 2000; Bigo 2002; Ceyhan and Tsoukala 2002). In these accounts, the migration–security nexus is not a post-9/11 phenomenon but a complex whose *durée* is somewhat longer; its formation being conditioned by the interplay of numerous events and processes operating on multiple scales and temporalities. The following quotation illustrates this point and is, I would venture, typical of the way in which a great deal of international relations and critical security studies has understood the context of the securitization of migration.

> The last decades of the twentieth century were marked by a dramatic change led by the development of globalization, the enhancement of transnational flows, and the end of bipolarity. The construction of the European Union, the emergence of new economic agreements such as NAFTA, the deterritorialization of markets, physical borders, and identities, the increase of migration flows, the construction of the Schengen area, and the fragmentation of major states (e.g., the Soviet Union and Yugoslavia) have raised questions about Westphalian state sovereignty and identity. ... In consequence, Western societies are witnessing the emergence of many existential and conceptual anxieties and fears about their identity, security, and well-being. As Martin Heisler asserts, migration is at the focal point of the interrelated dynamics of identity, borders, and orders. By its transnational character, its dynamics, and its impact on people and institutions at all levels, migration is

posing a serious challenge to the long-standing paradigms of certainty and order.

Ceyhan and Tsoukala (2002: 23)

Securitization theory is of course not a unified voice but, like any thriving intellectual enterprise, a space of lively and often productive disagreements. For instance, its practitioners may share the basic proposition that migration is not naturally a question of security but only becomes so subject to particular social processes. However, there is little common agreement on what the most relevant processes are. In one version, it is the successful performance of particular speech acts and discursive enactments which explains how an issue becomes securitized (Waever 1995; Buonfino 2004). In another, which draws its analytical insights from Foucault and Bourdieu, one finds the insistence that, besides the rhetorical configuration of security, it is necessary to consider the dynamics of institutional fields, including the inter-bureaucratic struggles of security professionals, certain technical practices of security and the constitution of specific security domains (Bigo 2000; Huysmans 2006b).

However, it is not such theoretical differences that interest me here, so much as one particular assumption that most participants in the securitization debate do happen to share. This is the assumption that it is now, in our time, in the recent present, that migration has become a security concern. It is the perspective that says migration only becomes a security issue in the period following the demise of geopolitical bipolarity, or perhaps in the period that began with the crisis of Keynesian welfarism. Before this time, the assumption goes, migration policy was much closer to labour policy. It was therefore less controversial and politicized than today. This is perhaps why students of security have largely confined their attention to the recent present, and left migration history to historians, and perhaps the occasional political scientist looking for patterns of path dependence.

Studies in the securitization of migration have privileged our own time, and shown little inclination towards undertaking historical reflection and analysis of earlier politicizations of migration. This is perhaps one reason why they have only partially grappled with the changing forms, objects and rationalities associated with securitization. But this is not because they have neglected the shifting thematic foci of security practices. After all, there is certainly an awareness in this literature that fields and objects of security can vary. For instance, in a particularly influential intervention, Waever (1995) identifies "societal security" as a growing concern within politics after the Cold War. Societal (in)security names a situation in which threats are less likely to be associated with aggression from other states, but instead with challenges to society and, in particular, cultural, national and social identity.

But, despite this sensitivity towards the existence of different, historically constituted security fields – societal, national, environmental, etc. – there is still a tendency in writing about the securitization of migration to attribute a core meaning to security, to find a kernel of security that remains unchanged across time and institutional space. For instance, Waever insists that ultimately "Security means survival, it means 'this is an existential threat with a point of no return'" (Waever 1996: 108). Often, insecurity is associated with the presence of dangerous others who pose existential threats to our survival.

This understanding of security as being, at its core, a matter of existential threat has influenced the way in which scholars of migration have understood risk. Although risk has not always been explicitly theorized in studies of the security–migration nexus, there seems to be an underlying assumption that risk is a question of danger and threat, and often contamination posed by foreign bodies. Ibrahim's discussion of the racial subtext of the securitization of migration is typical in this regard. "This [racialized] discourse has been possible through the broadening of the concept of security and the linking of risk and threat to migrants" (Ibrahim 2005: 164). Here, risk is understood as a potential for harm embodied in particular behaviours and/or types and classes of persons.

The problem with this understanding of risk is that it overlooks the multiple different ways in which risk has been interpreted and deployed as a political technology. For instance, it overlooks the fact that, within the logic of *social* security – and it is quite striking how rarely securitization theory has addressed this particular kind of security practice – the meaning of risk was displaced away from an association with types of persons and threats, and associated much more closely with the properties of social and economic processes under conditions of industrialism, urbanism and market capitalism (see also Aradau and van Munster, this volume).

This quite different understanding of risk is particularly evident in the conception of unemployment which became dominant within post-Second World War welfare states. Whereas once unemployment had been viewed as a risk to be borne by the individual and their community, the Beveridgean and Keynesian view which came to be inscribed in the design of much social and economic policy saw it as a risk to which workers were inevitably exposed under industrial capitalism, a risk which could be effectively mitigated by state systems of social insurance. Within the diagram of the social state, unemployment was governed not so much as an existential threat as an everyday risk, not dissimilar from personal theft or the work-related accident, susceptible to bureaucratic management through actuarial calculation and monetary compensation (Defert 1991; Ewald 1991; Walters 2000).

The argument of this paper is that by placing contemporary questions of migration in a broadened historical field of enquiry, it becomes possible to shed new light on issues of risk and security. It becomes possible to see, for instance, that what we today call "risk" and "security" are not at all constant but, in fact, the correlates of specific kinds of political games and governmental technologies; that migration has been politicized, dramatized and problematized through languages and technologies other than "security"; and that, by engaging with these other problematizations of migration, we get a sharper and more specific understanding of what security and risk mean today within the migration field.

With this aim in mind, this chapter calls for greater genealogical sensitivity in research on the migration–security nexus, the complex that I want to call, for want of a better term, "homeland security". If genealogy can be regarded as a "history of the present", this is because it seeks to "undertake an analysis of those objects given as necessary components of our reality" (Dean 1994: 33). Such a move entails that we make a conceptual shift: from an investigation that places the concept of "securitization" at its heart to one oriented by the idea of problematization. As Foucault has put it, this is "a matter of analyzing not behaviors or ideas ... but the *problematizations* through which being offers itself to be, necessarily, thought" (Foucault 1997: 11). It is not a matter of jettisoning the analytics of security so much as putting "security" in its place. It is a question of finding what happens once we treat the things that are today bundled under the rubric of security not as the self-evident response to a political event (e.g. "9/11") nor as the expression of a sociological process with roots in other macroprocesses (e.g. globalization or transnationalization), but as a particular and contingent form of problematization.

The aim of the chapter is to put the securitization of migration in its place. In order to do this, it is necessary to centre my discussion not on contemporary events within the migration field, but on a particular episode in the recent past. The event I have chosen is a specific episode in the interwoven histories of anti-immigrantism and immigration control in the United States – the so-called "Wetback crisis", which exploded into public life in the early 1950s.[2] As the following two sections of the chapter explain, this "crisis" centred upon the presence of legal and illegal seasonal migrant workers from Mexico toiling in the fruit and cotton fields of the Southwest US. Drawing upon newspaper reporting of this crisis, I seek to reconstruct certain aspects of the political imagination presupposed by the debate about the wetback. Among other things, this exercise reveals that, inasmuch as this crisis was debated as a question of security – and this was not always the case – this was frequently in terms of its implications for the *social* security of Americans, and also, to some degree, of the migrants themselves.

In a final section, I use this account of the "Wetback crisis" to pose a series of questions about the contemporary migration–security complex. By comparing the paradigm of homeland security, which has become quite central in thinking about migration today, with that of social security, it becomes possible to cast certain features of the former in a new light. I shall focus on three particular aspects of today's migration–security complex: its metagovernmental character; the centrality of a problematic of identity–security; and the political obsession with borders. In short, the chapter reveals that a more critical and reflexive account of the present requires us to recognize not a singular process of securitization, but the play of and between changing forms of problematization.

## The "Wetback crisis", 1951

From March 25 to March 29, 1951, the *New York Times* published a series of five investigative reports concerning "the economic and sociological problem of the 'wetbacks' – illegal Mexican immigrants in the Southwestern United States" (*New York Times* 1951a: 1). Authored by Gladwin Hill, this five-part series not only offers us a window on to the ways in which questions of illegal immigration were posed in the early 1950s. It was also something of a political event in its own right, bringing national attention to, and sparking widespread media interest in, the so-called "wetback problem", which had, until that time, existed largely as a local matter (Calavita 1992: 47; Flores 2004: 2). What can this series tell us about the ways in which certain forms of migration were problematized?

The situation in the Southwest, parts of the deep South and the Far West, according to Hill, is that of a "ceaseless and steadily increasing tide of illegal immigration from Mexico into the United States" (*New York Times* 1951a: 1). It is estimated at more than one million individuals per year. "They sneak across the thinly patrolled 1,600 mile border between Brownsville, Tex., and San Diego, Calif., in an unending hegira from Mexican unemployment and wage levels as low as 40 cents a day, seeking farm work and any other labor available in this country" (*New York Times* 1951a: 1). While the term "wetback" is deemed pejorative and offensive today, it seems to have been the standard description at the time. Writers such as Hill always placed the word in quotation marks, not to suggest a certain critical distance from it, but merely, it seems, to mark it as an unusual term, perhaps on the assumption that a national audience might be unfamiliar with it. Nearly every article uses the term but always feels bound to explain it – a reference to "those who swim the Rio Grande, the Texas–Mexico boundary" (*New York Times* 1951a: 1). In 1954, a mass deportation drive would take the name Operation Wetback.

Hill's series is highly critical of the situation he encounters. He goes to great lengths to challenge what had been the prevailing view, namely that this was just a "picturesque cat-and-mouse game on a grand scale between a mass of amiable Latins and an overwhelmed border patrol"; a regional curiosity in which an annual "invasion" of migrant labour crossed the border as a "regular essential and harmless supplement to the domestic harvest forces" (*New York Times* 1951a: 41). The situation was much more serious. At its heart was the vulnerable and hyper-exploited condition of the migrant worker by the large-scale agricultural industries, ranches and farms that were the principal magnet for, and indeed active recruiters of, this migrant labour. Prevailing wage levels are described as tantamount to peonage, and the working conditions are compared with *ante bellum* slavery. All of this was going on under the nose of the Immigration Service, the Border Patrol and local law authorities, leading Hill to make what would be a frequent analogy between the governance of illegal migration and the days of prohibition when "wholesale violation of the laws of the United States was being ignored, tacitly sanctioned or overtly encouraged by a large cross-section of the population" (*New York Times* 1951a: 1).

Hill and other journalists sought to force the wetback issue into the spotlight of national politics. But it was not as though this practice of utilizing Mexican workers – both authorized migrants and the "illegal" – was particularly new. On the contrary, immigration from Mexico had gained momentum since before the First World War. Whereas the Quota Restrictions of 1921 and 1924 reduced levels of European immigration, Mexicans and other migrants from the Western hemisphere were exempt. Within official circles, Mexico was regarded as a "back door" which, given its geographical proximity, offered a source of flexible and easily deportable labour for the expanding agricultural economy of the Southwest (Calavita 1994: 58–61). This "flexibility" was amply demonstrated in the 1930s when, in the context of the worsening economic depression, public charge clauses were activated as a pretence for "repatriating" approximately 400,000 Mexican and Mexican American workers and their families (Ngai 2004: 72) – an act which Ngai (2004: 75) describes as a "racial expulsion program exceeded only in scale by the Native American Indian removals of the nineteenth century".

This temporary importation of Mexican workers to meet the agricultural economy's demand for cheap, non-unionized labour was formalized in the 1940s in the form of the Bracero programme. This began in 1942 as a measure of expediency to meet war-related labour shortages with so-called "guest-workers", but proved useful enough to employers and state officials that it was placed on a more permanent footing following the end of the war. Bracero was expanded in 1951 in conjunction with the passage of Public Law 78, which legalized certain forms of quasi-bonded, "contract" labour in the agricultural sector of the US economy (Calavita 1992: 43–4). Referring literally to "one who works with their arms", Bracero has been described as "a labor contracting system by which the US government negotiated the temporary importation of 4.8 million Mexican workers" between 1942 and 1964, when the programme was eventually ended (Akers Chacón and Davis 2006: 140).

Together with undocumented "wetbacks" – and the line between them was typically very blurred – Bracero workers constituted a mass source of vulnerable labour that would fuel the growth of the agricultural industries in the postwar period.[3] In one of the most sophisticated historical accounts of this phenomenon, Ngai argues that this "transnational Mexican labor force" constituted "a kind of 'imported colonialism' that was the legacy of the nineteenth-century American conquest of Mexico's northern territories". For this was a workforce governed by new social relations "based on the subordination of racialized foreign bodies who worked in the United States but who remained excluded from the polity by both law and by social custom" (Ngai 2004: 129). It could certainly be argued that the history of illegal immigration since this time will be very much the story of changing forms of this inclusive–exclusionary practice.

The crisis of the 1950s was met with a dual-pronged response that in essence continues to set the terms of the politics of illegal immigration today. One prong would be a set of repressive measures, including the enhancement of border patrol agencies, and a mass "round up" and deportation under the auspices of Operation Wetback. It would invoke fears of the risk of communist infiltration and employ military-style tactics of enforcement. According to the INS, over one million migrants were apprehended during the fiscal year of 1954 alone (Nevins 2002: 34). The other prong was to refashion the Bracero programme, expanding it and moving it closer in form to state-managed recruitment. This move was rationalized by the argument that a state-guaranteed supply of flexible labour would wean farm employers away from their reliance upon illegal workers.

But while it is possible to identify these continuities with and anticipations of contemporary policy, there are a number of features concerning the political framing and "response" to the Wetback crisis that stand out as quite peculiar from the perspective of today. It is these that I highlight in the following section because of the way they serve to enhance the intelligibility of the current migration–security complex.

## Illegal immigration and the security of the social

As we noted at the outset, securitization theory tells a story of a migration field which *becomes* securitized. It is as though the rhetoric, practices and politics associated with security seep out from the geopolitical and military sectors and infiltrate a terrain that was previously unmarked by any security logic. Our encounter with the moment of the wetback suggests a need to amend this view. At least as far as the migration of Mexican workers was concerned, migration was certainly not framed as a security issue as it is today. But questions of illegal immigration and security were connected in a different sense. The so-called "wetback" issue was perceived as threatening *the security of the social*. To grasp the specificity of the wetback problem, and thereby to better particularize the nature of current security discourses, it is necessary to consider how the problem of illegal immigration came to be posed at the level of the social.

### Governing the social

The social is typically understood within the social sciences as referring to universal properties and characteristics of human existence. However, Foucauldian-inspired research has suggested a more specific and historicized understanding of the term (Donzelot 1988; Rose 1996a; Walters 2000). As Rose has argued, the social is best approached as a new formula of rule which materialized in multiple ways across countless institutional sites sometime around the middle of the nineteenth century. Its emergence is unthinkable outside its relationship to a whole series of intellectual machineries and political technologies, such as social statistics, the social survey, social work and social insurance, which together crystallized the possibility of new ways of governing human affairs. As the twentieth century progressed, the social would find its most influential political articulation in the guise of "welfare", a "formula of rule somewhere between classical liberalism and nascent socialism" (Rose 1996a: 48).

Among other things, social governance entailed a particular conception of risk. I have already touched on this above, but it deserves to be re-emphasized here as this approach to risk associated with the welfare state offers a point of contrast to the notion of risk at work in contemporary schemes and dreams of homeland security. It is nicely summarized by Simon when he notes that, whether we speak of Keynesianism, Fordism, collectivism or the social, it was a matter of depicting "social life as distributions of aggregate risks that could be governed by redistributing them", and engaging such social risks using technologies as varied as insurance, case work and urban planning (Simon 1997: 176).

The wetback issue condensed a whole series of concerns about work, crime, illness, morality, citizenship and security, much as the discourse about illegal immigration does today. However, the way in which these connections were imagined was definitely shaped by these logics of social security, broadly understood. We have already seen evidence of this logic in the particular style of reporting conducted by the *New York Times*. Here, I want to consider a further illustration that comes from a Presidential address before Congress on the subject of illegal immigrants from Mexico. The fact that no less an authority than the President of the USA could frame the discussion of illegal immigration in decidedly social terms attests, if nothing else, to the political normality of the social point of view at this time.

According to President Truman (1951), the problem of the wetback stemmed in considerable part from the fact of their impoverished living conditions, and the way in which such concentrated poverty bred related problems of unemployment, poor health and crime which rippled out into the broader society. Truman laments the situation of the illegal immigrant "left in abject poverty", but also how their presence fostered a situation in which "Thousands of our own citizens, particularly those of Latin descent, are displaced from employment or forced to work under substandard conditions". While Truman called for greater resources to prevent unauthorized border crossing and illegal employment, he noted that such prohibitive measures were not sufficient. Using a language that is strongly reminiscent of the dominant approach to another key "social" question in the 1950s, namely unemployment, he spoke of the need for better organization and regulation in the agricultural economy with, for instance, the surveillance of labour market needs so that a more "rational" assessment could be made of the balance needed between temporary foreign and domestic labour supply.

But the problem was not merely one of mitigating the poverty of migrant labour by improving standards and controls in the labour market. The illegal status that so many migrant workers endured was also a problem in its own right. The really interesting point to note here is that, at least as far as the Presidential address is concerned, illegality is registered as problematic not primarily because it symbolizes a violation of national law, a transgression of state borders or a criminal propensity on the part of its subjects – all perceptions that vitalize the politics of immigration today. It is a problem because of the way it places its subjects outside the regime of liberal citizenship. "Since these unfortunate people are here illegally, they are subject to deportation if caught by our immigration authorities. They have to hide and yet must work to live. *They are thus in no position to bargain with those who might choose to exploit them* ... They are unable, therefore, to protest or to protect themselves" (Truman 1951; my emphasis).

## Liberty–security

Truman's speech is significant in part because it suggests that discourse about illegal immigration was underpinned by a conception of a normal subject, which is in key respects quite different today. Underlying the President's remarks is the idea of the subject as a rights-bearing collective worker, capable of engaging in industrial bargaining and political activity. The illegal immigrant deviates from this norm. The significance of this deviation, and its relevance for our discussion of security, becomes apparent once we note that Truman's form of liberal reasoning contains more than a trace of the logic of liberal security which Foucault describes in his lectures on governmentality. Burchell has summarized this nicely when he observes that, under modern conditions, "The objective of a liberal art of government becomes that of securing the conditions for the optimal and, as far as possible, autonomous functioning of economic processes within society or, as Foucault puts it, of enframing natural processes in mechanisms of *security*" (Burchell 1991: 139). Put differently, the viability of market society depends upon the cultivation of free subjects capable of identifying and asserting their own interests. The security of state and society is thus pegged to the preservation of conditions in which the subjects of government are capable of fending for themselves. Illegal immigration appears as a problem precisely because it threatens to erode such a state of affairs. In other words, it threatens to undermine the delicate but dynamic balance between a socialized society and a capitalist economy that is the hallmark of governing according to the formulae of welfare.

Seen in the light of this social problematization of the illegal immigrant, certain features of the Bracero programme appear in a slightly different light. For one of its features was that it sought to establish certain minimum standards with regard to the employment and residence of its subjects. For instance, the version of the programme iterated in 1942 specified minimum wage and day rates, as well as a subsistence wage for workers unemployed for more than 25 percent of their contract period. It also conceded to the migrant workers the right to elect representatives to discuss complaints with employers and, in a later version, issued standards as to the provision of means and housing by employers (Calavita 1992: 19–20, 46). Scholars have documented the extent to which employers sought to circumvent or simply ignored these social regulations, and the reluctance of official agencies to enforce them. But, as inadequate as they may have been, the very existence of such regulations attests to the fact that the technology of the social provided a kind of repertoire of practices for the governance of illegal immigration at this time.

So it seems there was a discourse in the 1950s which saw illegal immigration as a set of processes endangering the security of the social. To recognize this is not to claim that such a discourse was universal or hegemonic, nor that all commentators expressed the relatively sympathetic position seemingly espoused by the President. For example, "Operation Wetback", the mass "repatriation" of workers to Mexico, was conceived and executed as though a military operation, and legitimated by the familiar language of undocumented migrants as "an actual invasion of the United States" (Head of INS, quoted in Ngai 2004: 155). Clearly, illegal immigration may have been officially perceived as a social problem, but it was at the same time imbricated in the logic of national security.

## Social or homeland security?

Our discussion of the Wetback crisis points to the existence of a migration–security nexus that significantly predates the period that many commentators associate with the securitization of migration. As we have seen, one possible explanation is the fact that we are dealing not with a singular securitization process but with the existence of multiple security formations. In this final section, I want to use the preceding sketch of a social problematic of illegal immigration to raise some questions about the nature of contemporary securitizations of migration and risk. My argument is that, although there is still a problematization of illegal immigration from the perspective of social security, this is not the dominant articulation of migration as a security issue today.[4] Instead, we are dealing with a different set of programmes and technologies, and a different politics of security. I want to call this, for want of a better term, the game of *homeland* security.

### *Fluid subjects*

While homeland security is no less messy and coherent as an assemblage of discourse, technology and subjectivity than social security, it is nevertheless possible to form at least a rough impression of how this paradigm intersects with questions of migration. Here, it is useful to briefly consider the political imagination presupposed in typical journalistic reports. Consider the following excerpt from *Newsweek* (2004: 32):

> How easy is it to make oneself over into a desperate Afghan refugee who deserves asylum in the West? Thousands of Pakistanis, Iranians, Central Asians and other Muslims have done it. Last week I did it, too. First, I found one of the dozens of underground 'travel agents' in Peshawar who specialize in smuggling illegal immigrants. Through him I arranged passport photos of me looking vaguely Afghan. . . . The photos were handed over to my agent, and a set of fraudulent documents ordered up. Now I was 'Mariana Ali' from Bamian, where many Afghans look vaguely Chinese.

Melinda Liu, the journalist in question, goes on to explain that she was then given additional documents that would be useful in fabricating a claim for asylum. These included a forged letter purporting to be from Taliban intelligence authorities threatening her with investigation for teaching English to girls. All this, of course, came at a price. For instance, a visa to Ukraine before September 11 would cost you as much as US$2,500 but could now reach US$4,000.

Or consider the following introduction to an article entitled "Why our borders are out of control":

> The headlines usually belong to the most desperate: to the Mexican border-jumpers, the Chinese entombed for months below deck, the Haitians who disembark from ramshackle freighters along the docks in Miami. . . . [But] While the United States seeks new ways to thwart gate-crashers, about half of all illegal immigrants walk unchallenged through the front door. Fraudulent passports and visas, questionable claims of asylum and bureaucratic bungling, help tens of thousands reach American soil and stay indefinitely.
>
> *Newsweek* (1993: 25)

The article goes on to note how Sheik Omar Abdel-Rahman, the "Egyptian fundamentalist cleric" whose followers were charged with the first attack on the World Trade Center, had been admitted into the country numerous times despite the revocation of his green card and the appearance of his name on a State Department watch list. This narrative of perpetrators slipping through the net to commit their crimes would be amplified a hundredfold following the second attack on the Twin Towers. One enduring feature of the narrative of "September 11" is the observation that the immediate perpetrators all entered the US legally.

These are merely two of countless journalistic reports concerning illegal immigration. But they reveal certain things. In the case of the wetback, the burden of insecurity fell mainly, though not exclusively, upon social and economic mechanisms of impoverishment. In this sense, there was a kind of family resemblance between illegal immigration and other social problems such as unemployment, literacy, infant mortality, regional under-development and poverty – all problems that were deemed manageable by the systems of welfare and social security. But, in the above quotes, it is possible to discern how the locus of insecurity has shifted. Although the ramifications of illegal immigration for the income and work of Americans continues to be at issue – according to *Time* (2004), the failure to control the border "holds down the pay of American workers and rewards the ille-gals and the businesses that hire them" – the terrain of the problem has clearly changed. It is no longer a matter of processes such as de-unionization and impoverishment working themselves out within a nationally unified socioeconomic system. Instead, there is a new political imagination pre-occupied with the play of mobilities, and populated by elusive persons (terrorists, asylum seekers, smugglers) and mercurial things (contraband, drugs, weapons) that are able to move about almost undetected, exploiting the smooth, networked spaces, but also the seemingly ungoverned border-lands of a "global" world. The governmental imagination moves from a focus on the deep, interior spaces of national societies and economies to the manifestly superficial, open space of the "transversal" (Bigo 2000: 171). Whereas before, insecurity was to be addressed by state bureaucratic inter-ventions aiming to restore the equilibrium between society and economy, under the paradigm of homeland security, it is much more a game of gov-erning access, targeting weak points and risk factors, preventing intrusion, tracking movement, verifying identity and detecting the undetected. Illegal immigration enters into a new problem series, a "paradigm of suspicion" which, through countless reports, enquiries and statistical experiments, generates a risk-oriented knowledge focused upon systematic affinities between certain forms of immigration, terrorism, organized crime, drugs and smuggling (Shamir 2005). The discursive relationships within this cluster of problems comes to the fore, while the socioeconomic context of migration is de-privileged and must settle for being only one among a host of factors. The strong identity which social security fostered between illegal immigration and the space of labour is almost entirely dissolved. In turn, illegal immigration itself becomes one more form of risky mobility, and a symptom of "our broken borders".

### Risky subjects

In her examination of what she calls "biometric borders", Louise Amoore does much to clarify the role that technologies of risk come to play in the governance of migration and the paradigm of homeland security. Noting how the "deployment of electronic personal data in order to classify and govern the movement of people across borders has become a key feature of the contemporary war on terror", she examines the case of the US VISIT programme (Amoore 2006: 341; see also Amoore, this volume). In many ways, both a public policy and a security "solution" marketed by management consultants and other technicians of risk, US VISIT works by utilizing and interfacing over twenty existing databases from travel, immigration, health, education, police and other authorities. Using this information, the itinerant subject is profiled and encoded in terms of degrees of risk. Logics of precaution and preemption come to the fore: "The guiding assumption ... is that encoded risk profiles can be used as a basis to predict and prevent future acts" (Amoore 2006: 340).

This account of US VISIT can be situated alongside a growing body of richly contextualized studies examining particular schemes, programmes and technologies of borders and bordering (Verstraete 2001; Salter 2004; Sparke 2006b). Such work represents an important contribution to our understanding both of the logic of homeland (or, in the European case, Schengenland) security and the way in which the war on terror is reshaping the securitization of migration. The focus on specific practices reveals that, if homeland security serves to govern illegal immigration as a form of risk that is isomorphic and integrated with other risks, it does so not merely through repeated discursive enunciations but at the level of durable, technical inventions (Huysmans 2006b). However, the intelligibility of the modes of governance associated with technologies such as US VISIT can be further enhanced when we place them in the kind of genealogical trajectory I have been outlining in this chapter. There are two points I want to make in view of the earlier discussion of social security and illegal immigration.

The first concerns what I want to call the *metagovernmental* character of the contemporary migration–security nexus. In the case of the Bracero programme, one sees how governmental intervention operates at the level of social and economic processes. For instance, a knowledge of the employment conditions of Mexican migrants has as its correlate certain attempts, however limited, to ensure minimum wage rates on farms. The governmental objective is to manage levels of poverty both among migrant workers and within the agricultural sector more widely. With US VISIT, as with many similar programmes of homeland security, governance operates at a somewhat higher order and at a greater remove from social processes. If we can speak of metagovernance, it is because US VISIT operates upon statistical and biographical knowledge generated by other governmental domains, such as education and travel, but puts this information to work for other purposes, namely the identification of anomalous or risky patterns of behaviour. US VISIT contributes to the wider phenomenon of "reflexive government" (Dean 1999), which treats existing governmental systems and practices, and their respective systems of identification, as a complex governmental domain in its own right.

Recognizing that identity, understood in a technical–administrative rather than a political–cultural sense, is now a domain of government with its own density, irreducibility and economy sheds new light on certain emerging issues in the migration field. First, it relates to the fact that see-mingly new kinds of problems such as "identity theft" and "identity fraud" have moved to the centre of migration and security agendas. Second, it also corresponds with the perception that the verification of identity – for example through the technologies of biometrics – is a new growth industry (Muller 2004; see also Epstein, this volume). Finally, it also helps to explain how terms such as "the undocumented" have emerged as new discursive markers for the subjects of illegal immigration, and even, in the case of the *"sans papiers"*, a site of political community and contestation (Balibar 2000; McNevin 2006). As the documentation of identity for governmental pur-poses is not at all recent, but in fact a feature of most modern, bureaucratic systems of rule (Caplan and Torpey 2000), the question of why identity security enjoys such a prominent status within contemporary security poli-tics is surely one that begs further scholarly analysis.

My second observation concerns a new kind of subject that is presupposed by the logics of risk that are so central to the game of homeland security. Certainly, on this note, we should not ignore the fact that the war on terror has added new identities and ethnicities to the long history of anti-immi-grantism (Gerstle 2004), a history that has played itself out around a series of racialized "Others". If the undocumented Mexican labourer was, as Ngai puts it, the "prototypical illegal alien" (Ngai 2004: 71), and while an equation between Latino/a identity and illegality persists, it is now that Arabic or Muslim identity is constituted as the dominant racial marker of insecurity in the age of terror (Ibrahim 2005).

However, while politically crucial, to focus only on the changing ethni-cizations of migration insecurity would lead us to overlook certain trans-formations at the level of the cultural and technological production of the subject. That is, it would lead us to neglect new forms of individuation. Here, Deleuze's brief but highly suggestive reflections on "control societies" are particularly helpful (Deleuze 1995). Deleuze does not speak of risk spe-cifically, but what he calls "control" certainly has strong affinities with risk-based governance. He observes that, whereas modern, disciplinary societies featured a productive tension between masses and individuals, today we are witnessing the emergence of the "dividual", the fragmentary subjective counterpart and effect of a society dominated by data banks, identity pro-files, samples and markets.

Deleuze's discussion of the dividual is provocative but somewhat vague. As I have argued elsewhere (Walters 2006: 191), it can be sharpened if we relate it to the changing aims and objectives of governance. It could be argued that the birth of the dividual corresponds with a certain scaling back of the ambition of governance. This is perhaps the case as we follow the line from social to homeland security. We saw in the case of the wetback that governmental intervention took the amelioration of poverty and the improvement of the general social condition of the population as a key aim. In contrast, while it is incredibly ambitious in terms of its will to know the riskiness of its populations, and in meeting the technical challenges this poses, the paradigm of homeland security is quite limited in another respect. It is interested only in practices of population division, segmentation, sorting and threat neutralization. Like a burglar alarm or a firewall, the security it offers to the privileged "inside" – an interior space it simultaneously constitutes – is the reduction of exposure to harm, and nothing more. This shift can be captured quite neatly by the changing significance of poverty. For the apparatus of social security, poverty is something to be managed and reduced. For homeland security, according to Roy (2004; cited in Shamir 2005: 202), "poverty is being slyly conflated with terrorism" so that merely possessing the nationality of a poor nation has the potential to mark the bearer as an elevated risk. Improving the condition of this subject is marginal to the political agenda; the only concern is to govern their access. This is perhaps another way in which poverty itself is shifted from the register of social security and development and moved towards the overlapping space of homeland and geo-military security; another way in which even poverty becomes securitized (Duffield 2001).

### Porous borders

This discussion of risk, profiling and dividualization leads me to the final point I want to make concerning homeland security, and what it is we gain by reading some of its features against my earlier historical moment. This final point concerns the extraordinary political, technological and symbolic importance that is today attached to borders. One feature of the burgeoning interest in border studies across the social sciences has seen scholars document the drawn-out processes through which a US–Mexico border in its current state has been assembled, and the implications of such processes for national identity, territory and sovereignty. For instance, Nevins observes how 1940 was a turning point for the institution of the Border Patrol. For it was in the context of the outbreak of the Second World War that the national administration "played an important role in constructing immigration and border enforcement as issues of national security" (Nevins 2002: 30). At this time, the INS would be transferred from the Department of Labor to Justice and 712 new border guards added, doubling its force. Elsewhere, researchers have begun to explore the seemingly paradoxical phenomenon of "rebordering" (Andreas 2000a), whereby processes of economic globalization and liberalization, and the demilitarization of many border areas, have been accompanied by the appearance of new forms of bordering directed towards the policing of risky mobilities. The apparent bounding of the EU with an "external frontier" is one example of this practice (Walters 2002; Anderson and Bigo 2003). But the prototype is the remaking of the US–Mexico border. While the NAFTA has been pursued to liberalize the movement of goods, there has been in parallel a dramatic escalation of border control. Describing the rise of a "border-centred strategy of immigration control", Cornelius (2005) offers a sense of this transformation when he notes that public expenditure on border enforcement quintupled from US$750 million in 1993 to US$3.8 billion in fiscal year 2004, and the size of the Border Patrol tripled to more than 11,000 agents (see also Sparke, this volume).

It seems that the advent of the war on terror, and its institutional embedding in systems of homeland security, has served not only to intensify this project of rebordering, but to accelerate its projection outwards across networks of surveillance as well as inwards throughout society, confirming that borders are not only territorial lines but complex networks of surveillance and control (Bonditti 2004). At the same time, the fact that President Bush has recently signed into law a plan to add an additional 700 miles of fortified fencing to the existing system of defence at the US–Mexico border (BBC 2006), coupled with the nightly TV images of border jumpers and the vigilantes who hunt them, means that a more traditional conception of the border has certainly not vanished. On the contrary, it has in certain respects only become more prominent. Hence, a more complex situation now exists in which we see a "vacillation of borders", meaning that they are "no longer localizable in an unequivocal fashion" (Balibar 2002: 91).

But one thing which has perhaps not always been sufficiently explored by this growing literature on border studies concerns the changing significance of the border within the political imagination. Reading contemporary news reporting about illegal immigration and comparing it with the reporting of the wetbacks, it becomes quite clear that the position of the border within political debate has changed quite significantly. The 1950s certainly saw renewed attempts to expand the Border Patrol and consolidate the border as a legal and territorial limit – a move that was at times politically contested by certain border communities. However, if news reporting is any guide, within the popular imagination, the border seems to have had a relatively minor status. Despite the fact that the pejorative name "wetback" referred to the phenomenon of migrants wading across the Rio Grande, it was only occasionally that reporting focused explicitly on the border crossing activities of migrants, and then only as one among many aspects of "wetbackism". Rarely did the border feature as a metaphor or a symbol.[5] On the contrary, one finds a very mundane and de-dramatized language, which speaks of the "international boundary" (*New York Times* 1951b: 31) or of actual border regions, such as the "Texas–Mexico boundary" (*New York Times* 1951a: 1). Public attention was far more focused on the living and working conditions of the migrants than it was on the journeys they made to reach the US, or the fact they had illegally crossed the border. The equation of borders and security had yet to become central within popular discourse about migration.

Compare this with media debates today in which the border has become a privileged signifier: it operates as a sort of meta-concept that condenses a whole set of negative meanings, including illegal immigration, the threat of terrorism, dysfunctional globalization, loss of sovereignty, narcotic smuggling and insecurity. For instance, for several years, the much watched *Lou Dobbs Tonight* show on CNN has almost nightly carried a segment entitled "Broken Borders", where it polemicizes against "illegal immigration" at the southern border. Popular reporting traffics under such titles as Broken Borders, Porous Borders, Borders out of Control, all terms that are interchangeable with "illegal immigration" in a way that was not common in the 1950s. At the same time, the border holds out the promise of a solution to these hazards. Within today's political culture in the US, and in many other liberal democracies, the border has been elevated to the point where it now sits proudly alongside the family, community, neighbourhood, flexibility and other key terms in the political lexicon that Bourdieu and Wacquant (2001) call the "new planetary vulgate". Like these other terms, the border does not have to justify itself. Public debate can appeal to it as a self-evident political value.

There are of course multiple ways of imagining and naturalizing the nation-state and its power to confer life and security on some while withholding such privileges from others. With the talk of broken borders, or whenever the question of security is posed as "who left the door open" (*Time* 2004), or with the very idea of homeland security, it seems that nation and state power come to be legitimated through a particular set of associations – the warm, intimate notions of *home*. Contemporary migration controls may or may not be biopolitical but, as I have argued elsewhere at greater length, they are certainly more and more *domopolitical* (Walters 2004b).

## Conclusion

A great deal of the literature on the securitization of migration tends to embody a tacit assumption. It is that we already know what security is. Different fields may come to be securitized, but we nevertheless know security when we see it. We know it because it speaks a certain language in which the grammar of threat and the idiom of risk are prominent. We recognize it because of how it identifies and almost requires the existence of certain enemies, be these anarchists, communists, illegals or, most recently, Islamicist terrorists. And it is evident to us because security employs characteristic moves, whether these are the call for better forms of identity profiling and inspection, or the sanctioning of exceptional measures, of Patriot Act expedited deportations and extraordinary renditions. The fact that we hear of these terms and practices on an almost daily basis encourages a certain kind of familiarity with them. We live in close proximity to this migration–security complex, so close that it is easy to takes its definitions and presuppositions about risk and security for granted.

Putting this migration–security complex in its place is a matter of using a certain kind of historical practice to establish a degree of critical distance from some of the elements which make up this complex. It is a matter not of denying its political importance so much as refusing its capacity to define the present in unequivocal terms, and hopefully lessening the hold which certain understandings of security exercise on our political imagination. It is matter of approaching the present from a slightly different direction so that its more prominent features can be apprehended in a different light. If the present could be likened to a city, then it's a question of discovering streets and other routes (tunnels, demolished buildings, catacombs?), or perhaps other modes of representation, that enable one to encounter that old town square at a different angle, to see its monuments from a different perspective. Using the "Wetback crisis" of the 1950s as my historical cut, I have tried to show that particular features of today's migration–security complex are far from self-evident. The fact that there was relatively little official or public concern with the identity documents of Mexican migrants then, or that there was not much of a language of "borders" in use to express generalized anxieties of insecurity and violated sovereignty, or that the migrants were almost axiomatically defined as "labour" and associated with "social" issues – all these findings suggest there is much about the migration–security nexus today that is not as obvious as it seems.

But, in addition to its potential as an instrument of defamiliarization, the kind of genealogical sensibility towards which I have gestured has a second significance. This is the possibility of identifying political logics and imaginations that are harder to see if we confine our analyses to the contemporary moment. Here, I want to elaborate the point I raised at the end of the previous section concerning the place of "home" within the complex of homeland security. One of the more striking things that emerges from a survey of news reporting about illegal immigration is the prominent role which images and metaphors of home play in constructing a notion of the space and the collective subjectivity that is to be secured. I would not want to give the impression that homeland security is a coherent discourse lacking any contradictions. It is probably better to see it as a rationalization of a whole host of contradictory political objectives and policy projects than a singular logic working itself out. But while we should not over-rationalize it, we can nevertheless note that this discursive space does serve to draw a set of associations and overlaps between the image of the state and that of the domestic space of the home. Hence, border control comes to be justified as a precaution against various types of criminal incursion, and risk management figures as a technique – not unlike the firewall on a home computer – of balancing openness towards a world of transactions and flows with the need to ensure the integrity of the space inside. This leads to a certain irony when we place the rise of homeland security alongside the political trajectory of the social security project. At the same time that the privatized logics of personal finance, risk management and other elements of "prudentialism" (O'Malley 1996) are taking over much of the terrain once governed by social insurance and other, related forms of social security, the image of the endangered household is going in the other direction. It is becoming mobilized (although surely not for the first time) as a figure of collective and public identity. For, in the figure of homeland security, the home becomes nothing less than the privileged signifier for collective identity and a revived politics of national and geopolitical in/security. The defence of society gives way to the protection of the home.

## Notes

1 I am grateful to William Biebuyck for providing research assistance for this paper, and Canada's SSHRC for research funding.

2 Rather than substitute less offensive proxies (e.g. undocumented migrant) for terms such as wetback and illegal immigrant, I retain them because, for historical and analytical purposes, I want to foreground how particular persons and acts are named and specified under particular historical and social conditions. Hence, if I write "illegal immigrants", this is not to affirm such terminology, but to use it as a shorthand for "those subjects known as or named 'illegal immigrants'". For an excellent discussion of the problematic political and epistemological status of terms such as "illegal immigration", see De Genova (2002).

3 The blurring of legal and illegal status was particularly evident in the practice of "drying out wetbacks": state officials would have illegal workers literally step over the border so they could be instantly readmitted legally for the purposes of temporary employment. See Calavita (1992).

4 It is much more common today that the illegal immigrant is problematized not just as one who undermines welfare through offering a source of low-wage competition, or whose substandard living conditions directly contaminate the community, but through their presence, and that of their children, within public education and welfare services where they drain away scarce resources. Accordingly, one sees a politicization of access and eligibility by grass roots movements. Just as "welfare fraud" comes to function as an explanation for the difficulties of welfare under neoliberal conditions, the eviction of the illegal from the welfare system serves to displace questions about social citizenship.

5 One of the few exceptions I have found is a *Business Week* article entitled "Wetbacks in Middle of Border War" (*Business Week* 1953).

# 9 Embodying risk

## Using biometrics to protect the borders[1]

*Charlotte Epstein*

In 2002, the US officially established biometrics at the heart of its new border security management practices when the President signed off the Enhanced Border Security and Visa Entry Reform Act. There is no shortage of explanations as to why the state turned to this new, private technology. Some emphasize the need to find the most efficient technology in a post-9/11 context of heightened insecurity and the "war on terror". Yet, while the terrorist attacks of September 11, 2001 may have legitimized it, they did not trigger the state's turn to biometrics: the first large-scale use of biometrics by US law enforcement agencies occurred in fact at the January 2001 Superbowl in Tampa, Florida; and biometrics-based trusted traveller schemes have been in place at certain US airports since 1993 (Woodward, Orlans and Higgins 2003: 248–95). Other explanations underscore a general "rolling back" of the state where traditional military and defence functions are increasingly contracted out to the private sector, specifically in high-risk activities (Mandel 2002; Singer 2004; Avant 2005). This chapter considers, rather, what biometrics does *for* the state. It explores the specific ways in which, far from signalling a retreat of the state, the introduction of biometrics into traditional border protection practices reinforces not merely the governance capabilities of the state, but its power. For biometric borders appear as a perfect marriage of convenience: with states as their client (a situation that was generalized when the US imposed the biometric passport on the twenty-seven allied countries of the Visa Waiver Program in 2006), the biometric industry is booming, with its market doubling between 2005 and 2007 alone (Epstein 2007). States, for their part, see biometrics as the high-tech solution for managing the increasingly intractable terrorist risk (US Congress 2005).

This particular convergence of state and new technology and the way it has impacted on contemporary border protection practices is the focus of this chapter. To analyse it, it reads two logics against one another: the functional logic of the technology itself, and the political logic of the modern state. It proceeds in four movements. It begins, first, by examining the US border security programme, US VISIT, as the most extensive application of the new biometric technologies. The purpose here is not to condone any kind of technological determinism (whereby the technology was adopted because of the efficiency gains it enabled in terms of maximizing border security), which would underplay the political significance of the state's turn to biometrics. Nor is the concern to grasp the material or social conditions that have enabled the technology's development. Rather, using the biometric engineering manuals, this first part unpacks the functional logic of biometric systems from the inside and on their own terms. The aim in this part is to critically examine both a technology and a literature that have so far remained largely beyond scrutiny.

In a second movement, the chapter turns to read the use of biometrics from the logic of the contemporary state. Michel Foucault's concept of "governmentality" provides a starting point for contextualizing these new border protection practices. His analytics of power are especially useful for examining the type of politics unfolding in a context where the technologies of risk by which we are increasingly governed home in ever more closely upon the human body. Biometric systems in particular are deployed around particular representations of the human body. The two main distinct figures of the human body that feature at the centre of the new border protection systems are thus considered successively. This second part unpacks the construction of the *foreign body* underlying the US VISIT Program. This body intimately scrutinized at the US borders features not as the recipient of political rights, but as a live, mobile object. In a third movement, the chapter then examines the *risky body*, the figure at the core of biometric systems, and offers two successive, and in some ways contrary, readings of the state's turn to biometrics. On a first level, the Foucauldian lenses highlight the development of biometric borders as a system of risk management geared towards *embodying* risk in the "risky body". They reveal how, in putting a body to the new face of risk, as it were, these new high-tech border protection practices have reinforced the state, by establishing risk – in the form of the risky body – as the third term articulating the relationship between the state and its population. However, the fourth and final movement of the chapter analyses the figure of risky body as that which fundamentally escapes modern power: it marks the inconceivable, the blind spot on the radar of modern power.

## Reading the new border security practices

### Biometric authentication systems

Starting from the biometric engineering manuals,[2] "Biometric authentication systems" are systems of surveillance designed to secure access to a space – whether a physical space, such as an office, or a logical space, such as a network – by controlling individuals' access to it (Zhang 2002; Woodward, Orlans and Higgins 2003; Ashbourn 2004; Bolle *et al.* 2004). They use "biometrics" to identify a person: these constitute sets of measurements derived from the print or photo of distinctive body parts (face, finger, the hand, the iris) or a behavioural trait (voice, signature or even keystroke) that constitute markers of individuality. Access is granted to that person once she has been correctly identified ("authenticated", in the engineering lingo). They are risk-based surveillance systems, where the risk-to-be-managed is the penetration into the secure space by an unauthorized or undesirable body. Central to the system is the compilation of databases collecting the designated biometrics of all the people susceptible of requiring access to that space. Initially developed as private technologies, to secure private spaces, the effects they exert are highly political, in that they constitute knowledge-based technologies of population control. In fact, as I have argued elsewhere (Epstein 2007), they tend to blur the distinctions between private and public. The making of the databases requires every person susceptible to need to enter the space to submit personal, and indeed sometimes very intimate, information to the registration process (known as "enrolment"). For example, the iris can reveal information about various kinds of medical conditions, such that the person is giving up much more than just her identity (Bolle *et al.* 2004: 148).

The scale upon which such information-based forms of control operated changed dramatically with the state's turning to biometrics: from visitors to a private space, the population pool had shifted to the visitors to an entire (and one of the largest) country. The US Congress' response to the 9/11 attack was to mandate a complete overhaul of the American border control system, to be fully implemented by the end of 2005 at the latest. "Biometric entry capabilities" were what the Departments of Justice and Homeland Security were charged with developing (US State Department 2006a). "Biometric borders" were thus Congress' dream of a perfect shield for the homeland (Amoore 2006). By January 2006, US authorities had fingerprinted over 44 million individuals, making the new border protection system, in the triumphant assessment of the US State Department (2006a), "the largest-scale application of biometrics in the world". This change of scale is in fact inscribed within the functional logic of the technology. Indeed, unlike how the state would have it (US State Department 2006a), for the biometric engineer, it is not strictly that the technology is adaptive to the security requirements of the state, but rather that the political application is already integral to the technology itself. In biometric manuals, "database W", where "W" stands for "world population", is the perfect database, the one that would enable biometric systems to perform at their best and eliminate all threats (Bolle *et al.* 2004: 157). In other words, in the biometric engineer's world, registering the intimate details of every single body on this planet is the solution to the problem of risk. The US authorities' new border protection programmes are thus one step closer to the industry analysts' fantasy of a perfect zero-risk system. This is a performative, self-fulfilling techno-logic that forecloses the possibility of failure from the onset: no matter how many mismatches or false positives may actually occur on the ground, in this functional logic, these errors are readily attributed to the notion that the usage of biometrics is not extensive enough. Both imperfection and danger are thus located *outside* the system, and failure can only arise from not enough biometrics, rather than too much.

## The US VISIT Program

Reading the biometric borders from the biometric engineering draws out the trajectory of this new border protection system in a new light. Let us retrace the stages of its development (see also Sparke, this volume). The first step in the elaboration of a comprehensive system of border protection centred on biometrics was the National Security Entry–Exit Registration program (NSEER), established on September 11, 2002 (US State Department 2003a). NSEER developed the first biometric database of risky aliens, by combining a new, biometrics-based registration process for travellers to the US broadly deemed potentially risky, with pre-existing databases that already used biometrics. The registration process operated in two ways. It designated certain nationalities (Iran, Iraq, Libya, Sudan and Syria) for automatic registration, and it singled out certain individuals "arriving from certain countries, or who [met] a combination of intelligence-based criteria, and [were] identified as presenting an elevated national security concern".[3] At registration, the individual's biometrics (fingerprint and faceprint) were collected, together with detailed biographic information.

NSEER was terminated in December, 2003, and progressively replaced by US VISIT (United States Visitor and Immigration Status Indicator Technology), which was piloted in 2004 and generalized throughout 2005 (US State Department 2005). For a significant problem with NSEER was that it still relied on broad categories: something more fine-grained was needed, capable of directly identifying the *actually* risky individual amid the fray of travellers, instead of operating in terms of broad "groups" of potentially risky travellers who were ranked according to their nationality or race. Indeed, an important weakness of the system was that it was left open to considerable criticism as to how these generic markers of "untrustworthiness" were determined: why certain nationalities were included and not others, such as Cuba or North Korea.[4] Or indeed Saudi Arabia, given that the stated rationale was, in the words of one official: "these are places where al Qaeda or other terrorist organizations have been active" (US State Department 2003a). The supplemental list of individuals was one step closer to being able to home in directly on the risky body; however, it too relied on categories that were not easily defined and exposed to injunctions of racial or religious profiling. In short, the system was discriminatory, as well as inefficient, as it could be defeated by individuals defying coarse categorizations. One such individual was Richard Reid "the shoe bomber", who had passed border controls undetected on his legitimate British passport: Mark Salter

(2003: 129) describes the subsequent coining of the awkward new category of "British Muslims of this militant stripe". In fact, NSEER's main function lay elsewhere: in the constitution of the database N of risky bodies.

In the biometric logic, database N corresponds to the first stage in the making of the biometric database, which is known as "negative enrolment". The enrolment process aims to constitute a pool of "trusted subjects", to whom access can be granted to the secure space, and who form database M (Bolle *et al.* 2004: 159). To this end, negative enrolment first weeds out the "questionable subjects" from the broader pool of potentially trusted subjects to form database N of individuals who present a risk – risky bodies. Positive enrolment can begin once the negative enrolment has been terminated, to constitute the actually trusted pool of subjects on database M. Considering NSEER application in the light of these dynamics reveals that the sixteen months when the programme was operational allowed for the orchestration into one immense dataset of all pre-existing criminal databases both national (FBI) and international (Interpol), in addition to a new database, created by the US military, who collected "un-named" fingerprints in identified sites of danger abroad, such as al Qaeda training camps, which provided a real "mine of fingerprints", according to one official from the Justice Department (Korbach 2003). In addition, a stated objective of NSEER was to make this monster database accessible to a vast array of US government agencies for a variety of purposes, including law enforcement within the US territory (US State Department 2002). From this perspective, then, NSEER was more than an imperfect scheme hastily thrown together while a better one was under way; it was a necessary step phase in the compilation of the largest ever biometric database.

Under US VISIT, *every* body is fingerprinted and photographed indiscriminately.[5] First, visitors from non-visa waiver countries, as well as those visitors from visa waiver countries who intend to stay over three months, are fingerprinted and photographed at the American Embassy where they apply for the visa (under the "BioVisa program") (Williams 2006). Second, short-term visitors from the twenty-seven visa waiver (i.e. closest allies) countries have their fingerprints and faces photographed and scanned at the port of entry. Hence, paradoxically enough, the extension to all non-US visitors did away with nationality or ethnically based discrimination. Again, I am not claiming that such discrimination does not actually occur on the ground but, rather, that it was written out of the system's design. In fact, what US VISIT did was to substitute a morally charged logic of discrimination with a technical, and thus seemingly apolitical, logic of "enrolment". Thus, if NSEER was the phase of "negative enrolment", US VISIT represents the "positive enrolment" of all travellers to the US. Every visitor is now automatically screened against the database N of risky bodies: should this yield a match, the visitor is denied entry. By January, 2006, the system had thus screened out 14,000 individuals at US embassies and 907 at the port of entry, according to Jim Williams (2006), US VISIT director. All the other visitors are "positively enrolled" into database M of "trusted subjects", albeit still not as trusted as the *really* trusted subjects of the "trusted travellers" programmes.

## Foreign bodies: political subjects or live objects?

Let us now turn to read the US Visit Program from a different logic altogether, that of the modern state. The use of biometrics at the borders suggests that, far from having been dis-invested (Salter 2003), the old border system is in fact the chosen site of development of these very particular practices of *governmentality*, by which I mean, following Foucault, modern technologies of population management and the new forms of power exerted in their wake. Foucault distinguishes between "sovereignty" and "governmentality" in the context of a broader historical enquiry into the emergence of the practices by which we are governed. He is concerned with the exercise of government in its most practical, concrete terms: *governing*, rather than government. That is, his focus is not on a set of institutions, nor on an ideological construct, but rather on the multifarious techniques and technologies progressively developed over time to orientate or guide the conduct of individuals. Hence, the starting point for his enquiry is located outside the state, in the dense fabric of social relations; and he proceeds from the bottom up: how come human beings form relationships that allow them to act upon or govern each other? What governs over the individual (this question also branches off in Foucault's thought into the issue of self-government)? How are children governed by their parents; how is a lover governed by his lover (Foucault 2001a: 1570)? With regard to the state, the question becomes: what exactly is the relationship between the state and its population whereby the former is able to govern over the latter? Coining the term "governmentality" was necessary to provide a counterpoint to the concept of sovereignty, which had tended to blinker political theorists to the nature of this bond between the modern state and its population. Moreover, the Foucauldian concept foregrounds the workings of power, which tend to be eclipsed in the policy turn increasingly implied by terms such as "governance" (see, for example, Bevir 2007). Governmentality regroups the polymorphous tactics and strategies of a managerial state, whose primary concern is no longer with "ruling over" its subjects, but rather with managing its population so as to maximize its productive capacities. A productive population is the key objective of the governmental state. Governmentality thus points to an overall tendency towards increasingly efficient forms of population management and to this incremental logic of the modern state. *Governmentalization*, rather than governmentality, marks the general orientation of the modern state; and it is indissociable from an incremental trajectory of power.

Whereas governmentality refers to the broad conceptual framework, discipline and biopower capture two concrete modalities of state power successively emerged within that framework. Both are productive powers – powers that enable production – that target the population, but they differ as to their points of application. The modern individual is created by disciplinary technologies deployed upon both body and mind. (Foucault 1977). The target of biopower, in contrast, is the population as a whole (Foucault 1990, 2001b). It is the form of power concerned with the life ("bios"), with the well-being and prosperity of the population. "Biopower" captures a fundamental shift whereby the main modality of state power was no longer the power *over* life – the power to kill – but rather the power to *make live*. It signals a state busying itself increasingly with birth and death rates, living conditions, issues of health, hygiene, reproduction and, indeed, population movements. Historically, discipline precedes biopower, but they co-exist; for biopower needs discipline, as the most effective and least costly means by which the population is managed from within. Thus, a productive population is the aim of the governmental state; discipline and biopower are the means to achieve it, ensuring docile (discipline) and healthy (biopower) individuals who produce.

To the governmental state, biometrics offers a technology centred around the human body as the ultimate marker of individuality (as it is premised on the fact that no two individuals have the same biometrics). In fact, biometrics hits both at once the objectives of discipline and biopower. For it features as the ultimate individualizing technology; yet it is also deployed to regulate entire populations. Returning to the US VISIT Program, discipline and biopower draw out the two axes along which it has developed: it encompasses an ever larger population of travellers, on the one hand, while constantly refining its capacity to home in on individual bodies (rather than groups). However, in the case of biometric borders, the target for these governmental practices constitutes non-citizen, *foreign* bodies. It is noteworthy in this regard that US citizens are spared the biometric scrutiny that their government subjects foreign travellers to. Nor does the US passport contain the biometric chip that the US government has imposed upon other states as a condition for allowing entry to their citizens (US Congress 2005). If, in a Foucauldian perspective, the political subject is created through individualizing technologies of power, in this relationship between the sovereign state and its citizen, the body of the citizen still features as the recipient of rights. With regards to the non-citizen body of the traveller, no such relationship exists, whereby the state remains the guarantor of those political rights. The state whose territory the traveller enters upon is under no such obligation to guarantee political rights that it did not grant in the first place. There may exist a customarily accepted obligation, upon which the whole passport system is premised, to grant protection to the citizen of another state, as formally requested by that state itself through the gesture of presenting the passport at the port of entry (Salter 2003).[6] But that obligation, and the relationship it rests upon, exists *vis à vis* other *states*; and it is merely the graceful granting of a request that may be revoked at any time (when the relationship between the two countries breaks down).

Between the US sovereign and the non-citizen traveller, no such relationship exists. Yet the traveller's body is scrutinized up close and controlled in intimate detail. In the absence of such a relationship, the traveller's body does not figure as the recipient of political rights. It is "just" a body; it has effectively been reduced to its sheer physical "thing-ness", stripped down to its bodily existence. Moreover, it is a body without a voice: In the US VISIT Program, the address from the state (in the person of the border guard) to the traveller to identify herself is posed directly to the body. For, contrary to what the biometrics literature claims, it is not so much about verifying that you are who you say you are, because more often than not you don't actually say anything; but that you are the "right" body, the one that yields a match (Muller 2004, 2005; Epstein 2007). At the biometric borders suddenly surface the "secret presupposition of the [modern] political domain" and the ultimate object of biopolitics: bare life (Agamben 1998: 130). These are not the spaces on the edges of politics or normally out of sight, such as the camps, where Agamben first located it, nor those of the asylum system, where it erupts in all its violence (Dauphinee 2007; Isin and Rygiel 2007). These are the places associated with the seemingly very mundane contemporary experience of travelling. That the US VISIT Program now applies to *all* foreign bodies, not merely those that have been identified as potentially "risky" or even "guilty" (see below), is all the more significant. In the new border protection practices, each visitor to the US features as a foreign body tagged with an individually calculated level of risk.

When the human body is no longer so clearly upheld as the recipient of rights, as the subject of politics, it is not so clear that it is anything more than just a living object, or indeed an animal-to-be-managed. Thus, in the manuals whose logic undergirds our contemporary border protection systems, the human population is envisaged as "a zoo". Human beings are divided into five groups: sheep, goats, wolves, lambs and chameleons. The sheep, which comprise the majority, are "the well-behaved subjects"; goats are "particularly difficult to identify ( ... ) perhaps due to physical damage to body parts"; wolves are "the subjects that attack other subjects in the population" by "imitating, impersonating or forging a biometric"; lambs are "easy to imitate" and thus "the subjects that are attacked by other subjects"; as for chameleons, they are "the subjects that both attack and are being attacked" because they are "both easy to imitate and good at imitating" (Bolle *et al.* 2004: 163–4). This is not because animal life has been elevated to the level of human life. Rather, it is because, in the logic of biometrics, "life" is nothing more than a functional attribute of the object that is key to the technology's efficiency. Thus, the iris is considered as the most efficient biometric identifier, because it is the only biometric for which the human body needs to be maintained alive – unlike the finger, which can be chopped off a dead body. What is the one remaining problem with the iris, for these manuals? "Some people are missing one or both eyes" (Bolle *et al.* 2004: 148). The technology that has been called upon to reinforce the borders is thus one that dehumanizes the human body and reduces it to bare life. Biometric borders thus reveal the type of politics underlying these biopolitical practices as one where "the individual" is delinked from "the human": individualization, here, emerges as a process of de-humanization and de-politicization.

## The risky body (I): the third term binding the state to its population

Biometrics promises an infallible, high-tech security in a context of heightened demand for security in a post-9/11 world. Yet the demand itself is nothing new; only the increased vigour with which it has been addressed by states since 9/11, not least in adding biometrics to its range of technologies of state power, has drawn into sharp relief the function of security under governmentality. In fact, guaranteeing security has always been central to the governmental state: the "security compact", as Foucault (2001c: 385) had named it already in 1977, is a key feature of the relation between the government and the population. This is not, however, security-as-sovereignty; not the "territorial compact", where the sovereign promises secure boundaries, or peace within those boundaries. The boundaries are long settled, and no civil strife looms in most of the states adopting biometrics today. The threat is different; or rather, the entire security logic is different. With security-as-sovereignty, what the state secured was the state itself: this was the self-referential circularity characteristic of sovereignty (Foucault 2001d: 644–6). Maintaining the boundaries, upholding law and order, was what mattered for the sovereign state. It readily exerted its right to kill (its own subjects) to protect these two markers of sovereignty. For the governmental state, in contrast, security is about keeping these subjects *alive*: live bodies, so to speak, are the objects of security. In the Hobbesian state, security was only a consequence of abiding by the law. You were safe because of the law, but also so long as you did not cross it. Here, security is a condition of possibility, or rather a condition of heightened productivity: the individual body is protected so that she can produce. There, power was at a bay. Here, biometrics work up close, right against the body, to *help* the individual feel safe, and thus better produce. There, furthermore, *everyone* was potentially destructive; hence, the law was so necessary to contain these wolfish tendencies.

The governmental state, in contrast, is solicitous. What Foucault pointed out in 1977 still holds true: the exceptional measures adopted in the name of security are seldom emphasized as a sovereign prerogative, a sign of arbitrariness, that is, as a demonstration of sovereign power. On the contrary, they are presented not only as necessary – vital even – but as an expression of solicitude. The solicitous state will secure the population by any means necessary. These may include the law, but are not limited to it. There, the law was instrumental to the sovereign's promise. Here, Foucault points to a security that no longer uses the law but operates above it (Foucault 2001e); and below it as well, up close against the body, as biometrics illustrate. That the security function appears to be evolving increasingly outside both territory and the law, as illustrated by war prisons at Guantánamo Bay, is a further confirmation that this is security-as-governmentality (Butler 2004). This reaches well beyond the political inclination of a particular administration; it lies at the heart of the way the governmental state is shaping out. For security is the one priority upon which all governments seem to agree, at least those investing heavily into security technologies such as biometrics.[7] One of the effects of the so-called "war on terror" has been to strip the definition of security to its bare essentials, such that all governments can agree, regardless of their political inclination: this is no longer about social security (as indeed it still was in Foucault's 1977 text), it has become quite adamantly about *physical* security, literally about life and death.

Securing the mass of productive bodies is thus the finality of governmentality today. But securing it against what? Against an "untraditional threat", to use the expression of NATO Supreme Allied Commander for Europe General James Jones (US Congress 2006); that is, no longer a sovereignty-type attack upon the borders, but rather a threat of disruption of the productive fabric, whether targeting productive bodies and/or the productive infrastructure. It is noteworthy that the expression was coined in the context of a US Army General submitting to Congress the necessity to redefine NATO's mandate away from traditional defence functions and towards internal security. For with this type of move, the army itself – the classic guardian institution of sovereignty – is seeking to invest the terrain of governmentality (see also Bigo 2006; Huysmans, Dobson and Prokhovnik 2006). Viewed from the relationship between the state and the population, this threat has also become the third term binding the state to its population. It has served to establish a new correlation between the degree to which the threat is wielded, and that to which it is responded to; such that *more* insecurity leads to *more* response – and thus more governmental state. In a context in which "governing" has come to mean containing the risk of a terrorist attack, biometric systems provide the perfect technology for managing such risk. For they define the risk, or rather *embody* it, in the risky body. By the same token, the risky body has become the central figure determining the entire design of security management. Or rather, the risky body features on two different levels: it is an abstract figure triangulating the relationship between the state and its population in a way that reinforces the state. It is also a foreign, de-humanized, bare body.

The biometric borders are not intended to stop the flow of "normal" travellers – in fact, they aim explicitly at minimizing the disruption to normal airport traffic. The system will only be alerted when it spots a potentially risky body. This obsession with risk, with the accident, the exceptional, is characteristic of risk technologies and, more broadly, of a society for which risk prevention is a key *modus operandi* (Beck 1992). In this particular instance, risk has been incorporated, made flesh, *as* a risky, foreign body; as such, the task of protecting the borders has been entirely cut out as finding the risky body. Ironically, in a system that tends towards total visibility (as per the endless proliferation of cameras in public or semi-public spaces), the "normal" traveller has become invisible, unnoticeable. The exception is the visible, or rather what the system seeks to *render* visible by, literally, putting a face (or a fingerprint) to a name.

## The risky body (II): the blind spot of power

These vast biometric databases serve to sift out risky bodies from the flow of travellers at the gates of the homeland. In effect, they are differentiating between two kinds of risky (foreign) individuals: "guilty" bodies, first, known transgressors of the law. Indeed, one of the celebrated advantages of US VISIT is its ability to "stop murderers and paedophiles from entering the United States" (US State Department 2006a). It is significant that that one of the first effects of the deployment of biometrics at the borders has been to reinforce the traditional law enforcement practices, which harks back to sovereignty. The second category seems more difficult to pin down: "immigration violators" is how these bodies are designated in the same press release celebrating the merits of US VISIT. But given that "immigration violators" are as old as the US itself, and that they have tended to be extremely productive, indeed cheap and economically indispensable bodies (Andreas 2000b), it is unlikely that such a hugely expensive border protection system was suddenly set up against them today merely because the technology has become available. In fact, the bodies that are sought out are the destructive bodies; not merely the unproductive ones, but those bearing intentions to rip apart the productive fabric of the homeland, as well as themselves. That these are presumed to be more likely immigration violators is in itself an interesting presumption, given that many September 11 attackers were not. Of course, "destructive bodies" is not how they are officially referred to: "immigrant violators" is the fall-back, familiar sovereignty category established in lieu of a new and still as yet not completely circumscribed type, despite the monster databases. This un-definability is significant; it is more than a linguistic or epistemological shortcoming: it points to a fundamental impossibility for a logic geared towards productivity to actually *conceive* these destructive bodies, even while it is effectively centred around them.

Already in the previous section, we saw surveillance systems geared towards rendering visible the risky body: in fact, they point to a blind spot on the radar of power. Invisible and inconceivable, these destructive bodies are the ultimate affront to governmentality; for they posit the limits of the conceivable. Foucault himself (1990: 138–9) had already remarked, *a propos* suicide and the obsession with studying it in the nineteenth century, how the body that kills itself is a fundamental defiance to a form of power that enables life; and suicide has indeed been analysed as a form of political resistance to the biopolitical state (Edkins, Pin-Fat and Shapiro 2004; Dauphinee 2007). In another text on "Security and the State" (2001c), Foucault points to the genuine anger of governments in the face of terrorism. For terrorism makes a lie of their promise of a secure life, the bond to their population. Yet these two strands, a body that kills itself but not others, and a terrorist that kills others but not (necessarily) itself, remained unconnected in Foucault's thought. Today, the new development that needs to be accounted for is the significance of this figure of the destructive body to the deployment of new forms of terrorism. And this begins with finding a name for it: hence the term "destructive body" proposed here, rather than "suicide bomber", because the bomb is no longer its defining feature, as the 9/11 plane attacks have shown. The target for these destructive bodies is the very same productive fabric upon which governmental technologies are deployed. They constitute a double defiance to biopower, the power fostering the life of the species man (Foucault 2001c: 242). First, the individual is reclaiming her/his body away from power, in a singular re-appropriation, and indeed reversal, of the sovereign's right of death (Dauphinee 2007). Second, killing *other* bodies generalizes the act to the level of humanity at large, and destroys (a least a part of) the species' productive and reproductive capacities.

The 9/11 terrorist actions defied the power of the state, in its sovereignty, by locating the attack on its territory; but also in its governmentality, by targeting a perfect emblem of productivity – the World Trade Center. It is significant that the only way the state knew to react was afforded by the old schemes of sovereignty: toughen the borders – all the more so as the attack did take place on the borders, both planes having been domestic flights. Yet the borders became the site of development of these new technologies of population control. Are they the same old borders, then? Yes, in that they have not altered the lines of the map. And yet the new borders are not just stronger physical barriers – no concrete walls built up here. They are flexible and high tech, infused with biopower. They are no longer the classic portals of sovereignty, where power was exerted by granting or withholding access at the gate, but did not extend far beyond the gate on either side. Rather, the borders have become nodes, or gateways, along the circuits of a more fluid and ubiquitous power; a power that now extends to foreign bodies abroad. They have been turned into strategic spaces for the collection of fingerprints. Governmentality has invested the borders. The old schemes of sovereignty have been reactivated by being placed within the field of governmentality. Indeed, the resurgence of "guilty bodies", a category pertaining to the sovereignty framework, in the new biometric border management system does exactly that. Nonetheless, the borders *are* strengthened, and sovereignty is reinvigorated, albeit reworked. In Butler's (2004: 93) words, "governmentality becomes the new site for the elaboration of sovereignty". Yet what re-emerges in the end is a bolder sovereign state – a state consolidated not merely in its governmentality, but in its very sovereignty: the "sovereign power" that Agamben (1998) and Edkins, Pin-Fat and Shapiro (2004) draw our critical attention to.

Sovereignty, that "anachronism that refuses to die", as Judith Butler (2004: 54) ironizes, indeed shows little sign of waning. No need to look for a neat break between sovereignty and governmentality; Foucault himself insisted on their co-existence. This, however, prompts a similar question to the one raised by the new borders: is this a new, fundamentally different sovereignty? Butler, for her part, captures one "reconstellation" of sovereignty operated by the war prisons, which have brought sovereignty a new lease of life. There sovereignty is revitalized, yet deeply deformed: we are in a new era of "petty sovereigns", to use her term. Yet the monstrous sovereignty she exposes is a sovereignty fully colonized by governmentality; and these petty sovereignties may distract from that other nexus, sovereignty/ law/rights, and thus from sovereignty's capacity to actually function as *resistance* to governmentality. In other words, maybe sovereignty persists today, not just because it is easily disfigured, but because it still continues to operate as the pole of resistance to governmentality. Indeed, historically, the evolution towards governmentality was accompanied by the appropriation of sovereignty by "the people" (Foucault 2003: 37–40). At that particular point, sovereignty became the critical instrument wielded against the excesses of (a monarchic) power. Undoubtedly, this democratization of sovereignty was a smokescreen for the rise of these new forms of disciplinary and regulatory power from within this same people; and Foucault (2003: 40) calls for moving away from *both* disciplinary powers and "the old right of sovereignty". Nonetheless, in the meantime, that "old right" is the only one we have, as Foucault himself recognizes (2003: 39; see also Shaw 2004).

Moreover, this other "piece of the real", biometric borders, reveals some very real points of tension between sovereignty and governmentality, which seem to indicate that sovereignty is perhaps not so easily reconfigured. Thus, perhaps sovereignty may still be more than an empty shell entirely hollowed out, but still somehow upheld, by governmentality. For why, then, would governmentality continue to uphold sovereignty at all? The latter's persistence suggests a more complicated relationship that needs to be further explored. Before nailing too hastily the lid on sovereignty's coffin, maybe we should see that "anachronism" instead as referring back to the form once taken by a democratized sovereignty, where it operated as a refuge from power. In a sense we – as modern political subjects – have no choice but to keep reclaiming the figure of the body as the recipient of rights. For letting go of that figure, in the face of a creeping biometricization of society (and not just at the borders; Epstein 2007), we risk leaving the body stripped bare and standing completely naked in the face of sovereign power.

Not only is the figure of the individual as subject of rights, entitled to bodily integrity, the only recourse against encroachments upon civil rights but, more concretely, and at the systemic level, sovereignty is what has effectively prevented the deployment of biometrics to its full capacity – the constitution of the perfect biometric database W that has registered all the fingerprints in the world, towards which governmentality, with its expansive trajectory, tends, as do biometric technologies. On the one hand, there is no doubt that a key effect of biometric borders was the mutual reinforcement of *all* governmentalities, and not just that of the US state. In this way, for example, some countries in the visa waiver scheme chose to exploit individually the possibilities offered by the "e-chip" embedded in the biometric passport far beyond what had been imposed upon them by the US government: the US only required the e-chip to contain a digitized replica of the photograph of the face, established since 2003 as the international biometric (by the International Civil Aviation Organization). Yet countries such as Australia, Belgium, Great Britain or Germany decided to include fingerprints. On the other hand, however, constitutional sovereignty still upholds very real hurdles to the full deployment of governmentality. Indeed, the main reason why the US subjected visa waiver country travellers to fingerprinting and digital photographing under US VISIT in the first place is that, even with biometric passports, the US depends upon other states' goodwill to access the biometrics on the chip. Even if another state includes fingerprints on the chip, these would need to be configured so as to allow US machines to read them.[8] In other words, behind the question of authorization, the US is coming up against *other* states' sovereignty. Having its own biometric systems circumvents these issues. This may be another reason why, while it collects fingerprints from "aliens", the US does not include its own citizens' fingerprints in their passport (US Congress, 2005) – effectively removing the risk that they may be read by other states. At play here is thus a competition between jurisdictions – who has access to whose citizens' biometrics – and thus between sovereignties. But this is also a sign of sovereignty's enduring resistance to governmentality: it is interesting that, on the related question of what passenger information should be made compulsorily available by the airlines to the US administration, the staunchest opposition has stemmed from the European *parliament*, the institution charged with guarding the sovereignty of the European peoples. Thus, sovereignty has so far effectively stalled the free flow of fingerprints from one database to another across the globe.

## Conclusion

This chapter sought to capture two logics that have found one another: that of biometric technologies and that of the modern state. It progressed from biometric systems to biometric borders, the site where this encounter occurred, and unpacked the US VISIT Program. A key concern, in analysing these new security practices that operate right up against the traveller's body, was to observe what happens to the classic figure of the body as the recipient of political rights – the figure of the modern political subject, in other words. In these biopolitical security practices that target foreign bodies, this figure is simply absent, and the body stands bare and voiceless before state power, a living object whose movements are to be monitored. This was not about the deviations, mistakes or grave mistreatments of travellers that have multiplied on the ground (Mutimer 2007); nor was it about whether the new border protection system actually works. Rather, it was about the logic that regulates the functioning of biometric systems and has, with the state's turning to biometrics, spilled over into the practices by which we are governed today; those same practices that are meant to make us feel "safe", "secure", "protected" against the terrorist risk. Thus, what is evacuated at the biometric borders, along with the figure of the human body as recipient of rights, is that other political logic that has historically acted as a counterweight to these governmentality dynamics: the logic of rights/laws/civil liberties that is pinned on to the framework of sovereignty. Hence, the need to reclaim that figure, and indeed the discourse of sovereignty from which it stems, as against the colonizing discourse of governmentality and these biopolitical security practices that de-humanize, and consequently de-politicize, the human body.

Furthermore, to understand the security logic under which we are governed today, this chapter focused not only on the body that biometric borders are looking *at* but on that which they are looking *for*. For all their efficiency, expediency and technological sophistication, the security logic underpinning these biometric border practices revolves around something it cannot name: the figure of the destructive body. On the one hand, the control of territorial access is entirely ruled by this exceptional figure – the flow of normal travellers goes unnoticed. And yet at the same time, it marks the blind spot on the radar of power, a fundamental inconceivable for a power geared towards producing productive bodies. Hence the need to mark it with a face or fingerprints, to contain it, in the risky body. While the figure of the risky body embodies the third term triangulated in a relationship between the governmental state and its population increasingly grounded in security, the body that really destroys itself and other productive bodies also marks the limit of that governmental logic.

## Notes

1 I would like to thank Louise Amoore and Marieke de Goede, as well as the participants in the 2006 ISA workshop "Governing by Risk in the War on Terror", for their helpful suggestions on a prior version of this chapter.

2 While as a technology biometrics uses knowledge from many different scientific domains (such as biology, computer science, mathematics, etc.), biometric engineering is the applied science concerned specifically with the transformation of these different types of knowledge into new technologies. Hence its corpus of manuals provides the material under examination here.

3 Thus, the registry was rapidly *de facto* expanded to include the following nationalities: Afghanistan, Algeria, Bahrain, Bangladesh, Egypt, Eritrea, Indonesia, Iran, Iraq, Jordan, Kuwait, Libya, Lebanon, Morocco, North Korea, Oman, Pakistan, Qatar, Somalia, Saudi Arabia, Sudan, Syria, Tunisia, United Arab Emirates and Yemen (US State Department 2003a). The legal basis for this national registry is the 1952 Immigration and Nationality Act, which requires "any alien over 14 years old who remains in the US for more than 30 days" be registered. Thus, technically, the new system merely requires cancelling the exemptions that were in place in practice, for those five "suspicious" nationalities enumerated above (US State Department 2002).

4 The point was made by, among others, Khaled Abdel Kareem, a journalist form the Middle East News Agency at a Foreign Policy Center briefing (US State Department 2003b).

5 With two exemptions: Canadian citizens and Mexican citizens who already have a "laser visa" (Border Crossing Card) – and thus whose fingerprints have been pre-recorded through a different system (US State Department, 2004).

6 In the first page of the British passport, this request to is explicitly laid out in the following terms: "Her Britannic Majesty's Secretary of State requests and requires in the name of Her Majesty all those whom it may concern to allow the bearer to pass freely without let or hindrance, and to afford the bearer such assistance and protection as may be necessary".

7 In fact, the failure to do so brought about the defeat of a right-wing government in Spain, illustrating that this lies beyond party political distinctions, as indeed does the US Democrats' aggressive attempt to take on the theme of "homeland security".

8 This transpired as a real concern at the US Congress (2005) Committee Hearing on Border Security/Biometric Passports with regard to the new European passports: when asked whether the US border system could not read the actual chip or would not be allowed information on the EU databases, the Department of Homeland Security official replied: "well, both actually".

# Part IV

# Risk, tactics, resistances

# 10 Border hacks

## The risks of tactical media

*Rita Raley*

## Introduction: symbolic performances

Leading up to Labor Day 2005, the Department of Ecological Authoring Tactics, Inc. (DoEAT) launched a border disturbance action with the yellow "Caution" signs mounted along the San Diego area highways. Introduced in the early 1990s, the signs were intended to function as warnings to drivers about the possibility of immigrants trying to cross the busy highways before border checkpoints. DoEAT's intervention was to defamiliarize the iconic silhouettes of three running figures, surprising drivers with the new titles: "Wanted," "Free Market," "No Benefits," and "Now Hiring." In the wake of Operation Gatekeeper (1994) and the construction of the "Iron Curtain," the 14-mile San Diego–Tijuana border fence, highway deaths are no longer as common as they once were. The scene of death has shifted eastward to the deserts and mountains – but the iconic signs remain (Robbins 2006). In the hands of the DoEAT group, the signs were no longer simply cautionary warnings; instead, they were a tactical art performance enacted with a sense of urgency that also resonates in the Spanglish word play in the group's acronym: "do eet." Reminiscent as it was of the Situationist technique of *détournement*, DoEAT's interruptive and resignifying art performance commented on the neoliberal economic policies that compel the forced movement of migrant labor. In its allusion to NAFTA and the "free market" that opens the US–Mexico border to commodities but reinforces its closure to people, the DoEAT tactic was truly site specific, situated both physically and socio-culturally. Highlighting the disparity between the mobility of capital and the immobility of people, the signs continue to speak both to the conditions of labor and to the criminalization of border crossings. The circulation of goods and capital has been enabled by the free trade agreement, the signs remind us, but border security practices, particularly walls and fences, continue to prohibit the circulation of people. At the new Iron Curtain, neoliberal market ideologies of liquid, free-flowing capital and open borders of labor come up against new policing tactics to regulate the movements of people.

*Figure 10.1* 'CAUTION', DoEAT, 2005.

DoEAT's border disturbance action thus raises a crucial question at the outset: in the new mode of Empire, have we in fact seen a fundamental shift from a territorial to a capitalist logic of power? We can start to address this problem with a critical look at the reinforcements of territory and national sovereignty along the US–Mexico divide. There is a complex history of securitization along this border, particularly complex with respect to the calls to preserve or otherwise defend the 66-mile stretch in San Diego County, but it is the post-Gatekeeper period that directly informs projects such as DoEAT's.[1] More than 3,500 people are reported to have died attempting to cross into the US since the implementation of Gatekeeper, far more than the dozens killed trying to cross the San Diego highways, the vagueness of both numbers speaking to the sense in which the migrants are not granted the dignity of singularity either in life or in death (Cooper 2003). Criminalizing movement – the visible manifestation of which would be miles of double and triple fencing, barbed wire, concrete pillars, light towers, helicopter patrols, and video-surveillance cameras – has also resulted in the Sisyphean task of capture and return of the anonymous swarms said to be "flooding" or "pouring" over the border. Surely this massive investment in border control and the assertion of territorial sovereignty, begin-ning again at precisely the moment that NAFTA is signed, indicates if not a shift, at least a complex imbrication, of territorial and capitalist logics of power. Further, the development of a "virtual fence" with remote-detecting sensors, remote-controlled cameras, and unmanned aerial vehicles (UAVs) along the US–Mexico divide, along with recent anti-immigration initiatives in the US and Secure Flight and other "trusted traveler" programs, remind us of the intensification of both biometric and territorial borders.

The sheer numbers of those who do not register in biometric testing or otherwise "slip through the fence" can only suggest an intensification, rather than a true fortification or securitization, of borders.[2] The new Iron Curtain has hardly stopped migration north – indeed, by all accounts, the numbers appear to be at an historic high – so what other purposes does it serve? Etienne Balibar writes in a different context about the symbolic power of "obsessive and showy security practices" at the border, which are "designed, indeed, as much for shows as for real action" (Balibar 2003: 40). What would be the sociocultural function of such "shows"? Peter Andreas' important study, *Border Games: Policing the U.S.–Mexico Divide*, provides some answers. Noting that "'successful' border management depends on successful image management [which] does not necessarily correspond with levels of actual deterrence," Andreas concludes that border control is a "public performance for which the border functions as a kind of political stage" (2000b: 9). In other words, the performance of security is more important than actual security, and the theatrical serves as a substitute for the real. The miles of razor wire, the ubiquity of "boots on the ground", the air support – they are all material entities, but they are also crucially part of what Andreas names as a "symbolic performance." "Border control efforts," he explains, "are not only *actions* (a means to a stated instrumental end) but also *gestures* that communicate meaning" (ibid: 11). If indeed it is the case that border control is an "escalating symbolic performance," then we would also have to understand the interventionist tactics of DoEAT and other art collectives in precisely the same terms. Their battle is at once material and symbolic, fought on the very "political stage" where power is exercised. Within a regime of signs, then, the gesture of re-naming the migrant family as "Wanted" is as provocative and significant as it is clever.

Andreas' thinking about the inverse relation between the "escalating symbolic performance" of border control and "actual deterrence" resonates with Ulrich Beck's noted articulation of the central problem for world risk society, which is "how to feign control over the uncontrollable" (Beck 2002: 41; see also the Introduction to this volume). As Beck notes, we have seen a shift from risks that can be calculated and controlled and about which one can make decisions to uncontrollable risks, which exceed rational calculation. The alarmist quality of mainstream media news may make us feel as if risk has increased but, in fact, as Beck explains, risk has simply been spatially, temporally, and socially unbounded. As a result of this de-bounding, Beck argues, "the hidden critical issue in world risk society is *how to feign control over the uncontrollable* – in politics, law, science, technology, economy, and everyday life" (ibid: 41). How, then, does a nation-state simulate control over the ultimately uncontrollable movement of people across borders? With "symbolic performances", military operations double as public relations (PR) campaigns.

And now the stage is set for my reading of a selection of new media art works and performances that critically respond to the securitization of the US–Mexico border. For the crucial problem is not whether or not we can articulate an exclusive logic of power for our historical moment, but how it is that we can understand the critical response to the manifestation and material consequences of that power. As securitization procedures and policies intensify, so, too, does the art-activist response, which gains not only an urgency but also a critical sophistication. As symbolic analysts, these artists are particularly well positioned to think about the deployment and manipulation of signs. Who better to inform such a campaign than the Critical Art Ensemble (CAE), the preeminent tactical media practitioners who for two decades have used theory and performance to alter our perceptions of normalized social practices? CAE's intervention is de-familiarization, to change the way we see the otherwise "transparent codes" of Empire. In an interview exchange, they outline the work of all socially engaged art practices: "Now domination is predominantly exercised through global market mechanisms interconnected with a global communications and information apparatus. Any type of resistant production of representation intervenes and reverse-engineers the displays, software, and hardware of this apparatus" (McKenzie and Schneider 2000: 137). Reverse engineering is most obviously at work in the DoEAT highway sign performance and, more subtly, in the other new media art projects I will discuss. What I will work to demonstrate is the way in which these new media artists utilize the virtuality of their medium in order to critique the immobility of material bodies. Their critique of the neoliberal ideologies of free-flowing virtual capital is manifest in their tactical use of the very technologies, techniques, and tools that late capitalism itself employs. It is even the case, as I will suggest at the end of this chapter, that tactical art practices can directly challenge the risk-based regulation of borders, and both the officials and the technologies used to sustain them.

There is a long-term discourse on the US–Mexico borderlands/*la frontera* as a space of conflict but also of negotiation, exchange, mixture, hybridity (Anzaldua 1987). As the border itself has become increasingly materialized as a fence, a wall, a line, there has of necessity been a shift to thinking of the border itself as a metaphysical binary. This is the point, then, to emphasize the situated aspect of my analysis. We can certainly see a more complex, integrative notion of borders at work in sites such as the Canary Islands or Melilla and Ceuta (Spanish enclaves in Morocco frequently used as passage from Africa to the EU), where this is not necessarily a clear binary logic at work. Different media forms, notably narrative cinema, have intervened with regard to these other borders (Dir. Julie Bertuccelli's *Since Otar*

*Left* (2003) is one example). The new media interventions I address in this chapter are not about the borderlands as a space of hybridity; rather, we will see the insistence on the binary structure of US/Mexico. In this respect, they perhaps indicate the extent to which tactical media in the US, as Geert Lovink has suggested, even now remain wedded to the singular campaign, "rooted in local initiatives with their own agenda and vocabulary;" unlike the media artists of former Communist countries, their terrain is not that of the broad social movement, or Revolution as such (Lovink 2003: 255).

Through an analysis of border disturbance actions initiated by the Electronic Disturbance Theater (EDT) – along with a succession of works situated on the line between artistic and political statements, particularly projects featured in the inSite_05 festival – we will be able to trace the contours of a new front in the battle over immigration and mobile labor populations. Instead of celebrating the crossing of literal and figurative borders (of disciplinary boundaries, genre, language, gender, race, sexuality), as has been the case within cultural criticism in recent decades, these projects serve as a reminder of the material border's irreducibility. No articulation of a space in between, of a third term, of any spatial or geometric metaphors for hybridity, can overcome the material fact of the new Iron Curtain. Reminiscent to some extent of the cultural nationalisms of Fanon and Césaire, such thinking marks a moment of anti-colonial art practice: the aim is not to theorize liminality but to force a rupture in the binaries of interiority/exteriority, here/there, native/alien, friend/enemy. The radical dichotomies integral to the war on terror – "you're either with us or against us" – find their counterpart in art practices that themselves depend on the solidarity of the "we" against the "them." A fence has been built, binaries constructed, and these artists intend to overturn them. Their struggle, while embedded in a binary, rather than a hybrid, cultural logic, nevertheless suggests a reconfigured notion of oppositionality. As we will see, both the "we" and the "them" in their projects and practices are understood to be diffuse, networked, and temporarily, rather than territorially, situated.

The imaginary of the new world order maintains territorial divisions as metaphysical divisions, informed as it has been in the last few decades by texts such as Samuel Huntington's *The Clash of Civilizations and the Remaking of World Order*, whose familiar thesis about civilizational identities and differences naturalizes the US–Mexico border, demarcating the putatively archaic and primal divisions between Anglo and Latino (Huntington 1998). But we must push further to recognize that the articulation of the US–Mexico border in terms of friend versus enemy is a hallmark of our Schmittian moment. Friend and enemy are not for Carl Schmitt private, individual, emotional, or psychological categories. It is not *my* enemy but *our* enemy. That is, "the enemy is solely the public enemy," and it is the defining of the enemy that unites "us" against "them" (Schmitt 1996: 28). In times of crisis, in a state of emergency, Schmitt claims, a political community must decide who is different or threatening enough to warrant the designation "enemy;" enemies, then, are those who threaten a community's security and economic prosperity. Friends are those who are sufficiently loyal and obedient to the commands of the sovereign, those who are willing to risk their lives in the defense of a community. It is in these morally absolutist terms that migrants, "illegals," have been figured not only as a contaminant of the social body but as a sinister threat to the political community in the US.

That citizens assume the responsibility of making sovereign decisions about the normal and abnormal, trusted and untrusted, is another hallmark of our current moment. It is not simply that citizens have been incorporated into the war on terror but that citizens assume the role of proxy sovereigns. As Judith Butler notes in *Precarious Life*, "when the alert goes out, every member of the population is asked to become a 'foot soldier' in the war on terror" (Butler 2004: 39). And as Giorgio Agamben observes in his analysis of the "state of exception," "every citizen seems to be invested with a floating and anomalous *imperium*" (Agamben 2005: 43).[3] With the US–Mexico border written under the sign of national security, we have seen paramilitary and vigilante organizations such as the Minutemen claim the right to make sovereign decisions about friend and enemy. We have also seen gubernatorial plans to broadcast live surveillance footage from the Texas border, allowing not just citizens but all web users to report supposed illegal crossings to an emergency hotline (BBC 2006). It is in these terms that we can revisit the DoEAT intervention: their "Wanted" sign directly invites citizens to be proxy sovereigns insofar as "illegals" are enemies in the war on terror. It reminds us that we are all invited to become, at times it seems almost required to become, proxy sovereigns. In an updating of Cold War logics, we are invited to join in the search for the enemy within.

How, then, are enemies contained and managed as the US national security state evolves? In January, 2006, the Department of Homeland Security awarded a US$385 million contract to Halliburton subsidiary Kellogg Brown & Root for the construction of new immigrant detention centers for future states of emergency:

> the contract, which is effective immediately, provides for establishing temporary detention and processing capabilities to augment existing ICE Detention and Removal Operations Program facilities in the event of an emergency influx of immigrants into the U.S., or to support the rapid development of new programs.
>
> *Business Wire* (2006)

We can call these planned detention centers what they are – camps – and thereby turn to Agamben's articulation of the concept of *homo sacer*, that which can be eliminated or killed but not sacrificed. The war on terror has necessitated extensive critical commentary on *homo sacer*, particularly in relation to camps and other contemporary states of exception (e.g. Butler

2004; Calarco and DeCaroli 2007), so it is perhaps sufficient to note that sacred life is the human body separated from its normal political circumstances. Immigrants become "sacred" in these terms at the moment of crossing the border, becoming "illegal" and "enemy."

We might probe more deeply into the relation between *homo sacer* and the migrant by situating it within Butler's commentary on violence and de-realization. For Butler, the migrant (which I address here as a representative instance of wretched, excluded, de-realized life) cannot simply be restored to or reinserted into the category of the human. Rather, the migrant poses the question of the human not in the exclusion it suffers from the normative condition of the human (the category which, by its very exclusion, it helps to constitute), but by operating as "an insurrection at the level of ontology" (2004: 33). The migrant, that is, forces upon us the question of whose lives remain real in light of those who have already suffered the violence of de-realization. "Violence," Butler asserts, "renews itself in the face of the apparent inexhaustibility of its object. The de-realization of the 'Other' means that it is neither alive nor dead, but interminably spectral. The infinite paranoia that imagines the war against terrorism as a war without end will be one that justifies itself endlessly in relation to the spectral infinity of its enemy" (ibid: 33–4). We might further generalize this condition of spectrality to the very institution of the border itself. Here, I do not mean to erase or negate the "real" material border with its powers of exclusion, but to insist that the border represents simultaneously a material space of violent exclusion as well as a space of exclusion that is haunted by the return of that which it has to exclude over and over again. This is to say the border is that which becomes spectralized by the very return of the migrant. The border, then, functions as a space that is both real and yet made unreal. This leads us to a strange relation between the material border and network traffic, between flooding a material border and flooding a server. Flooding, pulsing, "apparent inexhaustibility" – this is the mode of the swarm, the paradigmatic mode of conflict for "netwar" and for the Electronic Disturbance Theater in their strikes against the Minutemen.

## Swarm the Minutemen

On May 1, 2006, the Electronic Disturbance Theater (EDT) partnered with activists in the Tijuana–San Diego area for a virtual sit-in particularly directed against the websites of California and Arizona Minutemen organizations, "Save our State" initiatives, and Congressional representatives supporting anti-immigrant legislation. The "SWARM the Minutemen" action ("South West Action to Resist the Minutemen") targeted websites with a distributed denial-of-service attack (DDoS), specifically with a FloodNet application that is a hallmark of the EDT. Emerging from the research environment at CADRE in 1998, FloodNet began as a SuperCard script that was used playfully to upload secret messages to the error logs (Meikle

2002: 140–72). In the hands of Java programmer Brett Stalbaum, in collaboration with Carmin Karasic, Stefan Wray, and Ricardo Dominguez, himself a former member of the Critical Art Ensemble, FloodNet evolved into a
*hacktivist* tactic, an applet available to all those wishing to support the
Zapatista movement and social justice campaigns at the US–Mexico border.
The "SWARM the Minutemen" activists provide a succinct description of
FloodNet's operation:

> The software we are using requests files from the servers of the targeted
> websites that are not found – files like Justice, Freedom, and the names
> of those who have died crossing the border. In effect you will see the
> error message – "files not found." The sit-in will interfere with and slow
> down the servers of these various groups and individuals – much like a
> physical sit-in slows down the movement of people in buildings or on
> streets. In addition, the administrators of the servers will see logs of the
> action where the names of those who have died crossing, and the
> requested files like justice, appear repeated thousands upon thousands of
> times.
>
> SWARM the Minutemen Campaign (2005)

The orthographic formulation "hacktivist" suggests that a denial-of-service
attack, with its emphasis on interference and disturbance, can be considered
a legitimate means of social protest, but such a claim has met with some
resistance. For example, Oxblood Ruffin, a long-term member of the hacking collective Cult of the Dead Cow (cDc), from which the term "hacktivist"
originated, has argued that the primary target of hactivist actions ought to
be internet censorship. According to Ruffin, hacktivist networks are the
"blue helmets" of the internet and thereby ought to work toward open code
and peace rather than war (Ruffin 2004). As access to information is in
cDc's terms a fundamental human right, it follows that a DDoS attack is an
assault on free speech and a violation of the principle of free flow. DDoS
attacks have also been literally interpreted as assaults: at the time of Flood-
Net's initial deployment in 1998, it generated a great deal of publicity and
anxiety about possible terrorist applications (Denning 2000). More recently,
Estonia was the target of high-profile DDoS attacks apparently originating
in Russia, an event that now informs the many cyberwar game scenarios
between the US and China. Thus, it is the case that we are currently seeing
a massive private and public sector investment in the monitoring and controlling of risks related to computer use: InfoSecurity, especially data protection, is the currency of our moment.

Although there is an element of play at work in a FloodNet virtual sit-in,
EDT is adamant: "This is a Protest. FloodNet is not a game" (EDT 2005a).
It is indeed not a game but in fact the primary weapon in EDT's arsenal,
over time targeting various institutions and symbols of Mexican neoliberalism, NAFTA, CAFTA, the School for the Americas, the US Defense

Department, Samuel Huntington, and others. Although these targets appear singularly identified, SWARM's overall concern is not simply a set of antagonists or enemies but a broader "systemic logic." They seek to disrupt that which "'others,' migrant people and people of color in general," that which willfully erases the complex history of migration to the US in order to posit a rightfully native population (EDT 2005b).[4]

How is it that one battles a "systemic logic" rather than a clearly identifiable opponent, one that can be seen and therefore destroyed? What is the critical rationale for FloodNet as a mode of protest? To understand the rationale, we must understand the swarm as it has been theorized by RAND researchers John Arquilla and David Ronfeldt in their work on the effects of information technologies on conflict. Put simply, swarming is a mode of conflict in what has been called, variously, "cyberwar," "infowar," and "netwar" (1993). Such conflict has never been limited to traditional military warfare, nor does it necessarily need to be online; in fact, as Arquilla and Ronfeldt explain in *Networks and Netwars*, "we had in mind actors as diverse as transnational terrorists, criminals, and even radical activists" (2001: 2). Swarming, then, can be high, low, or no tech (ibid: 11). Regardless, it is a mode of attack, both a military tactic and a practice of political resistance: "Swarming is a seemingly amorphous, but deliberately structured, coordinated, strategic way to strike from all directions at a particular point or points" (ibid: 12). And in the context of their analysis of the Zapatista movement, they write:

> Swarming occurs when the dispersed units of a network of small (and perhaps some large) forces converge on a target from multiple directions. The overall aim is *sustainable pulsing* – swarm networks must be able to coalesce rapidly and stealthily on a target, then dissever and redisperse, immediately ready to recombine for a new pulse.
>
> Arquilla and Ronfeldt (1998: 15; 2000)

We can contrast the swarm with the wave-like structure of the phalanx: the swarm is the dispersion of force rather than its massification or concentration. It is also the paradigmatic figure for the common gateway interface (CGI) battle scene (e.g. *The Matrix Reloaded*) and, as such, its choreography – marked by convergence, "sustainable pulsing," even "apparent inexhaustibility" – has been firmly ensconced in our cultural imaginary. That it would similarly be lodged in our political imaginary is indicated by the EDT proposal for the development of "non-violent Electronic Pulse Systems (EPS)" (Dominguez *et al.* 1998). Themselves the kind of "radical activists" whose tactics Arquilla and Ronfeldt seek to describe, EDT in turn has recourse to the RAND papers on swarming in order to articulate their project of Digital Zapatismo.

Dominguez and his fellow tacticians work with some of the core principles of CAE: power is no longer centralized but has become networked and nomadic; the site of resistance has in turn shifted from the street to the network; the object of electronic civil disobedience (ECD) is disturbance and obstruction; and disturbance is necessarily temporary. In their first book, *The Electronic Disturbance*, CAE (with Dominguez on board) announces: power "has shed as many of its sedentary attachments as possible;" it is fluid, decentralized, capable of re-situating itself (CAE 1994: 111). For CAE, then, revolution is no longer a matter of spatialized expression; there is no longer a Winter Palace to storm. That is, "the architectural monuments of power are hollow and empty, and function now only as bunkers for the complicit and those who acquiesce. ... These places can be occupied, but to do so will not disrupt the nomadic flow" (ibid: 23). The architectural monuments are defunct and so, too, are the streets, which are "dead capital;" in fact, "the streets in particular and public spaces in general are in ruins" (CAE 1996: 11; 1994: 24). Or, as Michael Hardt and Antonio Negri will put it later in *Multitude*, "basic traditional models of political activism, class struggle and revolutionary organization have become outmoded and useless" (2004: 68). In his 1998 paper on the futures of electronic civil disobedience, EDT member Stefan Wray speculates that the wars of the future, our present, "will be protested by the clogging or actual rupture of fiber optic cables and ISDN lines – acting upon the electronic and communications infrastructure" (1998a). Such transgressive tactics shift the internet "from the public sphere model and casts it more as conflicted territory bordering on a war zone" (Wray 1998b). Wray takes care to stress that street protests will by no means disappear; rather, "we are likely to see a proliferation of hybridized actions that involve a multiplicity of tactics, combining actions on the street and actions in cyberspace" (ibid). ECD, then, will gradually develop as a "component" or "complement" to more established forms of civil and political protest. It may be the case that guerrilla action is limited but, as CAE notes, the "old school" of street protest "has plenty of currency in local affairs where problem institutions are present and concrete" (McKenzie and Schneider 2000: 144). On this point, we would certainly need to acknowledge both the street protests against proposed anti-immigration legislation in spring 2006 and the many school walkouts coordinated by web-to-SMS broadcasting and other social networking tools. Indeed, recent student protests in France and the mass protests against immigration policy across the US remind us that street-based protests are far from obsolete and can potentially have a material effect on public policy.

The use of ECD to thwart the flows of information, to obstruct, block, and otherwise disturb has been extensively documented, but what bears reiterating here is the notion, again articulated by CAE, that "blocking information access is the best means to disrupt any institution, whether it is military, corporate, or governmental" (1996: 13). Again, we see an adumbration and an echo of Arquilla and Ronfeldt's thinking on electronic activism (the theorists and activists in some sense produce each other): "It means disrupting if not destroying the information and communications systems, broadly defined to include even military culture, on which an adversary relies in order to 'know' itself" (1997: 30). The RAND authors leave open the possibility of outright destruction, but CAE and EDT will insist this is not their aim. Rather, the objective of a disruptive action or performance is the temporary reversal, not the cessation, of the flows of power.[5] In this respect, the threat of FloodNet applications is more symbolic than actual, however dangerous it may seem to disrupt server traffic for a few hours. Dominguez acknowledges the difference between the symbolic and the real:

> electronic civil disobedience has a certain symbolic efficacy against power. With the Mexican government, no matter what you do to their website, you're not going to disturb their tanks, their missiles. No matter how much you disturb Nike's website, you're not going to disturb their stores, because they have real exchange power on the ground.
>
> Meikle (2002: 170)

To put the inevitable question bluntly: what, then, is the point? The answer offered by Dominguez, EDT, and other tactical media practitioners is again informed by CAE but, to understand fully the investment in temporary provocations and disturbances, we need to return to Foucault, for whom

> there is no single locus of great Refusal, no soul of revolt, source of all rebellions, or pure law of the revolutionary. Instead there is a plurality of resistances, each of them a special case: resistances that are possible, necessary, improbable; others that are spontaneous, savage, solitary, concerted, rampant, or violent.
>
> Foucault (1990: 96)[6]

After Foucault, then, we have CAE – "resistance can be viewed as a matter of degree; a total system crash is not the only option, nor may it even be a viable one" – and Dominguez himself: "There is only permanent cultural resistance; there is no endgame" (CAE 1994: 130; McKenzie and Schneider 2000: 139).

In what are we investing, then, if not a revolution or an endgame? In sum, it is the "negation of negation:" "The hope is to try to maintain the open fields that already exist, and perhaps expand this territory and elongate its temporality, rather than insist that we can change the whole structure with some kind of utopian ideal" (CAE 1996: 24; McKenzie and Schneider 2000: 139). In David Garcia and Geert Lovink's manifesto, "The ABC of Tactical Media," we see a similar focus on an elongated temporality of the present, the provisional, the "here and now" (Lovink 1997). "Tactical Media are never perfect," never finished, they tell us. Rather, they are "always in becoming, performative and pragmatic, involved in a continual process of questioning the premises of the channels they work with" (Lovink 2003:

264). In all we can see the recognition that "revolution" as such does not need to be a singular temporal or spatial event, that it does not need to be a moment of spectacle. Instead, we can think, as does Dominguez, in terms of "symbolic efficacy." A temporary provocation, however momentary, can change the signifying field in which it occurs, although its material effects cannot be determined in advance. In this respect, the provocation has no necessary teleology; its outcomes are unpredictable and unforeseeable. Why else should the Amsterdam tactical media festivals be organized under the rubric "Next 5 Minutes?" This is not to say that utopian vision is somehow bounded or curtailed, but that a tactical media practitioner acts for the "here and now" with a fragmentary and hopeful vision of an ideal future, one that is not fixed on a future horizon but ever in flux.

## Crosser/*La Migra*

Judi Werthein's shoes – *Brinco (Jump)* – provide us with an entryway into the discourse on migrancy and mobility. Designed for the inSite_05 show and manufactured in China, the shoes were equipped with the necessary tools for crossing borders on foot, including a compass and a flashlight for night crossings. A small pocket on the tongue of the trainer holds either money or painkillers, and the removable insole is printed with a map of documented safe crossing points on the Tijuana–San Diego route. The movement of the migrants that wore them – a set number of pairs were distributed along the border as part of Werthein's intervention/show/project – is marked at three points along the shoe. On the back of the ankle is an image of Santo Toribio Romo, the Mexican patron saint of migrants, their guide and protector. An Aztec eagle is embroidered on the side, and the eagle of the US quarter appears on the toe, indicating or perhaps even propelling the migrant's movement toward the US. The artist designed 1,000 pairs for manufacture in China; after she distributed some along the border, the remainder were sold in a high-end boutique in San Diego. The contrast between the Chinese production costs – US$17 – and the resale costs in the boutique – US$215 – not only brings issues of outsourcing and wage inequities to the fore but also points to the inevitable commodification of the experience of the other.

The thematic significance of the shoe should be clear, its connection to the demand for the freedom to control one's own movement apparent. The canonical text on this issue of freedom of movement is Hardt and Negri's *Empire*. In their schema, Empire depends on a migrant labor force; it cannot then shut down the flows of autonomous movement without destabilizing itself. It is a bit of an understatement to say that they have a more optimistic than pessimistic view of nomadism, of the "specter of migration" and the "irrepressible desire for free movement" (2000: 213). On the issue of nomadism as a form of class struggle, they are unequivocal: "Mobility and mass worker nomadism always express a refusal and a search for liberation:

the resistance against the horrible conditions of exploitation and the search for freedom and new conditions of life" (ibid: 212). We might contrast their vision of the potentialities of free movement with the intensification of the biometric regulation of movement under the US VISIT and related programs, with the division of the population into trusted and untrusted travelers. The demand for freedom of movement is not a demand for movement as such; in fact, the freedom not to move might also be construed as expressive of a certain dignity. The withholding of movement is certainly a familiar practice of civil disobedience, wherein "I would prefer not to move" is a mode of refusal by withdrawal rather than confrontation. Like Bartleby's refusal, it is passive and dangerous, suggesting a certain decorum while also announcing that one is subject to power. In the ceding of power, what is left is the power to withhold. The *droit de cité* (rights to full citizenship) includes the freedom of movement for all, not simply for "migrants" of the global South, and it also includes residential rights, the freedom not to move, to remain settled. This is to say that we must also recognize the capitalist forces that compel movement and be wary of the equation of freedom with the ability to become nomadic. Mobility *per se* by no means endows the subject with an unconditional freedom. In fact, it is precisely the migrant's separation from the nation-state as the guarantor of human rights that places her at risk.

It is precisely the discourse on nomadism that informs Zygmunt Bauman's "liquid modernity" thesis, which holds that

> we are witnessing the revenge of nomadism over the principle of territoriality and settlement. ... It is now the smaller, the lighter, the more portable that signifies improvement and 'progress'. Traveling light, rather than holding tightly to things deemed attractive for their reliability and solidity – that is, for their heavy weight, substantiality and unyielding power of resistance – is now the asset of power.
>
> Bauman (2000: 13)

Coming at the end of the Wired 90s, the liquid modernity thesis is very much in the spirit of Hardt and Negri's synopsis of Empire's capitalist logic of power and their assertion that the "hardware era, the epoch of weight and ever more cumbersome machines," and "heavy modernity," "the era of territorial conquest" is coming to a close (2000: 113–14). Liquidity suggests a temporal rather than a spatial logic of power, a shift away from the management of material things to the management of mobility and speed. Anti-liquidity, then, is the space of EDT's intervention, as Dominguez explains: "The goal of EDT's disturbance is to block Virtual Capitalism's race toward weightlessness and the social consequences a totalized immaterial ethics creates" (Marketou 2002). Their object is not necessarily to emphasize the material basis of capitalism, but to disrupt the circulation and flow of virtual capitalism (Figure 10.2).

*Figure 10.2* Ricardo Dominguez & Coco Fusco, Turista Fronterizo, 2005.

Dominguez's border art-activism includes not only FloodNet perfor-mances but media art projects as well. *Turista Fronterizo*, his collaboration with Coco Fusco for the inSite_05 online exhibit, "Tijuana Calling/Lla-mando Tijuana," is, as its title suggests, an exercise in border tourism pre-sented in the form of a Monopoly-like game. Players choose one of four characters, all border crossers, and proceed on "a virtual journey through the San Diego–Tijuana borderlands," or, simply, around the board. As Gringa Activista, El Gringo Poderoso, El Junior, or La Todológa, players encounter various obstacles and windfalls according to type, adding to or depleting the initial monetary stake as the case may be. If you play in Spanish as El Junior (characterized as *huevón*, politely translated as "lazy"), you often end up at a strip club in Tijuana, under suspicion by the Drug Enforcement Adminis-tration (DEA), or back in the Detention Center. Clichéd this may seem, and indeed that is the point for a game that works with types so as to destabilize types. That is, the general, categorical aspect of the game play alludes to the reduction of real material lives to one-dimensional, pre-scripted characters.

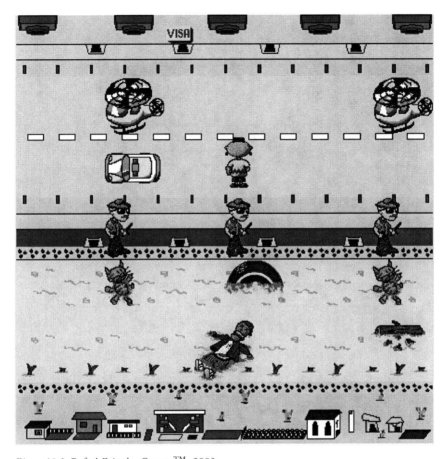

*Figure 10.3* Rafael Fajardo, Crosser™, 2003.

The project does not aim to grant a voice to the migrant or the citizen; rather, the project suggests that one cannot speak from within or outside of the scripted game play. As with a role-playing game, players are addressed in the second person, allowing for a kind of pedagogic experience – what happens if you are caught with cocaine at the border? – limited by the absence of source or reference material; that is, players wanting concrete information about cocaine traffic, for example, must conduct their own research. Although inSite had wanted projects that were exclusively online, Dominguez also built a 1970s-style Pac Man game box for the project and installed it at the Zapatista headquarters in Tijuana. The new computer that housed the game was also placed there to build up the local media lab, thus coordinating not only the material and "virtual" aspects of *Turista* but also *Turista* and Digital Zapatismo. Moreover, the physical placement of the computer game at EZLN (Zapatista Army of National Liberation) head-quarters forecloses the presentation of Mexico as a stable object of border tourism (Figures 10.3 and 10.4).

*Figure 10.4* Rafael Fajardo  La Migra™, 2003.

*Turista Fronterizo* is one of many "games with an agenda," and there are others directly concerned with the US–Mexico border, two of which are Rafael Fajardo's *Crosser*™ and *La Migra*™. Modeling the games on Frogger and Space Invaders, respectively, Fajardo works with basic game mechanics to stage the scene of border crossing as one of collision detection. Thus, the crosser must avoid both air and land border patrols, highway traffic, and dead bodies and other obstacles in the river; and *la migra* uses a car to block the descending bodies (an incomplete "hit" results in death). While one might think this seems a bit macabre, Fajardo self-consciously employs the garish colors and avatars particular to many games so as to preserve a game's basic antagonistic structure. Within these game spaces, border crossing is staged in unadulterated binary terms: US/Mexico, crosser/*la migra*, good/

*Figure 10.5* Anne-Marie Schleiner & Luis Hernandez, Corridos, 2005.

evil. This is migrancy and territorial sovereignty made starkly polarized – how else are we to understand the implications of rendering border crossing as a matter of obstacle avoidance? How, further, are we to understand that successful border crossers in *La Migra* – those not swatted back *à la* Pong – fall into a detention center for deportees? We might further address the use of a game, as Fajardo notes, to "create a subtle multi-level critique" by considering his statement on the matter:

> I've come to understand that the games, any games that attempt to deal with the real, will be incomplete. The map is not the territory, the stakes are not life and death, and a player can walk away when the thrill is gone ... Rather, I have come to understand *Crosser*™ and *La Migra*™ as poems, where the absences and silences are as important as that which is stated.
>
> Fajardo (2000)

Invoking Baudrillard on the simulacrum, Fajardo reminds us that the "map is not the territory," that we should clearly not conflate the border games with the "real" border. We should attend to, play, *Crosser*™ and *La Migra*™ as games – this much is indicated by the design – but as poems they are intended to have a memorializing capacity as well. What they cannot capture or represent are the "absences and silences" that demarcate the difference between a game and a game of life and death (Figure 10.5).

Having examined new media act's engagement with territorial borders, I want to move by way of a conclusion to an account of the complex entanglements of the territorial and the biometric brought to the fore by Anne-Marie Schleiner and Luis Hernandez's *Corridos*, a three-dimensional, open-source, cross-platform game also commissioned for the "Tijuana Calling" inSite exhibit. Taking its title from the *corrido*, a Mestiza narrative ballad traceable to the early modern Spanish ballad form of the romance, *Corridos* maintains a parallel investment in fostering cultures of resistance. As they functioned as a paradigmatic mode of itinerant storytelling, *corridos* played a significant role during the Mexican Revolution, their dispersal epitomizing the very decentralized modes of dissent that now inform EDT. As Américo Paredes has shown, *corridos* are particular to the populations around the US–Mexico border, where the "slow, dogged struggle against economic enslavement and the loss of their own identity was the most important factor in the development of a distinct local balladry" (1958). In the development of a resistant local balladry in the border regions geographically separated from Mexico's centers of power, we can see a clear antecedent to Digital Zapatismo and other tactical movements in the present.

The *corrido* has also been traditionally sung by migrants on the journey north, their narrative subjects outlaws and related legends. *Corridos* the project takes its thematic cue from narco-corridos, contemporary ballads that are often reverential toward drug traders, and, as the designers note, "tell the sometimes sad, cynical and romanticed adventures of narco traffikers who take great risks to deliver drugs across the mexican/us frontera" (Schleiner and Hernandez 2005). *Corridos* the game puts the player in the position of a drug smuggler along the Tijuana–San Ysidro border. As with the ballad, it situates the outlaw or criminal in an idealized subject position, yet also reminds us of the double figuring of people and drugs as undesirable. Indeed, both people and drugs are lumped together under the rubric of "illegal traffic." The language of drugs in the game also derives from the folklore of the ballad, wherein animals stand in for substances (the three animals, goat, rooster, and parrot, refer to heroin, marijuana, and cocaine, respectively). Invoking the complex and imbricated histories of the ballad and of drug trafficking, *Corridos* links both within the context of an open-source environment that allows for modification, somewhat in the way that ballad lyrics allow for musical variation.

More important for my purposes is the objective of the game, which is to find the secret tunnels – narco-tunnels – leading from Tijuana to San Ysidro and use them to run drugs and weapons between the two countries. Modeled on two area neighborhoods, or aspects of two area neighborhoods, *Corridos* has recourse to the material real in its presentation of secret tunnels that circumvent border controls, while nonetheless insisting that it is "just a game." As the designers note: "Corridos is basically a computer game about driving and listening to music." However, the putative discrepancy between a game and the migrant, material world collapsed at Denver Airport in November,

2005. En route to visit his wife and collaborator, Anne-Marie Schleiner, Hernandez was detained by Homeland Security Agents after a luggage search turned up copies of both the game and the inSite_05 brochure, which together rendered him an untrusted subject. Here, we must remember that the Department of Homeland Security's Automated Targeting System uses passengers' choice of reading material along with motor vehicle records, meal and seating preferences, and other personal data in order to assess risk. Hernandez (2005) describes the airport incident in detail in a post to the inSite group:

> In a luggage check at the Denver International Airport, the TSA/ immigration found both a "Tijuana Calling" brochure and a copy of the game that Anne-Marie and me produced for inSite. They searched the inSite website and all of its links and loaded the game and made me play it for them, they found that the game as most of the projects were posing a threat to the US national security and that they were "Anti-American", in speaking about illegal crossings and traffic, in their own words. One officer even told me to watch out who we were working for. I explained that the game as well as the other pieces of art had been commissioned by an art institution whose objective is to gain deeper cross understanding about life in the Mex–US border, for both the peoples of Mexico and the US. They said they didn't believe it and discredited the festival, evidently ignoring what art is. When I told them that the organization was run by US citizens, they replied that not all US citizens are prone to like the government and its policies and that actually a lot of them were working against it.

Were this to end in a spectacular confrontation and escape, it might even be the non-lyric text for a contemporary *corrido*, perhaps one might even call it a *ludo-corrido*. It is in fact both a story of a great battle and a story of risk, but crucially lacks a romanticized ending. To wit: after a lengthy interrogation about Hernandez's knowledge of secret tunnels and terrorist activities in the border regions, he was deported back to Mexico, barred from re-entering the US for a period of five years.

InSite festival projects such as *Turista Fronterizo* might initially raise the question of a discrepancy between the migrant, material world and the computer game, but Hernandez's detention is a clear moment of conjunction between them. The distinction between Hernandez the artist and the first-person perspective of *Corridos* collapsed, and Hernandez in a sense became embedded in his own game, thrust into the world that his project portrays. The temporal, epistemological, spatial, sociocultural gap between the "illegal" and the artist-activist closed, the latter thrown into the world of the former. The artist himself becomes enclosed within restricted borders, indicating that the radical dichotomy between the game and the "real" is ultimately not sustainable.

In the quotidian exercise of risk profiling and threat assessment, it is *Corridos* the game that renders Hernandez a dangerous, untrusted subject. The brochure and festival may be written under the sign of sedition, but the game is written under the sign of risk. I will hazard a generalization and say that our shared cinematic imaginary alone, much less the coverage of the Iraq war, ought to have made us all well versed in the use of games and simulations as training mechanisms for military activities. How else are we to understand the Transportation Security Administration (TSA) officials' mandate that Hernandez play the game in their presence? In this context, the game becomes the illegal substance, the undesirable, that which cannot cross the border, and the TSA mandate becomes part of a military operation. The newly amplified practices of state securitization and the issue of material border crossings come together in this complex instance of risk assessment.[7]

It is also important to take account of another aspect of risk embedded in the game. One of the risks run by hacktivist art projects is that they go unacknowledged, that their provocations are either unseen or dismissed as mere game playing. At the very moment that Hernandez is forced to play the game in the presence of TSA officials, the game succeeds in unfolding the very risk it was predicated upon. It succeeds, that is, in displaying the activist political potential coded within it. This, after all, is the audience that the game would most especially aim to provoke. It is not only Hernandez who is forced to play the game, but the TSA officials also become implicated in its structure and rhetoric. Hernandez's detention and deportation demonstrate the danger that the game presents in the eyes of the TSA officials: without this double risk of banishment and provocation, the game would fail to register any political or activist potential.

It bears repeating that *Corridos*, like the narco-corridos, was a commissioned work, its expressed pedagogic purpose, as Hernandez recounts, "to gain deeper cross-understanding" about the US–Mexico border, "for both the peoples of Mexico and the U.S." Even with the awareness that the insistence on an educative mission constitutes a kind of juridical defense, *Corridos*, and the festival of which it was a part, perform the very reverse engineering called for by CAE. Within a regime of signs, when border control is a "symbolic performance" of security, the (temporary) provocation of tactical media is to reveal those signs to be mutable. What DoEAT and the other artists here present is a mutability of signs, symbolic performances, that speak to material conditions that are far less plastic and mutable.

### Notes

1 For more on the history of securitization at the US–Mexico border, particularly in response to the 'Wetback crisis' in the early 1950s, see William Walters' contribution to this volume.

2 For a thorough account of the failures of biometric testing, see Charlotte Epstein's contribution to this volume.

3 On Agamben's reading of the role of *consuls*, proxy sovereignties, and the collapse of the "distinction between public and private authority," see Louise Amoore's contribution to this volume.

4 To fill out a taxonomy of wired activism on the issue of borders, one must mention other activist organizations that use new media for organizational purposes: deleteTheBorder. org, the Organic Collective, and noborder.org. The slogans and core principles of these (often civil disobedience-based) campaigns are as follows: an end to deportations and detentions; freedom of movement; papers for all.

5 It should be noted that disruption *per se* is not an unqualified good and certainly not always tactical. In fact, there is a certain capacity for banality and pettiness in the obstruction of network traffic.

6 Louise Amoore has written brilliantly of the impossible ideality of the great refusal, which promises a singular, cohesive, and locatable enemy, as well as of the momentary aspect of dissent in the Foucauldian tradition, specifically in relation to biometric borders and the regulation of the movement of people (2006, 2007b).

7 For a more detailed commentary on risk management in the context of the war on terror, see de Goede and Amoore's Introduction to this volume.

# 11 Subverting discourses of risk in the war on terror[1]

*Susan Bibler Coutin*

New discourses of risk and security create surreal forms of governance. Uncertainty is now a rationale for taking preemptive military actions (Aradau and van Munster, this volume), informality is considered potentially terrorist, profiling focuses on modeling the normal rather than the abnormal (de Goede 2003 and this volume), and surveillance is extended to entire populations (Amoore, this volume). When trained on risks that are deemed unquantifiable and dangers that are considered unknowable, surveillance, profiling, policing, and criminalization become something other than knowledge practices – perhaps what might be better termed forays into the unknown. Before the unknown can be entered, however, it must first be produced. This is accomplished through a time warp of sorts, in which future yet unspecified dangers are made ever present, and in which past actions are taken to have led to something other than current realities and can therefore no longer be considered valuable precedents (Beck 2000; O'Malley 2000). This break with the past (as referenced by the fact that, in the US, the attack on the US Pentagon and the World Trade Center is known by a *date*, 9/11) is taken to simultaneously have led the present and the future to converge. In this time warp, actions take on the character of gestures, grounded in both hope and despair. As Aradau and van Munster note in their contribution to this collection, British Prime Minister Tony Blair justified the decision to send troops to Iraq, despite a lack of proof that Iraq's government had weapons of mass destruction, by asking, "Would you prefer us to act, even if it turns out to be wrong? Or not to act and hope it's OK?" (quoted in Aradau and van Munster, this volume). Similarly, in a 2002 speech outlining the Iraq threat, US President George Bush stated, "Many people have asked how close Saddam Hussein is to developing a nuclear weapon. Well, we don't know exactly, and that's the problem. ... Facing clear evidence of peril, we cannot wait for the final proof – the smoking gun – that could come in the form of a mushroom cloud" (White House 2002). In the face of catastrophe, it is presumed better to do *something* than *nothing*, even if the consequences of doing something are not clear.

The temporalities at work in new security discourse can disable certain forms of critique, particularly those that rely on education and consciousness-raising. Social movements expend considerable resources attempting to "frame" issues in ways that promote their cause. The assumption behind such efforts is that, if the public really understood that immigrants benefit the economy, or that handguns are more likely to harm owners than burglars, or that the US supported Saddam Hussein in the Iran–Iraq war, then citizens would support immigration reform, hand-gun controls, and an end to the US presence in Iraq (see also Bigo 2002). Such forms of critique focus on *knowledge* – of trends, risks, and histories. Presumably, accurate understandings of past and present realities provide a guide to future actions. A break with the past, in contrast, creates the "unknown" and "unknowable," thus rendering such understandings obsolete. As Beck observes, "The concept of risk reverses the relationship of past, present and future. The past loses its power to determine the present. Its place as the cause of present-day experience and action is taken by the future" (2000: 214). Thus, if terrorists can potentially access weapons of mass destruction, then a new order prevails, immigrants must be evaluated as potential terrorists, and the history of US–Iraq relations, however sordid, has little bearing on the current need to prevent extremists from making Iraq "a base from which to overthrow moderate governments in the region and plan new attacks on the American people" (White House 2007).

As discourses of security shift, however, so too do means of subverting such discourses. The essays in this collection suggest that, when risk is rendered catastrophic yet incalculable, oppositional discourses and tactics, like security discourses themselves, must enter the unknown, not to minimize the unknown through knowledge, but rather to use its temporal rift to redefine the security project itself. Thus, if agents of surveillance can be repositioned as objects of surveillance, then the future converges with the present in ways that challenge, rather than support, the war on terror. Similarly, if current approaches to profiling attempt to "read" the future into the present, then disrupting the grid of intelligibility that underlies such reading makes classification and categorization impossible. Finally, to the degree that new tactics of governance depend on the unknown, the clandestine can potentially co-opt new forms of security.

The remainder of this essay explores these oppositional potentials by drawing on the contributions to this volume, examples from popular culture, and my own research regarding unauthorized migration from El Salvador to the United States. I begin by analyzing consciousness-raising strategies pursued by social movement activists during the 1980s. I then examine the potential for subverting discourses of risk associated with the war on terror, focusing on repositioning subjects, disrupting intelligibility, and co-opting forms of security. I conclude with reflections on the temporalities of both security and opposition.

## Consciousness-raising

During the 1980s, US social movements that sought to challenge security discourses associated with the Cold War used consciousness-raising and public education as key techniques for mobilizing activists and swaying public opinion. The premise of national security discourses during the 1980s was that the US and the Soviet Union were locked in a global struggle between democracy and communism – a struggle that, due to the nuclear threat, was waged indirectly in civil wars and political conflicts in Central America, Angola, Afghanistan, and various parts of the world. Grassroots activists in the US who were critical of such discourses sought to challenge the continued development and production of nuclear weapons as well as US support for authoritarian governments. As a technique, consciousness-raising was premised on the idea that the public was, to some degree, duped. Activists contended that government sources of information were used to justify officials' accounts of security threats and that the news media largely either conveyed these justifications or reported on situations in insufficient depth for readers to grasp the histories of and varied interests at stake in particular conflicts. Activists presumed that, if the US public were aware of the ulterior motives behind US military and foreign policies, then the public would demand policy changes. Here, I focus on the forms of critique used within two movements that were prominent during the 1980s: the anti-nuclear weapons movement and the US sanctuary movement, which sought refugee status for Central Americans who were fleeing civil wars in their countries of origin.

The anti-nuclear weapons movement drew on medical and therapeutic expertise to convey the overwhelming destructiveness of nuclear weapons, and the risks that these posed to civilian populations even if no war occurred. Anti-nuclear weapons activists used films such as *The Day After* and *The Last Epidemic*, lectures, books, and visual devices to demonstrate that the US possessed incredible destructive capacities and that, if deliberately or inadvertently released, these could destroy life on this planet. Experts, such as Dr. Helen Caldicott, told audiences of the medical effects of a nuclear explosion:

> Six miles from the epicenter, every building will be flattened and every person killed. Because the human body is composed mostly of water, when it is exposed to thousands of degrees Celsius, it turns into gas and disappears. ...

> Twenty miles from the epicenter, all people will be killed or lethally injured, and most buildings will be destroyed. People just beyond the 6-mile, 100-percent lethal range who happen to glance at the flash could have their eyes melted.

> Quoted in Gusterson (1996:199–200)

Visual devices were used to enable viewers to imagine the power of the global nuclear arsenal. For example, one chart represented the power of all of the bombs used during the Second World War (including those dropped on Hiroshima and Nagasaki) as a single dot. The destructive capacity of the entire nuclear force was represented in this chart as some 5,000 dots (see Gusterson 1996: 198–200). One viewer who viewed an anti-nuclear film commented that, after at first being grief-stricken at the prospect of a nuclear holocaust, "gradually there just comes an acceptance, not of the situation, but of the fact that you know about it, you can't get away from it, and you have to do something about it, and if you don't make it the highest priority in your life, what the hell does your life mean?" (quoted in Gusterson 1996: 201–2).

Through these educational techniques, anti-nuclear weapons activists sought to challenge the notion that nuclear weapons were a form of protection that increased US security, and to instead convince audience members that nuclear weapons were a source of danger, a danger that could only be reduced by dismantling nuclear weapons. These strategies were effective. Gusterson reports that "at the peak of this moment, in 1983, according to Lawrence Write (1989: 158), 'a poll taken in California ... found that eighty-five percent of the respondents expected a nuclear war in their lifetime'" (1996: 203). Like new security discourses, anti-nuclear activists' strategies sought to bring a possible future – nuclear annihilation – into the present but, in so doing, they sought to avoid, rather than justify, a break with the past. In other words, anti-nuclear activists sought continuity between the pre-nuclear past and present nuclear realities, a continuity that was to be accomplished through dramatic reductions, if not outright elimination, of nuclear stockpiles (Gusterson 1996).

Much like anti-nuclear activists, sanctuary activists sought to make the US public inescapably aware of a horrific social problem, namely human rights violations being committed by regimes that the US government supported. Through such awareness, sanctuary activists sought to secure asylum for victims of these violations and a moratorium on US aid to Central American governments. To promote public awareness, activists produced literature detailing the histories of Central American conflicts and US involvement in those conflicts, sent delegations to Central America, and publicized the "testimonies" of refugees who had escaped these conflicts (SCAAN 1983; Bau 1985; MacEoin 1985; Golden and McConnell 1986; Smith 1996). Histories were designed to demonstrate that, instead of being a conflict between the US and the Soviet Union, civil wars in El Salvador, Guatemala, and Nicaragua had been launched in response to state repression of peasant and worker movements. Delegations brought members of congregations that made up the sanctuary movement to Central American communities where they accompanied vulnerable groups, such as displaced peasants who were repopulating a village, and thus sought to protect them from persecution or military reprisals. After returning, delegation members gave public presentations about their experiences. Most central to the movement's consciousness-raising activities, however, were refugee "*testimonios*", public accounts of persecution and flight by Central Americans themselves (see also Arias 2001; Beverley 2004). Testimonies, like the act of offering sanctuary itself, brought Central Americans and US citizens into close contact, making the seemingly distant conflicts in El Salvador and Guatemala a reality.

Like the educational campaigns waged by anti-nuclear activists, the sanctuary movement's consciousness-raising activities were quite effective. Congregation members who traveled to Central America or heard the testimonies of Central American refugees found themselves inescapably aware of suffering in Central America. The minister of a Tucson, Arizona, sanctuary congregation reported,

> There was a period of about four months where I literally couldn't talk to people about it [the human rights situation in Central America]. I mean, I could talk to other people who were doing the work, but there was such a gap between the world that I was living in of crisis on the border and nice, content Tucson that I couldn't find the language to describe what I was experiencing.
>
> Coutin (1993: 162)

Similarly, a member of a sanctuary congregation in Oakland, California, commented that it was impossible for her to ignore the knowledge that she had acquired regarding civil wars in Central America: "Sometimes I wish I could [not know]. Sometimes I think, 'Oh, darn it! Why can't I just enjoy things? And live my life the way I used to! Why do I have to feel this responsibility for getting things done?' But I can't ignore it." For sanctuary activists, knowledge of human rights abuses being committed in Central America changed their social and political consciousnesses, which in turn demanded concrete actions. A woman who had been indicted on charges of conspiracy and alien-smuggling as a result of her sanctuary work assisting Central Americans to cross the US–Mexico border related "When I met Central American refugees face-to-face, it was transforming. When I heard their stories, when I saw them cry, it was gut-wrenching for me. I knew I had to do something" (Coutin 1993: 74).

Sanctuary and anti-nuclear activists' consciousness-raising strategies directly challenged Cold War security discourses. First, activists sought to defuse the risk that security discourses targeted, i.e., the possibility of a Soviet nuclear attack, or of guerrillas winning wars in Central America and establishing communist regimes in, to paraphrase former US president Ronald Reagan, the United States' "backyard." To defuse this risk, anti-nuclear activists redirected public attention toward the threat posed by nuclear weapons themselves, regardless of who wielded them. Sanctuary activists challenged Reagan's domino theory – the notion that, like dominos, a regime that gave way to communism could "topple" its neighbors, thus permitting communism to spread – by stressing the indigenous nature of Central American conflicts. US security, activists suggested, was not at stake within Central American wars. Second, activists challenged security discourses by exposing the horrific nature of security practices themselves. In the case of anti-nuclear activists, this was accomplished through graphic accounts of the effects of nuclear explosions. In the case of sanctuary activists, the horrors of torture, massacres, and human rights violations in Central America were recounted in order to convince listeners that supporting the governments that committed such abuses meant being complicit in atrocities. These consciousness-raising efforts suggested that US security practices – arms production and military support for Central American regimes – did not serve their ostensible purposes, but instead furthered US imperialism, supported the military industrial complex, or protected the interests of multinational corporations. This critique used knowledge of past and present realities to suggest future courses of action, namely the dismantling of nuclear weapons, granting refuge to Central Americans, and a moratorium on military aid to Central American governments. As activists had themselves been mobilized by knowledge, movement participants reasoned that knowledge could mobilize the broader public in support of movement goals.

These knowledge-based critiques contrast sharply with the effects of knowledge practices associated with the US invasion of Iraq. Prior to the invasion, US and other coalition officials justified military action on the grounds that the Iraqi government had provided support to the September 11, 2001 hijackers and the claim that Iraq possessed weapons of mass destruction. Following the invasion, the evidence that had supported these claims was found to be highly suspect, and no weapons of mass destruction were located within Iraq (Cable News Network 2005). Such revelations are precisely the sort of knowledge in which consciousness-raising strategies are grounded. Nonetheless, in the US, public support for the Iraq war as well as for internal security measures that some have characterized as a violation of civil liberties remained high (Farkas, Johnson and Duffett 2002; *USA Today* 2005; Schneider 2007), although it has since declined. The fear of an unspecified yet potentially catastrophic threat legitimized precautionary efforts to counter that risk (Aradau and van Munster, this volume).

If scientific uncertainty disables knowledge-based critiques that take the form of consciousness-raising, how then can new security discourses be challenged? Answering this question requires entering the realm of science fiction.

## Repositioning subjects: back to the future

A common plot in science fiction movies involves a temporal acceleration, in which an anticipated future is encountered in the present only to turn out to be erroneous. Within this scenario, the error is discovered by a security agent, the very individual responsible for ensuring that the anticipated future came about or was avoided. This discovery, much like consciousness-raising, entails a shift in subjectivity. Once the security agent is aware of the possibility for error, the legitimacy of the security apparatus evaporates, both for the agent and for the audience members viewing the film. The security agent now poses a danger to the system as a whole, and this character shifts from policing to being policed. By repositioning subjects, such films disable the logic of precautionary action. Instead of being the means to avoid calamity, precautionary actions, due to their potential for erroneously targeting the "innocent," *become* the calamity. Terrorism or crime, in this scenario, can no longer be distinguished from efforts to combat terrorism or crime, in that both destroy the civilian population. Knowledge of uncertainty, the potential for error, and the potential that this error will harm the very subjects that the security project was ostensibly designed to protect give security measures sinister connotations. Repositioning the agent of security simultaneously repositions the population, making it the potential victim of the security project itself.

An early film that followed this plot line was the movie *Logan's Run.* This film depicts a futuristic society in which everyone wears a crystal "life clock" that will alert them to the time when they are supposed to be renewed in a ritual known as "carousel." During carousel, which is watched and celebrated in a public stadium, the individuals whose life clock has run out slowly float upwards and then explode. The life clock runs out at age thirty, so there are no elderly people in the society. The main character is Logan, a "sandman" responsible for capturing runners, those individuals who abscond when their time for carousel has come. At the movie's outset, Logan believes in renewals, which are supposed to take people to a better life. Assigned the task of discovering the underground "sanctuary" where runners hide, Logan's crystal is set to go off four years prematurely, positioning him among the runners. Logan begins to have doubts – has anyone ever actually been renewed? Logan himself becomes one of the runners and participates in an effort to mobilize City residents to free themselves of the security apparatus that compels them to die at age thirty.

A more recent film with a similar plot line is *Minority Report* (see also Shapiro 2005). In this film, "pre-cogs" who can foresee the future are connected to a complicated surveillance system. When the pre-cogs see that a crime is about to be committed, they alert the pre-crime unit, which is dispatched to prevent the crime and capture the culprit-to-be. The pre-cogs' predictions have enabled the pre-crime unit to eliminate homicides in the Washington, DC area. The plot turns on the experiences of Detective Anderton, the head of the pre-crime unit, who is informed that he is going to commit a crime. While fleeing from his former colleagues, the detective re-examines the certainty of the pre-cogs' predictions, and learns that the pre-cogs are fallible. Horrified at his own role in capturing people who may have been innocent, and struggling to evade the pre-crime unit's pervasive surveillance apparatus, Anderton challenges the system in which he formerly served.

*Logan's Run* and *Minority Report* differ in that they speak to the political discourses of their day. *Logan's Run*, which was made in the 1970s, is steeped in the idealism of social movements that sought to challenge hegemonic structures that promulgated "false consciousness" and that placated the populace through hedonism and consumerism. Logan flees the powers-that-be and aligns his fate with an underground movement. Anderton, in contrast, wages his own individual battle against the system. Logan, like other runners, is marked by the crystal that announces that his time for renewal has come. Anderton is marked by biometric indicators detected at numerous surveillance points located throughout the city. His individual *identity* is known, and his movements are recorded by pre-crime agents. In *Logan's Run*, runners are pursued because of what they have done – they have evaded the requirement to be renewed. In *Minority Report*, criminals are pursued because of what they are *going* to do – their future, rather than past, actions are at stake. The surveillance technologies – such as retina scans – used in *Minority Report* are also similar to those currently being developed for ports of entry (see Epstein, this volume), whereas policing strategies in *Logan's Run* rely on practices more akin to profiling, such as the furtive behavior of runners, the flashing life clock that gives them away, and a giant radar-like map that pinpoints runners' locations. What these movies share, however, is that they bring the future into the present in a way that challenges the security apparatus. When Logan and Anderton become security targets, in Logan's case, because his life clock is accelerated and, in Anderton's case, because his future crime is foreseen, agents of policing become subjects, and policing itself is problematized.

As Amoore (this volume) notes, the war on terrorism has given rise to "proxy sovereignties," in that the general population is to be "vigilant" for signs of impending terrorist actions (see also Bigo 2002). Through bringing potential futures (e.g., becoming suspect, being detained) into the present, the duality of policing and being policed could, as occurred in the case of Logan and Anderton, reposition subjects such that the agents of policing – the "vigilant" population – could realize itself as object and thus make surveillance itself illegitimate.

Moving away from the realm of science fiction, the film *The Official Story* repositions subjects in ways that bridge consciousness-raising and potential subversions of current security discourses. In this film, Alicia, a bourgeois Argentine woman whose husband has military connections, discovers that her adopted daughter – a girl of five – may in fact have been the daughter of a *desaparecida*, a woman who was "disappeared" during the Argentine dirty war. Like the consciousness-raising model, the film focuses on the main character's quest to uncover the true past, her increased knowledge of her government's repressive practices, and the actions – such as inviting one of the *Abuelas de Plaza de Mayo*, the grandmothers of the disappeared, to her home – that this knowledge compels her to take. Knowledge of torture and disappearances repositions Alicia, giving her a connection to the targets of government repression. At the same time, Alicia, much like Logan and Anderton, becomes cognizant of her own complicity (through her silence, ignorance, and possible acquisition of one of the fruits – a child – of the dirty war) in repression. Alicia discovers that the tactics that were allegedly used to rid the country of subversives targeted innocent people, such as her childhood friend, Ana. "Precautionary" actions turned out to harm, rather than protect, society. This film, which was released in 1985, while the Argentine government was trying former military rulers for their roles in the repression, was largely seen as emblematic of the Argentine public's own reckoning with its complicity in the dirty war.

It is worth considering the role of *normalcy* within both consciousness-raising and current security discourses. Within consciousness-raising approaches, *normalcy* is equated with complicity, being "duped" and attempting to hide the truth. "No business as usual" has long been a slogan of movements for social justice. This slogan suggests that, beneath the veneer of normalcy lie atrocities and injustices, such as the accumulation of nuclear stockpiles or the persecution of guerrilla suspects in Central America. Preventing business as usual becomes a mechanism for exposing truth, for demonstrating that multiple realities (e.g., middle-class life in the US, warfare in El Salvador) are interlinked. In *The Official Story*, the "normalcy" of Alicia's life is disrupted by her knowledge of her daughter's possible origins – nothing will ever be "normal" again. Indeed, during the Argentine dirty war, observers commented on the bizarreness of normalcy, of some individuals going about their daily routines while others experienced torture or the sudden disappearance of a family member (Taylor 1997). In contrast, in the war on terror, *normalcy* becomes a political act, as George Bush insisted, "Now, the *American people have got to go about their business*. We cannot let the terrorists achieve the objective of frightening our nation to the point where we don't – where we don't conduct business, where people don't shop. That's their intention" (White House 2001, emphasis original; see also Amoore, this volume). Within this schema, normalcy becomes a strategy for warding off catastrophe and is always defined in relation to the impinging future that has worked its way into the present. Given the proliferation of proxy sovereignties and the pervasiveness of profiling (as discussed below), normalcy also becomes a way of defending oneself against suspicion of terrorism.

The potential for repositioning agents as subjects of surveillance is perhaps the flip side of ways in which current security discourses appropriate the language of human rights. Military leaders in Guatemala learned that they could more effectively repress the Guatemalan population if they eliminated the most egregious offenses and issued reports regarding their own "improving" human rights record (Schirmer 1998). The Guatemalan government, which initially resisted defining Guatemala as a Mayan nation, learned that it had more to gain by embracing and incorporating Mayanness (Nelson 1999). In the face of catastrophic environmental disasters such as Bhopal, chemical companies have developed "green" forms of consulting, according to which populations are "informed" of and have a role as "stake-holders" in assessments of risks associated with the production of chemicals (Fortun 2001). By appropriating oppositional discourses (of human rights, indigenous rights, environmental justice), authorities suggest that they have taken these critiques into account.

In contrast to such appropriations, when individuals are repositioned as the subjects rather than the agents of surveillance, practices that seek to prevent a catastrophic future themselves become the catastrophe (see also Simon, this volume). Repositioned subjects question how normalcy is to be inter-preted, and suggest ways in which new forms of profiling can be resisted.

## Unintelligibility

As Aradau and van Munster (this volume) and de Goede (this volume) suggest, current forms of surveillance attempt to read the present for the future, focusing not on risky social groups, but rather on "normal" popula-tions. Profiling examines normalcy out of a sense that the terrorist may be "unexceptional," someone who looks like "any of us" (Aradau and van Munster, this volume). Similarly, as de Goede points out, the "know your customer policies" currently utilized by banks are designed to document customers' identities. "The *absence* of information," she notes, "becomes regarded as suspicious in itself" (de Goede, this volume, emphasis original). Where previous profiling may have focused on abnormal behavior, current tactics are extended to entire populations, and the burden of proof shifts from the government, which is enjoined to cast its net as widely as possible, to the targets of surveillance, who must prove their own normality (Aradau and van Munster, this volume).

The papers in this volume suggest at least two potential responses to such profiling. One response focuses on the creation of *interstitial*, *hybrid* or *ambiguous* subjects, who are difficult to classify. Another response focuses on disrupting the *grid of intelligibility itself* (see also Edkins and Pin-Fat 2004). I take up these two responses in turn.

Interstitial, hybrid, or ambiguous subjects appear to defy classificatory grids in that they cannot be placed. Individuals may have multiple or unclear racial backgrounds, their origins may be unknown (as when indivi-duals lack birth certificates), or they may cross boundaries. As Gloria Anzaldúa (1987: 22) drew attention to the potentially counterhegemonic potential of such border crossings when she sought an

> accounting with all three [of my] cultures – white, Mexican, Indian. I
> want the freedom to carve and chisel my own face. ... And if going

> home is denied me then I will have to stand and claim my space,
> making a new culture – *una cultura mestiza* – *with my own lumber, my own*
> *bricks and mortar and my own feminist architecture.*

One danger of treating interstitiality as a form of resistance, however, is that those who are ambiguously positioned may be easier to destroy. This point was brought home to me at an academic conference when, after a series of papers that had discussed the multiplicity of identities, a scholar who was knowledgeable about the African National Congress in South Africa pointed out that individuals who had taken on *noms de guerre* were sometimes arrested on charges filed against the individuals that they had posed as being. In other words, having multiple identities or falling between categories can multiply the grounds on which authorities can apprehend an individual. My own research has examined how undocumented migrants are ambiguously positioned as physically in, but legally outside of, the spaces that they occupy (Coutin 2005). Such ambiguous positioning can lead to dis-memberment or death as migrants travel through space but outside of offi-cial routes. Migrants travel on top of rather than within trains, in cargo compartments rather than passenger seats, and through deserts rather than on established roads. Human, yet a good to be transported, migrants may suffocate, die of heat exhaustion, or lose limbs as their legs are sucked under moving trains that they attempt to board. Interstitiality and hybridity may defy classification, but can come at the expense of the individuals who are out of place. Interstitiality can be a space of death.

In contrast to the creation of interstitial subjects, which position certain people outside of categories giving them ambiguous profiles, disrupting the grid of intelligibility prevents profiling and thus puts everyone on an equal footing. Blurring the line between the suspect and the above-board makes it difficult to distinguish between the two. For instance, there are ways that law itself traffics in illegality. US immigration law draws a line between residents who are authorized and those whose presence is unauthorized. To draw this line, the unauthorized are situated in some respects as "outside" of the polity – they are denied rights and services, and are regarded as living in an "underground" even as they interact with those whose presence is "above board." Illegal presence is thus, in a sense, a product of law. US immigration laws also allow for "exceptions" that permit the line between law and illegality to be redrawn. For instance, individuals who had immi-grated to the US without authorization during the Salvadoran and Guate-malan civil wars were exempted from restrictive immigration policies adopted in the US. This exemption was granted on the grounds that these migrants had had temporary permission (a pending asylum application or temporary protected status) to remain in the US, and that they had there-fore put down roots. Thus, through this exemption, actions ("putting down roots") that had been prohibited were redefined as having been on the path of law. Illegality can thus be incorporated into law, and law itself can be a hidden presence within the prohibited, thus creating a "zone of indistinction" (Agamben 1998: 6) between law and illegality.

The potential for disrupting grids of intelligibility and making boundaries themselves indistinct suggests a third means of subverting security discourses: using the "pull" that the prohibited exerts on official accounts to incorporate the illegal into the official. Such incorporation, which is akin to co-optation, may have ambiguous political valences.

## Incorporation

New security discourses derive legitimacy from and thus depend on constructing a domain of the threatening and potentially catastrophic unknown (Bigo 2002). This unknown takes many forms – unbridled immigration, illicit financial transfers, alien presences, unauthorized movements, clandestine networks, undocumented transactions, paperless persons. Constructing this domain as a *threat*, as potentially terrorist and therefore *powerful*, increases its value. As transactions and movements are more fully prohibited and pushed further underground, their profitability can increase. Smugglers can raise their fees, smuggling networks can become more organized and thus more violent (Andreas 2000b). As Walters (this volume) points out, clandestinity is marketable. As it increases in value (a value that may be financial, psychological, and cultural), the prohibited exerts a pull on the very security measures that seek to prevent its existence. This pull can produce cross-cutting tendencies – in addition to prohibiting allegedly potentially terrorist practices, such as unrecorded financial transfers, security agents (including those entities on whom responsibility for security has devolved) may want to get their "cut." In the process, the prohibited can be incorporated into, and thus potentially shift, the security project itself. Incorporation plays against other readings of the informal or the clandestine as suspicious.

Instances of incorporation abound. In the US, as US immigration authorities have redoubled their efforts to locate and remove unauthorized immigrants, US banks have sought to devise ways to extend home loans, credit, and banking privileges to individuals who lack US identity documents. Programs directed at "the unbanked" encourage members of low-income communities to open savings accounts (see, e.g., FDIC 2003). I have attended meetings of Los Angeles-based community organizations at which immigrants, including those who were unauthorized, were encouraged to use banking services. As the US government increasingly restricted access to US identity documents, such as drivers' licenses, banks began to accept identity documents, such as the matricula consular, issued by foreign governments, as proof of identity for the purpose of opening bank accounts (see, e. g., Bank of America 2002). In an effort to benefit financially from "a market that has unmet banking needs," banks have accepted ITINs or "individual taxpayer identification numbers" in lieu of social security numbers. An individual quoted in one article about extending home loans to undocumented immigrants pointed out, "Illegal immigrants are a huge gray area and it becomes even more gray when you start issuing ITINs. . . . There's complicity already within the government in which they're saying that they're kind of fine with these people here as long as they pay their taxes" (Pasha 2005). Financial records, such as loan payments or evidence of financial assets, can be submitted as part of applications for legal permanent residency, as documentation of individuals' length of residence in and ties to the United States (Coutin 2000). Such banking practices have generated backlashes and boycotts on the parts of groups opposed to illegal immigration. Nonetheless, these home loan programs counter the claim that undocumented immigration is intrinsically immoral.

Migrant remittances are another transaction that financial institutions have sought to incorporate. As de Goede (2007: 147) notes, money can be perceived as "moral" or "ethical," and remittances are no exception. During interviews, a Central Bank official in El Salvador described remittances as "pure," a Salvadoran businessman described remittances as "fresh money . . . the true foreign currency, fresh, without cost," and a Salvadoran professor described remittances as foreign currency that enters the country "clean" (Coutin, forthcoming). Remittances' purity derives from removing the taint of origin by constituting remittances as the second half of a transaction in which the first half never occurred. The Central Bank official explained, "with remittances, it's like, you don't have to discount anything. . . . We never have to pay anything, it's not like a loan, or a sale of goods, in which we receive income but we have to give away the good, or a loan in which we receive currency but we have to pay it back in the future." Because the costs of migrating are born by migrants themselves, remittances appear to bank officials – and indeed are recorded in International Monetary Fund (IMF) reports – as "unrequited transfers" resulting from "noncommercial considerations, such as family ties or legal obligations, that induce a producer or owner of real resources and financial items to part with them without any return in those same forms" (IMF 1977: 71, quoted in Díaz-Briquets and Pérez-López 1997: 322). To maximize their ability to record remittance income in their balance of payment statements, countries have adopted measures to eliminate the black market in currency and to encourage migrants to use official means of transferring money. Although the effects of remitting on national economies are widely debated (see Hernandez and Coutin 2006), remittances position migrants, including those who are unauthorized, as key to their homelands' futures. Illicit practices (migration, informal financial transfer) that are targeted by security measures are also hailed for their development potential.

Governments have also sought to benefit directly through unauthorized migration. In the US, a controversial component of US immigration law known as "245(i)" has permitted unauthorized migrants who are the beneficiaries of family visa petitions to adjust their status to legal permanent residents without having to return to their country of origin to claim their visa. In exchange for this privilege, migrants have had to pay fines of US $1,000. Funds from these fines are used to support US border enforcement. One rationale for creating 245(i) in the first place was that US authorities, rather than airlines and travel agencies, would be able to profit from migrants' need to claim their visas. By enabling migrants to avoid making the journey home, 245(i) redirected funds that migrants would otherwise have had to spend on travel. Some migrants also consider the fees that the US government charges for renewing Employment Authorization Documents to be akin to the fees charged by alien-smugglers.

Security forces' dependence on the phenomena they seek to prohibit was graphically depicted in the film *A Day without a Mexican*. In this film, all individuals of Mexican descent mysteriously vanished from US territory in a single day. Lawns were left unmown, children were unsupervised, professionals disappeared from their offices, and US border patrol agents found themselves without work. At the end of the movie, when Mexicans reappeared and the border patrol encountered a would-be illegal migrant, the agents celebrated his return, carrying him on their shoulders like a hero. Their jobs were secure once more. This film suggested that, if they achieved 100 percent success rates, security measures barring illegal immigrants would also generate a public catastrophe.

## Conclusion: temporalities of security and subversion

Unlike sanctuary and anti-nuclear activists, who, in the 1980s, found that knowledge of persecution and nuclear weapons compelled them to act, US security personnel in the 2000s have been moved by what US Secretary of Defense Donald Rumsfeld referred to as pithily as "unknown unknowns," seemingly gaps in knowledge that are so extensive that they have not yet been identified as areas of investigation, or as Rumsfeld put it, "the ones we don't know we don't know." Unknown unknowns exert a pull on security agents, demanding knowledge practices that are after something other than knowledge – premonition, if you will, or a stab in the dark. Given that the precise target of investigation is unclear, surveillance blankets the population at large, treating all both as suspect and as potential informants. A recent plot to attack the Fort Dix Army Base in New Jersey, for example, was foiled through what one news report referred to as "John Q. Public," namely, "a Circuit City employee who reported a suspicious video" (Meyer 2007; Meyer and Hayasaki 2007). Security practices are forward looking, but non-linear, in that history is not necessarily a guide to future practices, and signs of future developments may not become legible until after the fact. As accounts of the Fort Dix plot noted, "even the FBI's most expert counter-terrorism profilers have no foolproof way of predicting which individuals might turn radicalized thoughts into deadly acts of violence, the officials say" (Meyer 2007). Potential futures are embedded in present realities, thus catapulting the present into an only somewhat preventable future that is itself dissociated with the past.

Challenges to the knowledge practices that the security project enables must also engage unknown unknowns. When agents who are responsible for surveillance find themselves objects of surveillance, they experience a break with their own past and, indeed, with the world as they know it. Inserted into an unimagined future, they discover that the catastrophe that they feared is already occurring, and is in fact the security project itself.[2] Such repositioning makes the boundaries between "suspicious" and "normal" behavior indistinct, as agents' own "normal" behavior turns out to be "suspicious." If the line between terrorists and their targets cannot be drawn, then the present turns out to already be the feared future, with the risks posed by security practices adding to, rather than minimizing or eliminating, the risks posed by terrorists. As such lines are rendered indistinct, security measures can be "pulled" by prohibited practices, which have been invested with some degree of value and power. As official practices come to incorporate elements of the prohibited, the security project can shift, acknowledging its dependence on some of the very practices – informal exchanges, illicit movements – that it seeks to prevent. Illegal persons may retrospectively turn out to have been on the path of law all along, just as unauthorized exchanges may turn out to be key to national and international economies. Such retrospective incorporation restores linkages between present and past by using the present to redefine or reproduce the past. Such non-linear temporal movements may hold out some hope for preventing security projects from realizing the very catastrophes that they ostensibly combat.

## Notes

1 I thank Marieke de Goede and Louise Amoore for inviting me to participate in the International Studies Association Workshop, 'Governing by Risk in the War on Terror', and for their comments on an earlier draft of this essay. I also thank the other workshop participants for the discussion, which stimulated the ideas presented in this chapter. The research on which this paper is based was supported by a grant from the National Science Foundation's Law and Social Science Program (awards #SES-0001890 and #SES-0296050) and a research and writing grant from the John D. and Catherine T. MacArthur Foundation.

2 For one sense in which such catastrophe may play out, note the role that an FBI informer played in the alleged Fort Dix bombing plot that was aborted in 2007. According to a *New York Times* article, an informer's job consists of "gaining access to the world of a possible threat, playing along to see just how far suspects were willing to go, and allowing the authorities to act before the potential terrorists." In this particular case, the informer seemingly encouraged suspects to move the plot forward and suggested using weapons that were more powerful than those that the suspects had been considering. See Kocieniewski (2007: A1).

# 12 Risk and imagination in the war on terror

*Mark B. Salter*

## Are you ready for this?

Risk management has been adopted by a host of state agencies and private corporations as the gold standard in dealing with the new terrorist threat; in large part because it is premised on the idea that increased interdependence brought about by globalization also yields increased vulnerability. The tighter our production chains, the more integrated our economies, the more frequent our mobility, the less slack in our society, and the less redundancy in our security measures: the greater the efficiency, the greater the susceptibility to attack. Risk management as a governance framework seeks to focus scarce resources on risks that are ranked according to frequency and impact. Focusing on a pragmatic assessment of the possible and likely sources of danger for an organization, institutions have been prompted to reconsider old models of governance to focus on the new environment of emergency and exception. Analyses of the 9/11 attacks, especially in the comparison with the Pearl Harbor attacks of 1941, conclude that, rather than a failure of policing, of empire, of society – the 9/11 attacks represent a failure of the imagination. If only the policing and military powers of the state had been directed at the eighteen hijackers or the one shoe bomber or the four transit bombers, then surely it would have been successful. To cover up the plain failure of the military might of the world's only superpower and its handmaidens to prevent the dramatic attacks in New York, Washington, Madrid, and London, the blame is assigned to those "managers of unease" for failing to convince policymakers that the sky was falling. And, now those self-same managers are made re-responsible for creating and legitimizing new nightmare scenarios (Amoore, this volume). The recent moral panics regarding border security, port security, container shipping, or explosive liquids are illustrative of the way in which the public imaginary of the war on terror is dominated by risk managers who, in Bigo's terms, "not only respond to threat but also determine what is and what is not a risk" (2002: 74). Faced with the failure of the policy imaginary (or rather the failure of policymakers to be convinced by the imagination of the analysts, as we see below), there was frantic securitization of a number of sectors. In our exuberance to embrace the new realities of living under threat of terrorism, a raft of invasive and emergency programs was suggested – but not all programs were successful. For example, the following programs were cancelled or curtailed due to political and public pressure: total-then terrorist-information awareness program; the terrorist futures markets; the terrorist information and prevention system; the color-coded threat advisory system; the "ReadyAmerica" program run by the Department of Homeland Security. In short, how do we analyze the politics of the risk imaginary in the war on terror?

Bigo (2002), Amoore (2004, 2006), de Goede (2003), and the contributions to this collection examine the extensive bleeding of the war on terror and its concomitant expansion of emergency surveillance, investigatory, and policing powers into new sectors of society and new aspects of behavior. The case that this expansion is in essence biopolitical is made by Dillon (2007), Dillon and Reid (2001), and others. Without diminishing the power of this thesis, I want to make a parallel argument – the battles over the commanding heights of the popular imagination are just as important as the struggle to control mobile bodies. Serious study of the consequences of imagination for conflict can be seen in Gregory (1994), Shapiro (1997), and Gregory and Pred (2007), in which the architectures of meaning for war or spatial politics are examined through a combination of cultural and governmental texts. Shapiro argues that

> to analyze how things in the world take on meanings, it is necessary to analyze the structure of imaginative processes. The imaginative enactments that produce meanings are not simply acts of a pure, disembodied consciousness; they are historically developed practices which reside in the very style in which statements are made, of the grammatical, rhetorical, and narrative structures that compose even the discourse of the sciences.
>
> Shapiro (1988: 7)

I want to push forward here an analysis of a particular set of popular risk imaginaries, as a complement to the critique of national or international imaginaries. This is a slight modification of a term both Said and Shapiro use: "international imaginary" (Said 1993: 310). Shapiro uses it to mean the structural and symbolic framework that gives meaning to, and perpetuates, the configuration of sovereign states and their international relations (1996: 3). While not disputing the importance of these concepts, the popular imaginary is also important, by which I mean non-elite international epistemology and ontology – how the multitude comes to authenticate knowledge about the world and the possibility for values within that world.

The discussion of the imaginary and, in particular, the American imaginary has become the object of more serious scholarly concern since the invocation of the war on terror. I want to move away from considering the general national subjectivity, the political "we" that is defined and reified as the subject and object of politics toward an analysis of more specific bureaucratic imaginaries and more particular cultures of risk. Der Derian provides several excellent analyses of simulation and dissimulation in war, including a very interesting analysis of DARPA – the Department of Defense's own imagination factory (2000). Aretxaga, for example, discusses both the specific imaginary of the US Department of State illustrated through its publications and forecasts, and the popular imagination that is characterized as an "invisible space of the terror imaginary of [t]he U.S. (attacks on buildings and government, germ infection, etc.)" (2002: 140–4). Also, Simon examines the way in which the American risk imaginary, defined as "deeply embedded and often highly coded cultural images of the natures of risk," after Hurricane Katrina was shaped by racialized tropes of law and order (2007b: 4; see also Simon, this volume). Heng (2006) and Rasmussen (2006) examine how the American military as an organization has adopted and adapted the risk management approach. To follow from Bigo's formative work in this area, this chapter asks what are the politics of this unease? What are the politics of the risk imagination? Why are some mobilizations of fear productive of the consent needed for exceptional measures, while others fail? What I propose here is an examination of three settings of the risk imaginary: official, *ex officio*, and popular.[1] An examination of the technique of risk management as a way of structuring imagination follows.

## Imaginaries of terror

One of most interesting dynamics of post-9/11 public discourse has been the faulting of imagination – not intelligence, policing, or military might. A key conclusion of the 9/11 commission was that the chief failure was one of the imagination.[2] But, to parse this further, we know that it is not the failure of science fiction writers or Hollywood executives in this regard (Stockwell and Muir 2003). Tom Clancy had predicted in 1997 an attack on the American capital using a civilian aircraft in *Executive Orders*, when a Japanese pilot kills the president, the majority of both legislatures, and the Supreme Court, ushering in a new era of uncorrupted politics. *The Siege* (1998) directed by Edward Zwick put suicide bombers in New York City in retaliation for an American army abduction of a terrorist leader, Sheik Ahmed Bin Talal. Weber points out that "the Pentagon formed the 9/11 Group ... composed of Hollywood filmmakers and directed them to brainstorm about future terrorist scenarios" (2006: 3). Moving toward the nonfiction section, a 2001 Presidential Daily Briefing described "Bin Laden Determined to Attack Inside the United States," specifically mentioning the possibility of hijacking American aircraft and the surveillance of Federal buildings in New York City. Thus, it is not imagination *per se* that was lacking – but rather a lack of convincing imaginings. This indictment of imagination is not really about imagining possible futures, or even about the ranking of possible risks. Rather, it is an attempt to blame the narrative or storytellers that, in the information-soaked decision-space, certain imaginings were not more persuasive. Following from Amoore (this volume), I argue that organizational culture is an important object of study. In particular, I am convinced that we need to analyze the popular imaginary as the universe of political actions that are possible and imagined, not simply as a subset of a national or international imaginary, but as a system of bureaucratic and popular imaginaries that condition the possibility of decisions about risk and security.

This is a vital addendum to the Copenhagen School's literature on securitization (Waever 1995; Williams 2003). Specifically, I want to pose the question of *why* certain securitizations are successful, while others fail (Balzacq 2005; Taureck 2006). Walter's critique hits the mark: securitization theory does not examine the "set" of the political drama, or rather limits the setting to one of five frames (this volume). To continue this dramaturgical analysis, securitization theory does not address the setting, the timing, or the audience response (Salter, forthcoming). Why are some securitizing speech acts welcomed and others derided? Why does domestic surveillance by the National Security Agency meet with only legalistic resistance from opponents, while the total information awareness program, later the terrorist awareness program, fails? Why does the standardization of drivers' licenses mandated by the RealID Act fail, but the border crossing card made mandatory by the Western Hemisphere Travel Initiative does not raise resistance? In essence, I am interested in supplementing the Copenhagen School's theory to examine the securitization of the American imagination. I am convinced that, in addition to the battles of entrenched interests and bureaucratic politics that structure these failures, the degree of public consent or resistance is conditioned by the deep structure of the popular imaginary. In this section, I want to look at three important imaginaries of terror attacks in the United States.

## Official imagination

An attack on the World Trade Center was certainly imaginable; it had happened in 1993 – however, the use of planes as weapons themselves was considered unimaginable. Why? There is a genuine question about why the Hart–Rudman Commission was ignored, although published in 2000, which specifically and precisely predicted terrorist attacks on the US (Flynn 2002). To push forward this critical appraisal of the moment of imagination – why some securitizations are successful – it is important to gauge why some judgments are "imaginable" and some "unimaginable." The presentation of the 9/11 Commission is specifically described as a "narrative," and the report has a narrative arc, jumping back and forth in time and using many conventions of traditional literature, as Klein (1989) would no doubt have predicted. The Commission explains the failure of imagination by describing the many threat analyses which predicted such an attack that were disbelieved (Kean and Hamilton 2004: 341–3). They describe the disconnect between analysts and policymakers: "those government experts who saw Bin Laden as an unprecedented danger needed a way to win broad support for their views ... " (Kean and Hamilton 2004: 343). It was precisely not a failure of imagining, but of failing to "win broad support" within the administration. Rice's imagination failed to be fired by the Presidential Daily Briefing about bin Laden's determination to strike within the US through hijacking planes. She said in her testimony before the 9/11 Commission:

> ... I said, "No one could have imagined them taking a plane, slamming it into the Pentagon ... into the World Trade Center, using planes as a missile." As I said to you in the private session, I probably should have said, "I could not have imagined," because within two days, people started to come to me and say, "Oh, but there were these reports in 1998 and 1999. The intelligence community did look at information about this."
>
> Rice (2004)

Rice argues that her individual failure of imagination was the result of the failed persuasive rhetorical power of those analyses. In her testimony, Rice displaces the failure of analysis into a failure of the imagination, and from there into a failure of narrative. The narrative failed to fire her imagination, which led to a subsequent un-imagining of the threat. Rice asked that Clarke's 1998 *Delanda Report* be recast – again a narrative issue – when he re-presented it to the executive when W. Bush assumed power. The report clearly set forth a strategy for the elimination of the bin Laden network very similar to the eventual shape of the war on terror. Rice's testimony continues:

> Part of the problem is – and I think Sandy Berger made this point when he was asked the same question – that you have thousands of pieces of information – car bombs and this method and that method – and you have to depend to a certain degree on the intelligence agencies to sort to tell you what is actually relevant, what is actually based on sound sources, what is speculative.
>
> Rice (2004)

Thus, it is not the experts who failed in their analysis or in their imagination, but it is the experts who failed in providing a compelling narrative for their analysis. Rice's public defense relied on a criticism of the overload of expert opinion, and the failure of narrative. I would argue that this is a direct consequence of the adoption of a risk management paradigm, which I explore below. It is a different kind of imaginary politics from the negotiation of the national "we" or the barbaric "them" (Salter 2007). The representation of the imagination as the site of policy analysis is fascinating in its implications, and indicates the degree to which affect, emotion, and narrative play a role in decision-making even for hard-hearted realists such as Dr. Rice. We see an adoption of this tactic in Richard Clarke's speculative fiction.

## Ex officio *imagination*

January 25, 2001, Clarke writes a memo to Rice, the newly installed national security advisor, "challenging Rice to image the day after an attack," which fails to be convincing (Kean and Hamilton 2004: 344). By 2005, Clarke is out of the bureaucracy, and is writing "Ten Years Later" for the *Atlantic Monthly*. Clarke (2005) places an historical analysis of the war on terror from the perspective of 2011 in a lecture given at the Kennedy School at Harvard by Professor Roger McBride. In presenting the argument in a remote authorial voice, Clarke distances his analysis from the personal and professional attacks he suffered after the publication of *Against all enemies*, and also places his predictions firmly in the realm of the imagination. Clarke seemingly embraces the problem of narrative in a particular effort to convince.[3] Although fiction, the article is full of footnotes to current sources which support the "realism" of these targets, tactics, or trends, and photomontages which illustrate these various attacks.

The fictional Professor McBride starts out his summary of 2005 with a series of suicide attacks by the al-Qaeda of America on vulnerable targets: casinos in Las Vegas, a water park in Florida, and an amusement park in New Jersey. The terrorists are specifically described as non-Arab representing other affiliates of al-Qaeda, which prompts wide-scale retaliations against Islamic sites. Paralleling the plot of *The Siege*, suspected individuals are put into camps. The campaign culminates with a Christmas bombing of the "Mall of the States" in Minnesota (plainly representing the Mall of America in Minneapolis) and other shopping centers. In his detailed descriptions of the tactics of the terrorists, McBride emphasizes how small teams (two to four) can easily obtain false identity documents, travel, firearms, and uniforms. By 2006, America has become an entirely militarized society with increased US military on national soil and the dramatic invention of new state militias. "Subway Day" eerily predicts the 7/7 bombings in London and leads to the creation of a new Federal transit police force – supplemented by the US military which is quickly withdrawing from Iraq. To supplement the additional police and paramilitary forces, a national ID card with RFID technology is made mandatory (a reference to the RealID Act), and is linked to various governmental databases including gun registries. In the alternate 2007, an American attack on an Iranian nuclear site, which failed due to faulty intelligence, leads to greater instability in the Middle East, which in turn prompts a fundamentalist coup in Saudi Arabia. Attacks on civilian aircraft within the US on "Stinger Day" illustrate the vulnerability of airliners to shoulder-launched missiles (MANPADs). Faced with a fundamentalist regime in Saudi Arabia, a new oil crisis caused the world economy to slow down. 2008 sees a cyberattack on America's critical infrastructure and an election bringing with it increased anti-terror policies. In 2009, this culminates in a new draft which generates military and public safety officers. A special court is established to decide on the status of prisoners (as enemy combatants or prisoners of war). Further impeding global commerce, fears of a nuclear weapon being imported into the US leads the Navy to implement a 200-mile *cordon sanitaire* in which all ships are subject to search. Unsecured general aviation and easy access to noxious chemicals are blamed for attacks in 2010. At the close of the piece, as McBride ponders on how we might have avoided this nightmare scenario, he combines chances missed by 2005 (the date of publication) and future opportunities. The war on Iraq is lamentable as it distracts from the war on terror and encourages *jihadis*; the lack of political engagement with Islam also reflects a weakness in American public diplomacy; the inability of the US to solve the Palestine and Chechnya issues adds to our international reputation; intelligence failures also lead America to be unprepared for major geopolitical shifts; dependence on oil and a lack of investment in critical infrastructure security also make America more vulnerable.

In a final footnote, Clarke reasserts his own authorial intent to say (distinct from the voice of his mouthpiece professor):

> *Author's note*: This scenario is intentionally very bad but not worst-case. (A nuclear or biological attack would be worst case.) The purpose of this article is to suggest that there are still opportunities to avoid such disasters without sacrificing our liberties, if we act now ...
>
> Clarke (2005: 77)

In this construction, Clarke poses a triple nightmare: the potential apocalypse which is at the limit of the imaginable, the inevitability of vulnerability, and the totalitarianism of reaction. The attack scenarios illustrate common wisdom among terror experts: small teams are most effective, it is easy to evade policing profiles, coordinated attacks cause greater chaos, economic uncertainty has ripple effects in an open society. The governmental response to militarize society and radically decrease civil rights is seen as the only way to react to the attacks, as prevention has failed. Clarke, then, is adding to our imagination new and various nightmares to prompt urgent policy actions. What is particularly useful here is that Clarke aims to convince by using fiction – supported by empirical evidence.

## Popular imagination[4]

To contrast with the near-future writing of Clarke, Ethan Reiff and Cyrus Voris created the mini-series "Sleeper Cell." The plot centers on a Muslim FBI agent who goes undercover to infiltrate an al-Qaeda sleeper cell in Los Angeles. The advertisements for this mini-series included "The enemy is here," "Friends. Neighbors. Husbands. Terrorists" and, finally, "Know your enemy," suggesting precisely the kind of generalized fear discussed by Amoore (this volume). The Los Angeles cell is composed of a former French skinhead who came to al-Qaeda through his Algerian wife, a Bosnian Muslim, and a disenfranchised son of a liberal Berkeley history professor, and is led by a Saudi veteran of the Afghani mujahadeen, Indonesia, and "Black Hawk Down" in Somalia (who himself masquerades as a Jewish security expert). One of the narrative hooks of this very popular series is the demonstration of terror tactics by the members of the cell: surveillance and countersurveillance, obtaining nondescript vehicles, hiding their victims, blending into society, gaining deadly chemicals, and, finally, staging an attack on an open target. Cells in Washington and New York attempt to coordinate their attacks on the same day of the Muslim calendar. The terrorists initially plan an attack on a shopping center, but then choose an LA Dodger baseball game. The attack is thwarted through the courageous actions of Darwyn, the undercover agent. Darwyn, a representative of the survival of the fittest ideology, is African American, whose cover identity emerges from prison to join the cell. In this move, the questions of the systemic alienation of race relations in the US, the disproportionately minority prison population, or jail house conversions to Islam are totally obscured (despite the clear parallel between Darwyn and Jose Padilla). Inspired by boxer Muhammad Ali's disavowal of the 9/11 attacks as "not really Islam," Reiff and Voris created the show with particularly pedagogical intent: to teach viewers about the varieties of Islam, the dedication of suicide bombers, and the difficulty in deterring a suicide bomber or cell that Epstein alludes to in her piece. They want to "break down" stereotypes of Muslims in America and create a sympathetic Muslim hero. Part of this pedagogical project is illustrating how the terrorists operate in America:

> the kind of ingenuity on display in "Sleeper Cell" is impressive; you want to tip your hat to it, and, at the same time, you want to grab your hat and run. But where to? The cell members hide in plain sight; they use PayPal to transfer drug money, and they pick up their packages at Mail Boxes etc.
>
> Franklin (2005: 111)

In the final episode as the leader is captured, shot by Darwyn's female handler (who is beheaded in the première of Season 2), the US military carries out the wishes of the President: Darwyn's undercover actions (he kills to maintain his cover) compromise the legal case against the terrorist, and so the military will take custody of the prisoner. The *post facto* appropriation of the legal case by the military mirrors the international war on terror. It is a naturalization of the state of exception applied outside of American territory at Guantánamo Bay and paves the way for the same kind of actions on American soil. And, as Leonard argues, over the course of the series, we move from gaining understanding about the motives of terror toward a profound lack of empathy for the prisoner: "Sleeper Cell tries laudably to entertain us and to complicate us simultaneously. But we also experience the Stockholm syndrome in reverse. The more time we spend with these people, the less we care about them" (2005). Erickson argues that two discourses of subversion and ambiguity mark the "[complex] field of interpretation" in the American popular imaginary of representations of counterterrorism (2007: 202).

Representations of terrorists in "Sleeper Cell" make racially determined physical descriptors difficult, which in turn enable the surveillance of the total population. But, these representations of terrorists as fundamentalists simultaneously render the terrorist psyche as unproblematic and simplistic – so inherently perverse that it renders guilt obvious or unnecessary. Katz follows this description of "banal terrorism" as "everyday, routinized, barely noticed reminders of terror or the threat of an always already presence of terrorism in our midst" (2007: 350).

These close readings of different kinds of popular imaginaries are not intended to poll the entire culture – but rather show the politics of imagining risk in the war on terror. In particular, these three texts detail the imagining of vulnerability and potential public and governmental responses. We can analyze these texts for their ideological meaning, as symptoms of broader sociopolitical trends, rather than intentional pieces of propaganda. Separate from the pedagogical or political intent of these texts, we can identify some deep structural elements of the way in which fear, uncertainty, and risk are being mobilized and used in the popular imaginary. Flynn, for example, argues in his conclusion: "Terrorism is only one of a growing list of potentially catastrophic events that threatens the public" (2007: 170). But he continues to argue that the solution lies in the wide-scale diffusion of "preparedness:" our greatest untapped asset is the American people. Agents and authorities who wish to increase their scope of movement or justification for the extension of powers require a generalized fear, but are wary of creating emergency fatigue: in this case, the fear of a terrorist attack is a resource that must be used judiciously (within a framework of liberal governance). To return to the question of securitization – why is this terror alert system contestable, while the use of planes is unimaginable? What uses are these differing imaginings of terror being put to?

## Ranking our nightmares

As Jonathan Simon says in his chapter, "it is more accurate to suggest that nightmares have been the driving force in inventing new forms of government" (this volume). Risk management provides a rationale, a calculus, a system within which these nightmares can be promulgated and regulated at the same time. With risk management, a structure for empirically ranking nightmares comes into play. Needless to say, this appeal to the "authority of statistics" (Bigo 2004) hides the incalculability in the ranking of risks. As Beck argues, "the hidden central issue in world risk society is *how to feign control over the uncontrollable* – in politics, law, science, technology, economy and everyday life" (2002: 41). Lee Clarke argues in his analysis of emergency planning that fantasy plans are laid "that grow out of a managerial need to *do something* about potentially grave danger. As these [high reliability] organizations do their planning they transform uncertainty into risk, and the main tool they use in that transformation is a rhetorical one" (1999: 19). Following Ericson (2006; this volume) and Aradau and van Munster (2007), reliable, mathematical calculation of the impact, frequency of, or vulnerability to terrorism is impossible. As a consequence, there is a fetish for the appearance of certainty and the management of unease. A key component of risk management as a *dispositif* is the acceptance of failure, the acceptance of certain disasters or emergencies. I argue that, within the security realm and, in particular, the diaphanous discourse justifying the war on terror, the logic of risk fuels the circulation of anxiety and the provision of governmental "solutions." Experts, firms, and agencies offer calculations of the costs and benefits of specific failures, with a view to providing resources appropriate to cost.

We can point to two practical dangers with the adoption of the risk management framework within the war on terror: an empirical or managerial critique, and a more abstract weakness. Inherent in risk management for security is conspicuous consumption of expertise. There is an organizational focus on development of expertise for low-n, low-probability events that cannot focus on prevention, but rather preemption. There is a limit to the efficacy of risk communication and the fetish for planning for the unexpected in the war on terror, as it is precisely not politically viable. Risk management supports both of these moves – the focus on measurable threats and the acceptance of failure. Thus, there is a managerial blind rush to action and an unfulfilled promise of control. As Aradau and van Munster argue in this volume, the doctrine of preemption continually drives the expansion of governance, surveillance, and interferences in greater areas of social life. Within the popular imaginary, there is a pressure to plan for every eventuality, what Grusin calls "premediation:" "part of a heterogeneous media regime whose fundamental purpose is to preclude that no matter what tomorrow might bring, it will always already have been premediated" (2004: 29). If every possibility has been pre-imagined, then focus can be directed on response management – making foreign policy always preemptive (occurring before proof) and reactive (to the imaginary). The metric for the ranking of these nightmares is always abstract and always already insufficient.

The imagination is becoming a more serious site of analysis for theorists and policymakers alike because terror is not a clear object of statecraft or public policy. The real enemy in the war on terror, as it were, is anti-Americanism, which is precisely not externally visible or provable. Consequently, the focus is on preemption, precaution, premediation, and imagination – those possible, potential signs of internal dissension. Terror is a tactic. We see in the official, *ex officio*, and popular representations of the popular imaginary that the focus of anxiety is on particular tactics. The Presidential memo, Clarke's intelligence estimate and fictional writings, and the mass media all focus on the tactics of terror – which consequently minimizes the consideration of the motives. All terrorists are described as "fanatical" – suicidal and thus always already alienated, with no need to comprehend the economic, social, political, or geopolitical motivation for attacks. Risk management renders the imaginary "real" – quantified, qualified, and defined – and provides an auditable plan to action.

## Mission: imagination

Increasingly, the international imaginary is also a crucial battlefield, especially as the war on terror is portrayed as a war of ideas. And, it is ideas and imagination that are described in the latest National Security Strategy as *causing* terrorism to spring from the dispossessed of globalization: "it is ideas that can turn the disenchanted into murderers willing to kill innocent victims" (White House 2006: 9). The target of war on terror is anti-Americanism – the doctrine of preemption mandates that action is always too late, which is particularly supported by risk management. In particular, this anti-American imagination is an anti-colonial imagination, and must be understood in reference to colonial and anti-colonial cultures (Barkawi and Laffey 2006; Salter 2007). The logic of preemption prioritizes the power of imagination over the power of fact – suspicions over evidence. The National Security Strategy argues that imagination and suspicion trump facts, even retroactively:

> It is an enduring American principle that this duty obligates the government to anticipate and counter threats, using all elements of national power, before the threats can do grave damage. The greater the threat, the greater is the risk of inaction – and the more compelling the case for taking anticipatory action to defend ourselves, even if uncertainty remains as to the time and place of the enemy's attack.
>
> White House (2006: 18)

As a *dispositif*, the colonial imaginary marshals the resource of premediation to generate fear and administer the "appropriate" responses. As a response, the anti-colonial imagination values resistance, surprise, and innovation. This is not to say that these colonial/anti-colonial discourses or strategies are coordinated or smooth, but rather there is a zone of contestation in which the public risk imaginary is debated. These imaginaries generate the fear of anti-Americanism and administer the appropriate responses, simultaneously embedding an acceptance of failure and a focus on those responses that are measurable.

There are a number of strategies for examining how these popular imaginaries manifest geopolitical narratives or identity schemes. The popular imaginary is akin to a market of ideas in which narratives, identities, and social scripts vie for adherents and credibility. Within international relations, Shapiro (1997) examines representations of violence in movies; Weber (2006) looks at discourses of sexuality and their connection to tropes of American national identity; Neumman and Nexon use the Harry Potter saga to focus scholarly attention (2006); Erickson (2007) compares representations of counterterrorism agencies in American television. One way that commonly accepted narratives are shattered and broken is through the use of humor, laughter, and parody that disrupts the flow of narrative. Foucault, for example, starts *Order of Things* by describing:

> the laughter that shattered ... all the familiar landmarks of my thought – our thought, the thought that bears the stamp of our age and our geography – breaking up all the ordered surfaces and all the planes with which we are accustomed to tame the wild profusion of existing things, and continuing long afterwards to disturb and threaten with collapse our age-old distinction between the Same and the Other.
>
> Foucault (1970: xv)

The laughter at the ridiculous or the unexpected reveals the inevitable slips and gaps in hegemonic narratives or discourses. I am not making any causal claim that a particular joke or artistic intervention changes popular culture, but rather that more analytical attention needs to be paid to the sensibility of humor in the popular imaginary.

I want to conclude by examining two precisely political representations in the risk imaginary: a Canadian sit-com *Little Mosque on the Prairie* and guerilla artist Banksy's intervention at Disneyworld. Based in the prairie town of Mercy, *Little Mosque* opens with the problems associated with the community finding a permanent mosque (which they do in a Church hall). In addition to presenting a caricature of a fundamental Muslim, out of step with the community, the question of radicalism and prejudice is demonstrated in the town "shock jock" and the placid mayor. More political, the new Imam is a lawyer from Toronto who has found a new calling. On his way from the modern city to the prairie town, he is questioned by police at the airport because a nervous passenger who overhears half a telephone conversation about his move and career change. The (white) passenger hears "I've been planning this for months; it's not like I dropped a bomb on him. If Dad thinks it's suicide, so be it. This is Allah's plan for me." The police arrive and tell him "you're not going to Paradise today." "What's the charge," says the Imam, "flying while Muslim"? During the interrogation by the bumbling police, the Imam jokes that "if my story doesn't check out, you can deport me to Syria." The police officer (not Royal Canadian Mounted Police) snaps back, "You do not get to choose which country we deport you to." Three recent cases demonstrate the imaginary in which this circulates. Individuals have been prevented from boarding planes due to the suspicion of other passengers. Raed Jarrar, a human rights activist, was barred from boarding a Jet Blue flight due to a T-shirt with Arabic script (Jarrar 2006). MacFarquhar reports that "six imams were hauled off a US Airways plane in Minnesota in November after apparently spooking at least one fellow passenger by murmuring prayers that included the word Allah" (2006). Two Canadians have been deported to Syria for detention and torture. Maher Arar, a Canadian software engineer, was deported to Syria while transiting through the United States (O'Connor, 2006). What is the effect of joking about this "banal terror?" The creator of *Little Mosque on the Prairie*, Zarqa Nawaz, was praised in the Canadian media for breaking taboos. In the press kit, Nawaz says her show "is a sitcom and not political satire. It is important to normalize the community within the greater community so as not to be seen as the 'other' but to recognize that we all have universal themes which exist in all communities" (2007: 6).

Banksy is the pseudonym of a British artist whose installations and graffiti often interrupt traditional urban or art spaces (2007). Well known in Britain, the reclusive artist has placed re-touched masterpieces in British museums (pastoral paintings with shopping carts or CCTV cameras added) and painted idyllic scenes on the Israeli–Palestinian separation barrier (see Collins 2007). In September 2006, Banksy introduced a hooded, orange jumpsuit-clad, inflatable figure of a Guantánamo Bay detainee into a ride at Disneyland in Florida.[5] Park-goers on the Big Thunder Mountain Railroad had their ride stopped "for security reasons" while facing the blow-up detainee. Petrides argues that this kind of intervention "is a political operation that removes an historical past of colonial imposition only to re-place it into an existing context, equally imposing, in order to comment on our present state of political affairs" (2006: 3). Banksy sets up a tension between the "security reasons" that the rollercoaster is stopped and the "security reasons" for the incarceration of detainees without trial in a military prison that interrupts the ride. These interventions occur within the realm of the imagination of risk in an attempt to disrupt the "banal terror" of the everyday. Banksy and Nawaz aim to remind us of the geopolitics and micropolitics at stake in representing culture as non-political. As with *Little Mosque on the Prairie*, the use of humor for shock tells us something about the way risk and imagination are at work. Without making a biological–essentialist argument, cognitively, we are adaptive thinkers. The paralysis and paranoia of September 12 has been replaced by the moral imperative to maintain "normal" life (Bush 2001). We come to accept the exceptional as mundane. In short, we do not fear the statistically "right" things: smoking less than skiing, driving less than flying (Myers 2001). Consequently, it is easy to shape the risk imaginary toward the mundane, to bracket both low-probability risks and potential catastrophic results. Within securitization studies and within our analyses of risk in the war on terror, we can observe entropy of risk perception, which leads (inadvertently or intentionally) toward the depoliticization of exception policies and politics. Our analysis of the popular imaginary must be contextually sensitive, but also carefully attuned to that which is depoliticized in culture by examining moments of laughter as potentially political interruptions of the everyday.

## Notes

1 See Grusin (2004: 25) who argues that the logic of premediation and remediation structure depictions of disaster in cinematography, television, and print media.
2 This is also true of the investigation of the 1982 bombings of the Marine barracks in Beirut (House Armed Services Committee 1983: 2).
3 S. E. Flynn avers a similar aim in *America the Vulnerable* and *The Edge of Disaster*. Flynn is an member of the Council of Foreign Relations, an ex-Coast Guard officer, and a researcher for the Hart–Rudman Commission.
4 See Erickson (2007) for other analyses of *24*, *The Agency*, and *The Grid* and Weber (2006) on *Minority Report*, *Behind Enemy Lines*, *Black Hawk Down*, and *Kandahar*.
5 Video is posted on his website: http://www.banksy.co.uk/films/movie5.html. This stunt was concurrent with an installation on global poverty that featured a mock-up of a sitting room with an elephant painted to blend in with the wallpaper.

# Bibliography

Abu-Laban, Y. and G. Christina (2002) *Selling Diversity: Immigration, Multiculturalism, Employment Equity, and Globalization*, New York: Broad View Press.

Accenture (2004) *2004 News Releases*, http://www.accenture.com/xd/xd.asp?it = enweb&xd =_dyn%5Cdynamicpressrelease_730.xml (accessed January 11, 2008).

Accenture Digital Forum (2004) 'US DHS to Develop and Implement US VISIT Program at Air, Land and Sea Ports of Entry', http://www.digitalforum.accenture.com.

ACE (2004) *Specialty Products. Property Terrorism*, http://www.aceterrorismrisk.com (accessed June 8, 2007).

Achelpöhler, W. and H. Niehaus (2004) 'Data Screening as a Means of Preventing Islamist Terrorist Attacks in Germany', *German Law Journal* 5 (5): 495–513.

Ackelson, J. (2005) 'Constructing Security on the U.S.–Mexico Border,' *Political Geography* 24 (2): 164–84.

Adam, B. and J. van Loon (2000) 'Introduction', in B. Adam and J. van Loon (eds) *The Risk Society and Beyond: Critical Issues for Social Theory*, London: Sage.

Adey, P. (2004) 'Surveillance at the Airport: Surveilling Mobility/Mobilising Surveillance,' *Environment and Planning A* 36 (8): 1365–80.

—— (2006) '"Divided we move": the *Dromo*-Logics of Airport Security and Surveillance,' in T. Monahan (ed.) *Security and Surveillance: Technological Politics in Everyday Life*, London: Routledge.

Agamben, G. (1998) *Homo Sacer: Sovereign Power and Bare Life*, Stanford: Stanford University Press.

—— (2002) 'Security and Terror', *Theory & Event* 5: 4.

—— (2004) 'No to Bio-Political Tattooing,' *Le Monde* January 10.

—— (2005) *State of Exception*, Chicago: University of Chicago Press.

Akers Chacón, J. and M. Davis (2006) *No One is Illegal: Fighting Racism and State Violence on the US-Mexico Border*, Chicago: Haymarket.

Alusuutari, P. (2005) *The Governmentality of Consultancy and Competition: The Influence of the OECD*. Paper presented at the 37th World Congress of the International Institute of Sociology, Stockholm, July 5–9.

Amin, A. (2002) 'Spatialities of Globalisation,' *Environment and Planning A* 34 (3): 385–99.

—— (2004a) 'Multi-ethnicity and the Idea of Europe,' *Theory, Culture and Society* 21 (2): 1–24.

—— (2004b) 'Regulating Economic Globalization,' *Transactions of the Institute of British Geographers* 29 (2): 217–33.

Amin, A. and N. Thrift (2004) *The Blackwell Cultural Economy Reader*, London: Blackwell.

Amin, A., D. Massey and N. Thrift (2003) *Decentering the Nation: A Radical Approach to Regional Inequality*, London: Catalyst.

Amoore, L. (2004) 'Risk, Reward and Discipline at Work', *Economy and Society* 33 (2): 174–96.

—— (2006) 'Biometric Borders: Governing Mobilities in the War on Terror', *Political Geography* 25 (3): 336–51.

—— (2007a) 'Vigilant Visualities: The Watchful Politics of the War on Terror', *Security Dialogue* 38 (2): 215–32.

—— (2007b) '"There is No Great Refusal": The Ambivalent Politics of Resistance,' in M. de Goede (ed.) *International Political Economy and Poststructural Politics*, London: Palgrave Macmillan.

Amoore, L. and M. de Goede (2005) 'Governance, Risk and Dataveillance in the War on Terror', *Crime, Law and Social Change* 43 (2): 149–73.

—— (2008, in press) 'Transactions After 9/11: The Banal Face of the Preemptive Strike', *Transactions of the Institute of British Geographers* 33.

Anderson, D. (1999) 'The Aggregate Burden of Crime', *Journal of Law and Economics* 42: 611–42.

Anderson, M. (1996) *Frontiers. Territory and State Formation in the Modern World*, Oxford: Polity/Blackwell.

Anderson, M. and D. Bigo (2003) 'What are EU Frontiers for and What do they Mean?' in K. Groenendijk, E. Guild and P. Minderhoud (eds) *In Search of Europe's Borders*, The Hague: Kluwer.

Andreas, P. (2000a) 'Introduction: The Wall after the Wall', in P. Andreas and T. Snyder (eds) *The Wall around the West: State Borders and Immigration Controls in North America and Europe*, Lanham, MD: Rowman and Littlefield.

—— (2000b) *Border Game: Policing the U.S.-Mexico Divide*, Ithaca: Cornell University Press.

Andreas, P. and T. J. Biersteker (eds) (2003) *The Rebordering of North America: Integration and Exclusion in a New Security Context*, New York: Routledge.

Andreas, P. and R. Price (2001) 'From War Fighting to Crime Fighting: Transforming the American National Security State', *The International Studies Review* 3 (3): 32–51.

Andreas, P. and T. Snyder (eds) (2000) *The Wall Around the West: State Borders and Immigration Controls in North America and Europe*, New York: Rowman and Littlefield.

Anzaldúa, G. (1987) *Borderlands/La Frontera: The New Mestiza*, San Francisco: Aunt Lute Books.

AON (2005) *Terrorism Risk Map*, http://www.aon.com/risk_management/terrorism_mitigation/terrorism_risk_map.jsp (accessed June 8, 2007).

Apted, M. (dir.) (2001) *Enigma*, Miramax Films.

Aradau, C. (2007) 'Law Transformed: Guantanamo and the "Other" Exception', *Third World Quarterly* 28 (3): 489–502.

Aradau, C. (2008) *Rethinking Trafficking in Women: Politics Out of Security*, Basingstoke: Palgrave.

Aradau, C. and R. van Munster (2007) 'Governing Terrorism through Risk: Taking Precautions, (un)Knowing the Future', *European Journal of International Relations* 13 (1): 89–115.

—— (2008, forthcoming) *The Politics of Catastrophe*,

Aretxaga, B. (2002) 'Terror as Thrill: First Thoughts on the "War on Terrorism"', *Anthropological Quarterly* 75: 139–50.

Arias, A. (ed.) (2001) *The Rigoberta Menchu Controversy*, Minneapolis: University of Minnesota Press.

Arquilla, J. and D. Ronfeldt (1993) 'Cyberwar is Coming!', *Comparative Strategy* 12 (April–June): 141–65.

—— (1997) *In Athena's Camp: Preparing for Conflict in the Information Age*, Santa Monica: RAND.

—— (1998) *The Zapatista "Social Netwar" in Mexico*, Santa Monica: RAND.

—— (2000) *Swarming and the Future of Conflict*, Santa Monica: RAND.

—— (2001) *Networks and Netwars: The Future of Terror, Crime, and Militancy*, Santa Monica: RAND.

Ashbourn, J. (2004) *Practical Biometrics: From Aspiration to Implementation*, London: Springer-Verlag.

Associated Press (1988) 'Bush [Nomination Acceptance Speech]: "Stakes Are High and Choice is Crucial"', *Los Angeles Times* August 19: 6.

Atia, M. (2007) 'In Whose Interest? Financial Surveillance and the Circuits of Exception in the War on Terror', *Environment and Planning D: Society and Space* 25 (3): 447–75.

Avant, D. (2005) *The Market for Force: the Consequences of Privatizing Security*, Cambridge: Cambridge University Press.

Baker, S. (2006) *Remarks*, Center for Strategic and International Studies, Washington, December 19, http://www.dhs.gov/xnews/speeches/sp_1166557969765.shtm (accessed October 8, 2007).

Baker, T. (2002) 'Liability and Insurance after September 11: Embracing Risk Meets the Precautionary Principle', *The Geneva Papers on Risk and Insurance* 27 (3): 349–57.

Baker, T. and J. Simon (eds) (2002) *Embracing Risk: The Changing Culture of Insurance and Responsibility*, Chicago: University of Chicago Press.

Balibar, E. (2000) 'What we Owe to the Sans-Papiers', in L. Guenther and C. Heesters (eds) *Social Insecurity; Alphabet City No. 7*, Toronto: Anansi.

—— (2002) *Politics and the Other Scene*, London: Verso.

—— (2003) 'Europe: An "Unimagined" Frontier of Democracy', *diacritics* 33 (3/4): 36–44.

Balzacq, T. (2005) 'The Three Faces of Securitization: Political Agency, Audience and Context', *European Journal of International Relations* 11 (2): 171–201.

Banfield, E. (1970) *The Unheavenly City: The Nature and Future of Our Urban Crisis*, Boston: Little, Brown and Company.

Bank of America (2002) 'Bank of America Reaffirms Commitment to Hispanic Community', *Press Release*, 23 April, http://newsroom.bankofamerica.com/index.php?s = press_-releases&item = 4936 (accessed May 1, 2007).

Banksy (2006) 'Disneyland', http://www.banksy.co.uk/films/movie5.html (accessed May 12, 2007).

—— (2007) *Wall and Piece*, London: Random House.

Barak, G. (2005) 'A Reciprocal Approach to Peacemaking Criminology: Between Adversarialism and Mutualism', *Theoretical Criminology* 9: 131–52.

Barkawi, T. and M. Laffey (2006) 'The Postcolonial Moment in Security Studies', *Review of International Studies* 32: 329–52.

Barry, A. (1993) 'The European Community and European Government: Harmonization, Mobility and Space', *Economy and Society* 22 (3): 314–26.

Bau, I. (1985) *This Ground Is Holy: Church Sanctuary and Central American Refugees*, New York: Paulist Press.

Baudrillard, J. (2003) *The Spirit of Terrorism and Other Essays*, London: Verso.

Baum, D. (1996) *Smoke and Mirrors: The War on Drugs and the Politics of Failure*, Boston: Little, Brown and Company.

Bauman, Z. (1998) *Globalization: The Human Consequences*, New York: Columbia University Press.

—— (2000) *Liquid Modernity*, Cambridge: Polity Press.

Bauman, Z., and L. Galecki (2005) *The Unwinnable War: an Interview with Zygmunt Bauman*, http://www.opendemocracy.net (accessed February 2, 2007).

Bayatrizi, Z. (2005) *Death Sentences: The Modern Ordering of Mortality*, PhD Thesis, Department of Anthropology and Sociology, University of British Columbia.

BBC (2005) *Dimbleby Lecture*, November 16, http://news.bbc.co.uk/1/hi/uk/4443386.stm (accessed January 11, 2008).

BBC (2006) 'Web Users to "Patrol" US Border', June 2, http://news.bbc.co.uk/1/hi/world/americas/5040372.stm (accessed January 11, 2008).

Beck, U. (1992) *Risk Society: Towards a New Modernity*, London: Sage.

—— (1999) *World Risk Society*, Cambridge: Polity Press.

—— (2000) 'Risk Society Revisited: Theory, Politics and Research Programmes', in B. Adam, U. Beck and J. Van Loon (eds) *The Risk Society and Beyond: Critical Issues for Social Theory*, London: Sage Publications.

—— (2002) 'The Terrorist Threat: World Risk Society Revisited', *Theory, Culture & Society* 19 (4): 39–55.

—— (2003) 'The Silence of Words: On Terror and War', *Security Dialogue* 34 (3): 255–67.

Beckett, K. (1997) *Making Crime Pay: Law and Order in Contemporary American Politics*, New York: Oxford University Press.

Belgian Privacy Commission/Commissie voor de Bescherming van de Persoonlijke Levenssfeer (2006) *Advies Nr 37 / 2006*, September 27.

Bennett, C. (2005) 'What Happens when you Book an Airline Ticket? The Collecting and Processing of Passenger Data Post-9/11', in M. Zureik and M. Salter (eds) *Global Surveillance and Policing: Borders, Security, Identity*, Cullompton: Willan.

Bennett, J. (2005) 'The Agency of Assemblages and the North American Blackout', *Public Culture* 17 (3): 445–65.

Berelowitz, J.-A. (2005) 'The Spaces of Home in Chicano and Latino Representations of the San Diego–Tijuana Borderlands (1968–2002)', *Environment and Planning D: Society and Space* 23 (3): 323–50.

Beverley, J. (2004) *Testimonio: On the Politics of Truth*, Minneapolis: University of Minnesota Press.

Bevir, M. (ed.) (2007) *Encyclopaedia of Governance*, Thousand Oaks: Sage Publications.

Bhabha, H. (1993) 'Culture's In Between', *Artforum* 32 (1): 167–70.

—— (1994a/2004) *The Location of Culture*, London: Routledge.

—— (1994b) 'Frontlines/Borderposts', in A. Bammer (ed.) *Displacements: Cultural Identities in Question*, Indianapolis: Indiana University Press.

Bhandar, D. (2004) 'Renormalizing Citizenship and Life in Fortress North America', *Citizenship Studies* 8 (3): 261–78.

Biersteker, T. J. (2002) 'Targeting Terrorist Finances: The New Challenges of Financial Market Globalisation', in K. Booth and T. Dunne (eds) *Worlds in Collision: Terror and the Future of Global Order*, Basingstoke: Palgrave.

—— (2004) 'Counter-Terrorism Measures Undertaken Under UN Security Council Auspices', in A. J. K. Bailes and I. Frommelt (eds) *Business and Security: Public-Private Relationships in a New Security Environment*, Oxford: Oxford University Press.

Biesecker, C. (2004) 'Congress Signals Strong Interest in UAVs for Border Security', *Defense Daily* 17 December.

Bigo, D. (2000) 'When Two Become One: Internal and External Securitisations in Europe', in M. Kelstrup and M. C. Williams (eds) *International Relations Theory and the Politics of European Integration*, London: Routledge.

—— (2001) 'The Möbius Ribbon of Internal and External Security(ies)', in M. Albert, D. Jacobson and Y. Lapid (eds) *Identities, Borders, Orders*, Minneapolis: University of Minnesota Press.

—— (2002) 'Security and Immigration: Toward a Critique of the Governmentality of Unease', *Alternatives* 27 (1, suppl.): 63–92.

—— (2004) 'Global (In)security: The Field of the Professionals of Unease Management and the Ban-opticon', *Traces: A Multilingual Series of Cultural Theory* 4: 109–57.

—— (2006) 'Global (In)Security: The Field of the Professionals of Unease and the Banopticon', in Bigo, D. and A. Tsoukala (eds) *Illiberal Practices of Liberal Regimes: The (In)Security Games*, Paris: Cultures et Conflits.

Bislev, S., D. Salskov-Iversen and H.-K. Hansen (2001) *'Government and Globalisation: Security Privatisation on the US–Mexican Border'*, Business Association of Latin American Studies Annual Conference, April 4–7, University of San Diego.

Blair, T. (2002) *Science Matters*, Speech delivered to the Royal Society, April 10, 2002, London: HMSO.

—— (2003) *Prime Minister's Speech to the US Congress*, July 18, http://www.number-10.gov.uk/output/Page4220.asp (accessed January 11, 2008).

—— (2004) *Prime Minister Warns of Continuing Global Terror Threat*, Prime Minister's Speech, March 5, http://www.number-10.gov.uk/output/Page5461.asp (accessed January 11, 2008).

—— (2005) *Statement to Parliament on the London Bombings*, July 11, http://www.number-10.gov.uk/output/Page7903.asp (accessed January 11, 2008).

BMSA (2004) *The Mathematical Sciences' Role in the War on Terror*, Washington, DC: National Academies Press.

Bolle, R. M., J. H. Connell, S. Pankanti, N. K. Ratha and A. W. Senior (2004) *Guide to Biometrics*, New York: Springer-Verlag.

Bonditti, P. (2004) 'From Territorial Space to Networks: A Foucauldian Approach to the Implementation of Biometry', *Alternatives* 29 (4): 465–82.

Borcila, R. (2006) 'Geography Lessons', videos available at http://www.borcila.tk/geographie/index.html (accessed April 2007).

Bougen, P. D. (2003) 'Catastrophe Risk', *Economy and Society* 32 (2): 253–74.

Bourdieu, P. and L. Wacquant (2001) 'Neoliberal Newspeak: Notes on the New Planetary Vulgate', *Radical Philosophy* 105: 2–5.

Bowe, C. (2004) 'Congress Targets Accenture Homeland Security Project', *Financial Times* June 10.

Brenner, N., B. Jessop, M. Jones and G. MacLeod (eds) (2003) *State/Space: A Reader*, Oxford and Boston: Blackwell.

Brodeur, J.-P. (1981) 'Legitimizing Police Deviance', in C. Shearing (ed.) *Organizational Police Deviance*, Toronto: Butterworths.

Brodeur, J.-P. and S. Leman-Langlois (2006) 'Surveillance Fiction or High Policing', in K. Haggerty and R. Ericson (eds) *The New Politics of Surveillance and Visibility*, Toronto: University of Toronto Press.

Brown, G. (2006) *Securing Our Future*, Speech to the Royal United Services Institute, February 13.

Brown, W. (2003) 'Neo-Liberalism and the End of Liberal Democracy', *Theory and Event* 7 (1).

—— (2006) 'American Nightmare: Neoliberalism, Neoconservativism and De-Democratization', *Political Theory* 34 (6): 690–714.

Buchanan, M. (2006) *Dirty Money, Part 3: Terrorism*, BBC Radio News, January 16, http://news.bbc.co.uk/1/hi/programmes/documentary_archive/4610276.stm (accessed January 11, 2008).

Buonfino, A. (2004) 'Between Unity and Plurality: The Politicization and Securitization of the Discourse of Immigration in Europe', *New Political Science* 26 (1): 23–49.

Burchell, G. (1991) 'Peculiar Interests: Civil Society and Governing "The System of Natural Liberty"', in G. Burchell, C. Gordon and P. Miller (eds) *The Foucault Effect: Studies in Governmentality*, Chicago: University of Chicago Press.

Burchell, G., C. Gordon and P. Miller (eds) (1991) *The Foucault Effect: Studies in Govern-mentality*, Chicago: University of Chicago Press.

Burke, J. (2004) *Al-Qaeda: Casting a Shadow of Terror*, London: I. B. Tauris.

Bush, G. W. (2001) 'Address to a Joint Session of Congress and the American People', Office of the Press Secretary, September 20, http://www.whitehouse.gov/news/releases/2001/09/20010920–28.html (accessed September 20, 2001).

—— (2002a) *President Bush Outlines Iraqi Threat*, http://www.whitehouse.gov/news/releases/2002/10/print20021007–8.html (accessed June 25, 2007).

—— (2002b) *President Signs Terrorism Insurance Act*, http://www.whitehouse.gov/news/releases/2002/11/20021126–1.html (accessed June 8, 2007).

*Business Week* (1953) 'Wetbacks in Middle of Border War', October 24.

—— (2001) 'The Price of Protecting the Airways', December 4.

—— (2004) 'Accenture Hits the Daily Double', 3891, p. 74.

*Business Wire* (2006) 'Homeland Security to Build Detention Camps in the United States', January 24.

Butler, J. (1990) *Gender Trouble: Feminism and the Subversion of Identity*, New York: Routledge.

—— (1993) *Bodies That Matter: On the Discursive Limits of 'Sex'*, London: Routledge.

—— (1998) 'Merely Cultural', *New Left Review* 227 (Jan/Feb): 33–44.

—— (2004) *Precarious Life: The Powers of Mourning and Violence*, London: Verso.

Cable News Network (2005) 'Official: U.S. Calls Off Search for Iraqi WMDs', http://www.cnn.com/2005/US/01/12/wmd.search/index.html (accessed April 13, 2007).

CAE, Critical Art Ensemble (1994) *The Electronic Disturbance*, Brooklyn: Autonomedia.

—— (1996) *Electronic Civil Disobedience and Other Unpopular Ideas*, Brooklyn: Autonomedia.

Calarco, M. and S. DeCaroli (2007) *Giorgio Agamben: Sovereignty & Life*, Stanford: Stanford University Press.

Calavita, K. (1992) *Inside the State: The Braceero Program, Immigration and the INS*, New York: Routledge.

—— (1994) 'US Immigration and Policy Responses: The Limits of Legislation', in W. A. Cornelius, J. F. Hollifield and P. L. Martin (eds) *Controlling Immigration: a Global Perspective*, Stanford: Stanford University Press.

Calhoun, C. (2003) 'The Class Consciousness of Frequent Travellers: Towards a Critique of Actually Existing Cosmopolitanism', in D. Archibugi (ed.) *Debating Cosmopolitics*, New York: Verso.

Cameron, A. and R. Palan (2004) *The Imagined Economies of Globalization*, London: Sage.

Cameron, I. (2003) 'UN Targeted Sanctions, Legal Safeguards and the European Convention on Human Rights', *Nordic Journal of International Law* 72: 159–214.

—— (2006) *The European Convention on Human Rights, Due Process and United Nations Security Council Counter-Terrorism Sanctions*, Report for the Council of Europe, February 6.

Campbell, D. (1998) *Writing Security: United States Foreign Policy and the Politics of Identity*, Minneapolis: University of Minnesota Press.

—— (2005) 'The Biopolitics of Security: Oil, Empire and the Sports Utility Vehicle', *American Quarterly* 57 (3): 943–72.

Campbell, R. (2002) 'America Acts: the Swift Legislative Response to the September 11th Attack on America', Paper to the conference, Liability and Insurance after September 11th, Insurance Law Center, University of Connecticut School of Law, March 21–22.

Canadian Air Transport Security Authority (2004) *Frequently Asked Questions*, http://www.catsa-acsta.gc.ca/english/help_aide/faq.htm (accessed July 19, 2004).

Canadian Air Transport Security Authority (2005) *2005 Annual Report Canada*, Ottawa: CATSA.

Caplan, J. and J. Torpey (eds) (2000) *Documenting Individual Identity: The Development of State Practices in the Modern World*, Princeton, NJ: Princeton University Press.

Carson, R. (1962/2002) *Silent Spring*, Boston: Houghton Mifflin.

Castel, R. (1991) 'From Dangerousness to Risk', in G. Burchell, C. Gordon and P. Miller (eds) *The Foucault Effect. Studies in Governmentality*, Chicago: Chicago University Press.

Center for Immigration Studies (2005) *Terrorism & National Security*, Center for Immigration Studies, http://www.cis.org/topics/terrorism.html (accessed January 11, 2008).

Ceyhan, A. and A. Tsoukala (2002) 'The Securitization of Migration in Western Societies: Ambivalent Discourses and Policies', *Alternatives* 27: 21–39.

Cheah, P. (1998) 'Introduction Part II: the Cosmopolitical – Today', in P. Cheah and B. Robbins (eds) *Cosmopolitics: Thinking and Feeling Beyond the Nation*, Minneapolis: University of Minnesota Press.

Cheah, P, and P. Robbins (eds) (1998) *Cosmopolitics: Thinking and Feeling Beyond the Nation*, Minneapolis: University of Minnesota Press.

Chediak, M. (2005) 'Following the Money: Tracking Down Al Qaeda's Fundraisers in Europe', *PBS Frontline: Al Qaeda's New Front*, http://www.pbs.org/wgbh/pages/frontline/shows/front/special/finance.html (accessed September 17, 2007).

Chertoff, M. (2005) 'Testimony by Secretary Michael Chertoff Before the Homeland Security Subcommittee of the Senate Appropriations Committee', http://www.dhs.gov/dhspublic/display?theme = 45&content = 4475 (accessed January 11, 2008).

—— (2006) 'A Tool we Need to Stop the Next Airliner Plot', *Washington Post* August 29: A15.

—— (2007) 'Remarks by Secretary Michael Chertoff to the Johns Hopkins University Paul H. Nitze School of Advanced International Studies', May 3, 2007, http://www.dhs.gov/xnews/speeches/sp_1178288606838.shtm (accessed May 2007).

Chesney, R. M. (2005) 'The Sleeper Scenario: Terrorism Support Laws and the Demands for Prevention', *Harvard Journal on Legislation* 42: 1–89.

Childs, B. (2006) 'A New Standard Formula: Social + Responsibility = Reward', *International Herald Tribune* March 16.

*CIO Insight* (2004) 'Beta', August, 42, p. 22.

Clarke, L. (1999) *Mission Improbable: Using Fantasy Documents to Tame Disaster*, Chicago: University of Chicago Press.

Clarke, R. (2004) *Against All Enemies: Inside America's War on Terror*, New York: Free Press.

Clarke, R. A. (2005) 'Ten Years Later', *The Atlantic Monthly* 295: 61–77.

Clifford, J. (1998) 'Mixed Feelings', in P. Cheah and B. Robbins (eds) *Cosmopolitics: Thinking and Feeling Beyond the Nation*, Minneapolis: University of Minnesota Press.

Cohn, T. (1999) 'Cross-Border Travel in North America: the Challenge of U.S. Section 110 Legislation', *Canadian American Public Policy* 40 (October): 1–70.

Coker, C. (2002) *Security, Independence and Liberty after September 11: Balancing Competing Claims*, 21st Century Trust, http://www.21stcenturytrust.org/post911.htm (accessed January 11, 2008).

Cole, S. (2001) *Suspect Identities: A History of Fingerprinting and Criminal Identification*, Cambridge, MA: Harvard University Press.

Coleman, M. (2005) 'US Statecraft and the US–Mexico Border as Security/Economy Nexus', *Political Geography* 24 (2): 1–25.

Collins, L. (2007) 'Banksy was Here', *The New Yorker* May 14.

Condon, B. J. and T. Sinha (2003) *Drawing Lines in Sand and Snow: Border Security and North American Integration*, New York: M. E. Sharpe.

Connolly, W. E. (2004) 'The Complexity of Sovereignty', in J. Edkins, V. Pin-Fat and M. J. Shapiro (eds) *Sovereign Lives: Power in Global Politics*, London: Routledge.

—— (2005) *Pluralism*, Durham, NC, and London: Duke University Press.

Cooper, M. (2003) 'On the Border of Hypocrisy', *LA Weekly* December 4.

—— (2004) 'On the Brink – From Mutual Deterrence to Uncontrollable War', *Contretemps* 4: 2–18.

Cornelius, W. (2005) 'Controlling "Unwanted" Immigration: Lessons from the US 1993–2004', *Journal of Ethnic and Migration Studies* 31 (4):775–94.

Council on Foreign Relations (2007) 'The War on Terrorism: the Financial Front', Transcript, January 10, http://www.cfr.org/publication/12432/ (accessed September 17, 2007).

Coutin, S. B. (1993) *The Culture of Protest: Religious Activism and the U.S. Sanctuary Movement*, Boulder: Westview Press.

—— (2000) *Legalizing Moves: Salvadoran Immigrants' Struggle for U.S. Residency*, Ann Arbor: University of Michigan Press.

—— (2005) 'Being en Route', *American Anthropologist* 107 (2): 195–206.

—— (forthcoming) *Nations of Emigrants: Shifting Boundaries of Citizenship in the United States and El Salvador*, Ithaca: Cornell University Press.

Coutin, S. B., B. Maurer and B. Yngvesson (2002) 'In the Mirror: The Legitimation Work of Globalization', *Law and Social Inquiry* 27: 801–43.

Coward, M. (2006) 'Securing the Global (Bio)Political Economy: Empire, Poststructuralism and Political Economy', in M. de Goede (ed.) *International Political Economy and Poststructural Politics*, London: Palgrave.

Crandall, J. (2005) 'Envisioning the Homefront: Militarization, Tracking and Security Culture', *Journal of Visual Culture* 4 (1): 17–38.

Crary, J. (2004) 'Conjurations of Security', *Interventions: International Journal of Postcolonial Studies* 6 (4): 424–30.

Curry, M. R. (2004) 'The Profiler's Question and the Treacherous Traveler', *Surveillance & Society* 1 (4): 475–99.

Danna, A. and O. H. Gandy (2002) 'All that Glitters is not Gold: Digging Beneath the Surface of Data Mining', *Journal of Business Ethics* 40: 373–88.

Dauphinee, E. (2007) 'Living Dying Surviving II', in Dauphinee, E. and C. Masters (eds) *Logics of Biopower and the War on Terror*, New York: Palgrave Macmillan.

Dean, M. (1994) *Critical and Effective Histories*, London: Routledge.

—— (1999) *Governmentality: Power and Rule in Modern Society*, London: Sage.

Defert, D. (1991) '"Popular Life" and Insurance Technology', in G. Burchell, C. Gordon and P. Miller (eds) *The Foucault Effect: Studies in Governmentality*, Chicago: University of Chicago Press.

de Genova, N. (2002) 'Migrant "Illegality" and Deportability in Everyday Life', *Annual Review of Anthropology* 31: 419–47.

de Goede, M. (2003) 'Hawala Discourses and the War on Terrorist Finance', *Environment and Planning D: Society and Space* 21 (5): 513–32.

—— (2005) *Virtue, Fortune and Faith: A Genealogy of Finance*, Minneapolis: University of Minnesota Press.

—— (2007) 'Underground Money', *Cultural Critique* 65: 140–63.

—— (2008) 'The Politics of Preemption and the War on Terror in Europe', *European Journal of International Relations* 14 (1): 161–185.

Deleuze, G. (1995) 'Postscript on Control Societies', in G. Deleuze (ed.) *Negotiations 1972–1990*, New York: Columbia University Press.

Denning, D. (2000) 'Hacktivism: An Emerging Threat to Diplomacy', *Foreign Service Journal*, http://www.afsa.org/fsj/sept00/Denning.cfm (accessed January 11, 2008).

DePalma, A. (2001) 'Slow Crawl at the Border', *The New York Times* October 21: A1.

Department of Homeland Security (2003) 'Remarks by Secretary Tom Ridge to the Council for Excellence in Government', http://www.dhs.gov/dhspublic/display?content = 1597 (accessed March 1, 2005).

Department of Homeland Security (2004) *We the People: Homeland Security from the Citizens' Perspective*, Washington, DC: Council for Excellence in Government.

Department of Homeland Security (2006) *Survey of DHS Data Mining Activities*, Washington, DC: Office of the Inspector General.

Der Derian, J. (2000) 'Virtuous War/Virtual Theory', *International Affairs* 75: 771–88.

—— (2001) *Virtuous War*, Boulder, CO: Westview Press.

DeRosa, M. (2004) *Data Mining and Data Analysis for Counterterrorism*, Washington, DC: Centre for Strategic and International Studies.

Derrida, J. (1994) (in conversation with Richard Beardsworth) 'Nietzsche and the Machine', *Journal of Nietzsche Studies* 7: 7–65.

—— (1992) 'Force of Law: The "Mystical Foundation of Authority"', in D. Cornell, M. Rosenfeld and D. G. Carlson (eds) *Deconstruction and the Possibility of Justice*, London and New York: Routledge.

Dershowitz, A. (2002) *Why Terrorism Works: Understanding the Threat, Responding to the Challenge*, New Haven, CT: Yale University Press.

—— (2006) *Preemption: A Knife that Cuts Both Ways*, New York: Norton.

Desforges, L., R. Jones and M. Woods (2005) 'New Geographies of Citizenship', *Citizenship Studies* 9 (5): 439–51.

Dezalay, Y. and B. G. Garth (2002) *The Internationalization of Palace Wars: Lawyers, Economists, and the Contest to Transform Latin American States*, Chicago: University of Chicago Press.

Díaz-Briquets, S. and J. Pérez-López (1997) 'Refugee Remittances: Conceptual Issues and the Cuban and Nicaraguan Experiences', *International Migration Review* 31 (2): 411–37.

Diken, B. and B. Lautsen (2005) *The Culture of Exception: Sociology Facing the Camp*, London: Routledge.

Dillon, M. (1996) *Politics of Security: Towards a Political Philosophy of Continental Thought*, London: Routledge.

—— (2004a) 'Correlating Sovereign and Biopower', in J. Edkins, V. Pin-Fat and M. J. Shapiro (eds) *Sovereign Lives: Power in Global Politics*, London: Routledge.

—— (2004b) 'The Security of Governance', in W. Larner and W. Walters (eds) *Global Governmentality: Governing International Spaces*, London: Routledge.

—— (2007) 'Governing through Contingency: The Security of Biopolitical Governance', *Political Geography* 26: 41–7.

Dillon, M. and J. Reid (2001) 'Global Liberal Governance: Biopolitics, Security and War', *Millennium* 30: 41–66.

Dobrowolsky, A. and J. Jenson (2004) 'Shifting Representations of Citizenship: Canadian Politics of "Women" and "Children"', *Social Politics* 11 (2): 154–80.

Dominguez, R., S. Wray, B. Beestal and Osea (1998) 'SWARM: An ECD Project for ARS Electronica Festival 1998', http://www.thing.net/%7Erdom/ecd/swarm.html (accessed January 11, 2008).

Donohue, L. K. (2006) 'Anti-Terrorist Finance in the United Kingdom and United States', *Michigan Journal of International Law* 27 (4): 303–435.

Donzelot, J. (1984) *L'Invention du Social: Essai sur le Declin des Pasions Politiques*, Paris: Fayard.

—— (1988) 'The Promotion of the Social', *Economy and Society* 17 (3): 395–427.

Douglas, M. and A. Wildavsky (1982) *Risk and Culture: An Essay on the Selection of Technological and Environmental Dangers*, Berkeley: University of California Press.

Dratel, J. (2005) 'The Legal Narrative', in K. Greenberg and J. Dratel (eds) *The Torture Papers: The Road to Abu Ghraib*, Cambridge: Cambridge University Press.

Duffield, M. (2001) 'Governing the Borderlands: Decoding the Power of Aid', *Disasters* 25 (4): 308–20.

*The Economist* (2005) 'New-look Passports; Border Controls', February 19: 75.

Edkins, J. (1999) *Poststructuralism and International Relations: Bringing the Political Back In*, Boulder, CO: Lynne Rienner.

Edkins, J. and V. Pin-Fat (2004) 'Introduction: Life, Power, Resistance', in J. Edkins, V. Pin-Fat and M. J. Shapiro (eds) *Sovereign Lives: Power in Global Politics*, London: Routledge.

Edkins, J., V. Pin-Fat and M. J. Shapiro (2004) *Sovereign Lives. Power in Global Politics*, London: Routledge.

Edley, C. (2003) 'The New American Dilemma: Racial Profiling Post-9/11', in R. Leone and G. Anrig (eds) *The War on Our Freedoms: Civil Liberties in an Age of Terrorism*, New York: Public Affairs.

EDT (2005a) 'FloodNet Foyer', http://www.thing.net/~rdom/zapsTactical/foyer3.htm (accessed January 11, 2008).

—— (2005b) 'What this Action is About', http://swarmtheminutemen.com/cartography/about.html (accessed January 11, 2008).

Elden, S. (2007) 'Rethinking Governmentality', *Political Geography* 26 (1): 29–33.

Elliot, L. (2006) 'Brown to Use Classified Intelligence in Fight to Cut Terrorist Funding', *The Guardian* October 11.

Epstein, C. (2007) 'Guilty Bodies, Productive Bodies, Destructive Bodies: Crossing the Biometric Borders', *International Political Sociology* 1 (2): 149–64.

—— (forthcoming) *The Power of Words in International Relations: Birth of an Anti-Whaling Discourse*.

*Equity International* (2005) 'The Center for Homeland and Global Security', http://www.globalsecurity.bz/ (accessed January 11, 2008).

Erickson, C. W. (2007) 'Counter-Terror Culture: Ambiguity, Subversion, or Legitimization', *Security Dialogue* 38: 197–214.

Ericson, R. V. (2006) 'Ten Uncertainties of Risk Management Approaches to Security', *Canadian Journal of Criminology and Criminal Justice* 48: 345–57.

—— (2007) *Crime in an Insecure World*, Cambridge: Polity.

Ericson, R. V. and A. Doyle (2004a) 'Catastrophe Risk, Insurance and Terrorism', *Economy and Society* 33 (2): 135–73.

—— (2004b) *Uncertain Business: Risk, Insurance and the Limits of Knowledge*, Toronto: University of Toronto Press

Ericson, R. V. and K. D. Haggerty (2002) 'The Policing of Risk', in T. Baker and J. Simon (eds) *Embracing Risk: The Changing Culture of Insurance and Responsibility*, Chicago: University of Chicago Press.

Ericson, R. V., A. Doyle and D. Barry (2003) *Insurance as Governance*, Toronto: University of Toronto Press.

Escobar, A. (1995) *Encountering Development*, Princeton: Princeton University Press.

Ettlinger, N. and F. Bosco (2004) 'Thinking Through Networks and their Spatiality: A Critique of the US (Public) War on Terrorism and its Geographic Discourse', *Antipode* 36 (2): 249–71.

European Commission (2000) *Communication from the Commission on the Precautionary Principle*, Brussels, February 2, COM (2000) 1.

Ewald, F. (1986) *L'État Providence*, Paris: Editions Grasset.

—— (1990) 'Norms, Discipline, and the Law', *Representations* 30: 138–61.

—— (1991) 'Insurance and Risk', in G. Burchell, C. Gordon and P. Miller (eds) *The Foucault Effect: Studies in Governmentality*, Chicago: Chicago University Press.

—— (1993) 'Two Infinities of Risk', in B. Massumi (ed.) *The Politics of Everyday Fear*, Minneapolis: University of Minnesota Press.

—— (2002) 'The Return of Descartes' Malicious Demon: An Outline of a Philosophy of Precaution', in T. Baker and J. Simon (eds) *Embracing Risk*, Chicago: Chicago University Press.

Fajardo, R. (2000) '*Crosser*$^{TM}$ and *La Migra*$^{TM}$', http://www.sudor.net/games/crosser_lamigra/index.html (accessed January 11, 2008).

Fall, J. (2005) *Drawing the Line: Nature, Hybridity and Politics in Transboundary Spaces*, Burlington, VT: Ashgate.

Farkas, S., J. Johnson and A. Duffett (2002) *Knowing it by Heart: Americans Consider the Constitution and its Meanings*, Public Agenda, http://www.publicagenda.org/specials/constitution/constitution4.htm (accessed April 13, 2007).

FDIC, Federal Deposit Insurance Corporation (2003) 'Tapping the Unbanked Market, Symposium', November 5, http://www.fdic.gov/consumers/community/unbanked/index.html (accessed May 1, 2007).

FinCen, or Financial Crimes Enforcement Network (2006) *Feasibility of a Cross-Border Electronic Funds Transfer Reporting System under the Bank Secrecy Act*, US Department of the Treasury, October.

Find Biometrics (2005) *Nexus Air*, http://www.findbiometrics.com/Pages/feature%20articles/nexus.html (accessed January 11, 2008).

Flanagan, R. (2006) *The Unknown Terrorist*, London: Atlantic Books.

Flores, L. (2004) 'Negotiating Entry, Bordering Whiteness: Rhetorical Subjectivity and the "Wetback Problem"', National Communication Association Annual Conference.

Flynn, S. (2003) 'The False Conundrum: Continental Integration Versus Homeland Security', in P. Andreas and T. Biersteker (eds) *The Rebordering of North America: Integration and Exclusion in a New Security Context*, New York: Routledge.

Flynn, S. E. (2002) 'America the Vulnerable', *Foreign Affairs* 81: 60–74.

—— (2007) *The Edge of Disaster: Rebuilding a Resilient Nation*, New York: Random House.

Fortun, K. (2001) *Advocacy After Bhopal*, Chicago: University of Chicago Press.

Foucault, M. (1970) *The Order of Things: An Archeology of the Human Sciences*, New York: Pantheon.

—— (1977) *Discipline and Punish: The Birth of the Prison*, New York: Pantheon.

—— (1980a) 'The Confessions of the Flesh', in C. Gordon (ed.) *Power/Knowledge. Selected Interviews and & Other Writings 1972–1977*, New York: Pantheon Books.

—— (1980b) 'Two Lectures', in C. Gordon (ed.) *Michel Foucault: Power/Knowledge, Selected Interviews 1972–1977*, Brighton: Harvester Press.

—— (1983) 'Afterword: The Subject and Power', in H. L. Dreyfus and P. Rabinow (eds) *Michel Foucault: Beyond Structuralism and Hermeneutics*, Chicago: University of Chicago Press.

—— (1990) *History of Sexuality, Vol. 1*, translated by R. Hurley, New York: Random House/Vintage.

—— (1991) 'Governmentality', in G. Burchell, C. Gordon and P. Miller (eds) *The Foucault Effect: Studies in Governmentality*, Chicago: University of Chicago Press.

—— (1994) 'Critical Theory/Intellectual History', in M. Kelly (ed.) *Critique and Power: Recasting the Foucault/Habermas Debate*, Cambridge, MA: MIT Press.

—— (1997) 'Polemics, Politics and Problematizations', in P. Rabinow (ed.) *Michel Foucault: Ethics, Subjectivity and Truth*, New York: New Press.

—— (2001a) 'Michel Foucault, une Interview: Sexe, Pouvoir et la Politique de l'Identité', in *Dits et Ecrits II*, pp. 1154–571, Paris: Editions Gallimard.

—— (2001b) 'Les Mailles du Pouvoir', in *Dits et Ecrits II*, pp. 1001–20, Paris: Editions Gallimard.

—— (2001c) 'Michel Foucault: la Sécurité et l'Etat', in *Dits et Ecrits II*, pp. 383–8, Paris: Editions Gallimard.

—— (2001d) 'La Gouvernementalité', in *Dits et Ecrits II*, pp. 635–57, Paris: Editions Gallimard.

—— (2001e) 'Désormais, la Sécurité est au-dessus des Lois', in *Dits et Ecrits II* , pp. 366–8, Paris: Editions Gallimard.

—— (2003) *Society Must be Defended*, translated by D. Macey, New York: Picador.

—— (2004) *Naissance de la Biopolitique: Course au College de France, 1978–1979*, Paris: Seuil/ Gallimard.

—— (2007) *Security, Territory, Population: Lectures at the Collège de France 1977–78*, Basingstoke: Palgrave.

Franklin, N. (2005) 'L.A. Outlaws: Showtime Brings International Terrorism Home', *The New Yorker* 81: 110–11.

Fraser, N. (2003) 'From Discipline to Flexibilization? Rereading Foucault in the Shadow of Globalization', *Constellations* 10 (2): 160–71.

—— (2005) 'Reframing Justice in a Globalizing World', *New Left Review* 36: 69–89.

Fraser, N. and L. Gordon (1998) 'Contract versus Charity: Why is There no Social Citizenship in the United States?' in G. Shafir (ed.) *The Citizenship Debates: A Reader*, Minneapolis: University of Minnesota Press.

Frears, S. (dir.) and S. Knight (writer) (2002) *Dirty Pretty Things*, Miramax Pictures.

Friedman, T. (2002) 'Techno Logic', *Foreign Policy* 129: 64–5.

Fukuyama, F. (1992) *The End of History and the Last Man*, New York: Free Press.

Gandy, O. (2006) 'Data Mining, Surveillance and Discrimination in the Post 9/11 Environment', in K. Haggerty and R. Ericson (eds) *The New Politics of Surveillance and Visibility*, Toronto: University of Toronto Press.

Garreau, J. (2001) 'Disconnect the Dots', *Washington Post* 17 September, http://www.casos.cs. cmu.edu/news/disconnect_wp.html (accessed January 11, 2008).

General Accounting Office (2003) *Homeland Security: Challenges Facing the Department of Homeland Security in Balancing its Border Security and Trade Facilitation Missions*, Washington, DC: GAO-03–902T, http://www.gao.gov/new.items/d03902t.pdf (accessed January 11, 2008).

—— (2005) *Homeland Security: Agency Plans, Implementation, and Challenges Regarding the National Strategy for Homeland Security*, Washington, DC, http://www.gao.gov/new.items/ d0533.pdf (accessed January 11, 2008).

Gerstle, G. (2004) 'The Immigrant as Threat to American Security: An Historical Perspective', in J. Tirman (ed.) *The Maze of Fear: Security and Migration After 9/11*, New York: New Press.

Gibbs, N. and M. Duffy (2002) 'Trust Me, He Says', *Time* November 11: 42.

Gibson-Graham, J.-K. (1996) *The End of Capitalism (as we knew it)*, Blackwell: London.

—— (2006) *Post-Capitalist Politics*, Minneapolis: University of Minnesota Press.

Gilbert, E. (2007) 'Leaky Borders and Solid Citizens: Governing Security, Prosperity and Quality of Life in a North American Partnership', *Antipode* 39 (1): 77–98.

Gill, S. (2003) *Power and Resistance in the New World Order*, Basingstoke: Palgrave Macmillan.

Golden, R. and M. McConnell (1986) *Sanctuary: The New Underground Railroad*, Maryknoll, NY: Orbis Books.

Gordon, C. (1991) 'Governmental Rationality: An Introduction', in G. Burchell, C. Gordon and P. Miller (eds) *The Foucault Effect: Studies in Governmentality*, Chicago: University of Chicago Press.

Graham S. (ed.) (2004) *Cities, War and Terrorism: Towards an Urban Geopolitics*, Oxford: Blackwell.

—— (2005) 'Software Sorted Geographies', *Progress in Human Geography* 29 (5): 562–80.

Graham, S. and D. Wood (2003) 'Digitising Surveillance: Categorisation, Space, Inequality', *Critical Social Policy* 23 (2): 227–48.

Gray, J. (2001) 'The Era of Globalisation is Over', *The New Statesman* September 24.

Green, M. (2002) 'Cat Models Look to Predict Losses from Future Attacks', *Best Wire* August 29.

Greenberg, K. and J. Dratel (eds) (2005) *The Torture Papers: The Road to Abu Ghraib*, Cambridge: Cambridge University Press.

Gregory, D. (1994) *Geographical Imaginations*, Cambridge: Blackwell.

—— (2004) *The Colonial Present. Afghanistan, Palestine, Iraq*, London: Blackwell.

—— (2006) 'The Black Flag: Guántanamo Bay and the Space of Exception', *Geografiska Annaler* 88 B (4): 405–27.

Gregory, D. and A. Pred (eds) (2007) *Violent Geographies: Fear, Terror, and Political Violence*, London: Routledge.

Grewal, I. (2005) *Transnational America: Feminisms, Diasporas, Neoliberalisms*, Durham, NC: Duke University Press.

Grusin, R. (2004) 'Premediation', *Criticism* 46: 17–39.

*The Guardian* (2005a) 'Plan to Improve Relations with Muslim Communities', August 1.

—— (2005b) 'Brazilian did not Wear Bulky Jacket', July 28, http://www.guardian.co.uk/uk_news/story/0,1537457,00.html (accessed January 11, 2008).

—— (2005c) 'It Could be You', April 20.

—— (2005d) 'US Vigilantes begin Border Stake-out', April 2.

Gusterson, H. (1996) *Nuclear Rites: A Weapons Laboratory at the End of the Cold War*, Berkeley: University of California Press.

Hacking, I. (1990) *The Taming of Chance*, Cambridge: Cambridge University Press.

Haggerty, K. and R. V. Ericson (2000) 'The Surveillant Assemblage,' *British Journal of Sociology* 51: 605–22.

Haggerty, K. and R. V. Ericson (eds) (2006) *The New Politics of Surveillance and Visibility*, Toronto: University of Toronto Press.

Haiman, J. (1980) 'The Iconicity of Grammar: Isomorphism and Motivation', *Language* 56 (3): 515–40.

Haney, C. (2005) *Statement to the House Judiciary Subcommittee on Immigration, Border Security, and Claims*, March 10.

Hannah, M. (2000) *Governmentality and the Mastery of Territory in Nineteenth-Century America*, Cambridge: Cambridge University Press.

Hansen, T. B. and F. Stepputat (2001) *Sovereign Bodies: Citizens, Migrants and States in the Postcolonial World*, Princeton: Princeton University Press.

Hardt, M. and A. Negri (2000) *Empire*, Cambridge: Harvard University Press.

—— (2004) *Multitude: War and Democracy in the Age of Empire*, New York: Penguin.

Harvey, D. (2003) *The New Imperialism*, Oxford: Oxford University Press.

Hay, J and M. Andrejevic (2006) 'Introduction: Toward an Analytic of Governmental Experiments in These Times: Homeland Security as the New Social Security', *Cultural Studies* 20 (4/5): 331–48.

Hays, R. J. (1996) *INSPASS: INS Passenger Accelerated Service System*, Washington, DC: Department of Justice, available from the Biometric Consortium http://www.biometrics.org/REPORTS/INSPASS.html (accessed January 11, 2008).

Hays, S. P. (1987) *Beauty, Health, and Permanence: Environmental Politics in the United States, 1955–1985*, Cambridge: Cambridge University Press.

Heisler, M. and H. Z. Layton (1993) 'Migration and the Links between Social and Societal Security', in O. Waever, B. Buzan, M. Kelstrip and P. Lemaitre (eds) *Identity, Migration and the New Security Agenda in Europe*, London: Pinter.

Heng, Y.-K. (2006) *War as Risk Management: Strategy and Conflict in an Age of Globalised Risks*, London: Routledge.

Herbert, B. (2005) 'It's Called Torture', *New York Times* February 28: A 25.

Hernandez, E. and S. B. Coutin (2006) 'Remitting Subjects: Migrants, Money, and States', *Economy and Society* 35 (2): 185–208.

Hernandez, L. (2005) 'InSite_05 brochure = game = terrorism', *inSite post* December 5.

Hillis, K., M. Petit and A. J. Cravey (2001) 'Adventure Travel for the Mind: Analyzing the United States Virtual Trade Mission's Promotion of Globalization through Discourse and Corporate Media Strategies', in A. Herod and M. Wright (eds) *Geographies of Power: Placing Scale*, Oxford: Blackwell.

Hindess, B. (1996) 'Neo-liberal Citizenship', *Citizenship Studies* 6 (2): 127–43.

—— (1998) 'Neo-liberalism and the National Economy', in M. Dean and B. Hindess (eds) *Governing Australia: Studies of Contemporary Rationalities of Government*, Cambridge: Cambridge University Press.

Hirst, P. and G. Thompson (1996) *Globalization in Question*, London Polity Press.

Holton, R. (2005) 'Network Discourses: Proliferation, Critique and Synthesis', *Global Networks* 5 (2): 209–15.

Home Office (2006) *Report of the Official Account of Bombings in London on 7 July*, http://www.homeoffice.gov.uk/about-us/news/7-july-report (accessed January 11, 2008).

House Armed Services Committee (1983) 'Summary of Findings and Conclusions', *Adequacy of U.S. Marine Corps Security in Beirut* 98th Congress, First Session, Washington: US Government Printing Office.

Hughes, C. (2002) 'Reflections on Globalisation, Security and 9/11', *Cambridge Review of International Affairs* 15 (3): 421–33.

*Human Rights Watch* (2005) 'Witness to Abuse: Human Rights Abuses under the Material Witness Law since September 11', 17 (2), June.

Huntington, S. (1998) *The Clash of Civilizations and the Remaking of World Order*, New York: Simon & Schuster.

Huysmans, J. (1995) 'Migrants as a Security Problem: Dangers of "Securitizing" Societal Issues', in R. Miles and D. Thranhardt (eds) *Migration and European Integration: Dynamics of Inclusion and Exclusion*, London: Pinter.

—— (2000) 'The European Union and the Securitization of Migration', *Journal of Common Market Studies* 38 (5): 751–77.

—— (2004) 'Minding Exceptions: Politics of Insecurity and Liberal Democracy', *Contemporary Political Theory* 3 (3): 321–41.

—— (2006a) 'International Politics of Insecurity: Normativity, Inwardness and the Exception', *Security Dialogue* 37 (1): 11–29.

—— (2006b) *The Politics of Insecurity*, London: Routledge.

Huysmans, J., A. Dobson and R. Prokhovnik (eds) (2006) *The Politics of Protection. Sites of Insecurity and Political Agency*, London: Routledge.

Hyndman, J. (2005) 'Migration Wars: Refuge or Refusal?', *Geoforum* 36: 3–6.

Ibrahim, M. (2005) 'The Securitization of Migration: A Racial Discourse', *International Migration* 43 (5): 163–87.

Ignatieff, M. (2004) *The Lesser Evil: Political Ethics in an Age of Terror*, Princeton, NJ: Princeton University Press.

Inda, J. I. (2006) *Targeting Immigrants: Government, Technology, and Ethics*, Oxford: Blackwell.

Intelligence and Security Committee (2006) *Report into the London Terrorist Attacks on 7 July 2005*, London.

Isin, E. (2004) 'The Neurotic Citizen', *Citizenship Studies* 8 (3): 217–35.

Isin, E. F. and K. Rygiel (2007) 'Abject Spaces: Frontiers, Zones, Camps', in E. Dauphinee and C. Masters (eds) *Logics of Biopower and the War on Terror*, New York: Palgrave Macmillan.

Janus, E. (2004) 'The Preventive State, Terrorists and Sexual Predators: Countering the Threat of a New Outsider Jurisprudence', *Criminal Law Bulletin* 40: 576–98.

Jarrar, R. (2006) 'Back from the MidEast', *Raed in the Middle*, http://raedinthemiddle.blogspot.com/2006/08/back-from-mideast.html (accessed August 10, 2006).

Jenson, J. and S. D. Phillips (1996) 'Regime Shift: New Citizenship Practices in Canada', *International Journal of Canadian Studies* 14 (Fall): 111–35.

Jessop, B. (2004) 'Critical Semiotic Analysis and Cultural Political Economy', *Critical Discourse Studies* 19 (2): 159–74.

Joh, E. (2004) 'The Paradox of Private Policing', *The Journal of Criminal Law and Criminology* 95: 49–131.

Johns, F. (2005) 'Guantánamo Bay and the Annihilation of Exception', *The European Journal of International Law* 16 (4): 613–35.

Johnson, R. (2002) 'Defending Ways of Life: The (Anti-)Terrorist Rhetorics of Bush and Blair', *Theory, Culture and Society* 19 (4): 211–31.

Kaplan, A. (2003) 'Homeland Insecurities: Reflections on Language and Space', *Radical History Review* 85: 82–93.

Katz, C. (2007) 'Banal Terrorism: Spatial Fetishism and Everyday Insecurity', in D. Gregory and A. Pred (eds) *Violent Geographies: Fear, Terror, and Political Violence*, London: Routledge.

Kean, T. and L. Hamilton (2004) *The 9/11 Report: The National Commission on Terrorist Attacks Upon the United States*, New York: St. Martin's Press.

Keil, R. and R. Mahon (eds) (2008) *Leviathan Undone? Towards a Political Economy of Scale*, Vancouver: University of British Columbia Press.

Kestelyn, J. (2002) 'For Want of a Nail', *Intelligent Enterprise* 5 (7): 8.

Klein, B. (1989) 'The Textual Strategies of the Military: Or Have You Read Any Good Defense Manuals Lately', in J. Der Derian and M. J. Shapiro (eds) *International/Intertextual Relations: Postmodern Readings of World Politics*, New York: Lexington.

Knight, F. (1921) *Risk, Uncertainty and Profit*, Boston and New York: Houghton Mifflin.

Knorr Cetina, K. (2005) 'Complex Global Microstructures: The New Terrorist Societies', *Theory, Culture and Society* 22 (5): 213–34.

Knox, H., M. Savage and P. Harvey (2005) *Social Networks and Spatial Relations: Networks as Method, Metaphor and Form*, CRESC Working Paper, University of Manchester, May.

Kocieniewski, D. (2007) 'Informer's Role Draws Praise and Questions', *New York Times* May 10: A1.

Kofman, E. (2005) 'Citizenship, Migration and the Reassertion of National Identity', *Citizenship Studies* 9 (5): 453–67.

—— (2003) 'Rights and Citizenship', in J. Agnew, K. Mitchell and G. Toal (eds) *A Companion to Political Geography*, New York: Routledge.

Korbach, K. (2003) 'National Security Entry–Exit Registration System', *Foreign Press Center Briefing*, Washington, January 17, http://fpc.state.gov/fpc/16739.htm (accessed October 8, 2007).

Krane, J. (2002) 'Terrorism Worries Bring Big Business: Pitch the Product the Right Way and "You'd be Amazed as What you Sell"', *Toronto Star* August 29.

Krebs, V. (2002) 'Uncloaking Terrorist Networks', *First Monday* 7 (4).

Kunreuther, H. and E. Michel-Kerjan (2005) 'Terrorism Insurance 2005', *Regulation* Spring: 44–51.

Lafer, G. (2004) 'Neoliberalism by Other Means: the "War on Terror" at Home and Abroad', *New Political Science* 26 (3): 323–46.

Lakoff, A. (2006) 'Techniques of Preparedness', in T. Monahan (ed.) *Surveillance and Security: Technological Politics and Power in Everyday Life*, New York: Routledge.

Lapham, L. (1998) *The Agony of Mammon: the Imperial Global Economy Explains Itself to the Membership in Davos, Switzerland*, New York: Verso.

Laplante, L. (1999) 'Expedited Removal at U.S. Borders: a World Without a Constitution', *New York University Review of Law & Social Change* 25 (2): 213–70.

Larner, W. (1998) 'Hitching a Ride on a Tiger's Back: Globalisation and Spatial Imaginaries in New Zealand', *Environment and Planning D: Society and Space* 16: 599–614.

—— (2000) 'Neo-Liberalism: Policy, Ideology, Governmentality', *Studies in Political Economy* 62: 5–25.

—— (2007) 'Expatriate Experts and Globalising Governmentalities: The New Zealand Diaspora Strategy', *Transactions of the Institute of British Geographers* 32 (3): 331–45.

Larner, W. and R. Le Heron (2002) 'The Spaces and Subjects of a Globalising Economy: Towards a Situated Method', *Environment and Planning D: Society and Space* 20 (6): 753–74.

Larner, W. and W. Walters (2002) 'The Political Rationality of the "New Regionalism": Towards a Genealogy of the "Region"', *Theory and Society* 31 (3): 391–432.

—— (2003) 'Globalisation as Governmentality', in M. Dean and P. Henman (eds) Special edition of *Alternatives* 29 (5): 495–514.

—— (eds) (2004) *Global Governmentality: New Perspectives on International Rule*, London and New York: Routledge.

Larner W., R. Le Heron and N. Lewis (2007) 'Co-constituting "After Neoliberalism": Political Projects and Globalising Governmentalities in Aotearoa New Zealand', in K. England and K. Ward (eds) *Neo-Liberalization: States, Networks, People*, London: Blackwell Publishers.

Latham, A. (2002) 'Re-Theorizing the Scale of Globalization: Topologies, Actor-Networks, and Cosmopolitanism', in A. Herod and M. Wright (eds) *The Geography of Power: Making Scale*, Oxford: Blackwell.

Le Billon P. (2006) 'Fatal Transactions: Conflict Diamonds and the (Anti)Terrorist Consumer', *Antipode* 38 (4): 778–801.

Lemke, T. (2001) '"The Birth of Bio-Politics": Michel Foucault's Lecture at the Collège de France on Neo-Liberal Governmentality', *Economy and Society* 30 (2): 190–207.

Leonard, J. (2005) 'There Goes the Neighborhood', *New York Magazine* December 5.

Levi, M. and D. Wall (2004) 'Technologies, Security and Privacy in the Post 9/11 European Information Society', *Journal of Law and Society* 31 (2): 194–220.

Levy, S. (2007) 'Geek War on Terror', *Newsweek* March 22.

Lewis, A. (2005) 'Introduction', in K. Greenberg and J. Dratel (eds) *The Torture Papers: The Road to Abu Ghraib*, Cambridge: Cambridge University Press.

Lind, E., K. Nightengale and J. F. Schmitt (1989) 'The Changing Face of War: Into the Fourth Generation', *Marine Corps Gazette* October: 22–6.

Lobo-Guerrero, L. (2007) 'Biopolitics of Specialized Risk: an Analysis of Kidnap and Ransom Insurance', *Security Dialogue* 38 (3): 315–34.

Lovink, G. (1997) 'The ABC of Tactical Media', *Nettime* May 16.

—— (2003) *Dark Fiber: Tracking Critical Internet Culture*, Cambridge, MA: MIT Press.

Lupton, D. (2006) 'Sociology and Risk', in G. Mythen and S. Walklate (eds) *Beyond the Risk Society*, Maidenhead: Open University Press.

Lyon, D. (ed.) (2002) *Surveillance as Social Sorting: Privacy, Risk and Automated Discrimination*, London and New York: Routledge.

—— (2003) *Surveillance after September 11*, London: Polity.

Lyon, D. and C. Bennett (eds) (2008) *Playing the Identity Card*, New York: Routledge.

Mandel, R. (2002) *Armies Without States: The Privatization of Security*, Boulder, CO: Lynne Rienner.

Mantas (2003) 'Money Laundering – Keep it Clean', *Banking Technology*, November 30, http://www.mantas.com/NewsEvents/News/BankingTechnology113003.html (accessed October 8, 2007).

Marion, N. E. (1994) *A History of Federal Crime Control Initiatives, 1960–1993*, Westport, CT: Praeger Press.

Marketou, J. (2002) 'Where Do We Go From Here?', *Net Art Commons* July 23, http://netartcommons.walkerart.org (accessed January 11, 2008).

Marshall, T. H. (1998) 'Citizenship and Social Class', in G. Shafir (ed.) *The Citizenship Debates: A Reader*, Minneapolis: University of Minnesota Press.

Marston, S. (1994) 'Who Are "the People?": Gender, Citizenship and the Making of the American Nation', *Environment and Planning D: Society and Space* 8: 449–58.

Marston, S. and K. Mitchell (2004) 'Citizens and the State: Contextualizing Citizenship Formations in Space and Time', in C. Barnett and M. Low (eds) *Spaces of Democracy*, London: Sage Publications.

Martin, E. (1994) *Flexible Bodies: Tracking Immunity in American Culture from the Days of Polio to the Age of AIDS*, Boston: Beacon Press.

Massey, D. (2005) *For Space*, London: Sage.

Massumi, B. (2007) 'Potential Politics and the Primacy of Preemption', *Theory & Event* 10: 2.

—— (2005) *Parables for the Virtual*, Durham, NC, and London: Duke University Press.

Maurer, B. (2005) *Mutual Life, Limited*, Princeton: Princeton University Press.

Mayer, J. (2005) 'Outsourcing Torture: The Secret History of America's "Extraordinary Rendition" Program', *The New Yorker* February 14.

McCormick, J. (2000) 'Schmittian Positions on Law and Politics? CLS and Derrida', *Cardozo Law Review* 21: 1693–722.

McCurdy, P. (1975) 'The PVC Puzzle: Some Pieces Are Still Missing', *Chemical Week* September 24: 5.

MacEoin, G. (1985) *Sanctuary: A Resource Guide for Understanding and Participating in the Central American Refugees' Struggle*, San Francisco: Harper & Row.

MacFarquhar, N. (2006) 'Sitcom's Precarious Premise: Being Muslim Over Here', *New York Times* December 7.

McKenzie, J. and R. Schneider (2000) 'Critical Art Ensemble: Tactical Media Practitioners', *TDR* 44 (4): 136–50.

McNeill, W. (1977) *Plagues and People*, New York: Anchor.

McNevin, A. (2006) 'Political Belonging in a Neoliberal Era: The Struggle of the Sans-Papiers', *Citizenship Studies* 10 (2): 135–51.

Mehta, U. S. (2000) *Liberalism and Empire: A Study in Nineteenth Century British Legal Thought*, Chicago: University of Chicago Press.

Meikle, G. (2002) *Future Active: Media Activism and the Internet*, New York: Routledge.

Meyer, J. (2007) 'As Terrorism Plots Evolve, FBI Relies on Agent John Q. Public', *Los Angeles Times* May 12.

Meyer, J. and E. Hayasaki (2007) '6 Charged in Plot to Strike Army Base', *Los Angeles Times* May 9.

Miles, D. (2006) *Deputy Secretary: 9/11 Changed America Forever*, US Department of Defense, http://www.defenselink.mil/News/NewsArticle.aspx?id = 726 (accessed June 25, 2007).

Miller, P. (1992) 'Accounting and Objectivity: The Invention of Calculating Selves and Calculable Spaces', *Annals of Scholarship* 9 (1/2): 61–86.

Minca, C. (2005) 'The Return of the Camp', *Progress in Human Geography* 29 (4): 405–12.

Mitchell, D. (2005) 'The S.U.V. Model of Citizenship: Floating Bubbles, Buffer Zones, and the Rise of the "Purely Atomic" Individual', *Political Geography* 24 (1): 77–100.

Mitchell, K (2003) 'Educating the National Citizen in Neoliberal Times', *Transactions of the Institute of British Geographers* 28 (4): 387–403.

—— (2004) *Crossing the Neo-liberal Line: Pacific Rim Migration and the Metropolis*, Philadelphia: Temple University Press.

Mitchell, T. (2002) *Rule of Experts: Egypt, Techno-Politics, Modernity*, Berkeley: University of California Press

Moss, F. (2005) 'Life in the Fast Lane: RFID Powers Border-Crossing Program', *Mobile Enterprise Magazine*, http://whitepapers.zdnet.com/whitepaper.aspx?docid = 174601 (accessed January 11, 2008).

Moyers, B. (2005) 'Welcome to Doomsday', *New York Review of Books* 52 (5): 8–10.

Muller, B. J. (2004) '(Dis)Qualified Bodies: Securitization, Citizenship and "Identity Management"', *Citizenship Studies* 8 (3): 279–94.

—— (2005) 'Borders, Bodies, and Biometrics: Towards Identity Management', in E. Zureik and M. B. Salter (eds) *Global Surveillance and Policing: Borders, Security, Identity*, Cullompton: Willan Publishing.

Mutimer, D. (2007) 'Sovereign Contradictions: Maher Arar and the Indefinite Future', in E. Dauphinee and C. Master (eds) *Logics of Biopower and the War on Terror*, New York: Palgrave Macmillan.

Myers, D. G. (2001) 'Do We Fear the Right Things', *American Psychological Society Observer* 14 (10).

Mythen, G. and S. Walklate (2006) 'Communicating Terrorist Risk: Harnessing a Culture of Fear?', *Crime, Media, Culture* 2 (2): 123–42.

Nagel, C. R. (2002) 'Geopolitics By Another Name: Immigration and the Politics of Assimilation', *Political Geography* 21 (8): 971–87.

Nawaz, Z. (2007) *Little Mosque on the Prairie Press Kit*, http://www.cbc.ca/littlemosque/pdf/presskit.pdf (accessed March 15, 2007).

Naylor, R. T. (2006) *Satanic Purses: Money, Myth and Misinformation in the War on Terror*, Montreal and Kingston: McGill–Queen's University Press.

Neal, A. (2004) '"Cutting off the King's Head": Foucault's Society must be Defended and the Problem of Sovereignty', *Alternatives* 29 (4): 373–98.

Nelson, D. M. (1999) *A Finger in the Wound: Body Politics in Quincentennial Guatemala*, Berkeley: University of California Press.

Neocleous, M. (2000) *The Fabrication of Social Order: A Critical Theory of Police Power*, London: Pluto Press.

NetEconomy (2005) *White Paper: Fighting Financial Crime*, October, http://www.neteconomy.nl (accessed January 11, 2008).

Neumman, I. and D. H. Nexon (eds) (2006) *Harry Potter and International Relations*, Lanham, MD: Rowman & Littlefield.

Nevins, J. (2002) *Operation Gatekeeper: The Rise of the 'Illegal Alien' and the Making of the U.S.-Mexico Border*, New York: Routledge.

Newman, D. and A. Paasi (1998) 'Fences and Neighbours in the Post-Modern World: Boundary Narratives in Political Geography', *Progress in Human Geography* 22 (2): 186–207.

*Newsweek* (1993) 'Why our Borders are Out of Control', August 9.

*Newsweek* (2004) 'All Papers in Order', November 5.

*New York Times* (1951a) 'Million a Year Flee Mexico only to Find Peonage Here', March 25.

—— (1951b) 'Southwest Winks at Wetback Jobs', March 28.

Ngai, M. (2004) *Impossible Subjects: Illegal Aliens and the Making of Modern America*, Princeton, NJ: Princeton University Press.

NIC (2005) *Mapping the Global Future: Report of the National Intelligence Council's 2020 Project*, Pittsburgh: Government Printing Office.

NPR (2003) *The 'Conspiracy' Art of Mark Lombardi*, November 1, http://www.npr.org/templates/story/story.php?storyId = 1487185 (accessed January 11, 2008).

Nyers, P. (2006) 'The Accidental Citizen: Acts of Sovereignty and (Un)making Citizenship', *Economy and Society* 35 (1): 22–41.

O'Brien, R. (1992) *Global Financial Integration: The End of Geography*, London: Pinter.

O'Callaghan, E. M. (2004) 'Expedited Removal and Discrimination in the Asylum Process: the Use of Humanitarian Aid as a Political Tool', *William and Mary Law Review* 43 (4): 1747–73.

O'Connor, D. R. (2006) *Commission of Inquiry into the Actions of Canadian Officials in Relation to Maher Arar*, Ottawa: Gilmore Print Group.

OECD, Organization of Economic Cooperation and Development (2002) 'Economic Consequences of Terrorism', *OECD Economic Outlook* 71: 117–40.

OECD Observer (2002) *Globalisation and its Enemies*, http://www.oecdobserver.org/news/fullstory.php/aid/682/Globalisation_and_its_enemies.html (accessed February 2, 2007).

Office of the President of the United States (2002a) *Border Security – Smart Borders for the 21st Century*, Washington, DC: The White House.

—— (2002b) *President Signs Border Security and Visa Entry Reform Act*, Washington, DC: The White House.

O'Harrow, R. (2005) *No Place to Hide*, New York: Free Press.

Ohmae, K. (1995) *The End of the Nation-State: The Rise of Regional Economies*, New York: Free Press.

Olds, K. and N. Thrift (2005) 'Cultures on the Brink: Reengineering the Soul of Capitalism – on a Global Scale', in A. Ong and S. Collier (eds) *Global Assemblages: Technology, Politics and Ethics as Anthropological Problems*, Oxford: Blackwell.

Olgun, A. (2006) 'Hofstadgroep: Voor deze Jongens is het Nu Echt Afgelopen', *NRC Handelsblad* April 21.

Olson, M. (2001) 'Larsen Asks INS to Reopen Tighter PACE', *The Northern Light* October 11.

—— (2002) 'Nexus Tweaking Should Speed-up Enrollment Process', *The Northern Light* July 4.

O'Malley, P. (1992) 'Risk, Power and Crime Prevention', *Economy and Society* 21 (3): 252–75.

—— (1996) 'Risk and Responsibility', in A. Barry, T. Osborne and N. Rose (eds) *Foucault and Political Reason: Liberalism, Neo-liberalism, and Rationalities of Government*, Chicago: University of Chicago Press.

—— (2000) 'Uncertain Subjects: Risks, Liberalism and Contract', *Economy and Society* 29 (4): 460–84.

—— (2002) 'Imagining Insurance: Risk, Thrift and Life Insurance in Britain', in T. Baker and J. Simon (eds) *Embracing Risk: The Changing Culture of Insurance and Responsibility*, Chicago: Chicago University Press.

—— (2004) *Risk, Uncertainty and Government*, London: Cavendish Press/Glasshouse Press.

OMB Watch (2005) *Safeguarding Charity in the War on Terror: Anti-Terrorism Financing Measures and Non-Profits*, Washington, October.

—— (2006) *Muslim Charities and the War on Terror: Top Ten Concerns and Update*, Washington, March.

Ong A. (1999) *Flexible Citizenship: The Cultural Logics of Transnationality*, Durham, NC: Duke University Press.

—— (2006) *Neoliberalism as Exception: Mutations in Citizenship and Sovereignty*, Durham, NC: Duke University Press.

Owen, J. (2005) 'NAFTA Partners for New Pact', *Seattle Post-Intelligencer* March 24: A3.

Paasi, A. (1996) *Territories, Boundaries, and Consciousness: the Changing Geographies of the Finnish-Russian Boundary*, New York: J. Wiley & Sons.

Paredes, A. (1958) *'With his Pistol in his Hand': A Border Ballad and its Hero*, Austin, TX: University of Texas Press.

Park, R., E. Burgess and R. D. McKensie (1925) *The City*, Chicago: University of Chicago Press.

Pasha, S. (2005) 'Banking on Illegal Immigrants', *Cable News Network*, http://money.cnn.com/2005/08/08/news/economy/illegal_immigrants/ (accessed May 1, 2007).

Patterson, J. (1987) *The Dread Disease: Cancer and American Culture*, Cambridge: Harvard University Press.

Peck, J. (2001) *Workfare States*, New York: Guilford Press.

—— (2004) 'Geography and Public Policy: Constructions of Neoliberalism', *Progress in Human Geography* 28 (3): 392–406.

Peppard, J. (2000) 'Customer Relationship Management (CRM) in Financial Services', *European Management Journal* 18 (3): 312–27.

Perera, S. (2006) 'Race, Terror, Sydney, December 2005', *Borderlands e-journal* 5 (1), http://www.borderlandsejournal.adelaide.edu.au (accessed February 2, 2007).

Peterson (1988) 'Bush Vows to Fight Pollution, Install "Conservation Ethic"; Speech Distances Candidate from Reagan', *The Washington Post* September 1: A1.

Petrides, M. (2006) 'Chadors and Graffiti, EU Flags and Iconic Bodies: Four Contemporary Visual Artists', *Opticon 1826* 1, http://www.ucl.ac.uk/ics/opticon1826/VfPChadorsand-GraffitisPDF.pdf (accessed March 29, 2007).

Pieth, M. and G. Aiolfi (2005) *Anti-Money Laundering: Levelling the Playing Field*, Basel: Basel Institute for Governance.

Posner, M. (2004) *Catastrophe: Risk and Response*, New York: Oxford University Press.

Pred, A. (2005) 'Situated Ignorance and State Terrorism: Silences, W.M.D., Collective Amnesia, and the Manufacture of Fear', in D. Gregory and A. Pred (eds) *Inhuman Geographies: Spaces of Terror and Political Violence*, New York: Routledge.

Purcell, M. and J. Nevins (2005) 'Pushing the Boundary: State Restructuring, State Theory, and the Case of the U.S.–Mexico Border Enforcement in the 1990s', *Political Geography* 24: 211–35.

Pynn, L. (1997) 'Without Politicians, Cascadia is Just a Dream', *Vancouver Sun* November 12: A1.

Raban, J. (2005) 'The Truth about Terrorism', *New York Review of Books* 52 (1): 22–6.

Rajaram, P. K. (2003) '"Making Place": The "Pacific Solution" and Australian Emplacement in the Pacific and on Refugee Bodies', *Singapore Journal of Tropical Geography* 24 (3): 290–306.

Raley, R. (2004) 'eEmpires', *Cultural Critique* 57 (Spring): 111–50.

—— (2008, in press) *Tactical Media*, Minneapolis: University of Minnesota Press.

Ranstorp, M. (2007) 'The Virtual Sanctuary of Al-Qaeda and Terrorism in the Age of Globalisation', in J. Eriksson and G. Giacomello (eds) *International Relations and Security in the Digital Age*, London: Routledge.

Rasmussen, M. V. (2006) *The Risk Society at War: Terror, Technology and Strategy in the Twenty-First Century*, Cambridge: Cambridge University Press.

—— (2004) '"It Sounds Like a Riddle": Security Studies, the War on Terror and Risk', *Millennium* 33 (2): 381–95.

Regosin, R. L. (2006) 'Rusing with the Law: Montaigne and the Ethics of Uncertainty', *L'Esprit Créateur* 46 (1): 51–63.

Reuter, C. (2004) *My Life as a Weapon: A Modern History of Suicide Bombing*, Princeton, NJ: Princeton University Press.

Rice, C. (2004) 'Transcript of Rice's 9/11 Commission Statement', *CNN.com*, http://www.cnn.com/2004/ALLPOLITICS/04/08/rice.transcript (accessed March 15, 2005).

RMS (n.d.) 'Advisors Network', http://www.rms.com/Terrorism/Advisors/Default.asp (accessed October 8, 2007).

Robbins, B. (1998) 'Comparative Cosmopolitanisms', in P. Cheah and B. Robbins (eds) *Cosmopolitics: Thinking and Feeling Beyond the Nation*, Minneapolis: University of Minnesota Press.

Robbins, T. (2006) 'San Diego Fence Provides Lessons in Border Control', *NPR* April 6.

Roberts, S. (2004) 'Global Strategic Vision, Managing the World', in B. Maurer and R. W. Perry (eds) *Globalization Under Construction: Governmentality, Law and Identity*, Minneapolis: University of Minnesota Press.

Robertson, R. (1992) *Globalization: Social Theory and Global Culture*, London: Sage.

Rodríguez, J. A. (2005) *The March 11 Terrorist Network: Its Weakness Lies in Its Strength*, Working Paper EPP-LEA, Department of Sociology, University of Barcelona.

Rose, N. (1996a) 'Governing "Advanced" Liberal Democracies', in A. Barry, T. Osborne and N. Rose (eds) *Foucault and Political Reason*, London: University College London Press.

—— (1996b) 'The Death of the Social? Re-figuring the Territory of Government', *Economy and Society* 25 (3): 327–56.

—— (1999) *Powers of Freedom: Reframing Political Thought*, Cambridge: Cambridge University Press.

—— (2001) 'The Politics of Life Itself', *Theory, Culture & Society* 28 (6): 1–30.

Rose-Redwood, R. (2006) 'Governmentality, Geography and the Geo-coded World', *Progress in Human Geography* 30 (4): 469–86.

Ruffin, O. (2004) 'Hacktivism, From Here to There', Yale Law School Conference on Cybercrime, http://islandia.law.yale.edu/isp/digital%20cops/papers/ruffin_hacktivism.pdf (accessed January 11, 2008).

Rumsfeld, D. (2002) *Briefing to the US Department of Defense*, February 12, 2002, Washington, DC: Department of Defense.

Said, E. W. (1993) *Culture and Imperialism*, New York: Random House.

Salter, M. B. (2003) *Rights of Passage: The Passport in International Relations*, Boulder, CO: Lynne Rienner.

—— (2004) 'Passports, Mobility and Security: How Smart can the Border be?', *International Studies Perspectives* 5 (1): 71–91.

—— (2007) 'No Waiting for the Barbarians', in M. Hall and P. T. Jackson (eds) *Civilizational Identity: The Production and Reproduction of 'Civilizations' in International Relations*, New York: Palgrave.

—— (forthcoming) 'The Setting of Securitization and Desecuritization', *Journal of International Relations and Development*.

SCAAN, Stanford Central American Action Network (1983) *Revolution in Central America*, Boulder, CO: Westview Press.

Schell, P. (1990) 'Bulldozing Borders', *The New Pacific* Summer: 5–10.

Schell, P. and J. Hamer (1995) 'Cascadia: the New Binationalism of Western Canada and the U.S. Pacific Northwest', in R. Earle and J. Wirth (eds) *Identities in North America: The Search for Community*, Palo Alto: Stanford University Press.

Scheuer, M. (2004) *Imperial Hubris: Why the West is Losing the War on Terror*, Dulles, VA: Brassey's.

Schirmer, J. (1998) *The Guatemalan Military Project: A Violence Called Democracy*, Philadelphia: University of Pennsylvania Press.

Schleiner, A., and L. Hernandez (2005) *Corridos*, http://www.ungravity.org/corridos/htm/situation.htm (accessed January 11, 2008).

Schmidt, R. (2003) 'US Expands Clandestine Surveillance Operations', *Los Angeles Times* March 5.

Schmitt, C. (1996) *The Concept of the Political*, translated by G. Schwab, Chicago: University of Chicago Press.

Schneider, B. (2007) 'Poll: Support for the Iraq War Deteriorates', *Cable News Network* March 19, http://www.cnn.com/2007/POLITICS/03/19/iraq.support/index.html (accessed April 13, 2007).

Schram, S. (2000) *After Welfare: the Culture of Postindustrial Social Policy*, New York: New York University Press.

Scott, J. (1998) *Seeing Like a State: How Certain Schemes to Improve the Human Condition Have Failed*, New Haven: Yale University Press.

—— (2005) 'Afterword to Moral Economics, State Spaces and Categorical Violence', *American Anthropologist* 107 (3): 395–402.

Shamir, R. (2005) 'Without Borders? Notes on Globalization as a Mobility Regime', *Sociological Theory* 23 (2) 197–217.

Shane, S., S. Grey and F. Fesenden (2005) 'Detainee's Suit Gains Support from Jet's Log', *New York Times* March 30: A1.

Shapiro, M. J. (1988) *The Politics of Representation: Writing Practices in Biography, Photography, and Policy Analysis*, Madison: University of Wisconsin Press.

—— (1996) 'Introduction to Part I', in M. J. Shapiro and H. R. Alker (eds) *Challenging Boundaries: Global Flows, Territorial Identities*, Minneapolis, University of Minnesota Press.

—— (1997) *Violent Cartographies: Mapping Cultures of War*, Minneapolis: University of Minnesota Press.

—— (2005) 'Every Move you Make: Bodies, Surveillance, and Media', *Social Text* 23 (2): 21–34.

—— (2007) 'The New Violent Cartography', *Security Dialogue* 38 (3): 291–313.

Sharma, A. and A. Gupta (eds) (2006) *The Anthropology of the State*, London: Blackwell.

Shaw, K. (2004) 'Creating/Negotiating Interstices: Indigenous Sovereignties', in J. Edkins, V. Pin-Fat and M. J. Shapiro (eds) *Sovereign Lives: Power in Global Politics*, London: Routledge.

Shields, P. (2004) 'When the "Information Revolution" and the US Security State Collide', *New Media & Society* 7 (4): 483–512.

Shiva, V. (2006) 'Globalisation and Terrorism', *Resurgence* 218, http://www.resurgence.org/resurgence/issues.shiva218.htm (accessed February 2, 2007).

Simon, J. (1997) 'Governing Through Crime', in L. Friedman and G. Fisher (eds) *The Crime Conundrum: Essays in Criminal Justice*, Boulder, CO: Westview.

—— (2007a) *Governing Through Crime: How the War on Crime Transformed American Democracy and Created a Culture of Fear*, New York: Oxford University Press.

—— (2007b) 'Wake of the Flood: Crime, Disaster, and the American Risk Imaginary after Katrina', *Issues in Legal Scholarship: Catastrophic Risks* 10: 1–17.

Singer, P. (2004) *Corporate Warriors: The Rise of the Private Military Industry*, Ithaca: Cornell University Press.

Sklair, L. (2001) *The Transnational Capitalist Class*, Oxford: Blackwell.

Slaughter, A.-M. (2004) *A New World Order*, Princeton: Princeton University Press.

Smart Border Declaration (2001) *Canada–United States Smart Border Declaration*, http://webapps.dfait-maeci.gc.ca/minipub/Publication.asp?Filespec = /Min_Pub_Docs/104780.htm.

Smith, C. (1996) *Resisting Reagan: The U.S. Central America Peace Movement*, Chicago: University of Chicago Press.

Smith, N. (2004) *Global Executioner: Scales of Terror*, http://www.ssrc.org/sept11/essays/nsmith_text_only.htm (accessed January 11, 2008).

—— (2005) *The Endgame of Globalization*, London: Routledge.

Smith, R. (2003) 'How Authentication Technologies Work', in J. D. Woodward, N. M. Orlans and P. T. Higgins (eds) *Biometrics: Identity Assurance in the Information Age*, Berkeley, CA: McGraw-Hill/Osborne.

Sniffen, M. J. (2006) 'Massive Terror Screening Draws Outrage', *Washington Post* December 1.

Sparke, M. (2000) 'Chunnel Visions: Unpacking the Anticipatory Geographies of an Anglo-European Borderland', *Journal of Borderland Studies* 15 (1): 2–34.

—— (2002) 'Not a State, but a State of Mind: Cascading Cascadias and the Geo-Economics of Cross-border Regionalism', in M. Perkmann and N. Sum (eds) *Globalisation, Regionalisation and Cross-border Regions*, New York: Palgrave Publishers.

—— (2003) 'American Empire and Globalisation: Postcolonial Specialisations on Neo-colonial Framing', *Singapore Journal of Tropical Geography* 24 (3): 373–89.

—— (2004a) 'Political Geographies of Globalization (1): Dominance', *Progress in Human Geography* 28 (6): 777–94.

—— (2004b) 'Passports into Credit Cards: on the Borders and Spaces of Neoliberal Citizenship', in J. Migdal (ed.) *Boundaries and Belonging*, Cambridge: Cambridge University Press.

—— (2005) *In the Space of Theory: Postfoundational Geographies of the Nation-State*, Minneapolis: University of Minnesota Press.

—— (2006a) 'Political Geographies of Globalization (2): Governance', *Progress in Human Geography* 30 (3): 357–72.

—— (2006b) 'A Neoliberal Nexus: Economy, Security and the Biopolitics of Citizenship at the Border', *Political Geography* 25 (2): 151–80.

Sparke, M., J. Sidaway, T. Bunnell and C. Grundy-Warr (2004) 'Triangulating the Borderless World: Geographies of Power in the Indonesia–Malaysia–Singapore Growth Triangle', *Transactions of the Institute of British Geographers* 29: 485–98.

Spence, K. (2005) 'World Risk Society and War Against Terror', *Political Studies* 53 (2): 284–302.

Stafford Smith, C. (2005) 'Representing "the Enemy": Human Rights and the War on Terror', *Criminal Justice Matters* 58: 44–7.

Standard and Poor's (2002) 'Terrorism Insurance Coverage Remains in Doubt', *Standard and Poor's Insurance* April 15.

Stanley, J. (2004) *The Surveillance–Industrial Complex*, American Civil Liberties Union, August.

Staps, F. (2007) 'De Geheime Schat' ['The Secret Treasure'], *NRC Handelsblad* July 14 and 15: 34.

Stark, J. (2001) 'Security Stifles Fast Lane Plans', *The Bellingham Herald* November 28.

Stehr, N. and R. V. Ericson (2000) 'The Ungovernability of Modern Societies', in R. V. Ericson and N. Stehr (eds) *Governing Modern Societies*, Toronto: University of Toronto Press.

Steinhardt, B. (2007) 'The Automated Targeting System – A Violation of American Law, the US–EU PNR Agreement and Basic Human Rights', presented to the European Parliament, Brussels, March 27.

Stern, J. and J. Wiener (2006) 'Precaution Against Terrorism', *Journal of Risk Research* 9 (4): 393–447.

Stevenson, M. (2007) 'Globalisation is Good for You', http://commentisfree.guardian.co.uk/merril_stevenson/2007/02/globalisation_is_good (accessed February 2, 2007).

Stiglitz, J. (2002) 'Globalization's Last Hurrah?', *Foreign Policy* January /February.

Stockwell, S. and A. Muir (2003) 'The Military–Entertainment Complex: A New Facet of Information Warfare', *fibreculture* 1: online.

Sunstein, C. R. (2005) *Laws of Fear. Beyond the Precautionary Principle*, Cambridge: Cambridge University Press.

Suskind, R. (2004) *The Price of Loyalty*, New York: Simon & Schuster.

Suzuki, T. (2006) 'Accountics: Impacts of Internationally Standardized Accounting on the Japanese Socio-Economy', *Accounting, Organizations and Society* 32 (3): 263–301.

SWARM the Minutemen Campaign (2005) 'How This Action Works', http://swarmtheminutemen.com/cartography/how.html (accessed January 11, 2008).

Taureck, R. (2006) 'Securitization Theory and Securitization Studies', *Journal of International Relations and Development* 9: 53–61.

Taylor, C. (2004) *Modern Social Imaginaries*, Durham, NC: Duke University Press.

Taylor, D. (1997) *Disappearing Acts: Spectacles of Gender and Nationalism in Argentina's 'Dirty War'*, Durham, NC: Duke University Press.

Taylor, J. B. (2007) *Global Financial Warriors: The Untold Story of International Finance in the Post-9/11 World*, New York: W. W. Norton.

Thompson, Jr, W. (2002) *One Year Later: The Fiscal Impact of 9/11 on New York City*, New York: Comptroller of the City of New York.

*Time* (2004) 'Who Left the Door Open?', September 20.

Tirman, J. (2004) 'Introduction: The Movement of People and the Security of States', in J. Tirman (ed.) *The Maze of Fear: Security and Migration after 9/11*, New York: New Press.

Torpey, J. (2000) *The Invention of the Passport: Surveillance, Citizenship and the State*, Cambridge: Cambridge University Press.

Truman, H. S. (1951) *Migratory Labor in American Agriculture, President's Commission on Migratory Labor*, Washington, DC: US Government Printing Office.

Turow, J. (2006) 'Cracking the Code: Advertisers, Anxiety and Surveillance in the Digital Age', in K. Haggerty and R. V. Ericson (eds) *The New Politics of Surveillance and Visibility*, Toronto: University of Toronto Press.

UK Treasury (2007) *The Financial Challenge to Crime and Terrorism*, London, February.

United Nations (1992) *Rio Declaration on Environment and Development*, General Assembly, 12 August 1992, http://www.un.org/documents/ga/conf151/aconf15126–1annex1.htm (accessed January 11, 2008).

United Press International (2004) 'U.S. Beefs up Canadian Border Security', *United Press International NewsTrack* August 19.

Urry, J. (2002) 'The Global Complexities of September 11th', *Theory, Culture and Society* 19 (4): 57–69.

—— (2005) 'The Complexities of the Global', *Theory, Culture & Society* 22 (5): 235–54.

US Congress (2005) *Infrastructure Protection and Cybersecurity*, House Committee on Homeland Security, Subcommittee on Economic Security, June 22.

US Congress, Senate Armed Services Committee Hearing (2006) *FY 2007 Defense Authorization*, March 7.

US Customs (2005a) *NEXUS Air*, http://www.customs.ustreas.gov/xp/cgov/travel/frequent_traveler/nexus_air.xml (accessed January 11, 2008).

US Customs (2005b) *SENTRI: Technical Process*, http://www.customs.ustreas.gov/xp/cgov/travel/frequent_traveler/sentri.xml.

US Department of Homeland Security (2004) *Securing Our Homeland: US Department of Homeland Security Strategic Plan*, Washington, DC: Department of Homeland Security.

US State Department (2002) *National Security Entry–Exit Registration System*, June 2, http://usinfo.state.gov/is/Archive_Index/EntryExit_Registration_System.html (accessed February 20, 2006).

—— (2003a) *US Changes National Security Entry/Exit Registration System*, December 1, http://usinfo.state.gov/gi/Archive/2003/Dec/02–374945.html (accessed February 20, 2006).

—— (2003b) *The US-VISIT Program*, December 22, http://fpc.state.gov/fpc/27524.htm (accessed February 20, 2006).

—— (2004) *Dept. of Homeland Security Offers Overview of US-VISIT Program*, March 11, http://usinfo.state.gov/gi/Archive/2004/Mar/12–88051.html (accessed February 21, 2006).

—— (2005) *U.S. Entry–Exit System Hailed for 'Unprecedented Results'*, May 18, http://usinfo.state.gov/gi/Archive/2005/May/19–588378.html (accessed February 20, 2006).

—— (2006a) *Biometric Entry System Installed at Final U.S. Land Border Ports*, January 2, http://usinfo.state.gov/gi/Archive/2006/Jan/03–63171.html (accessed February 20, 2006).

—— (2006b) *Visa Waiver Program*, October, http://travel.state.gov/visa/temp/without/without_1990.html (accessed February 20, 2006).

*USA Today* (2005) 'USA Today/CNN Gallup Poll Results', May 20, http://www.usatoday.com/news/polls/tables/live/0602c.htm (accessed April 13, 2007).

USCIRF (2005) *Report on Asylum Seekers in Expedited Removal: A Study by Refugee and Asylum Experts appointed by the Commission, as authorized by Section 605 of the International Religious Freedom Act of 1998*, US Commission on Religious Freedom, http://www.uscirf.gov/countries/global/asylum_refugees/2005/february/index.html (accessed January 11, 2008).

Valdés, J. G. (1995) *Pinochet's Economists: The Chicago School in Chile*, Cambridge and New York: Cambridge University Press.

Valverde, M. and M. Mopas (2004) 'Insecurity and the Dream of Targeted Governance', in W. Larner and W. Walters (eds) *Global Governmentality: Governing International Spaces*, London: Routledge.

Van Der Ploeg, I. (1999) 'The Illegal Body: "Eurodac" and the Politics of Biometric Identification', *Ethics and Information Technology* 1 (4): 295–302.

Van Houtum, H. and T. Van Naerssen (2002) 'Bordering, Ordering and Othering', *Tijdschrift voor Economische en Sociale Geografie* 93 (2): 125–36.

Van Munster, R. (2004) 'The War on Terrorism: When the Exception Becomes the Rule', *International Journal for the Semiotics of Law* 17 (2): 141–53.

—— (2008, forthcoming) *Immigration, Security and the Politics of Risk in the EU*, Palgrave.

Vaughan, J. (2005) *Modernizing the Welcome Mat: A Look at the Goals and Challenges of the US-VISIT Program*, http://www.cis.org/articles/2004/usvisittranscript.html (accessed January 11, 2008).

Verstraete, G. (2001) 'Technological Frontiers and the Politics of Mobility in the European Union', *New Formations* 43: 26–43.

Vlcek, W. (2006) 'Acts to Combat the Financing of Terrorism: Common Foreign and Security Policy at the European Court of Justice', *European Foreign Affairs Review* 11 (4): 491–507.

Waever, O. (1995) 'Securitization and Desecuritization', in R. D. Lipschutz (ed.) *On Security*, New York: Columbia University Press.

—— (1996) 'European Security Identities', *Journal of Common Market Studies* 34 (1): 103–32.

Wallach, L. and P. Woodall (2004) *Whose Trade Organization? A Comprehensive Guide to the WTO*, New York: The New Press.

Walker, R. B. J. (2006) 'Lines of Insecurity: International, Imperial, Exceptional', *Security Dialogue* 37 (1): 65–82.

Walters, W. (2000) *Unemployment and Government: Genealogies of the Social*, Cambridge: Cambridge University Press.

—— (2002) 'Mapping Schengenland: Denaturalizing the Border', *Environment and Planning D: Society and Space* 20 (5): 561–80.

—— (2004a) 'The Political Rationality of European Integration', in W. Larner and W. Walters (eds) *Global Governmentality: Governing International Spaces*, New York: Routledge.

—— (2004b) 'Secure Borders, Safe Haven, Domopolitics', *Citizenship Studies* 8 (3): 237–60.

—— (2006) 'Border/Control', *European Journal of Social Theory* 9 (2): 187–203.

Ward, D. (2002) 'Using Fast Lane is in the Cards', *Vancouver Sun* June 27: A4.

*The Washington Times* (2007) 'Imams' Suit risks "Chill" on Security', March 16.

Waters, M. (1995) *Globalization*, London: Routledge.

Weber, C. (2006) *Imagining America at War: Morality, Politics, and Film*, London: Routledge.

Weber, S. (2005) *Targets of Opportunity: On the Militarization of Thinking*, New York: Fordham University Press.

Welch, M. (2002) *Detained: Immigration Laws and the Expanding I.N.S. Jail Complex*, Philadelphia: Temple University Press.

—— (2005) *Ironies of Imprisonment*, Thousand Oaks, CA: Sage.

Whitaker, R. (2006) 'A Faustian Bargain? America and the Dream of Total Information Awareness', in K. Haggerty and R. V. Ericson (eds) *The New Politics of Surveillance and Visibility*, Toronto: University of Toronto Press.

White House (2001) *President Holds Prime Time News Conference: The East Room*, October 11, http://www.whitehouse.gov/news/releases/2001/10/20011011–17.html#Resume-business (accessed April 27, 2007).

—— (2002) 'President Bush Outlines Iraqi Threat', Remarks by the President on Iraq, Cincinnati Museum Center, Cincinnati, OH, October 7, http://www.whitehouse.gov/news/releases/2002/10/20021007–8.html (accessed April 13, 2007).

—— (2006) *National Security Strategy*, Washington, March, http://www.whitehouse.gov/nsc/nss/2006/ (accessed October 8, 2007).

—— (2007) 'Pursuing a Strategy for Success in Iraq', Remarks to the American Legion's Annual Convention in Washington, DC, March 6, http://www.whitehouse.gov/infocus/iraq/ (accessed March 29, 2007).

Wilhelm, S. (1997) 'Future Border Procedures Concern Trade Advocates', *Puget Sound Business Journal* 16 (October): A6.

Williams, J. (2006) *Coming to America: US-VISIT and US Visa Waiver Countries Update*, January 10, http://fpc.state.gov/fpc/58824.htm (accessed February 8, 2006).

Williams, M. C. (2003) 'Words, Images, Enemies: Securitization and International Politics', *International Studies Quarterly* 47: 511–31.

Williams, R. (1962) *The Long Revolution*, Harmondsworth: Penguin.

—— (1965) *Culture and Society 1780–1950*, Harmondsworth: Penguin.

Willis, C. (1997) *Yellow Fever, Black Goddess: The Coevolution of People and Plagues*, Reading, MA: Addison Wesley Publishing Company.

Willis, S. (2003) 'Old Glory', in S. Hauerwas and F. Lentricchia (eds) *Dissent from the Homeland: Essays After September 11*, Durham, NC, and London: Duke University Press.

Wilson, J. Q. (1997) *Moral Judgment: Does the Abuse Excuse Threaten Our Legal System?*, New York: Basic Books.

*Wired* (2004) 'Big Bucks for Biometric Screening', June 1, http://wired-vig.wired.com/news/privacy/0,1848,63683,00.html (accessed January 11, 2008).

Woo, G. (2002) 'Quantifying Insurance Risk', Paper prepared for the National Bureau of Economic Research meeting, February 1.

Woods, N. (2006) *The Globalizers: The IMF, The World Bank and Their Borrowers*, Ithaca: Cornell University Press.

Woodward, J. D. (2003a) 'Government and Military Programs', in J. D. Woodward, N. M. Orlans and P. T. Higgins (eds) *Biometrics: Identity Assurance in the Information Age*, Berkeley, CA: McGraw-Hill/Osborne.

—— (2003b) 'Private Sector Programs', in J. D. Woodward, N. M. Orlans and P. T. Higgins (eds) *Biometrics: Identity Assurance in the Information Age*, Berkeley, CA: McGraw-Hill/Osborne.

Woodward, J. D., N. M. Orlans and P. T. Higgins (2003) *Biometrics: Identity Assurance in the Information Age*, Berkeley, CA: McGraw-Hill/Osborne.

Wray, S. (1998a) 'On Electronic Civil Disobedience', http://www.thing.net/~rdom/ecd/oecd.html (accessed January 11, 2008).

—— (1998b) 'Electronic Civil Disobedience and the World Wide Web of Hacktivism: A Mapping of Extraparliamentarian Direct Action Net Politics', *Switch* 4 (2), http://switch.sjsu.edu/web/v4n2/stefan/ (accessed January 11, 2008).

Yaghmaian, B. (2006) 'Borderline Case', *Le Monde Diplomatique*, English edition, March.

Young, N. (2002) 'Hatred as Ambivalence', *Theory, Culture and Society* 19 (3): 71–88.

YVR (2005) 'Fast Track Border: Vancouver: Vancouver International Airport', http://www.yvr.ca/flightinfo/fastrackborder.asp (accessed January 11, 2008).

Zhang, D. D. (ed.) (2002) *Biometric Solutions of Authentication in an E-World*, Boston: Kluwer Academic.

Zehfuss, M. (2003) 'Forget September 11', *Third World Quarterly* 24 (3): 513–28.

Žižek, S. (1998) 'For a Leftist Appropriation of the European Legacy', *Journal of Political Ideologies* 9 (2).

—— (2004) *Iraq: The Borrowed Kettle*, London: Verso.

—— (2005) 'The Constitution is Dead – Long Live Proper Politics', *The Guardian* June 4.

Zureik, E. and M. B. Salter (2005) *Global Surveillance and Policing: Borders, Security, Identity*, Cullompton: Willan.

# Index

Lightning Source UK Ltd.
Milton Keynes UK
30 March 2010

152128UK00001B/64/P